Do the Amer
Common Lite

Gustavo Pérez Firmat, editor

Do the Americas Have a
Common Literature?

Duke University Press   Durham and London   1990

© 1990 Duke University Press
All rights reserved
Printed in the United States of America
on acid-free paper ∞
Library of Congress Cataloging-in-Publication Data
appear on the last printed page of this book.

For Jorge Olivares
For Michelle and Heather Smith

Contents

Acknowledgments

I would like to thank the John Simon Guggenheim Memorial Foundation and the Duke University Research Council for fellowships that allowed me to begin working on this collection. Several friends and colleagues gave generously of their time and expertise: Rosa Perelmuter Pérez, Jorge Olivares, Roberto González Echevarría, and James McIntosh. Reynolds Smith, my editor at Duke University Press, saw the project through from beginning to end. To them all I am grateful. Lastly, I would like to thank the authors of the essays for making the book possible.

Gustavo Pérez Firmat

Introduction: Cheek to Cheek

A few years ago, the "nuyorican" musical group Los Amigos and the Bad Street Boys had a hit record entitled "Bailando pegaíto." The Spanish title of the song was intended as an idiomatic translation of "Cheek to Cheek," for the Bad Street Boys took the old Irving Berlin standard, revised and updated some of the lyrics, and set the whole thing to a salsa rhythm. The result was a transculturated, Latinized version of the tune (whose title the Bad Street Boys pronounced, of course, "chik to chik") in which a young man from the barrio tries to convince a sophisticated American girl to dance with him. The new lyrics include such memorable lines as: "It feels like heaven dancing with you tonight; / take off your shoes, I know they are getting tight"; or, "Tighter and tighter as we can get; / your hips are moving like a speeding jet." In light of the earthy poetry of these lines, it is not surprising (though it may well be offensive) that the cover of the record album consisted of a photograph of the backside of several young women standing "cheek to cheek."

I open with this tongue-in-cheek anecdote because, both in its intention and in its content, it summarizes the aims of this volume. The subject of "Bailando pegaíto" is the contact—and perhaps the clash—between some of the cultures of the Americas. That is also our subject. "Cheek to Cheek" begins, "Heaven, I'm in heaven." What the Bad Street Boys have done is to bring heaven down to earth by lodging the barrio inside Berlin, by lacing Broadway melodies with ghetto beats. In the song, North and South, Anglo and Latin, are made to dance cheek to cheek. For this reason, the Latinized Berlin standard can serve here as something of a critical model: the purpose of the essays in this book is also close dancing; they aim to couple the literatures and cultures of

I

this hemisphere—particularly their North American and Latin American sectors—in order to find regions of agreement or communality. Thus, like the Bad Street Boys, the contributors make their moves at the borderline, in the juncture between North and South.

"Bailando pegaíto" also suggests the novelty, and even the irreverence, of such moves. The fact is that the field of inter-American literary studies is something of a terra incognita. Other than a few pioneering influence studies, scholarly forays in this field have been few and mostly very recent.[1] Unlike the contemporary literature of the hemisphere, whose breadth of interest and ambition is well-known, the criticism of American literature (using the adjective in its genuine, hemispheric sense) remains largely confined to well-established and long-standing disciplinary borders, with the result that contacts between scholars working on different areas of the New World have been rare and occasional. The most glaring instance of this institutional and scholarly isolation, perhaps, is the lack of dialogue between "Americanists" and "Latin Americanists." On the one hand, scholars of North American literature, while they have been much concerned with the "Americanness" of their domain, have usually neglected to consider this notion in anything other than the narrow nationalistic and anglophone sense, where America becomes a synonym for the United States. On the other hand, students of Latin American literature have for the most part not looked northward in search of significant contexts for their texts. The obvious language barriers, as well as the equally obvious economic and political differences among different parts of the hemisphere, have been decisive factors in discouraging Latin Americanists from engaging North American texts. It is deliberate, therefore, that in this book some of the contributors are writing "out" of their field: the reader will find Americanists writing about Borges and Latin Americanists writing about Hawthorne or Cooper.

Even comparatists working on New World literature have shown relatively little interest in inter-American investigations. Since in academic study the lines of literary comparison have generally run East to West, comparative discussions of the literatures of the Americas have primarily looked at the relationship between the New World and the Old World. Much has been written, for instance, on the European roots of New England transcendentalism or of the Spanish-American *nueva novela*. In fact, however, the Americas' cultural indebtedness to Europe is but one feature that the literatures of the New World have in common. And not enough has been said about this commonality, about the intersections and tangencies among diverse literatures of the New World considered apart from their extrahemispheric antecedents and analogues. The goal of the essays in this book is to participate in correcting this imbalance by adopting a North-South orientation and looking at New World literature in a Pan-American or inter-American context. Needless to say, the subject is imposingly and even impossibly broad, and each contributor has addressed only a limited aspect of it. Moreover, the volume as a whole makes no attempt at comprehensiveness, and even though an effort has been made to represent both "major" and "minor" literatures (and languages other than Spanish and English), exclusions have been inevitable. Nonetheless, considered collectively, the essays endeavor to lay some of the groundwork for further discussion of New World literature in a hemispheric context.

The essays themselves adopt four distinct approaches, which can be labeled *generic, genetic, appositional,* and *mediative.* The *generic* approach attempts to establish a hemispheric context by using as a point of departure a broad, abstract notion of wide applicability. One example is Lois Parkinson Zamora's demonstration that there exists a New World historical consciousness that cuts across national boundaries. Another example is Eduardo González's discussion of racial and cultural miscegenation; by focusing on what he terms "American theriomorphia"— that is, the figuration of racial and cultural crossings as mulattoness (a term derived from "mule")—González is able to make connections between such different writers as Cirilo Villaverde, José Lezama Lima, Melville, and Hawthorne. Similarly, José Piedra's inquiry into a "neo-African logic of performance" allows him to link the North American "blues" with the Cuban *son.* David T. Haberly's essay is generic in the literary sense: he studies the American mutations of the romantic genre of the legend in texts by North American, Spanish-American, and Brazilian writers from the last century.

A second approach is to get down to cases and examine actual *genetic* or causal links among authors and texts. The aim here is less to track down sources or influences—although both of these enterprises are more useful than some contemporary theories are willing to allow—than to record the uses to which a given author or text have been put by his or her successors. Illustrative of this method are Doris Sommer's essay on Faustino Domingo Sarmiento and James Fenimore Cooper, Enrico Mario Santí's essay on the complicated history of Latin American readings and misreadings of Whitman, and John T. Irwin's examination of Borges's rewriting of Poe's "The Purloined Letter."

Complementary to genetic studies are the essays that focus on non-genetic affinities. I have called this approach *appositional* since it involves placing works side by side without postulating causal connections. From this perspective confluence takes precedence over influence, and causal links, even when they exist, are deemed less relevant than formal or thematic continuities. In this group one can include Wendy B. Faris's discussion of the problematic of textual and territorial appropriation in Carpentier and Faulkner, René Prieto's mapping out of the areas of agreement in the poetics of Severo Sarduy and Nicole Brossard, and Jonathan Monroe's joint reading of poems by Adrienne Rich and Aimé Césaire. Taken together, the genetic and appositional methods are valuable not only for the light they cast on individual texts, but also for helping to create a sense of a distinctly American literary tradition.

The fourth approach, which one may call *mediative,* concentrates on texts that already embed an inter-American or comparative dimension. In this case the cross-country or cross-cultural appositions are internal to the works themselves; thus, instead of juxtaposing texts or authors, the critic addresses texts that place themselves at the intersection between languages, literatures, or cultures. Examples of this approach are José David Saldívar's discussion of the hemispheric significance of the thought of José Martí or my own exposition of the Pan-American poetics of José Lezama Lima. In this group one would also include Antonio Benítez-Rojo's discussion of Caribbean culture, which argues that the Caribbean is an "island bridge" that binds the Northern and Southern segments of the hemisphere. It is also to this last category that this volume as a whole belongs, since it too aspires to mediate or bridge geographical and cultural distances.

These four approaches to the issue of hemispheric literary communality—generic, genetic, appositional, and mediative—are not mutually exclusive nor do they (for this reason) necessarily appear in pure form. In addition, they can be placed in the service of differing critical agendas, as the ideological diversity of the following essays will testify. These approaches do, however, outline the methodological options available to inter-American comparatism, and the reader of this book should be able to form an idea of the advantages and limitations of each approach.

The title of this collection was inspired by that of another collection, Lewis Hanke's *Do the Americas Have a Common History?* (1964). Hanke's volume was devoted to a discussion of Herbert Eugene Bolton's controversial thesis, first set forth in 1932, that the frontier experience gives uniformity to New World history.[2] Many of the contributors to Hanke's volume take issue with Bolton, arguing that the specific historical circumstances are so diverse that it makes no sense to speak of a "common history." According to the Mexican philosopher Edmundo O'Gorman, for example, the unity of the Americas is no more than a "beautiful, fallacious illusion" (107) and a "geographical hallucination" (109). Similar arguments might be made against the title and intent of the present collection. Indeed, they have already been made: Roberto Fernández Retamar, the well-known Cuban poet and essayist, believes the histories of the United States and the rest of the hemisphere are so unlike that the corresponding literatures are therefore incommensurable.[3] Fernández Retamar is certainly correct in pointing to the huge historical and political differences between the United States and Spanish America (his principal points of reference); even so, historical position is not always identical with cultural position, and the essays in this volume tend to demonstrate that even when the comparison involves authors and texts from the First and Third Worlds it is possible to find substantial common ground.

Having said this much, I should point out that the book's title is not intended as a question to which its contents provide an answer. In fact, the essays themselves raise questions that suggest how difficult it would be to answer the title, both because of the scope of the question and because of the terms in which it is couched. The idea of a common literature, like that of a common history, may not be a "beautiful illusion" (though beautiful illusions also have their value), but neither is it a self-evident proposition. Given the recentness of inter-American comparatism, work in this area must be speculative and susceptible to revision. For this reason, the essays collected here should be perceived much as the lyrics in "Bailando pegaíto." They are intended as an invitation or come-on, as a proposition in the other sense; and the editor and contributors can only hope that the reader will be intrigued enough by their proposition to face the music and dance.

Gustavo Pérez Firmat

Lois Parkinson Zamora

The Usable Past: The Idea of History
in Modern U.S. and Latin American Fiction

If Death and Liberty
Can be personified,
Why not History?

It's got to be a fat old man
In faded overalls
Outside a house trailer
On a muddy road to some place
          called Pittsfield or Babylon.

He draws the magic circle
So the chickens can't get out,
Then he hobbles to the kitchen
For the knife and pail.

Today he's back carrying
a sack of yellow corn.
You can hear the hens cluck,
The young cocks strut their stuff.
    —Charles Simic, "Severe Figures"

That fat old man in the faded overalls is well suited to introduce my essay on historical consciousness in modern U.S. and Latin American fiction. History has indeed been one of the most severe—and recurrent—figures of America's collective imagination. The barnyard fairly reeks of that familiar historical anxiety, the motivation and theme of so much of our fiction. There he goes now, clutching his instruments, terrorizing those dumb clucks whose collective fate he seals. Then again, he's fickle, so tomorrow we may get corn. But what's this? History hobbles? Or is he hobbled by the writers who write him? After all, they too travel along that apocalyptic road to Pittsfield or Babylon. We might easily mistake the old man for the eighth deadly sin in some medieval morality play, ready to take the stage with the likes of gluttony and lust and avarice. But no, he is in fact the first deadly sin of the novel.

So we begin by recalling that the rise of the novel coincided with the impact of the idea of history upon modern consciousness. The reading and writing of history were prominent features of the culture of eighteenth-century Europe. Voltaire's *Charles XII* and Gibbon's *Decline and Fall of the Roman Empire* were international best-sellers, as were the forged histories of Macpherson and Chatterton. About England, Hume would declare, "I believe this to be the historical age and this the historical nation," an assertion that might have been made about France and Germany as well.[1] In London, the Society of Antiquaries was founded in 1718, but the startling innovation that was to become characteristic of all modern philosophies of history occurred later, not before the last third of the eighteenth century, and departed distinctly from the historical thinking of Voltaire and Gibbon and Hume. The idea that the meaning of history resides and reveals itself in the historical *process,* rather than in isolated events, has its roots in the historiographic thinking of Hobbes and Vico, but it found its culminating expression in Hegel's philosophy. Hannah Arendt asserts that the central concept in all of Hegel's metaphysics is history: "This alone places it in the sharpest possible opposition to all previous metaphysics, which since Plato had looked for truth and the revelation of eternal Being everywhere except in the realm of human affairs—of which Plato speaks with such contempt precisely because no permanence could be found in it and therefore it could not be expected to disclose truth."[2] The revolutionary idea that the particular occurrence derives its intelligibility from the process of history as a whole strongly influenced the developing genre of the novel. In his classic exposition of the connection, *The Historical Novel,* Georg Lukács refers specifically to the Hegelian foundations of the late-eighteenth- and early-nineteenth-century historical novel, and much of what he says can be related to the development of the genre in general.

Lukács is concerned with novelistic representation that is radically and uniquely historical; the development of this representational mode he associates directly with the first generalized—that is, modern—European war. If the *idea* of history had been revolutionized in the late-eighteenth century, the revolutionizing of the *experience* of history was soon to follow: Lukács describes the "mass experience of history" occasioned by the French Revolution and the subsequent Napoleonic wars, when for the first time the individual was confronted with the direct reality of world history. The advent of mass conscriptions and unlimited geographical warfare made people think globally, and historically. They realized that similar upheavals were taking place everywhere, a realization which must have, Lukács posits, "enormously strengthen[ed] the feeling first that there is such a thing as history, second that it [was] an uninterrupted process of changes and finally that it [had] a direct effect upon the life of every individual."[3] The generalized conflict also awakened national, and nationalistic, sensibilities in Europe: there were altogether new appeals to national character and national history, to past greatness and past dishonors—in short, to the particularities of ethnic and cultural heritage. Thus communities as well as individuals were being made aware of their relationship to world history, a relationship in which change was increasingly viewed qualitatively as well as quantitatively. This nascent ideology of progress also found expression in Hegel's philosophy, in his vision of the "world spirit" which is embodied in the dialectics of historical development. Lukács directly links this Hegelian idea to the development of the novel: "According to the new interpretation, the reasonableness of human progress develops ever increasingly out of the inner conflict of social forces in history itself; according to this interpretation history itself is the bearer and realizer of human progress" (25). In a critical discussion too well known to need reiteration here, Lukács makes us aware of the ways in which the basic generic conditions and characteristics of the novel developed alongside the Hegelian concept of the historical character of existence.

If in the mid- to late-eighteenth century the development of modern historical consciousness and the development of the novel impinge and intersect, we would have to say that they *parallel* the emergence of independent national identities in the Americas. Lukács completely ignores the possible influences of the Americas on European historiography and historical fiction, and Hegel treats America as an exception to his theory of historical dialectics. In *The Philosophy of History,* Hegel refers generally to the New World, moves to a contrast of English and Spanish America, then returns to generalize about America's lack of a usable history: "It is for America to abandon the ground on which hitherto the History of the World has developed itself. What has taken place in the New World up to the present time is only an echo of the Old World—the expression of a foreign Life; and as the Land of the Future, it has no interest for us here, for . . . our concern must be with that which has been and that which is."[4] To participate in the dialectical movement of history, a nation must assimilate and preserve its past by negating it, a process which allows a nation to free itself of its past while at the same time making it an integral part of the present continuity of existence. For Hegel, America had no assimilated past, hence no possibility of historical continuity or national identity: does not the very term "New World" seem to contain and confirm this fact? Hegel concludes: "America is therefore the land of the future, where, in the ages that lie before us, the burden of the World's History shall reveal itself—perhaps in a contest between North and South America" (86).

We will overlook Hegel's depreciation and dismissal of America's indigenous cultural past and observe instead that he correctly foresaw what would become a principal theme of both North and South American literature, the question of America's historical identity.[5] He also foresaw that this American anxiety of origins would be intimately related to the New World's uses of its Old World predecessors, that is, to the historical processes of colonialism and independence in this hemisphere. For though the European concepts of history and nationality to which I have referred evolved without substantial reference to America, the reverse is certainly not true. America's ideas about history and its own historical identity are, of course, profoundly rooted in European philosophy; though almost two hundred years have been added to our history since Hegel's assertion and the directions of domination and influence have changed considerably, the relation of American identity to European cultural models continues to be problematic. Indeed, Hegel himself has proved one of the most difficult of our European predecessors to negate and assimilate. I will refer in some detail to novels by Willa Cather and Carlos Fuentes which specifically address residual Hegelian suspicions that America does not really exist as an intellectual culture: both of these writers place European history and historiography in an indigenous American context in order to investigate the particular character of the American past. Cather and Fuentes will lead me to other writers who have recently written "metahistories" which shift the historical focus from the sources and substance of American history to the means of its narration. These works, like Cather's and Fuentes's, posit history not only as background and cause, but as the very condition of their existence. Because of the particular challenges of historical self-definition in the New World, such fiction is common in (and to) the Americas.

One more relevant idea evolves coincidentally with the historical developments that I have touched on here by way of introduction: the idea of comparative literature. The growing sense of the relation of historical process to national identity in Europe raised questions about how to define national culture and how to understand differences among cultures. During the last quarter of the eighteenth century (and again, primarily in Germany), Herder, the Schlegels, and others developed influential theories which conceived of literature as the voice of a nation or culture, or even as a power which shaped it, and they promoted the comparative discussion of literature by epoch and ethnicity in these terms. A growing appreciation of various folk literatures, and the comparative study of ancient, Eastern, and modern foreign literatures contributed to the idea of literature as an expression of the characteristics of culture. Although questions of national identity are now relatively rare in comparative studies of European literature, they are very current in areas where national identity is in more formative stages of development, as it is in Latin America, and where literary criticism is effectively redefining concepts of national literature, as it is in the U.S. We may, then, understand Hegel's questions about American identity not only in an eighteenth-century historiographic context, but also in a contemporary comparative one. The novelists whom I will discuss here are impelled by such comparative questions, as I am in this essay.

The title of this collection, and the intent of my own essay, obviously enlarge the territory of comparative literary inquiry from its original national parameters to hemispheric ones. It is a significant expansion, since "America" encompasses thirty-five countries and fifteen territories or protectorates, four principal Indo-European languages and countless indigenous languages, 676 million inhabitants, and more than sixteen million square miles of land. The extent of this territory, not to mention the radical diversity of its economic, governmental, and educational systems, may begin to suggest the difficulties of inter-American comparative studies, particularly if they are broadly generalizing in intent. The very inadequacies of the terms "North American" and "South American" suggest the problems facing the critic or reader who is interested in evolving a comprehensive American critical context. Though "American" does, after all, apply to the whole hemisphere, the term is rarely used in the U.S. to refer to anything beyond its own borders. To call Carlos Fuentes or Gabriel García Márquez or Jorge Luis Borges "American" writers, while correct, may be confusing. Nor will "North American" be a useful term in this study, because I do not deal with Canadian fiction at all, and the Mexican fiction which I discuss is not properly speaking either North *or* South American, but rather Central American.

The term "inter-American" suggests my comparative context, but it too may be misleading, since it is sometimes applied to relations among countries *within* North or South America, as well as to relations *between* North and South America. I will use "Latin American" to refer to the fiction of both Central and South America, but at the risk of being too inclusive, because I do not deal with fiction from all the countries contained in that term. Even my use of the term "U.S. fiction" is ambiguous in this comparative context because Mexico is also a "United States"— "Los Estados Unidos de México." This interweaving of names may serve to suggest the complexity of our comparative enterprise here, as well as the ways in which our American identities have historically overlapped, impinged, reflected, and modified each other, as often unconsciously as consciously. Perhaps Hegel foresaw even this, in his reference to the revelation of historical meaning in the potential dialectic between North and South America.

I

We are worried about redeeming the past.
They are accustomed to acclaiming the future.

Their past is assimilated; and, too often, it is simply forgotten.
Ours is still battling for our souls.
  —Carlos Fuentes, *Latin America: At War With the Past*

In these schematic sentences, Carlos Fuentes places in opposition what he proposes as the current conceptions of history in the U.S. and Latin America.[6] And in what after four decades is still the single most influential comparative treatment of the cultures of the Americas, *El laberinto de la soledad* (*The Labyrinth of Solitude*, 1950), Octavio Paz precedes Fuentes in contrasting the historical visions of the U.S. and Mexico. Paz too assigns to the U.S. the historical character which Hegel imputed to the entire hemisphere: a place without a past, with only a future.[7] But if Latin America's view of the past is first presented as starkly opposed to that of the U.S., a second look reveals that the two views share a common characteristic: their lack of resolution. Fuentes follows Hegel strikingly in his assertion that the past is not yet usable anywhere in America: if the U.S. has *too* completely assimilated its past, rendering it inaccessible, Latin America has *in*completely assimilated its history, to the same effect.

Fuentes elaborates history's "battle for our souls" in Latin America by asserting that no stage of Latin America's past has yet been fully assimilated.

Each new historical project not only replaces the foregoing, it annihilates, rejects, and obliges it to start again from the beginning. The Conquest tries to wholly deny the existence of the indigenous world, Independence denies the Colonial world, and the Revolution rejects nineteenth-century positivism. While yet claiming to be orphaned, each of Mexico's historical projects is open, *nolens volens,* to the secret contamination of the traditions thus denied.[8]

Latin America has not properly negated its past, so it cannot fully integrate the past into the present to realize what Hegel defined as the continuity of its being. Almost all of Fuentes's novels depict Mexico's past, and Latin America's, as a series of ruptures, of discontinuous fragments. In fact, precisely because it is unresolved, history has provided the tensions and ironies of much of the best of recent Latin American fiction: the past is always present, and origins are always problematic, in Juan Rulfo's *Pedro Páramo* (1955), Elena Garro's *Los recuerdos del porvenir (Recollections of Things to Come,* 1962), Ernesto Sábato's *Sobre héroes y tumbas (On Heroes and Tombs,* 1962), Alejo Carpentier's *Los pasos perdidos (The Lost Steps,* 1953), and *El siglo de las luces* (translated as *Explosion in the Cathedral,* 1962), Gabriel García Márquez's *Cien años de soledad (One Hundred Years of Solitude,* 1967), Reinaldo Arenas's *El mundo alucinante* (translated as *The Ill-Fated Peregrinations of Fray Servando,* 1969), Augusto Roa Bastos's *Yo el supremo (I the Supreme,* 1974), José Donoso's *Casa de campo (A House in the Country,* 1978), Mario Vargas Llosa's *La guerra del fin del mundo (The War of the End of the World,* 1981), Isabel Allende's *La casa de los espíritus (The House of the Spirits,* 1982), among others. These novelistic explorations of the national and regional past often project expansive mythic histories for their American territory: Fuentes argues that Latin America's unresolved history can only be encompassed by an inclusive mythic vision and its consequent narrative modes.

If Fuentes describes Latin America's historical dilemma in what are undeniably Hegelian terms, he emphatically rejects dialectical idealism as a solution to that dilemma, and looks back before Hegel to Giambattista Vico's *New Science* (1744). Like Hegel, Vico locates historical significance in the process of history as a whole; but unlike Hegel, Vico's historical process is not essentially linear, nor does it privilege a progressive dialectic. In Vico's metaphoric expression of history as a spiral,

Fuentes finds a model capable of encompassing the linear time of Western thought and the circular times of indigenous mythology which meet in Mexico. And in Vico's investigation and presentation of the "poetic" origins of human history and his privileging of fictional texts (one entire section of the five of *New Science* is devoted to Homer and Greek fables), Fuentes finds support for his belief that history can—and must—be written by novelists. Fuentes uses Vichian historiography explicitly in *Terra nostra* (1975) and *Una familia lejana* (*Distant Relations*, 1980); both are novels about the European historical origins of Mexican and Spanish-American culture, and both oscillate back and forth between the Old and New Worlds.[9] Vico's rejection of eighteenth-century scientific empiricism and the Cartesian conception that the intellect can apprehend first principles intuitively, without reference to historical experience, coincides with Fuentes's rejection of similar ideas in this century—ideas which he summarizes as the "bastardization of the philosophy of the Enlightenment"[10] and which he implicitly associates with what he sees as the cancellation of history in the U.S.

But are our historical sensibilities in the Americas really as divergent as Fuentes insists? Do we seriously entertain the schematic opposition which he proposes, or accede to his idea that U.S. history is only the history of forgetting? Are Fuentes, and we, simply (perhaps oversimply) fulfilling Hegel's prediction, opposing North and South America for the purposes of historical self-definition?

Fuentes *does* make an exception to his generalization for Faulkner and the writers of the U.S. South on the grounds that the South shares with Latin America the historical experience of colonial exploitation and political failure as the rest of North America does not.[11] And he *does* recognize that the U.S. is not the only place where the past may be subsumed by an illusory future. One of his Mexican characters in *Distant Relations* speaks globally about this century's habit of divorcing the past from the present "con el propósito de que el pasado sea siempre algo muerto a fin de que nosotros mismos seamos siempre algo nuevo, diferente del pasado despreciable, nuevos y en consecuencia hambrientos de novedades en el arte, la ropa, la diversión, las máquinas. La novedad se ha convertido en el certificado de nuestra felicidad ("with the proposition that the past must always be something dead and we always something new, something different from that much-to-be-scorned past— new, and consequently thirsting for the latest innovations in art, clothing, entertainment, machines. Novelty has become the blazon of our happiness").[12] In Mexico, as in much of the world, novelty is advertised, packaged, marketed, and consumed, though the U.S. has of course taught the world how. It is also true that the triumph of technology tends to emphasize innovation rather than preservation and, again, the U.S. undeniably leads the way. It was, after all, one of the most important of U.S. technologists of progress, Henry Ford, who in the 1920s declared that "history is more or less bunk."

Still, Fuentes is not unaware that the relation of the present to the past is a major theme in U.S. literature, and has troubled more U.S. writers than those from the South. In the nineteenth century we need only think of the major U.S. writers to recognize a continuous strain of historical consciousness in their fiction: Cooper's outraged defense of America's indigenous history and resources, Hawthorne's guilt-ridden explorations of the Puritan past, Twain's nostalgia for the freedom of the untrammeled land (a fiction based on the illusion of America's par-adisal past, which Twain was himself instrumental in creating and which finds its culminating lyrical expression just forty years later in Fitzger-ald's famous conclusion to *The Great Gatsby*), and Henry James's elegant regret for a European cultural heritage which never fully took in the New World. In our own century the sense of U.S. history conveyed in literature has shifted in significant ways. The historical uneasiness of many of our modernist writers results less from the past's multilayered and unresolved presence (this was, after all, Hawthorne's dilemma as much as Faulkner's and Fuentes's) than from the the thinness of the past, or even its perceived absence. There is an acute sense of missing history among U.S. modernists, which must be recognized as a historical prob-lem and the result of historical conditions. Henry James was the first to leave for Europe for explicitly historical reasons, and Eliot and Pound followed him, looking for the past which they could not seem to locate in America. Referring to Oakland but epitomizing the attitude toward American culture generally, Gertrude Stein spoke for a whole "lost gen-eration" of writers when she concluded, "There is no there there." Henry Adams, whom Alfred Kazin calls "the Gibbon, the Voltaire, the Proust and the doom-filled Oswald Spengler" of his time, was also impelled to search for U.S. historical origins, which he found in medieval Europe rather than the more recent national history which his own family had been so instrumental in constructing; William Carlos Williams too found in other historical traditions (including those of Latin America) the means to critique his own. For many modernists, U.S. history be-came a photographic negative, the reverse side of a tapestry. The outlines did not reveal what was there, but what was *not,* and should have been.

Since World War II, U.S. fiction has in fact generally shifted from the collective historical preoccupations of these earlier writers to the more private realms of psychology and ontology. And what we selectively call postmodernist fiction—the term remains more descriptive of an aesthetic sensibility than of a temporal period—emphasizes the self-reflexive linguistic and literary structures of the work rather than its mimetic and historiographic capacities. In Latin America, on the contrary, questions of national identity and political self-definition have increased in both complexity and urgency since World War II and have increasingly served as subjects for fiction. But even if we agree that post–World War II fiction differs in the U.S. and Latin America in its historical charge, surely we can also agree that it is wrong to say that U.S. writers have generally or traditionally been unconscious of history. We may, therefore, wonder why we have been so willing to accept Fuentes's and Paz's characterizations to that effect. There are, it seems to me, two general areas of explanation for our tendency to agree with them, despite ample evidence to dispute the simplification of their oppositions.

The first lies in the nature of U.S. literary criticism, not in the nature of U.S. literature. Until about fifteen years ago, prevailing literary critical thought in the U.S.—New Critical, formalist, and structuralist thought—encouraged readings of American literature which minimized the complex influences of the historical context in and on the literary text. These critical theories fostered an American canon comprised of modern works which foreground aesthetic and psychological concerns rather than historical or social ones (or works which were, in any case, the object of critical discussions which foregrounded these issues), and university courses which approached literature rhetorically rather than socially or politically. Many of the most influential critics and theorists of American literature during this century have sought to define what Nina Baym calls the "myth of America":

> The myth narrates a confrontation of the American individual, the pure American self divorced from specific social circumstances, with the promise offered by the idea of America. This promise is the deeply romantic one that in this new land, untrammeled by history and social accident, a person will be able to achieve complete self-definition. Behind this promise is the assurance that individuals come before society, that they exist in some meaningful sense prior to, and apart from, societies in which they happen to find themselves.[13]

Baym is only one of the more materially and historically minded critics who have recently reacted against the "derealization" of U.S. literature, and who are directing attention toward its social and historical subjects and contexts. Even so, the impulse of U.S. critical theory to oversimplify or dismiss ("to forget," as Fuentes would have it) the historical subjects and contexts of U.S. literature remains strong. Thus, J. Hillis Miller, a prominent U.S. literary critic, has recently lamented "the incommensurability between the sign system and the material base" and "the apparent canyon between history and language" in the U.S.: he both reflects and reinforces the modernists' historical anxiety when he writes, "We can remember the beginnings of American civilization. It is recent, datable, relatively simple. It has not been accumulating long enough to be thick on the ground."[14] Latin American literary critics, like U.S. critics, have been persistently concerned with tracing an essential identity in their literature, but they have never conceived that identity apart from complex communal historical pressures and circumstances.[15] They have, of course, also noted the seeming historical discontinuity between America and its European and indigenous roots, but they do not conceptually detach their literature from those histories, or assume that American culture was created *ex nihilo,* as a topological gesture rather than as a historical and cultural process.

The second and more important area of explanation for the perceived dichotomy between U.S. and Latin American historical understanding lies in our conceptions of historical process. The U.S. and Latin America have different philosophical lineages and, particularly in the twentieth century, different historiographic descendancies from Hegel and German idealism. It is these differences which I will pursue in the following pages.

II

German historical idealism developed during the formative period of U.S. national self-definition, and its essentially progressive dialectics supported and then supplanted the Puritan sense of America as the latest stage of a universal historical process.[16] In the U.S. the charting of universal history became by the mid-nineteenth century a means of explaining its secular destiny, as it had been for the Puritans a means of explaining their divine destiny. Following Hegel, Lessing and Herder applied to history the concept of development, and Friedrich Schlegel and Schiller the idea that humanity outgrows forms of belief and seeks newer and more adequate expressions of his spirit: the process of history itself came to be viewed as possessing an inner and active purpose which made it intelligible and assured its advance toward truth. These thinkers found in the past experience of mankind the repository of communal wisdom, but it is the future which inevitably receives systematic emphasis in their dialectical historiographies. Their emphasis on the ideal movement of history has been construed as an emphasis on the future by U.S. prophets of progress from the mid-nineteenth century to the present. A blatant example is "The Progress of Mankind," an address given by U.S. historian George Bancroft before the New York Historical Society in 1854: "Everything is in motion, and for the better. The last system of philosophy is always the best. . . . The last political state of the world likewise is ever more excellent than the old."[17] I cite this futuristic bombast to create a contrast with what we know to be the complexities of historical consciousness in U.S. literature, and also to acknowledge the undeniable conversion of German idealism into a facile doctrine of progress in the U.S.—in other words, both to contest and confirm Fuentes's assertion about the extreme future orientation of the United States. As we will see, Willa Cather's fiction also contests Fuentes's assertion.

Geoffrey Hartman reminds us of the dangers of "those picaresque adventures in pseudo-causality which go under the name of literary history," but he might agree that there are instances of influence and confluence which comparative literary studies are in the business of noticing.[18] German philosophical idealism was directly imported into British literature by Coleridge and Carlyle, and via Carlyle into American literature by Emerson, who in turn influenced much subsequent U.S. literature directly and indirectly through his influence on William James's phenomenological psychology.[19] These writers view history as propelled by a progressive and universal force which may be conceived in religious, biological, psychological, or aesthetic terms, or all of them at once: Carlyle fuses history, poetry, and religion; Emerson yokes Lamarckian evolutionary beliefs to his conception of the Oversoul operating in both history and art; James's "stream of thought" flows forward even as it accumulates in each instant the whole history of the individual. Though Willa Cather was not a systematic or programmatic thinker (as are Fuentes and many other contemporary Latin American writers, with their more political contexts and imperatives), she nonetheless read, admired, and cited Carlyle, Emerson, and James, and her novelistic portrayals of U.S. historical reality clearly reflect this lineage of transcendental idealism.[20]

In a broadly generalizing essay such as this, the question of how the comparatist chooses examples is crucial. I have chosen to discuss Cather's work because it illuminates the European historiographic heritage that I am proposing as central to U.S. modernism. Furthermore, Cather has not, to my knowledge, been placed in a comparative American context, though her southwestern settings are themselves inter-American in their examination of the mixture of indigenous, Hispanoamerican, and European cultures and characters.[21] Her fiction was very popular at the time of its publication, and it continues to appeal to both popular and scholarly audiences (a dual audience less usual in the case of U.S. literature than of recent Latin American literature). Nonetheless, it seems to me that until relatively lately Cather's work has not received the kind of academic attention it deserves, in part, perhaps, because its profoundly historical character did not easily conform to the prevailing aesthetic and mythic criteria of the American New Criticism that I mentioned earlier. In the U.S., Cather has been treated either as a regional writer or as a domestic one; in Latin America, she has been completely overshadowed by English and American modernists whose themes are more overtly political and/or whose narrative strategies are more overtly experimental than hers. Though this earlier neglect or relegation is now being redressed by feminist criticism and by the current critical shift that I have noted toward historicist and materialist approaches to U.S. literature, it is nonetheless one more reason for my choice of Cather's fiction in this comparative discussion of American literature.

Cather wrote twelve novels and several collections of short stories between 1905 and her death in 1947; most of her fiction is set in the nineteenth century or earlier. Her basic narrative impulse is to look back to the indigenous and the European roots of American culture, and then to follow their complex historical branchings and bloomings over time in a particular character and/or place. In all but two of her novels about the American past, she either locates the narrative situation in a contemporary setting or brings the story itself into the present: she clearly wished to avoid romanticizing the past by separating it from the present, a tendency of popular historical romance which she recognized and self-consciously rejected. Among U.S. writers her only equal in constituting a cultural memory from *both* native and imported matrices is Faulkner, and she has no equal, in my opinion, in combining the problematics of historical consciousness with those of artistic activity in what was still a relatively young and unformed culture. Her search for a usable past allies her to the major writers of her time, but she never shared the modernist suspicion (though she was certainly aware of it) that the American past was thin or nonexistent. We might consider this difference in the terms suggested by feminist criticism. Those who have never possessed a history—here the reference is not to Americans but to women—naturally prefer to recover the past before dismissing it as inadequate. The retrieval of lost history becomes an essential part of the process of liberation, for an unexamined past operates as fate rather than revelation. Though this observation applies not only to women but also to many contemporary postcolonial writers—it is a theme running throughout contemporary Latin American fiction—I would nonetheless point out that Cather's most fully drawn characters are women, often artists or aspiring artists, who must search their past in order to establish their place in the as-yet inchoate present of American culture.

Cather's best novels are set in the nineteenth-century Midwest and Southwest, but she does not glorify the westward movement in the nationalistic terms of manifest destiny, as did Whitman and Frederick Jackson Turner,[22] or in the progressive terms of scientific materialism of Bancroft and many others. Rather, she casts it in terms of Carlyle's conception of the hero and the hero's transcendental historical capacities.[23] Her European immigrants are hardly huddled masses yearning to be free, nor do they incarnate the banality of hurrying to America to forget their Old World pasts in exchange for New World futures. The Czech settlers in the Nebraska territory in *My Ántonia* (1918), the Swedes in *O Pioneers!* (1913), the French settlers in Quebec in *Shadows on the Rock* (1931), and the French missionary priests in the southwestern Mexican territory in *Death Comes for the Archbishop* (1927) are at once fugitives from and creators of history. They long (in one case, tragically) for the civilization which they left behind, and at the same time they attempt to transplant it or, in the most successful instances, to adapt it to their American circumstances. Cather attributes the strength of frontier culture to the special interaction of the European character and the American land, an interaction which does not really have a historical analogue in Latin America.[24] However, the towns which are subsequently created and populated by second- and third-generation immigrants are depreciated by Cather precisely because their various European heritages have been squandered, and nothing has arisen to replace them. Cather joins Hegel and Fuentes in finding that in these frontier towns, the past has been inadequately negated and hence inadequately assimilated into a genuinely American culture. But Cather does not stop here: her novels contain individuals—often artists or characters with special aesthetic sensibilities—who *are* heroes in a Carlylean sense, who *are* capable of historical assimilation. It is they who participate in what Carlyle (and following him, Emerson and James) conceived as the soul of history, they who assure that "one form passes into another, nothing is lost . . . and the Present is the living sum-total of the whole Past."[25]

In *The Song of the Lark* (1915, rev. 1937), Thea Kronberg is born of second-generation Swedish parents in the small town of Moonstone on the western plains of Colorado. The novel recounts her struggle to free herself from the vacuous (yet encumbering) culture of Moonstone and to realize herself as a great artist; she manages to do this through her artistic medium, music, and through her special capacity to intuit and integrate her cultural past into her own creative art. She has the good fortune to find two European music teachers, a German and a Hungarian, who introduce her to the European aesthetic tradition which is already lost to Moonstone.[26] It is in a concert hall in Chicago, using a ticket given to her by her Hungarian teacher, that she experiences her first, almost mystical intuition of the historical nature and imperatives of art. While listening to Dvorak's Symphony in E Minor, she senses "the amazement of a new soul in a new world; a soul new and yet old, that had dreamed something despairing, something glorious, in the dark before it was born; a soul obsessed by what it did not know, under the cloud of a past it could not recall."[27] She eventually goes to Germany to study voice: she begins her operatic career there, and then returns to interpret the great roles of German opera to American audiences—in New York and Chicago and San Francisco.

If Thea intuits the historical imperatives of her art in Dvorak's New World Symphony, she finds the strength to act upon them—to go to Germany and commit herself fully to her art—in the ruins of an ancient city of Indian cliff dwellers in Arizona. The short middle section of the novel, "The Ancient People," contains the account of Thea's stay in Panther Canyon (based on Walnut Canyon, the site of the city of the Sinagua Indians, near Flagstaff). In the majestic architectural ruins she finds shards of beautifully wrought pottery, the "fragments of desire" of this disappeared people; in these fragments she recognizes a continuity, an "older and higher obligation" than any other she has ever experienced. She intuits the past mystically—in the dreams and whispers of "the night of ages" which surround her, in visions of an Indian youth and an eagle. Then she enters imaginatively into that history. While bathing in the stream at the bottom of the canyon, she joins "a continuity of life that reached back into the old time. The glittering thread of current had a kind of lightly worn, loosely knit personality, graceful and laughing. Thea's bath came to have a ceremonial gravity. The atmosphere of the cañon was ritualistic" (378). Thea recognizes that "under the human world there was a geological world, conducting its silent, immense operations which were indifferent to man" (388–89). The "silent, immense operations" of historical process, recorded in the archaeological imprint of Panther Canyon, transcend individual consciousness and provide the continuity which neither individuals nor civilizations can sustain.

Clearly Cather is doing far more in this section than simply introducing a historical background for her character. She is dramatizing a concept of American history as unconscious racial and cultural memory, a temporal mode which she embodies and makes visible in the unmistakably American space of Panther Canyon. (She also does this in *The Professor's House* [1925], using the site of the Mesa Verde cliff dwellings in Colorado as the crucial space for her historian protagonist.) Cather's description of Thea's experience in Panther Canyon explicitly echoes William James's theory of the unconscious as it was presented in *Principles of Psychology* (1890), particularly in chapter 10, entitled "The Stream of Thought": his ideas and imagery are explicitly present in Cather's descriptions of Thea's experiences in Panther Canyon. For James, the past is unrepeatable, but it is always present in the unconscious: "Experience is remolding us every moment, and our mental reaction on every given thing is really a resultant of our experience of the whole world up to that date."[28] Thea has earlier had the sensation of having been in the canyon before. James discusses and rejects such sensations on the basis that psychic experience is temporally continuous: psychic history is not static but is constantly being modified by its integration into the present stream of thought. Each "brain-state" is therefore a record of the entire history of its owner, so it is out of the question, James asserts, that a "total brain-state" should recur identically. James was arguing against the functional psychology of his day, which divided perceptions into discrete units, and it is in this disciplinary context that he gives his now-famous definition of the stream of thought as flowing, as constantly in motion. As Thea bathes in the stream at the bottom of Panther Canyon, she intuits, in Jamesian fashion, that the past is not discontinuous or fragmented, but rather a continuous stream which flows in the present of mental experience. She is able to imagine the presence of the ancient civilization of the cliff dwellers, and make them a part of her own cumulative psychic history. Intuition and imagination are the bases of her historical understanding, the bases upon which "the Cliff-Dwellers had lengthened her past" (383): the American cultural heritage provides for Thea a mystical antithesis to European rationalism. Thus Cather dramatizes Thea's artistic synthesis of cosmic and collective history (Carlyle) and individual phenomenological and psychic time (James), a synthesis which can only occur for her on the terra firma of America's own cultural territory.

It is not enough, then, for the American artist to discover the European past and master its artistic and cultural legacy; she must also come to terms with the American past (as Cather's aspiring artist in *Lucy Gayheart* [1935] is tragically unable to do). Because Thea has left the impoverished present of Moonstone and gone back to the rich communal and mythic roots of America, she is able to rejoin and enrich contemporary American culture. We are told that while she is in Panther Canyon she clings to "whatever was left of Moonstone in her mind," and she does ultimately return to Moonstone—not in person, but in the town's communal memory. Referring to the news of Thea which reaches Moonstone through her aunt, the novel concludes:

> Her stories give them something to talk about and to conjecture about, cut off as they are from the restless currents of the world. The many naked little sandbars which lie between Venice and the mainland, in the seemingly stagnant water of the lagoons, are made habitable and wholesome only because, every night, a foot and a half of tide creeps in from the sea and winds its fresh brine up through all the network of shining waterways. So, into all the little settlements of quiet people, tidings of what their boys and girls are doing in the world bring refreshment; bring to the old, memories, and to the young, dreams (581).

This final geographical and topographical metaphor places in a communal context the dialectic between past and present, and between Europe and America, that we have followed in the individual character's life and art. The renewing tidal waters reiterate Thea's own experience of the past's regenerative force, and recall the everyday struggle of a community (comprised of neither artists nor heroes) to assimilate America's divergent and often buried pasts into their own ongoing present.

In Cather's willingness to posit for Thea in Panther Canyon a kind of Hegelian "absolute knowledge"—a union of subject and object, individual and collective consciousness—she may represent the end of the nineteenth century more fully than the first decade of the twentieth, despite the fact that she was writing contemporaneously with Faulkner, Fitzgerald, Hemingway, and Dos Passos. It is true that she still believed in the possibility of finding a historical center that would hold, a possibility which most European and U.S. modernists had, at the time Cather was writing, largely dismissed. It is also true that her fiction is untouched by the physics of relativity, or by the mechanics of entropy, a scientific metaphor for historical process introduced by Henry Adams into U.S. literature in 1907 in *The Education of Henry Adams*. And though subtle narrative ambiguities and ironies abound, her fiction does not self-consciously or self-reflexively call into question the mimetic capacities of language, as U.S. modernist literature so often does. Nonetheless, Cather's work *does* contain and exemplify the European historiographic heritage of U.S. literary modernism, and it *does* suggest the ways in which that heritage has been—must be—assimilated in order to be useful in America. It suggests, furthermore, the essential historical and historiographic concerns of many of her successors. Flannery O'Connor, Saul Bellow, Walker Percy, Robert Coover, among other U.S. writers, have continued to work both through and against the tradition which Cather's fiction so clearly embodies: in their work, as in Cather's, philosophical thinking inevitably becomes historical thinking. It is relevant here that the same European philosophical heritage has recently served as the basis for an important historicist reorientation in U.S. literary criticism. The "dialectical criticism" of Fredric Jameson is, of course, deeply rooted in Hegelian historicism, as modified by Marx and interpreted by Lukács, Adorno, Benjamin, and Marcuse.

III

The U.S. tradition of historical idealism which I have just traced may seem to differ considerably from the vision of history impelling recent novelistic practice in Latin America. For example, contrast Cather's acceptance of Carlyle's transcendental historicism to Augusto Roa Bastos's explicit rejection of it in *I the Supreme*. Roa Bastos makes ironic use of Carlyle's 1843 "Essay on Dr. Francia" to undermine the Carlylean conception of epic and prophetic history: Latin American history is portrayed as having produced few heroes, much less a dialectical progression toward truth. Nonetheless, Roa Bastos consistently treats history not as a record of civilization but as the process of civilization itself, and art as its necessary embodiment. These are undeniably the intuitions at the heart of Carlylean and German historical idealism, as is the conviction that the past is always present, that history is necessarily cumulative. In fact, I have already observed that recent Latin American writers often engage history as a primary and primal force: Roa Bastos is no exception, his dismissal of Carlyle notwithstanding. Still, there are significant variations in lineage and, before going further, I want to trace the outlines of that lineage as I have just done in modern U.S. literature.

Nineteenth-century sources of Latin American historiography are well documented: European positivism was adopted again and again—as Leopoldo Zea has shown in his seminal study, *The Latin American Mind*—to suggest more rationalistic and democratic models of government and education than those provided by the Spanish tradition of centralized power and culture.[29] The overarching transcendental idealism of German historiography was generally rejected in favor of the scientific modes of French positivism, but the progressive character of German historiography was nonetheless attractive to nineteenth-century political leaders throughout Latin America because it allowed the errors of past governments to be discounted, new orders to be justified, and reforms to be submitted to empirical criteria. The late Angel Rama, in his study of Latin American literary culture, describes the differences between these French and German imports. He is concerned less with differences in their historiographic patterns than in their attitudes toward individual and collective identity: in Latin America,

> we did not have the idealistic and individualistic German romanticism, but rather the socialistic French romanticism which made of Victor Hugo an American hero, in the same way that positivistic sociology engrained itself with enormous success in the Latin American mind, making of Comte and Spencer thinkers to whom obeisance was paid, not only for their clear explicative virtues but also because that doctrine adapted itself to the collectivized patterns of regional culture, permitting interpretations based on groups and classes as had always been done . . . (78).

Rama's focus is on the collective and empirical orientation of French positivism, but he does not entirely dismiss German historicism as an influence in Latin America. Comte was no less convinced than the German idealists that phenomena could be understood philosophically only if they were first understood historically through a demonstration of their temporal derivations and destinations, that is, through their relative positions in the whole course of history. Furthermore, Comte, like his predecessors Condorcet, Turgot, and St. Simon, was a social evolutionist with a strong secular faith in progress and human perfectibility.[30] As was Spencer, whose statements about the future's superiority to the past are in the same vein as the futuristic bombast of the American historian Bancroft, whom I have cited above.[31] In fact, it was Spencer rather than Marx who focused the ambitions of the working class in Argentina late in the century: socialism rather than communism was the desired goal of historical change. Marxist historiography was considered abstract and philosophical in comparison to Spencerian empiricism, despite Marx's repeated rejection of the intellectual abstraction of Hegelian idealism in favor of dialectical materialism. (Marx became an important historiographic source for Latin American literature only during the 1920s and 1930s as Latin American artists and writers involved themselves in the international communist movement: Pablo Neruda and Diego Rivera are important early examples.) There are, then, more similarities than differences in the nineteenth-century European historiographic imports into the Americas, despite the sociological orientation of Latin America's choices. It is only during *this* century that positivism has been self-consciously challenged and systematically rejected by Latin American philosophers and writers. It is in the context of this relatively recent negation and assimilation that we may find (*pace* Hegel) a genuine American historiography.

In the early decades of this century Latin America ceased to be Europe's monologue (as Leopoldo Zea has put it) and entered into a dialogue and then an argument with imported concepts of progressive history. The most visible arguers were Alejandro Korn in Argentina, Carlos Vaz Ferreira in Uruguay, Alejandro Deústua in Peru, Enrique Molina in Chile, and Antonio Caso, José Vasconcelos, and Octavio Paz in Mexico. Mexicans had more cause than most Latin Americans to reject positivism, for though it had been the basis for educational reforms under Benito Juárez in the mid-nineteenth century, it had also provided the philosophical justification for the subsequent dictatorship of Porfirio Díaz, with its accompanying racial and social theories of intellectual and political domination.[32] Furthermore, the model of the U.S. was often invoked in nineteenth-century Mexico to suggest the advantages of scientific positivism and a forward-looking mentality, a fact which no doubt gave impetus to the subsequent rejection of positivism as such, and to

Paz's and Fuentes's proposition that historical attitudes in the U.S. and Latin America are diametrically opposed. During this century, establishing and maintaining a distance from imported and imposed histories has come to be considered essential to the process of national self-definition in Latin America.

In the U.S. during this period there was also a reaction against the empirical positivism variously referred to as "mechanism," "rationalism," and "materialism." Unlike the reaction in Latin America, however, the U.S. reaction was not based on a specific sense of national historical necessity. Nor did it result in a coherent shift in historiographic attitudes based on evolving national identity, a failure which may explain the feeling of so many U.S. modernist writers that they were lacking a usable history in America. What they may have been lacking was a usable historiography.[33]

The positivism imported into Latin America in the nineteenth century has encountered strong and widespread resistance in the twentieth. The case of Mexico in particular, and the philosophical and humanistic reaction against positivism in Latin America generally, have been discussed by Michael Weinstein in his useful study, *The Polarity of Mexican Thought.* Weinstein has grouped several of the most important Mexican antipositivists and explored in detail their related philosophies of history.[34] He argues that they rejected existing positivist attitudes which focused on the efficient use of means to attain material and social ends, and developed instead a doctrine of human action which privileges the realization of intrinsic human values:

> The evolutionary philosophies of history propounded by such thinkers as Comte, Marx, and Spencer all had as their focus the progressive and self-conscious control of human beings over their material circumstances. The principle for conquering nature is the rule of economy, embodied in technologies resulting from applied natural science. . . . The Mexican finalists were well schooled in nineteenth-century evolutionary philosophies, since the doctrines of Comte and Spencer had provided the foundation for public education during the Díaz era, and Marxism was used to legitimize many of the actions of post-Revolutionary governments. Their antipositivism was based on their observation that the public situation in the twentieth century was not evolving in the directions of love, justice, and peace, but was marked by the emergence of more refined techniques of domination. The perfection of science, the so-

cialization of production, and economic development (industrialization) seemed to result in the appropriation of human beings-as-instruments by elites rather than in the liberation of humanity, the proletariat, or the individual (4–5).

The Mexican antipositivists also rejected concepts which posited human history as unfolding in accordance with an immanent or predetermined norm, whether the mechanism for the unfolding was metaphysical (Hegel) or sociological (Comte). They sought to create a national philosophy by analyzing the Mexican personality in its historical context, and by invoking humanistic and ethical precepts which would condition the context. But even this specifically American project was not conducted without the intermingling of European philosophical currents.

Weinstein names the Spanish philosopher José Ortega y Gasset and the French philosopher Henri Bergson as two of the most important European influences on Mexican and Latin American historiographic thinking generally in this century. Via a brief discussion of their philosophies of time, I will approach more specifically the nature of Latin American antipositivism. Furthermore, because I am comparing European sources of American historical consciousness, I will entertain for a moment the idea that Ortega and Bergson have served analogous *functions* in contemporary Latin American literary culture to those served by Carlyle and James in modernist U.S. literary culture, though the substance of their historiographic conceptions differs considerably. It also seems possible in this comparative context to juxtapose the essayists and poets Paz and Emerson: Paz has adapted a European historiographic tradition to suit the Latin American literary imagination of this century, as Emerson did in the U.S. in the last century.

IV

Ortega's influence on Latin American literature and philosophy has remained a controversial question, in part because of his conservative political and cultural ideas, in part because of his condescending (or perhaps more accurately, his paternalistic) attitude toward Latin America.[35] Paz and the Cuban novelist Alejo Carpentier have proclaimed Ortega an essential influence on their entire generation, but my interest here is not only in his influence but also in his function as mediator among cultures.[36] It is universally agreed that Ortega provided the essential conduit for German philosophy into Spanish and Latin American culture in this century, as did Carlyle (whom Ortega greatly admired) into British and American culture in the previous century. As editor and founder (1923) of the *Revista de Occidente,* Ortega introduced English and German philosophers, as well as the great European modernists (Valéry, Kafka, Huxley, Lawrence, Proust, Joyce), into Spain and, more importantly, into Spanish.[37] His own views were conveyed to Latin America in his voluminous writings, particularly *Meditaciones del Quijote (Meditations on Quixote,* 1913), *El tema de nuestro tiempo (The Modern Theme,* 1923), *La rebelión de las masas (The Revolt of the Masses,* 1930), *En torno a Galileo* (translated as *Man and Crisis,* 1933), and also in the actual migration of Spanish intellectuals to Latin American universities during the Spanish Civil War. All of them would have known Ortega's work, and many of them had been his students. If the specific nature of Ortega's influence remains open to question, his widespread presence in modern Latin American culture does not.

Ortega was not a systematic philosopher but an essayist whose profound interest in the nature of Hispanic culture he persistently couched in historiographic terms. In his essay "History as a System" (1935), he summarizes the concept of history which runs throughout his work. He writes, "Man is what has happened to him, what he has done. . . . *Man, in a word, has no nature; what he has is . . . history.* Expressed differently: what nature is to things, history, *res gestae,* is to man."[38] To attribute to human history an intrinsic or necessary character is an error: every person is "a drama": "each one in his turn is nothing but happening" (200). Like Vico, Ortega insists upon the primacy of historical research and experience, explicitly rejecting Descartes's identification of truth with subjective certainty; like Heidegger (with whom he associated his work), Ortega rejects the culmination of the Cartesian tradition, Hegel's identification of the subject and object in an all-inclusive knowledge. Instead, he proposes an essentially phenomenological "disintellectualization of the real": his theory of the *razón vital* ("vital reason" or "rational vitalism") of history depends upon a phenomenological understanding of man in his social and historical context. Ortega displaces Hegelian (and Carlylean) idealism and adopts instead a view which resembles the Husserlian (and Bergsonian) phenomenological insistence on the existence of the object world as well as the subject's perception of it. This view is epitomized in Ortega's famous slogan, "Yo soy yo y mi circunstancia" ("I am myself and my circumstances").[39] For Ortega, historical process is not ideal but phenomenological, not metaphysical but specifically located in geographical and political space.

For the Mexican antipositivists engaged in the attempt to create a genuinely American history and historiography, this idea of the specificity of historical experience provided essential impetus. Paz writes that for Latin American intellectuals, Ortega inserted ideas into a lived and living context, thus changing them from abstractions into "instruments, weapons, mental objects which we use and live. . . . His lesson consisted in showing us what ideas were used for and how to use them: not for the purpose of knowing ourselves or contemplating essences, but to clear a way through our circumstances, to dialogue with the world, with our past and our fellow men."[40] Paz's own contribution can, of course, be understood in exactly these terms. Furthermore, multiperspective narratives like Rulfo's *Pedro Páramo*, Vargas Llosa's *La guerra del fin del mundo* (*The War of the End of the World*), or García Márquez's *El otoño del patriarca* (*The Autumn of the Patriarch,* 1975) are Ortegan in their sense of circumstantial history: these novels filter history through the divergent consciousnesses of various groups or representative individuals, and show that each is unavoidably subject to particular (and often conflicting) historical circumstances which operate as fate. For despite Paz's reference to dialogue, Ortega's historiography also forcefully conjures up the idea of monologue: individuals and groups are inevitably encased and isolated by their own historical circumstances, in their own labyrinths of solitude. This idea, very current in contemporary Latin American fiction, may also contribute to dichotomies such as Paz's and Fuentes's, which oppose U.S. and Latin American cultural attitudes without entertaining the possibility of a third and synthesizing term. Paz summarizes Ortega's historical vision, and in his statement we again see reflected his own historical vision, and that of many contemporary Latin American writers: "A Promethean vision and also a tragic one. . . . History is our condition and our freedom: it is where we find ourselves and what we have made" (104).

Along with Ortega's concept of circumstantial history, the Mexican antipositivists found the philosopher's rejection of linear, progressive history congenial. Ortega conceived of history as a series of epochs, and within them generations, which reiterate certain basic civilizational patterns, a model of recurrence akin to that of Vico or Spengler or Nietzsche in its cyclical conception of human civilization and in its description of periods of historical plenitude and crisis.[41] Ortega refused to posit an intrinsic movement of history, but he nonetheless observed the recurrent nature of human activity. Each generation both argues and collaborates with the generations which precede and follow it: each generation is both a continuation and a beginning. The past is active in the present ("The past is I—by which I mean my life" [223]) in ways which are not so much progressive as cumulative—one might almost say rhythmic, given his reference to the "vital pulse" of human history. Ortega's *razón vital* is not dialectical in a Hegelian or Carlylean sense, and he carefully differentiated between his own concept and "the facile anticipations of logical dialectic": "The idea of progress, placing truth in a vague tomorrow, has proved a dulling opiate to humanity. Truth is what is true now and not what remains to be discovered in an undetermined future" (182).

Ortega's oblique reference to Marx in this statement is revealing, for though he was not a Marxist and rejected the historical discontinuity implied by the revolutionary utopianism of Marxism, he nonetheless coincided with Marx in challenging Hegelian idealism on materialist grounds. Ortega follows Marx, who praises Hegel ("that mighty thinker") and then negates and assimilates Hegelian idealism in order to "discover the rational kernel within the mystical shell."[42] Ortega and Marx coincide, furthermore, in their essentially Hegelian understanding of alienation as a function of historical and material circumstance: Ortega repeatedly insists that historical circumstance may be the source of social and political alienation, as well as the cause of eventual social and political integration. Indeed, Paz cites Ortega on just this point to conclude the essays in *The Labyrinth of Solitude*: "The sterility of the bourgeois world will end in suicide or in a new form of creative participation. This is the 'theme of our times,' in Ortega y Gasset's phrase; it is the substance of our dreams and the meaning of our acts" (212). My aim here is to suggest that Ortega's conception of history complements and reinforces other historiographic conceptions in modern Latin American literature and culture: not only Paz, but also Carpentier, García Márquez, and Cortázar might be profitably examined via Ortegan ideas of historical alienation and cyclical recurrence. In the case of Fuentes, I would argue that Ortega's presence in Latin American historiographic thinking generally, and in Paz's work particularly, creates an intellectual medium by and in which Fuentes can reject progressive, dialectical historical models in favor of Vico's spiraling history.

If Ortega's *razón vital* has been assimilated in a number of ways into contemporary Latin American literary embodiments of *communal* history, Bergson's creative vitalism has been assimilated into contemporary Latin American literary embodiments of *individual,* subjective time. Both philosophers conceive of history in explicitly vitalistic terms. Bergson's theory of *la durée* proposes a continuous temporal current of psychic experience which is both different from and yet conditioned by communal historical experience. While Bergson's ideas do not need detailed exposition here, the issue of Bergson's cultural *function* in Latin America may. Weinstein states simply: "Henri Bergson was the leader of the revolt against nineteenth-century absolutism in the West. His notion of spontaneous and improvisible creative evolution freed the concept of becoming from subordination to static truth systems."[43] Though it is possible that Weinstein overstates the case, it is nonetheless clear that Bergson's vitalism, like Ortega's *razón vital,* provided an essential source of European philosophical support for the Latin American critique of the linear and normative structures of nineteenth-century positivistic historiography.[44] As James's phenomenological psychology complements the larger Carlylean and Hegelian patterns of universal history in Willa Cather's fiction, so it is also arguable that Bergson's theory of individual temporal experience accompanies and conditions the Ortegan and Vichian patterns of collective historical experience embodied in Carlos Fuentes's fiction. Fuentes's *Distant Relations* implicitly reflects this European historiographic lineage of Latin American literature as Willa Cather's *The Song of the Lark* reflects the different yet related lineage of U.S. literature. And like *The Song of the Lark, Distant Relations* dramatizes the ways in which America's own indigenous cultural heritage modifies and conditions its received European tradition.

V

In *Distant Relations,* American culture contains (and is in some sense contained by) the European past. If German arias resound magisterially and symbolically in *The Song of the Lark,* it is a French air which provides the leitmotif for *Distant Relations*: "A la claire fontaine, en m'allant promener, j'ai trouvé l'eau si belle, que je m'y suis baigné. Il y a longtemps que je t'aime, jamais je ne t'oublierai." The fountain of the children's song suggests symbolically the French *sources* (literally, the wellsprings) of Latin American literary culture, and the renewing American sources for French literature as well. For Fuentes illustrates (as Cather, writing seventy years earlier, did not) that the intellectual current now flows strongly from West to East. *Distant Relations* alludes centrally to nineteenth- and twentieth-century Latin American writers who were influenced by French literature and who also went to France to add their Hispanic voices to the French literary tradition: Isidore Ducasse (the Comte de Lautréamont, "el francés de Montevideo" ["Frenchman from

Montevideo"]); José María de Heredia ("el francés de La Habana, el conquistador entristecido que regresa al viejo mundo . . . ebrio de . . . el sueño del continente nuevo, la pesadilla del continente viejo" ["Frenchman from Havana, the disconsolate conquistador who returns to the Old World . . . drunk with . . . the dream of the new continent, the nightmare of the old"]); Alexandre Dumas (whose father went to France from Haiti); Jules Laforgue (who went to France "a apresurar el paso de su 'juventud trieste y hambrienta' junto al Plata a esa trama temprana de la ilusión universal que se llama la muerte junto al Sena" [who "exchanged the passage of a 'sad and insatiable youth' beside the River Plate for the speedier universal illusion called death beside the Seine" [120–21, 123–24]). A poem by Jules Supervielle, another "Frenchman from Montevideo," serves as the epigraph to the novel's English translation. The relation of Europe and America comes full circle: the Latin American poets reach out to Europe and then back again; new worlds grow old and old worlds are renewed in Fuentes's spiraling history.

Fuentes's characters live not on the new and sparsely settled frontier, but in the largest city in the world, and one of the oldest. The Mexican family, the Heredias, have roots and branches in France and Spain, and they know the history of French and Spanish exploitation in the Caribbean, a history in which their forebears participated profitably. They themselves travel to Europe frequently and know it intimately, if not comfortably: like cultural influences, tourism now moves in both directions across the Atlantic, a fact that only increases the difficulty of historical assimilation for the father of the Mexican Heredias, Hugo. Hugo Heredia is an archeologist, and as he speaks about Mexico's pre-Cortesian past, a Frenchman who is listening thinks (not condescendingly but admiringly) that Heredia has

> esa característica de los latinoamericanos cultos: sentirse obligados a saberlo todo, leerlo todo, no darle al europeo cuartel ni pretexto, conocer igualmente bien lo que el europeo ignora y lo que considera propio, el Popol Vuh y Descartes. Sobre todo, demostrarle que no hay excusa para desconocer a los demás (15).

> (that quality so characteristic of cultured Latin Americans: the passion to know everything, to read everything, to give no quarter, no pretext, to the European, but also to know well what the European does not know and what he considers his own, the Popol

Vuh *and* Descartes. And, above all, to demonstrate to the European that there is no excuse not to know other cultures [9–10]).

Hugo is burdened by the irony of his own Spanish heritage in Mexico: he believes that the foundations of the land and its greatest cultural achievements are to be found in the very monuments buried or destroyed by the Spanish invaders, the monuments of the cultures indigenous to Mexico. Heredia laments the expulsion of the ancient gods from the modern city, and the replacement of mythic time by mere chronological sequence: there is no longer an accreting present which would recuperate and revitalize the mythic Mexican past. Nonetheless, he insists that the ruins of ancient civilizations in Mexico testify to the fact that "las civilizaciones no mueren del todo; perduran, pero sólo si no progresan" ("civilizations do not die completely; they endure, but only when they do not progress" [12, 6]). Unfortunately, Hugo has not adequately assimilated this past: in attempting to educate his son to revere the past, he sacrifices the present, teaching him to scorn his contemporaries. Hugo's attempt to find a satisfactory position between the colonizer and the colonized fails. It is not an antiquarian devotion to monuments of stone which should determine one's relation to cultural history, Fuentes suggests, but rather the conviction that the present will remain incomprehensible, incomplete, *except* in the context of the past.

There is in Fuentes's novel, as in Cather's, a particular ancient site which the characters must recognize and internalize if they are to participate fully and consciously in American historical reality. The site is Xochicalco, the ruins of a splendid city near Cuernavaca. In a country of hundreds of excavated sites, Fuentes's choice of Xochicalco is revealing. Xochicalco reflects a late mixture of cultures: in a *cámara de ofrendas* (room of sacrifices), objects have been found which attest the presence of elements from the Mayan, Teotihuacán, Mezcal, Totonaca, Zapotec, and Nahua cultures. Furthermore, it is known to have been an important center for astronomical, hence historiographic, research; congregations of astronomers are believed to have met there to determine the fifty-two-year Aztec "century." A cave with a hexagonal perforation through the top of the mountain was used to calculate solar cycles: on the twenty-second of September, the sun's rays penetrate perpendicularly, totally illuminating the subterranean room. What strikes the contemporary visitor to the site is not only the astronomical and cultural wealth and diversity represented in Xochicalco, but also the quantity of artifacts and edifices that still lie buried under the sediment of centuries. Architectural forms are softened, rounded, disguised by the accretion of dirt, vegetation, and stones extraneous to the original constructions. The past seems literally to await recuperation and assimilation into the present, as Fuentes's novel continually suggests.

So we understand that if the French and German cultures are *sources* of the American worlds depicted by Fuentes and Cather, the ancient cultures of Xochicalco and Panther Canyon are their *genesis*. And if their European sources can be visited and studied, the American sites must be dreamed: the former are, finally, a question of education, the latter of psychic energy. Without an imaginative re-creation of the native substratum, no European culture can be fruitfully assimilated in America, nor can the process work in the other direction.

That Fuentes portrays Mexico's contemporary national identity as embedded in its indigenous past reflects the Ortegan idea of the utter specificity of historical circumstance, an idea also consistently engaged in the essays of Octavio Paz. Paz has written that "every history is a geography and every geography is a geometry of symbols"; Mexico's pyramids represent the cyclical time of myth, "the end and the beginning of movement. An immobility which terminates and re-engenders the dance of the cosmos."[45] More specifically than Cather in *The Song of the Lark,* Fuentes dramatizes in *Distant Relations* this translation of time into space. In his own essay, Fuentes, like Paz, describes the particular chronotopic configuration of Mexico as round and recurring: "ancient Mexican art consists precisely in creating a great area, space and time, which may contain the implacable *circle* of the subsistence of the cosmos, as well as the *circularity* of a perpetual return to one's origins, and the *circulation* of all those mysteries that cannot be limited by rationalization. . . . Mexico's ancient art contains a secret tension which cannot be admitted by positivistic thinking. . . ."[46]

To this vision of the communal and racial past, Fuentes joins a Bergsonian theory of personal memory to suggest the complexity of historical remembering. Bergsonian philosophy is integrated into *Distant Relations* by means of references to Bergson's closest literary kin, Marcel Proust, and also by references to the multiple narrators who will tell and retell the history which the novel contains. In *Creative Evolution,* Bergson's seminal work on subjective temporal apprehension, time is defined as "the continuous progress of the past which gnaws into the future and which swells as it advances. And as the past grows without ceasing, so also there is no limit to its preservation."[47] In *Distant Relations* there is a metaphor which self-consciously reflects this definition, and (despite

Fuentes's rejection of linear temporality) reflects as well Bergson's description of duration as "a stream against which we cannot go." One character tells another, whose name is Fuentes, to retell the history that he has just heard, for each version is

> un río más de esta carta hidrográfica que estamos dibujando, desde hace varias horas, usted y yo; sí, usted también, usted lo sabe, no puede escharse para atrás ahora, usted es ya otro río de esta cuenca cuyos verdaderos orígenes aún desconocemos, como ignoramos la multiplicidad de sus afluentes y el destino final al cual desemboca (157).

> (another river in the hydrograph we have been tracing for the past few hours, you and I. Yes, you as well, you know it; you cannot turn back now. You, too, have become a river in this watershed whose true source we still do not know, as we do not know the multiplicity of its tributaries or the final destiny toward which it flows [162]).

To the geographical and cultural renewal contained in Cather's image of the canals of Venice at the end of *The Song of the Lark,* Fuentes's image adds narrative and textual renewal. The past is the sum of the narrative modifications and transformations of present consciousness, a sum which never decreases, which perpetually increases. If an Ortegan sense of the circumstantial specificity of historical experience contributes to the solitude which afflicts the Heredias in *Distant Relations,* then the Bergsonian telling and retelling of that experience is the antidote to their solitude. One character says that narration is "un desesperado intento por restablecer la analogía sin sacrificar la diferenciación" ("a desperate attempt to reestablish analogy without sacrificing differentiation" [191, 200]). Fuentes's novel dramatizes the ways in which the perpetually regenerative process of narrative remembering makes distant relations less so.

It is clear that my own comparative study also attempts to "reestablish analogy without sacrificing differentiation": I will state explicitly what I have already implied, that the visions of history in the U.S. and Latin America seem to me to be less distant than Fuentes's and Paz's oppositions allow. Despite their different heritages and contexts, and their different political purposes, the novelistic engagements of American history by Cather and Fuentes are surprisingly congruent. Cather's final image of the canals of Venice, like Fuentes's fluvial image, suggests the ebb and flow (not the progress) of culture, the intermingling of various cultural currents (not a single, impelling source), and the expansive flow of individual and communal historical experience in expressive forms (both narrative and musical). Cather and Fuentes are united in their conscious reaction against the tenacious ideal—first made explicit by Hegel and still held in America in obvious and manifold ways—that our American pasts have been little more than an unrequited love affair with the European past. Their novels do not deny this love affair—indeed, they acknowledge and incorporate it in the ways I have suggested, and in others which I have not—but they also know that the American historical experience moves along more than just a transatlantic axis. Precisely because they share a Hegelian awareness of the interrupted history of the New World, they understand the consequent need to discover or invent a usable past from both European *and* native materials. Their novels posit art as the means of recuperating and assimilating the sundered pasts of America, and are themselves examples of that process. So they contest the assertion that the past is unusable in America: in their form and their content, the historical anxiety so typical of American self-definition is confronted, negated, assimilated. Such works as these, set in a comparative context, may themselves serve as the third, synthesizing term of the necessary dialectic between U.S. and Latin American historical consciousness.

VI

Neither Cather nor Fuentes, in the novels I have discussed, insists on the equation of history to its narrated versions: on the contrary, both posit external histories which precede narration and which must be discovered by the characters *before* they can be narrated. In a considerable number of recent Latin American and U.S. works, however, that order has been reversed. Critical terms like "documentary fiction," "nonfiction novel," and "metahistory" are frequently used, and are useful, to describe literature in which textual definition precedes historical definition, an order which is also basic to postmodernist aesthetics.[48] Such literature clearly continues the particularly American literary concern with the usable past, but it is now a question of narrative assimilation rather than of a process of cultural assimilation. García Márquez's *Crónica de una muerte anunciada* (*Chronicle of a Death Foretold*, 1981), Vargas Llosa's *Historia de Mayta* (*The Real Life of Alejandro Mayta*, 1984) and *¿Quién mató a Palomino Molero?* (*Who Killed Palomino Molero?* 1986), and Cortázar's *Libro de Manuel* (*Man-

ual for Manuel, 1974) foreground narrators who search for historical truth and find that it resides only in the volatile sum of its narrated versions. In the U.S., Norman Mailer, Truman Capote, and E. L. Doctorow write novels which modify generic categories because, as Doctorow has argued, there is no difference between "history" and "fiction," there is only narrative, only constructed versions of the world.[49] And in both the U.S. and Latin America, the creative journalism of writers like Joan Didion, Joyce Carol Oates, and Elena Poniatowska also contains the inherent premise that we can engage the past only by inventing it, never by discovering it. This realization is often presented as disillusioning rather than liberating because it inevitably undermines the possibility of knowledge and, with it, all claims to an unproblematic mimesis.

I do not mean to suggest that the blurring of historical truth and narrative truth is a recent phenomenon.[50] Nor would I suggest that the blurring of generic distinctions begins in American literature with postmodernism: Herman Melville's *Moby Dick* (1851), Domingo Faustino Sarmiento's *Facundo o Civilización y barbarie* (*Facundo, or Civilization and Barbarism,* 1845), Euclides da Cunha's *Os Sertões* (translated as *Rebellion in the Backlands,* 1902), John Dos Passos's trilogy, *USA* (1930–36), or James Agee's *Let Us Now Praise Famous Men* (1941) would belie such a suggestion. What I *do* wish to suggest here is that the postmodernist shift in emphasis from historical to narrative issues may be an indication that Hegel's question about the nature of America's past has been superseded by Barthesian and Derridian questions about the nature of language per se. This shift implies the possibility that the concept of universal historical process, which Lukács believed fundamental to the novel, has been replaced by processes which are linguistic and literary rather than historical in the sense that Lukács intended. A brief essay, "El pudor de la historia" ("The Modesty of History," 1952), by Jorge Luis Borges, will allow me to entertain this possibility, and conclude my discussion.

Much of Borges's work presents an assiduous investigation of America's cultural origins: "El escritor argentino y la tradición" ("The Argentine Writer and Tradition") is his best-known and most explicit essay on the subject, but it is only one among a great many which explore the historical and cultural traditions inherited by the American writer.[51] Borges is consistently and brilliantly impelled by the American anxiety of origins which I have been tracing here, but his investigation is rarely embodied in terms as specifically geographical as Cather's or Fuentes's, and rarely engaged by such localized ideological and cultural oppositions as those proposed by Fuentes and Paz.[52] Borges's approach to historical definition is instead suggested in the oxymoron of his title, *Historia de la eternidad* (*History of Eternity*, 1953). This title (and the work itself) embody Borges's characteristic oscillation between the poles of phenomenological particularity and philosophical abstraction, between the finite and the infinite: they reiterate the sense we so often have when reading Borges that we are entering into a discussion which is simultaneously about America and the cosmos. Borges entertains ideas, texts, events, settings, which are localized in time and place, and which are also lifted to a universal plane by the author's narrative practice of "deliberate anachronism and erroneous attribution." In the introduction to his 1932 collection, *Discusión*, Borges states that his essays are "resignados ejercicios de anacronismo: no restituyen el difícil pasado—operan y divagan con él" ("resigned exercises in anachronism: they do not restore the difficult past—they work and wander with it").[53] His imaginative historiography, which we might call philosophical anachronism, rejects overarching European paradigms of world-historical process and instead attaches upon the fragments of postmodern historical experience.

"El pudor de la historia" ("The Modesty of History") begins with Goethe. On September 20, 1792, after witnessing a battle in which some few French militiamen improbably defeat the German army, Goethe is reported to have observed, "En este lugar y el día de hoy, se abre una época en la historia del mundo y podemos decir que hemos asistido a su origen" ("In this place and on this day, a new epoch in the history of the world is beginning, and we shall be able to say that we have been present at its origin").[54] By quoting Goethe's statement, which is anything but modest, Borges acknowledges the late-eighteenth-century German source of positivist historiography so basic to American modernism but immediately amends Goethe by asserting that since that time, historic days have been fabricated regularly by governments, newspapers, and Cecil B. DeMille. "Real history," according to Borges, is more modest, and it is principally textual. He offers a phrase from the *Poetics,* another from the *Tusculanea,* yet another from the *Seven Pillars of Wisdom,* to suggest that history is a matter of linguistic use rather than of empirical data. And heroism is a matter of heroic fictions: the *Poema del Cid,* the *Aeneid,* the *Chanson de Roland,* Whitman, Hugo, Faulkner, and Housman convey to the author "el elemental sabor de lo heroico" ("the fundamental flavor of the heroic"). Carlyle appears here too, but this writer who provided Emerson's and Cather's literary archetype of historical heroism is relegated by Borges to a footnote that documents Carlyle's inadequate translation of a phrase from the Icelandic saga, *Heimskringla*. So Borges modestly sets to one side the Hegelian mainstream of universalizing historical order which Carlyle represented to his nineteenth-century American readers.

Borges's central example of history's modesty is from the *Heimskringla*. He cites a passage which details an exchange of words before a skirmish in 1225 between Saxon and Norse armies, a skirmish which the Norsemen subsequently lost. It is not the skirmish with its preceding verbal exchange which is significant, however, but the fact that it was recorded at all, for the author is an Icelander—that is, "un hombre de la sangre de los vencidos" ("a man of the lineage of the vanquished"). Snorri Sturluson records the defeat of his own people, a gesture which Borges treats as prophetic of a time when the distinction between nations will be effaced, when "la solidaridad del género humano" ("the solidarity of all mankind") will be established. Having undermined Hegelian historiography, Borges nonetheless concludes by observing the Hegelian dialectic of negation and assimilation which Snorri's text embodies. The skirmish between the Saxons and the Norsemen attests to nationalistic self-interest; the *recording* of the event attests to the transcendence of that self-interest: "Snorri, por el hecho de referirla, lo supera y trasciende" ("by relating it, Snorri surmounts and transcends that concept") [233, 170]). It is the text itself which exists in dialectical relation to history, incorporating it, transforming it, renewing it. History is advanced not by mere history but by narrative, which "surmounts and transcends" the events it describes. The writer's language does not so much represent history as signify it.

In accordance with the Latin American antipositivism which I have discussed here, Borges's history is circumstantial rather than ideal. Like literature, it is subject to many minor adjustments, to many readings, because the loci of culture are as numerous and widespread as language itself. Borges's history operates by small shifts in a centerless universe where all is margin, where there is no longer any heart of anything. This is not cause for disillusionment, as it sometimes is in postmodernist texts, but cause instead for imaginative recuperation and revitalization. Like Charles Simic's personification of history in the poem which introduces my essay, Borges's modest history is also clad in work clothes, but he is much less severe: instead of a knife and pail, he carries books, and his magic circle limns infinity, not apocalypse. His distracted gaze only sharpens his historical vision, for he knows that history is mythic and malleable, and that narrative form is responsive and responsible to such history. In his creative decentering of historical process, and in his insistence on the historicity of all narrative, Borges's figure provides material for the most usable American past of all.

David T. Haberly

Form and Function
in the New World Legend

During the course of the nineteenth century, writers throughout
the Americas faced a common task: to re-create or create a national past,
and to use that past as a means to understand the present. This endeavor
is generally associated with the common goal of achieving cultural as
well as political independence, and is a feature of the developing national
literatures of the hemisphere. Quite obviously, there was enormous diversity in the histories of English, Spanish, and Portuguese America; it
would seem equally obvious that nineteenth-century efforts to turn those
histories into literature should reflect that diversity. It is my purpose here,
however, to argue that one literary form, the legend, was of fundamental
importance in explorations of the past throughout the Americas; and that
the nature and requirements of that form, contrary to our expectations
of diversity, in fact imposed a remarkable degree of uniformity upon
those explorations. I will begin by seeking to define what the term
"legend" meant in the context of the nineteenth century, and will then
endeavor to exemplify the form through close readings of three well-
known legendary texts taken from various literatures of the Americas.

The meaning of the term "legend" might well appear, from much of
recent criticism, to be far too vague to define clearly. Twentieth-century
critical discourse tends to lump "folktales," "legends," and "myths"
together, as narrative forms which are presumably of popular rather than
erudite origin and which possess some sort of symbolic rather than
purely descriptive function. Northrop Frye, for example, notes that "The
difference between such terms as myth, folktale, and legend begins to
blur as soon as we think of such things formally, as types of stories."
Frye goes on to describe the word "legend" as "perhaps more proto-
historical in reference" than the word "myth," applied to "culture-

heroes or figures whose descendants can still be pointed to as long as the legend and the culture are connected." But Frye insists repeatedly that "the boundary line between myth and legend is impossible to draw."[1] Frye's confusion may reflect the difficulties inherent in the highly complex, multifaceted text which inspired these comments, the Bible. For the simpler, nineteenth-century texts I will be discussing in this essay, however, it is clear that distinctions between myth and legend can be made—and, more importantly, that those distinctions are faithful to nineteenth-century definitions.

From our contemporary perspective, it is sometimes hard to realize that intellectual interest in postclassical popular culture is a relatively recent phenomenon; the term "folklore" itself was coined by a British antiquarian, W. J. Thoms, in 1846.[2] In the years just before 1800, educated Europeans were familiar with the myths of Greek and Roman antiquity, and clearly identified them as myths—that is, as stories not to be taken as literally true, dealing with events set in very distant times and places and relating the deeds of divine or semidivine characters. Nonetheless, myths remained relevant because their primary function was to illustrate or personify universal ideas. The significance of the word "legend" and its cognates in Western European languages was far less clear. Dictionaries of the period generally provided two primary meanings for the term: an inscription on a coin; and a long-winded and wordy story.[3]

This second definition is of considerable interest, for it clearly expresses a disparaging attitude toward a form which was very shortly to become a focal point of European romanticism. At least part of this negativism about the legend, however, may have been due to the kinds of legends with which educated eighteenth-century readers had at least a passing familiarity. One major corpus of legends—and the etymological origin of the term itself—was composed of medieval narratives of the lives and miracles of the Virgin and of large numbers of saints; these prose or verse accounts were collected into anthologies, like the famous *Legenda aurea* of Jacobus de Voragine (1229–1298), and read aloud during mealtimes in monasteries all over Europe. A second corpus of texts defined as legendary contained prose and verse accounts of the deeds of heroic figures associated with medieval European history. These two categories allow us to posit the essential preromantic meaning of the term legend: a narrative of events of local rather than universal importance, taking place within the limits of historical time and involving characters who are capable of extraordinary and even improbable actions, often as the result of divine intervention, but who are nonetheless clearly human. And the dictionary definitions of the term make it clear that educated eighteenth-century Europeans found all such narratives antiquated, illogical, and largely irrelevant.

The shift in attitudes toward the legend and other popularly based narratives occurred very quickly, primarily as the result of the coincidence of German nationalism and the beginnings of romanticism at the very end of the eighteenth century. In their search for origins, for the authentic Teutonic *Völk*, a series of writers collected and published a very large body of narratives. The most famous of these collections is the *Kinder- und Hausmärchen* of Jakob and Wilhelm Grimm,[4] but a number of other texts were of equal importance: Johann Karl August Musäus, *Volksmärchen der Deutschen* (most influential in its revised form, rewritten by C. M. Wieland);[5] Johann Karl Christoph Nachtigal, *Volkssagen nacherzählt von Otmar*;[6] Johann Gustav Gottlieb Büsching, *Volkssagen, Märchen und Legenden*;[7] and the Grimms' *Deutsche Sagen*.[8] Within the space of a few decades, then, dozens of folk-based texts of Germanic origin became available; many of the works cited above were quickly translated into other European languages, and the search to find similar narratives quickly spread to other European cultures.

The numbers and the diversity of such texts required some sort of organization, and several major subcategories of folk narratives were at least tentatively established by the earliest German anthologists; these categories, while not always as clear or consistent as one would like, remain fundamental constants in folklore studies, and were defined concisely by Stith Thompson in 1946. The German term *Märchen* (generally translated as "fairy tale" in English), is applied to a tale set "in an unreal world without definite locality or definite characters and is filled with the marvelous"; it is obvious that stories like "Snow White" or "Cinderella," for example, have no connection with real places or actual events.[9] The German *Legend* or, more commonly, *Sage* ("legend" in English, "lenda" in Portuguese, "leyenda" or "tradición" in Spanish), on the other hand, is a structurally simple narrative which relates "an extraordinary happening believed to have actually occurred." *Sagen* may include both supernatural elements and historical characters and events, and are almost always firmly linked to a specific place and time; they frequently purport to explain local customs, beliefs, sayings, or placenames. The subcategory *Natursagen* specifically provides etiologies for local crops, geological anomalies, weather patterns, and so on.[10]

It is clear, then, that the basic parameters of the *Sage* had been established by 1800. Whether written in prose or in verse, a *Sage* mixed the real and the unreal, but consistently focused upon the specifically local rather than the universal. As important as the nature of the text, however, was the strongly ideological character of the subtext, and this too was implicit or explicit from the end of the eighteenth century onward. Moreover, this subtextual ideology was not at all what the last few decades of the twentieth century have conditioned us to expect; when we think of folk-based culture—of such well-known practitioners and interpreters of that culture as Pete Seeger or Víctor Jara, for example—we tend to associate an interest in or respect for such culture with socially progressive or even revolutionary ideologies.

In Germany in the period around 1800, however, the idealization of the *Volk* and the collection and study of materials presumably created or transmitted by that *Volk* were inextricably bound to an ideological stance which was frequently not merely conservative, but reactionary. The connection between the rise of romanticism and intellectual disquiet about the long-range consequences of the Industrial Revolution is a commonplace of literary history, but one which has particular relevance to the origins of the legend. *Sagen* and *Märchen* alike were viewed as the products of an authentic and specifically localized culture which was largely preliterate, definitively preindustrial and precapitalist, and inherently conservative. That culture preserved elements which dated from the Middle Ages and even beyond—back to a pre-Roman, pre-Christian society.[11]

These relics of the Teutonic past were of particular interest to the Brothers Grimm, who were endeavoring to use the linguistic and narrative forms of the *Volk* to establish the language, beliefs, and character of what Wilhelm Grimm defined as "the great race which is commonly called Indo-Germanic"; later writers substituted the term "Aryan."[12] This protoracism, however, was only one component of early German romanticism; of equal importance, in the subtext of much of the legendary material collected and published during the period around 1800, are religious devotion (antirationalist and proclerical), barter economies (anticapitalist), loyalty to monarchs and nobles (antidemocratic), and nationalistic views of a new Germany restored to its lost unity, military might, and territorial hegemony. And while the evolution of romanticism in nineteenth-century Europe moved it far away indeed from the specific concerns of a handful of German writers around 1800, the ideological subtext of the legend appears to have survived as an inherent component of the form itself as it spread throughout the literatures of the continent;

the most influential non-German exponent of the legend was, of course, Sir Walter Scott. Most writers of legendary texts, as they utilized materials of popular origin or invented stories which sought the appearance of popular origin, approached the text as an exercise in nostalgia for a lost world, a kind of Golden Age in which beliefs were simpler and more deeply held, customs were more authentic and characteristically national. The durability of this vision of the legend can be seen in the intense traditionalism of the *Leyendas* of Gustavo Adolfo Bécquer, first collected in book form in 1871.[13]

German romantic utilization of the legend as a key to unlock the past, reinforced by the immense prestige and popularity of Scott, made the form immediately and powerfully attractive to writers in the Americas. The problem that confronted American authors throughout the hemisphere, however, was the nature of the past that was to be unlocked—and, in fact, whether a past in the accepted, European sense of the word even existed on this side of the Atlantic. After all, one of the primary metaphors of independence in the Americas, repeated almost endlessly by both writers and politicians, was that the new nations of the hemisphere were children—gigantic, potentially powerful children, but children nonetheless, children without a past. Yet the European example appeared to suggest that literature, which American authors agreed was essential to the formation of independent national identities and cultures, could not exist in the absence of a past. In his famous preface to *The Marble Faun,* Hawthorne complained that the United States (like the other new nations of the hemisphere) contained "no shadow, no antiquity, no mystery, no picturesque and gloomy wrong," and concluded that "Romance and poetry, like ivy, lichens, and wallflowers, need Ruin to make them grow."[14]

For American writers—trapped between the felt need to possess a valid, usable past comparable to that of Europe and the insistence of logic and history that no such past existed on this side of the Atlantic—the literary legend offered a way out. The definition of the legend as a story which is based upon historical fact but which may contain parahistorical elements (magic, the supernatural, and so on) and which therefore requires the willingness to suspend logic defined as typical of the *Volk* allowed New World writers considerable creative space: their legends could appear to be historically based, but there was no requirement that they or their readers accept the characters or events described as historically accurate. In short, in the absence of a real past, the legend could be used to create the *appearance* of a past. In addition, the strongly local nature of the traditional European legend allowed writers in this hemisphere to finesse the issue of a national past by focusing on the past of a specific area within the nation. Furthermore, because any legend implied the existence of a folk tradition as its ultimate source, the use of the form by American authors—even if the texts they created were borrowed directly from European collections or created out of whole cloth—suggested that while national literary cultures equal to those of Europe were not yet established in this hemisphere, a nonliterary or preliterary culture did exist.

Despite its obvious utility, however, the legend as a literary form possessed its own dynamic. The legend, as it arrived from Europe, not only looked to the past, but also implied a clearly defined attitude toward that past—a lost Golden Age of strengths and virtues. Thus, borrowing Hawthorne's imagery, New World legends were not only required to uncover or construct the ruins necessary to support the growth of independent literatures; they were also required by the dynamics of the form itself to argue the superiority of the culture which survived only in those ruins. This inherent conflict between function and form is, I believe, the essence of the literary legend in the nineteenth-century Americas; it is also the source of the creative dynamism that makes the best examples of the genre in this hemisphere far more original and interesting than their European counterparts.

One of the earliest and most extraordinary of New World legends is Washington Irving's "Rip Van Winkle," written in June of 1818;[15] it also exemplifies a number of the theoretical issues I have raised, and I will discuss it in considerable detail. While "Rip Van Winkle" is widely admired and anthologized as one of the most representative North American texts, its origins are entirely European. One of the notes appended to "Rip Van Winkle" somewhat coyly admits that "The foregoing tale, one would suspect, had been suggested . . . by a little German superstition about the Emperor Frederick *der Rothbart,* and the Kypphauser mountain" (41). His contemporaries seem to have been well aware of the fact that Irving's story is in fact largely based on the "Peter Klaus" legend in Büsching's anthology, which in turn utilized material first published in Otmar's *Volkssagen.*[16] Irving sought to neutralize accusations of plagiarism in an 1835 footnote to his *Bracebridge Hall*:

> I find that the tale of Rip Van Winkle, . . . has been discovered by divers writers in magazines, to have been founded on a little German tradition, and the matter has been revealed to the world

as if it were a foul instance of plagiarism marvelously brought to light. In a note which follows that tale, I had alluded to the superstition on which it is founded, and I thought a mere allusion was sufficient, as the tradition was so notorious as to be inserted in almost every collection of German legends. I had seen it myself in three. I could hardly have hoped, therefore, in the present age, when every ghost and goblin story is ransacked, that the origin of the tale would escape discovery. In fact, I had considered popular traditions of the kind as fair foundations for authors of fiction to build upon, and made use of the one in question accordingly.[17]

We know, then, that Washington Irving did not invent the story of Rip Van Winkle; the plot—and a great deal of supportive information and description—can be found in his German source. At first glance, it might appear that all Irving added was local color, Americanizing the texture of his narratives through references to specific customs and artifacts of the Hudson Valley. In fact, however, Irving's innovations are far more profound, transforming both the form and the theme of the German original.

The most important formal element which Irving added is an extremely complex set of frames for the narrative. Some sort of simple frame was common in European narratives based upon popular tradition; such devices allowed both the writer and the reader to distance themselves from the story and from the belief systems of those who had presumably created and preserved the story. The idealized *Volk* were authentic, admirable, and inherently poetic—but it was important to make it clear that reader and compiler alike were socially and intellectually apart from and superior to the *Volk*, who, after all, really believed in ghosts, witches, goblins, and the like. Irving's frame, however, goes well beyond the formal expression of the benevolent if slightly patronizing skepticism found in the simple framing devices sometimes used by Musäus or the Brothers Grimm.

To begin with, Irving himself does not accept authorship of "Rip Van Winkle." Within the larger frame of *The Sketch Book,* the volume which contains the story, the putative author is the fictional "Geoffrey Crayon, Gent."—an American who has traveled to Europe and hereby offers us his impressions of the continent, as well as a few apparently unrelated texts, notably "Rip Van Winkle" and "The Legend of Sleepy Hollow," set in his native New York. However, within the smaller frame of the preface and notes to "Rip Van Winkle," Irving—as Crayon—

describes the text, in its preface, as "found among the papers of the late Diedrich Knickerbocker, an old gentleman of New York," who was the fictional author of Irving's 1809 *History of New York . . . by Diedrich Knickerbocker* (28). Irving thus places himself formally at two removes from the story, and distances himself still further—if somewhat more accurately—in the final note to "Rip Van Winkle," in which Crayon suggests that Knickerbocker borrowed the plot from a German legend, but deliberately misleads us about which legend the old gentleman might have used.[18]

Moreover, the smaller frame—the preface, final note, and postscript—contains a bewildering variety of information and allusion, and shifts abruptly and unpredictably from seriousness to satire, from statement to contradiction. The preface begins by characterizing and implicitly praising Knickerbocker's interest in history—not written history, but the orally transmitted "legendary lore so invaluable to true history." This praise is partially negated by the second paragraph of the preface, which mentions that the "literary character" of the fictive Knickerbocker's "history of the province, during the reign of the Dutch governors" is a matter of controversy, and notes that the work "is not a whit better than it should be." Nonetheless, Crayon insists that the *History*'s "chief merit is its scrupulous accuracy, which indeed was a little questioned on its first appearance, but has since been completely established; and it is now admitted into all historical collections as a book of unquestionable authority."

Having lauded the "scrupulous accuracy" of a work which is a hilarious and totally improbable fiction just barely disguised as history, Irving then denies the validity of Knickerbocker's nonaccomplishment: ". . . his time might have been much better employed in weightier labours." All in all, however, the preface concludes that the old gentleman never meant to offend, that his "errors and follies are remembered 'more in sorrow than in anger.'" Crayon notes, moreover, that Knickerbocker's memory is "still held dear by many folk whose good opinion is well worth having," but gives as an example of such folk only "certain biscuit bakers, who have gone so far as to imprint his likeness on their new year cakes—a kind of immortality almost equal to being stamped on a Waterloo medal or a Queen Anne's farthing" (28).

The note which directly follows "Rip Van Winkle" reinforces the ambiguity of the preface. After suggesting that Knickerbocker might have been influenced by a German legend about Emperor Frederick Barbarossa, who was popularly believed to be sleeping in the Kypphauser mountains, destined to reawaken in the future and restore Germany to its ancient glory, Crayon contradicts this suggestion by transcribing a note Knickerbocker supposedly appended to the manuscript of "Rip Van Winkle": Knickerbocker not only asserts that the old Dutch settlements along the Hudson were "very subject to marvellous events and appearances," but insists that he has personally spoken to old Rip Van Winkle, is convinced of his sanity and veracity, and that he has even "seen a certificate on the subject taken before a country justice and signed with a cross in the justice's own hand writing." The historical validity of the events described, Knickerbocker concludes, are "beyond the possibility of doubt" (41).

The preface and final note are not the only elements which comprise the inner frame of "Rip Van Winkle," nor are they the only source of ambiguity. There is, first, a final "Postscript," presented as "travelling notes from a memorandum book of Mr. Knickerbocker." These notes define the Kaatsberg or Catskill mountains as "a region full of fable," and then relate a series of Indian *Natursagen*: the old squaw-spirit who was the mother of the mountain spirits and who controlled the weather; a mischievous manitou or spirit who lived in the loneliest part of the mountains, a sacred place still known as "the Garden Rock"; and the origin of the stream, the Kaaters-kill, which gave its name to the mountains (42). In addition, the frame to this "Posthumous Writing of Diedrich Knickerbocker" also includes its epigraph, which quotes William Cartwright (1611–1643):

> By Woden, God of Saxons,
> From whence comes Wensday, that is Wodensday,
> Truth is a thing that ever I will keep
> Unto thylke day in which I creep into
> My sepulchre—(29)

What, however, is the point of all of this material, which most readers tend to skip over and which has been largely ignored by critics? What, if anything, does it have to do with the adventures of Rip himself, which I have not described simply because Irving's text is so well known? One obvious answer is that Irving is endeavoring to distance himself from the text itself—but we still need to ask why he felt it necessary to do so. Irving's earlier work was openly and intentionally comic, and certainly many elements in both the frame and the story of Rip Van Winkle are ironic and satirical, but almost all the other essays and stories included in *The Sketch Book* are obviously meant to be taken seriously; Irving was determined to establish himself as an important American writer rather than as the author of comic texts of local interest. If the purpose of the frame is merely to amuse us, moreover, the joke is needlessly convoluted and complex and goes on far too long.

The primary reason for the frame and for its insistent distancing is that Irving's story is an intensely subversive text on several different levels. First, and most obviously, it is politically subversive. As a number of critics have noted, the changes brought by revolution and independence are described either as superficial (King George replaced by Washington on the inn's sign, in a blue suit rather than a red) or as negative. Nicholaus Vedder's "quiet little Dutch inn" has been replaced by the Yankee Jonathan Doolittle's Union Hotel, "a large, rickety wooden building . . . with great gaping windows, some of them broken, and mended with old hats and petticoats. . . ." The noble tree in front of the inn is gone, and in its place is "a tall naked pole with something on top that looked like a red night cap. . . ." Worst of all, as a result of the arrival of democracy and its accompanying politics, "The very character of the people seemed changed. There was a busy, bustling disputatious tone about it, instead of the accustomed phlegm and drowsy tranquility" (37).

Irving's view of the revolution which began forty-two years before he wrote "Rip Van Winkle" is thus typical of the conservative, even reactionary tendency which I have argued was inherent in the tradition of the legend, a tradition which viewed the past as superior to the present. But while some critics have read the story as anti-Federalist, as pro-British, or as a monarchist fantasy, this political subtext is only one aspect of the story.[19] It is also profoundly subversive of history. Like many New World legendary texts, "Rip Van Winkle" necessarily endeavors to replace what we think of as history with parahistory—since the Golden Age which is the central locus of such texts either did not exist, in orthodox historical terms, or was historically unsuitable for literary utilization. In his various frames, Irving seeks, first, to disconcert us, to undermine our concept of history—and of truth itself, since the basis of orthodox history is that it is presented as a true account of the past. The frames are designed to make us uncertain about the story's authorship, about its validity as fact, even about the exact name of the mountains which are its physical setting.[20] Irving strongly implies that history taken from books—that is, printed or imprinted history—is an unreliable guide to events: the New Year's cakes imprinted with Knickerbocker's image are, perhaps, as enduring as coins (Queen Anne's farthings, issued in 1713–1714, had in fact almost disappeared from circulation in England by 1818) or as medals struck to commemorate an 1815 battle.[21] Irving is attempting to force us to accept his terms, to rely upon oral history, "that legendary lore so invaluable to *true* [my italics] history," and his careful design of that history allows him to create and situate the Golden Age which the legend form required.

That Golden Age is located in the small towns and rural expanses of the Hudson Valley, inhabited by the distant descendants of Dutch colonists. The putative chronological setting is the end of the eighteenth century, but any Golden Age is necessarily outside of time. Rip Van Winkle's world, rather, exists in a parahistorical continuum which transcends the written historical sequence of Dutch colonization, English colonization, and revolution; in it, the Amerindian past (the *Natursagen*) coexists with seventeenth-century New Holland (Hendrick Hudson, Peter Stuyvesant, and so on) and with a Teutonic past that is both pre-Dutch and, more importantly, pre-English ("Woden, God of Saxons").

The final and most important level of subversion in "Rip Van Winkle" is ideological. The story is designed to negate two diametrically opposed visions of the future of America, both of which are discussed elsewhere in *The Sketch Book*. One, inescapably, is the nationalistic postrevolutionary view of the United States as a swarming beehive of practical and productive activity, predestined to expand physically and to prosper materially: in short, the gigantic child coming of age. The second vision, which Geoffrey Crayon ascribes to various European philosophers, is based upon the pseudoscientific theory of New World degeneracy: ". . . that all animals degenerated in America, and man among the number" (9).

Both ideologies of the American future are based upon the concept of fundamental, enduring change—whether for better or for worse. Irving, however, carefully structures his text in order to suggest that no change has taken or will take place in Rip Van Winkle's Golden Age world. Previous ages have ended, he admits: the Indians of the appended *Natursagen* have ceased to exist—although the natural world they sought to explain still exists, to be explained in other ways, and although certain parallels between their world and Rip's can be found: the squaw-spirit whose demanding capriciousness survives in the shrewish Dame Van Winkle and the nascent shrewishness of Rip's daughter, for example. The world of seventeenth-century New Holland has also come to an end, surviving only in memories and legends, but deprived of its essential character: Hudson and his crew, reflecting that loss, go through the motions of drinking and playing, but do so in grim silence.

But Rip Van Winkle's world survives—despite the march of time, the Yankee invasion, political change, and progress. The central characteristic of that world—and nothing in the context of the early nineteenth-century United States could be more subversive—is a happy combination of unregenerate idleness and semiliterate or preliterate ignorance. Rip and his buddies, as described in the first pages of the story, personify those traits, but Rip's worthlessness is of heroic stature. Most of his cronies die, but Rip—like the Emperor Frederick (and this parallel between Rip and the Emperor is the essence of the legend), like Diedrich Knickerbocker, who survives in the "Posthumous Writing" of the text—only appears to die. In fact he is merely asleep, waiting until his world is on the brink of destruction by democracy, bustle, and progress. He returns to provide continuity and to reconstruct the world of the past and ensure its survival—and the inevitability of that survival, which no longer depends upon Rip's physical presence, is underlined by Irving's creation of both a second-generation *and* a third-generation Rip, son and grandson. The world to which Rip returns after the revolution has changed in appearance and in character—but our hero quickly puts things to right. Before long, Rip is back idling away the days on a bench in front of the inn, "reverenced" by the town's inhabitants and influencing "the rising generation, with whom he soon grew into great favor" (40). The inn over which he presides is no longer the Union Hotel, but "Mr. Doolittle's Hotel," and the owner's name, despite its Yankee origins, suggests the triumph of idleness. The ultimate proof that Rip has managed to defeat the forces of progress and to restore the Golden Age of blissful sloth and ignorance is not Knickerbocker's claim to have met Rip Van Winkle in the flesh, but his assertion that he "has seen a certificate on the subject taken before a country justice and *signed with a cross in the justice's own hand writing*" [my italics].[22]

This reading of Irving's story tells us a good deal about the legend and what it was to become in the New World. The other two examples of the form I have chosen, I believe, make it clear that while the Golden Ages envisioned by writers elsewhere in the hemisphere were very different from Irving's Hudson Valley, the legend as a literary form conditioned both the character and the presentation of the past. One of the most famous nineteenth-century Latin American legendary texts is *Iracema*, published in 1865 by the Brazilian José de Alencar (1829–1877).[23]

This text, described in its subtitle as a legend of Alencar's native province of Ceará, is set in the early sixteenth century at the moment of first contact between the Portuguese and the Indian inhabitants of Brazil.[24] In essays and reviews written well before *Iracema,* Alencar had made clear his vision of the Indian world as a Golden Age equivalent to the Middle Ages of European romantics like Scott; he insisted, for example, that "As leis da cavalaria no tempo em que ela floresceu na Europa, não excediam, por certo, em pundonor e brios à bizarria dos selvagens brasileiros" ("the rules of chivalry, in the days when European knighthood was in flower, most assuredly did not surpass the gallantry of the savages of Brazil in either dignity or mettle").[25] He further declared that those who wished to write works "nativamente brasileira de inspiração e forma" ("inherently Brazilian in inspiration and in form") had no choice but to focus on the world the Indians had created.[26] And, finally, while logic and history agreed that the Indian world had disappeared, at least in all but the most distant recesses of the nation's interior, Alencar believed that the purpose of the new national literature he was helping to create was to provide evidence—emotional, parahistorical evidence—that that world, as "o berço de nossa nacionalidade" ("the cradle of our nationhood"), still survived in nineteenth-century Brazil.[27]

Unlike Irving, Alencar does not openly negate written history. Rather, he uses the apparatus of written history to validate a story which is largely invented—and to mislead the unwary reader about the essential nature of the text. *Iracema,* despite its subtitled description as a legend, purports to be fact; a large number of detailed, scholarly footnotes serve as one frame for the text, presenting it as a historically accurate account of the first European settlement of Ceará and explaining the etymologies and meanings of the dozens of Indian words and names which appear in the text.[28]

The plot of *Iracema,* however, has very little indeed to do with the reality of Portuguese conquest. A handsome, heroic, and sensitive Portuguese soldier, Martim Soares Moreno, meets and falls in love with Iracema—an incredibly beautiful Indian girl sworn to chastity as a vestal priestess. The two have almost nothing in common except their mutual passion, but Iracema is compelled by that passion to leave her tribe and her religion and live with Martim and his Indian sidekick, Poti. Martim, driven by loyalty and ambition, leaves Iracema to return to the Portuguese conquest of Indian Brazil; she gives birth, in his absence, to their son, Moacir. Iracema dies of pain and sorrow just as Martim returns; he buries her beside the sea, and sails away with Moacir.

Alencar concludes that the meaning of this story is that "Tudo passa sôbre a terra" ("All things upon this earth must pass" [309]). The preface invokes the forces of nature, the land and sea of Ceará, to help the author reconstruct this past world, this Golden Age of Indian Brazil at the very moment of its extinction. The footnotes, with their emphasis upon chronology and a dead language, reinforce the theme of the passage of time and the passing of Indian civilization. As we have seen, however, the function of the literary legend in the New World is not simply to create and admire a lost Golden Age, but to relate it to the present— even to insist that it is not in fact lost. Alencar frames the context of the survival of Indian Brazil through the symbolic structure of his plot, through a decidedly nonscholarly use of history and linguistics, and, most remarkably, through the language of the text itself.

First, Martim Soares Moreno was a real person, but the evidence of the text suggests that Alencar chose him as the hero of *Iracema* because of the linguistic possibilities offered by his name. He stands for Portugal as a nation of warriors (Martim, derived from Mars) and seafarers (*mar*, in Portuguese, means "sea"); Martim is consistently described within Alencar's text by the epithet "the warrior of the sea." Thus it is clear that Martim, whatever his historical reality, is not intended to be viewed as an individual but as the symbol of a nation.

There is no historical evidence for Iracema's existence, but Alencar goes to great pains to explain her name as the combination of two Tupi words: *ira* (honey) and a variant form of the word *tembe* (lips)—therefore, "lips of honey" (312). Iracema is sweet and pure, but the scholarly apparatus which frames her name is designed to give her reality. She is, nonetheless, at least as symbolic as Martim; she is "the virgin of the forests," "the virgin of the jungle," and her name is in fact an anagram of "America"—the Indian America she represents. Her conquest by Martim and her death symbolize what happened to that America with the arrival of the Portuguese.

Iracema's death, however, does not mean that the Golden Age of Indian Brazil does not survive. She leaves a son, Moacir—whose name means "son of pain," the pain of the Portuguese conquest (319). Moacir is both Indian and Portuguese, the creature of both the jungle and the sea. He is, in short, the first Brazilian, and Iracema and Indian Brazil survive through him. Nor is Moacir the only source of survival. The Golden Age also survives in the original and remarkable language of Alencar's text. Over and over, perhaps hundreds of times in this brief work, Alencar makes a statement in standard Portuguese: for example, "Iracema dobrou a cabeça sôbre a espádua" ("Iracema bent down her head"). He then places a comma as a form of equation, and then essentially translates his Portuguese statement, through simile, into a new language—not Tupi, although it contains Indian words still commonly used to refer to flora and fauna, but the present-tense language of the enduring reality of Brazil itself, of the land and its creatures and plants, unchanged despite the historical accidents of conquest and settlement: "Iracema dobrou a cabeça sôbre a espádua, como a tenra palma da carnaúba, quando a chuva peneira na várzea" ("Iracema bent down her head, like the delicate *carnaúba* palm tree when the rains spatter the riverbanks" [263]). Thus, symbolically and linguistically, the Golden Age remains, able to serve as "the cradle of our nationhood," and the function of both the structure and the language of *Iracema* is to prove that survival.

The last New World legend I have chosen to describe in detail is "La fiebre amarilla" ("Yellow Fever"), by the Mexican Justo Sierra (1848–1912).[29] The first, most distant part of the frame—and the various parts of the complex frame make up about one-fourth of this brief narrative—begins by defining the text: the author wrote it a number of years previously, in an *Álbum de Viaje* (*Travel Album*), forgot about it for years, and only recently came across it by chance. The second frame, taken from the *Álbum,* describes a stagecoach ride from Veracruz to Mexico City. Accompanying the author on this trip is a young German with "cabellos de oro gris, ojos azules, grandes y sin expresión" ("grey-gold hair and large, expressionless blue eyes" [436]). Shortly after leaving Veracruz, the travellers are trapped by a violent tropical storm. The coach stops to wait for the tempest to pass, and the German complains, before he drops off to sleep, that he is burning up with fever. A branch happens to push through the leather flap that covers the coach window, and the narrator stares at a drop of water, "lágrima postrera de la tormenta" ("the storm's last tear"), trembling on a yellowed leaf. What he sees within that drop of water is the third, innermost frame for the invented legend which is the real focus of the text.

The drop of water is the Gulf of Mexico, filled with islands—including an imaginary, nameless island which even the hurricanes avoid; it is gold-colored, surrounded by a yellow aura, and is described in terms of death and sickness. "Una voz infinitamente triste, como la voz del mar, sonaba en aquella isla perdida" ("An infinitely sad voice, like the voice of the sea, echoed through that lost island" [437]). That voice is the ultimate source of the narrator's account of miraculous and mysterious events which took place on the island of Cuba in 1492. An indescribably beautiful thirteen-year-old girl, Starei (which Sierra explains means "star"), appears by magic on the island, and is adored as divine by the inhabitants. Sierra's description of Starei reinforces the priestly consensus that she is the creation and symbol of the Gulf: her eyes are like those of the Aztecs, her skin like that of the maidens who bathe in the Meschacebe or Mississippi (437–38).

Starei's arrival changes Indian life in Cuba; the entire male population of the island follows her around: old men die of weariness, young men commit suicide at her feet, and the women mourn the fact that their husbands have permanently abandoned them. The supreme god of the Antilles, Hurakán (the hurricane), attacks the island, as the priests speak of a new Deluge and the inhabitants spend the night in prayer and sacrifice. When the storm passes at dawn of the next day, Starei calls the Indians to the beach; she is holding a young and handsome white man, who appears to be dead. Starei vows that whoever saves the white man's life will be her husband, and a stranger—with huge golden eyes, a sensual and ironic face, and red tattoos covering his body, which is naked except for a breechcloth made of feathers from the Mexican Plumed Serpent— appears to take up her challenge. The stranger touches the white man's chest, but pulls back in fear from a strangely shaped wooden talisman, a cross. Once the cross is removed, the stranger brings the dead Spaniard back to life, and declares that he will hold Starei to her promise.

Starei instantly loathes the stranger, defined in the text as "the son of Heat," and falls madly in love with the Spaniard. She proposes marriage to him, but he reveals that he is a priest and cannot marry. The stranger, Zekom, returns to demand Starei's hand, revealing that they are both gods—she of the Gulf, he of the Tropics—and are destined to rule together. Starei still desires the Spanish priest, however, and when he again refuses, she curses him. That night, as another storm rages over Cuba, Starei and Zekom consummate their marriage. When the couple bids farewell to the Indians the next day, Starei's eyes too have become golden. They sail away in a magic canoe to the unknown island in the gulf, which we learn from this mysterious voice "es el centro del imperio de Starei, desde aquí irradia su eterna venganza contra los blancos" ("is the center of Starei's empire, from [which] spreads her eternal vengeance against the white man"). The Spanish priest soon dies of a new and horrible disease, his body turning as yellow as Zekom's eyes. Starei still mourns his death, and "sus lágrimas, evaporadas por el calor del trópico se evaporan y envenenan la atmósfera del Golfo, y ay de los hijos de las tierras frías!" ("her tears, evaporated by the heat of the tropics, are distilled and poison the air of the Gulf and—woe betide the sons of the cold lands!" [441]).

The drop of water which has contained all this finally rolls to the ground, and the last part of the frame begins. The carriage starts moving again, and the narrator looks at his companion, whose skin is now completely yellow. As the carriage arrives at the town of Córdoba, the German asks the narrator to look at the yellow woman. " '—Quién?'—le pregunté—'es Starei?' " (" 'Who?,' I asked; 'is it Starei?' "). The young man replies that it is. The narrator leaves his companion in Córdoba, and goes on to Mexico City; a Veracruz newspaper informs him that "El joven alemán Wilhelm S., de la casa Watermayer y Cía., que salió de esta ciudad bueno en apariencia, ha muerto en Córdoba de la fiebre amarilla" ("Wilhelm S., a young German employed by the Watermayer Company, left this city in apparent good health, but died in Córdoba of yellow fever. R.I.P." [442]).

Sierra's text, like Alencar's *Iracema,* is an effort to re-create the lost Amerindian past. In this case, however, the legacy of that past to the present—yellow fever—appears, rationally and logically, to be entirely negative; it is even more difficult to accept as a positive than the happy-go-lucky idleness and ignorance of Irving's Dutch New York. Nonetheless, this entirely invented Mexican *Natursagen* contains a subtext, primarily communicated through the frames of the narrative, which conforms to the model of the New World legend.

Sierra, through his frames, stresses that the events he is describing are entirely parahistorical—found not in books but in a drop of rainwater; their truth derives from Nature rather than from Man. The frames also define the essential characteristics of his highly unorthodox and ambiguous Golden Age: unity and independence. The geographical and ethnological information provided is disjointed, illogical, and disconcerting, but Sierra uses it to create a past in which what is now Mexico lay at the center of a world and a culture which included both the Atlantic Antilles and the Gulf of Mexico from Florida to Veracruz and which stretched as far north as the mouth of the Mississippi. The inhabitants of that world were independent of external human control, their lives affected only by nature and by the deities who represented its forces. This authentic and passionate world came to an end when the Spanish arrived—symbolized within the text by the priest whose alien religion leads him to deny both Starei and his own natural instincts.

Sierra also presents a present through his frames. The geographical and cultural unity of the past has disappeared. More importantly, independence has been replaced by the reality or the possibility of external domination. The Spaniards still hold the island of Cuba, "la esclava servida por esclavos" ("the slave served by slaves"), and other "sons of the cold lands" have come as well—Europeans and North Americans, all represented here by the almost anonymous young German business-man, Wilhelm S. The enduring vengeance of Starei is tropical America's safeguard against permanent absorption by these alien forces, and yellow fever not only secures the future, but also allows the past to survive into the present—even the blond, blue-eyed Wilhelm S. is able to see Starei just before he dies. The narrator is preoccupied by his traveling com-panion's illness, but the decidedly unscientific point of the first and last portions of the framing devices is that the narrator has no reason to fear yellow fever. An educated, even Europeanized Mexican, he is still a son of the tropics rather than of the cold lands; yellow fever cannot touch him, therefore, and he survives to read the news of the German's death and, years later, to discover this narrative in a box of long-forgotten papers.

I have attempted to show, through these brief analyses of three New World literary legends, that underlying superficial diversity is a remark-able unanimity of purpose and technique. I would stress, moreover, that in the New World legend purpose and technique are inseparable. In order to achieve their shared goal—to recover or create a past and to relate that past to the present—the writers of these legends felt it necessary to use complex framing devices, either external to the text or internalized in the language of the text itself. Those devices first seek to disconcert, forcing us to suspend logic and reason and to accept a nonrealistic, distorted, or subversive vision of the past; such formal devices also serve to establish, in the author's own terms, the relationship between that past and the present which is the ultimate function of the legend.

During the course of the nineteenth century, the legend slowly dis-appeared from the literature of the United States, or changed in purpose and in form. In can be argued, in part, that the legend—which by definition looked backward rather than forward—did not have much of a chance against the forces of optimism, materialism, and progress, forces defeated only within Washington Irving's legendary texts. Beyond this, however, the example of Nathaniel Hawthorne suggests that few American writers found it possible to discover a usable national past. Early legendary texts like "The Maypole at Merrymount" and the "Leg-ends of the Province House," all in *Twice-Told Tales,* show Hawthorne digging through the remains of colonial New England in search of a past he could utilize; at the end of his career as a novelist, he gave up the search and turned to Italy. The legend, as well, was exploited and trivialized to serve nonliterary ends—from Davy Crockett's election campaign to Paul Bunyan and the Jolly Green Giant. And, finally, it can be argued that the legend eventually moved outside literature entirely, to become a fundamental component of the cinema—a form in which the medium itself creates a frame which is far more concrete and immediately effective than the literary frames I have discussed.

In the rest of the hemisphere, the literary legend survived and flourished in the nineteenth century, reaching its peak in the *Tradiciones peruanas* of Ricardo Palma (1833–1919). Like earlier New World legends, the *Tradiciones* establish a past Golden Age—in this case, colonial Peru—and endeavor to link that past to the present. Palma, however, goes beyond his predecessors and contemporaries in fusing frame and narrative; in a number of *Tradiciones*, for example, the frame for the legend—the historical background—becomes the center of the text, and the nonhistorical or parahistorical events narrated serve as the frame. Moreover, the unique language of the *Tradiciones*—a language without fixed register, which jumps wildly from poetic descriptions to slang to Latin tags to verses from popular songs—is an integral part of the text, designed to disorient us and to prepare us to accept fiction as history and history as fiction.

Nor did the literary legend in Latin America end with Ricardo Palma. In literary history as in legend, the past survives into the present. That survival can be seen, first, in one of the most influential texts of twentieth-century Brazilian literature, Mário de Andrade's 1927 *Macunaíma*. Like Alencar, Andrade uses the structure and the language of the text to re-create Brazil's Indian past; he concludes, however, that the past has become meaningless, because Brazil itself has no future. And in Spanish America, I would suggest, the literary legend was rediscovered or reinvented in 1943, when a young Cuban wrote that "Vi la posibilidad de establecer ciertos sincronismos posibles, americanos, recurrentes, por encima del tiempo, relacionando esto con aquello, el ayer con el presente" ("I saw the possibility of establishing certain potential synchronic relationships—recurring, American relationships, existing beyond time—linking this to that, yesterday to the present").[30] This "revelation," Alejo Carpentier has declared, was the beginning of what he and many others have called "*lo real maravilloso*" (frequently translated as "Magic Realism") as the central focus of Spanish American fiction; it is also a restatement of the underlying purpose of the literary legend. Moreover, major texts of *lo real maravilloso*, from Carpentier's *El siglo de las luces* (*Explosion in the Cathedral*) and *Los pasos perdidos* (*The Lost Steps*) to

Gabriel García Márquez's *Cien años de soledad* (*One Hundred Years of Solitude*), not only continue the tradition of the legend by attempting to create a Spanish American past and to link that past to the present, but also utilize many of the formal devices—the creation of historical or pseudohistorical frames, the seamless mixing of history and parahistory, the disconcerting juxtaposition of reality and fantasy, the use of the language of the text itself as an integral part of the frame—that we have seen in the legends of Irving, Alencar, and Sierra.

José David Saldívar

The Dialectics of Our America

> In the absence of a pope, what are we to do about the problem of
> the canon in rewriting American literary history?
> —Werner Sollors, *Beyond Ethnicity: Consent and Descent*
> *in American Culture*

In light of the developments which have recently taken place
within the American literary historical community, Sollors's rhetorical
question about the American canon provides us with an appropriate
frame of reference. Indeed, the new "ideological" school of American
literary history led by Sacvan Bercovitch and Myra Jehlen, among others,
has, in many ways, underlined and strengthened the need to study our
American literary and historical past.[1]

The new American literary history has proceeded to do so by directing its attention to new writers, by addressing itself to new problems
in literary history, and, above all, by sharpening its methodological tools.
For example, Sacvan Bercovitch in *Reconstructing American Literary History* (1986) has argued for what he calls a "dialogic mode of analysis" in
the writing of the new literary history. Put more precisely, Bercovitch's
own history of American literature resembles Bakhtin's description of
the novelistic form: it is often marked by a clashing plurality of discourses, fragments, and a polyethnic system of American codes in what
he sees as our age of "dissensus."[2] Other Americanists, among them
Paul Lauter, Juan Bruce Novoa, Jane Tompkins, and Houston A. Baker,
Jr., have centered their "dialectics of validation" around aspects of American literature—such as race, class, gender, and difference—which had
so far received little attention; such scholars have given a new impulse
to the study of a variety of subjects ranging from the reevaluation of

what constitutes a "classical" American text to the role of a distinctly slave "vernacular" in American discourse in general, and in Afro-American literature in particular.[3] The theoretical boundaries within which American literary history and interpretation unfold have been redefined in the American theoretical works of Fredric Jameson, Frank Lentricchia, Hayden White, and Edward Said. Each in his own way has questioned the very premises upon which the concepts of American hermeneutics, alterity, history, and historiography rest.[4] It is within the ideological framework of these varied tendencies in American literary history that I would like to add two oppositional voices to our new literary history—namely, the Cuban poets and revolutionaries José Martí and Roberto Fernández Retamar.

What lies behind this essay, then, is a growing awareness on my part of the extremely narrow confines and conservative practices of literary study as it is now performed in the academy, and with that, a growing conviction about the social and political implications of this exclusionary practice. As a literary theoretician outside the mainstream and educated in a segregated farm society in south Texas, I have been particularly sensitive to the absence of writers from what Martí called "our America"—a Pan-American culture of descendants, both ethnically and culturally speaking, of aborigines, *mestizos,* Africans, and Europeans. It is my view that the greatest shortcoming of the literary historical work being done on the American canon is not its lack of theoretical rigor but rather its parochial vision. American literary historians (even the newer ones) and critics working on the reconstruction of American literary history characteristically know little in depth about the history, cultures, and discourses of the Americas as a totality. One of the values of a comparative focus is that it permits us to escape, at least to some extent, from the provincialism and limiting set of tacit assumptions that tend to result from perpetual immersion in the study of a single American culture or literature.

Martí's Manichean Allegory: Destructuring the U.S. Empire As a Way of Life

What is apparent is that the nature of the North American government is gradually changing in its fundamental reality. Under the traditional labels of Republican and Democrat, with no innovation other than the contingent circumstances of place and character, the republic is becoming plutocratic and imperialistic.

—José Martí, "North American Scenes"

It is not a case of [Martí] rejecting the United States mechanically, en masse; rather it is a case of underlining the negative aspects born in the country's breast.

—Roberto Fernández Retamar, "Introducción a Martí"

The point seems to be, one must be willing to begin an argument, and so formulate questions that will redefine the context, displace the terms of the metaphors, and make up new ones.

—Teresa De Lauretis, *Alice Doesn't*

During the past generation the new cultural history of America has been fractured into various professional shards: social history, ethnic history, women's history, Afro-American history, and Chicano history. No longer is American history conceived exclusively as the story of Anglo-Saxon men from the first settlements in the Chesapeake Bay area in 1607 to the present. Looking at American history "from the bottom up," this "revisionist" scholarship has shattered the traditional American consensus.[5] But in American literary studies there has not been enough major historical scholarship that can be called revisionist. In order to avoid the stark fragmentation of American intellectual history that has plagued our historians, however, I want to begin to make the literary history of the Americas whole again, first, by turning to the genealogical texts of José Martí and Roberto Fernández Retamar who, in their oppositional discourses, have attempted to unify the history of the Americas. Only when we begin to look at the history of the Americas as a hemisphere, and when we begin to analyze the real and rhetorical, often hostile, battles between the United States and what Martí called "Nuestra América"—"Our America"—can we begin to perceive what the literatures of the Americas have in common. After all the U.S. codes of reification—transforming the realities of dependency, conquest, and military intervention into the American rhetoric about freedom, virtue, and an "Alliance for Progress"—have been negated, Martí's "Nuestra América" (1891) and Fernández Retamar's *Caliban* (1971), "Nuestra América y Occidente" (1976), and "Algunos usos de civilización y barbarie" (1977) are illuminating texts upon which to base an indigenous American cultural critique. After analyzing Martí's and Fernández Retamar's deconstruction of "the America which is not ours," I will then examine what I see as some important literary and cultural connections between Fernández Retamar's Casa de las Américas publishing house in Havana, the Latin American *nueva narrativa,* and postmodernist North American literature: namely, the radical ethnopoetics of Rolando Hinojosa and Ntozake Shange. In my conclusion, I will also analyze a political cartoon in the *Washington Post* entitled "Ronald Reagan's World," and Gabriel García Márquez's ideological response to such a vision of Latin America in his 1982 Nobel Prize address, "The Solitude of Latin America."

At the outset, let me emphasize my goals in this reconstruction of American literary history: first, to place the leading oppositional intellectual figures from Our America within a limited genealogy of their discursive and nondiscursive practices; and second, to show how responsive to their historical situations of hegemony and hostility they have been. Like Nietzsche's genealogist, Martí and Fernández Retamar are always concerned in their cultural essays with the material configurations of power, the possibility and legitimacy of certain tropes and interpretations, and the concrete human efforts of such power structures. As we will see below, both Martí and Fernández Retamar assume authority to displace it.[6]

My brief exegesis of Martí's cultural criticism in "Nuestra América" does not pretend to meet the degree of historical completeness necessary to demonstrate the complex literary and ideological importance of his work. But, as Jean Franco explains in *An Introduction to Spanish American Literature* (1969):

> Only Martí [in the late-nineteenth century] significantly enriched and transformed the [Spanish literary tradition] on which he drew. He saw art neither as propaganda tools nor as play but as the expression which was communicable because universal. Yet this genuinely original poet and thinker had no followers and it was to be some time before his own optimistic statement [in "Nuestra América"] that "el libro importado ha sido vencido en América por el hombre natural" ("the imported book has been vanquished in America by natural man") was truly applicable to the literature of the continent.[7]

Enrico Mario Santí suggests, moreover, that because Martí never collected his prose works in book form, the "piecemeal, fragmented, and foreign publication of the first edition of Martí's collected works between 1900 and 1933 constitute both a cause and effect of this initial vacuum."[8]

Because I do not attempt to catalogue much that is positive in Martí's remarks about North American culture in the Gilded Age, this section of my study is not a "balanced" reading of Martí. Rather, my purpose is to focus on Martí's cultural critique of the U.S. "empire as a way of life."[9] As the U.S. underwent the transition from "competitive" capitalism to "monopoly" capitalism in the 1880s, Martí grew more critical about the bourgeois way of life there. In "The Modernity of Martí," Fernández Retamar argues that Martí "identified and denounced the characteristics of what we now recognize as the beginnings of the last stage of capitalism: the rise of the monopolies ('The monopoly,' says Martí, 'sits like an implacable giant at the door of the poor'), and the fusion of banking capital with industrial in a financial oligarchy ('those iniquitous consortia of capital')."[10] In "Nuestra América" and in his newspaper analyses of the U.S., Martí constructed a powerful cultural critique of imperialism, twenty-one years before Lenin diagnosed the mature features of imperialism in *Imperialism: The Highest Stage of Capitalism*.

From 1881 until just before his death in 1895 (he died battling the Spanish empire in Cuba), Martí rarely left the U.S. As one Martí scholar put it, "In the U.S., Martí became a politician, a chronicler of North American history, and a man of action."[11] Although Martí as chronicler wrote on a variety of North American topics (for instance, Grant's tomb), on Whitman as the great poet of the Americas, on Emerson as philosopher, and on more scientific and political subjects such as Charles Darwin and Karl Marx, he emerges in "Nuestra América" as a firm anti-imperialist, who once wrote about the emergent empire, the United States: "I know the monster; I have lived in its entrails."[12]

Emerson's "The American Scholar" (1837) established the grounds for a national, popular American literature—"Each age must write its own books; or rather, each generation for the next succeeding. The books of an older period will not fit this."[13] Martí's "Nuestra América" similarly provided a base for a national, Latin American literature that was capable of incorporating both the Spanish and First American experiences in the New World. In "Nuestra América" and "Madre América," as well as elsewhere, Martí's view of the American hemisphere is cast in a Manichean struggle. As he proposed in *La Nación*:

> On the one hand, there is in [the Americas] a nation proclaiming its right by proper investiture, because of geographical morality, to rule the continent, and it announces . . . that everything in North

America must be its, and that this imperial right must be acknowledged from the Isthmus all the way south. On the other hand, there are the nations of diverse origins and purposes . . . [Nuestra América].[14]

Any revisionist literary history of the Americas would have to contend with Martí's conviction of a profound gap between "Our America" and the other America, which is not ours. "Nuestra América" in particular can provide us with the central oppositional codes upon which to base a dialectical view not only of the American continent but of the many literatures of the Americas.

Seen in this light, "Nuestra América" marks the beginning of a new epoch of resistance to empire in the Americas. As a specific intellectual in Foucault's sense, Martí stands between two ways of thinking: the last representative of a nineteenth-century romantic idealism, and the first forerunner of a Latin American socialist ideology of continental solidarity. As Raúl Roa, Cuban foreign minister, speaking to the United Nations in May 1968, emphasized, "At the level of international relations, the fundamental antagonism of our epoch is expressed in the struggle between imperialism and the peoples of the underdeveloped world."[15] Martí is the first cultural critic from Our America bold enough to document to the rest of the American hemisphere what he saw as the United States's emerging ideas, languages, and reality of empire. (As a parenthetical note, the Nicaraguan *modernista* poet, Rubén Darío, would join Martí in attacking Teddy Roosevelt's "Big Stick" policy in his 1903 poem entitled "To Roosevelt.") As Martí prophetically stated in "Nuestra América":

> Our America is running another risk that does not come from itself but from the difference in origins, methods, and interests between the two halves of the continent, and the time is near at hand when an enterprising and vigorous people who scorn or ignore Our America will even so approach it and demand a close relationship. And since strong nations, self-made by law and shotgun, love strong nations, and them alone; since the time of madness and ambition—from which North America may be freed by the predominance of the purest elements in its blood, or on which it may be launched by its vindictive and sordid masses, its tradition of expansion, or the ambitions of some powerful leader—is not so near at hand, even to the most timorous eye, that there is no time

for the test of discreet and unwavering pride that could confront and dissuade it; since its good name as a republic in the eyes of the world's perceptive nations puts upon North America a restraint that cannot be taken away by childish provocations or pompous arrogance or parricidal discords among Our American nations—the pressing need of Our America is to show itself as it is, one in spirit and intent, swift conqueror of a suffocating past, stained only by the enriching blood drawn from the hands that struggle to clear away ruins, and from the scars left upon us by our masters. The scorn of our formidable neighbor who does not know us is Our America's greatest danger. And since the day of the visit is near, it is imperative that our neighbor know us, and soon, so that it will not scorn us.[16]

Stylistically the passage is typical of Martí's rhetorical grace, power, and lexical play: the balanced schemes of repetition, especially anaphora; the willingness to use alliteration to present harsh judgments; the amused, delicate use of litotes ("an enterprising and vigorous people . . . will demand a close relationship"); the tropical cadence of apostrophe; and the active use of a binary methodology. Its content, however, is a striking description of "the development of underdevelopment" in Latin America, for Martí's primary concern in the passage is the reality of relentless expansion by the North Americans. No Cuban (perhaps not even Fidel Castro at his rhetorical, vituperative best) has ever surpassed Martí in his lucid denunciation of American empire. No writer has been more graceful and clear than Martí in describing the negative way of life in the U.S.

By 1882 Martí had become convinced that the U.S. had given up its rhetoric of freedom and dignity. In New York he had witnessed the huge influx of European immigrants bringing with them "their wounds [and] their moral ulcers." Describing the miserable life of the underclass there, he wrote: "He who can observe the deplorable life of today's wretched workingman and woman in the cold latitudes without feeling his soul wrenched with pity, is not only barely insensitive, but commits a criminal act."[17] He had also observed the rise of blatant forms of white dominance over nonwhite populations in the urban metropole—blacks, Chinese, and the "First Americans" (Amerindians) were characteristically discriminated against by a white supremacist ideology.[18] So it came as no surprise to Latin American readers of "North American Scenes" when, in 1886, he wrote the following about the prototypical North

American character: "[Achieving a] fortune is the only object of life. . . . Men, despite all appearances, are tied together here only by interests, by the cordial hatreds that exist between those who are bargaining for the same prize. . . . It is urgent to feed the lamp of light and reduce the beast."[19]

Thus, in order to understand fully Martí's call for Latin American cultural autonomy, nationalism, and self-determination in "Nuestra América," it is essential to note his emergent sociopolitical radicalization in the U.S. His anti-imperialism was at once a close reading of U.S. "manifest destiny" doctrine.[20] His allegory of reading the imperial designs of North American foreign policy became a warning to Our America to prepare itself to withstand the relentless expansion of its neighbor to the north. From 1881 to 1889, then, Martí clearly perceived that U.S. foreign policy and industry would need both a cheap source of raw material, and a world market for their surplus goods. Our America, he predicted, was ripe for both: "The descendants of the pilgrim's father had their celebrations. What a difference though! Now they are no longer humble, nor tread the snow of Cape Cod with workers' boots. Instead they now lace up their military boots aggressively and they see on one side Canada and on the other Mexico."[21]

What Martí dramatizes for us in his voluminous essays, letters, and journalistic pieces (collected in seventeen volumes by Cuban publishers) is this: as an alienated Cuban exiled in the homemade ghettos of New York, he is the only Latin American intellectual of his time audacious enough to confront the U.S.'s imperial history, its imperial ethic, and its imperial psychology. Imperialism, Martí suggests, had penetrated the very fabric of North American culture and had infected its imagination. The U.S. metropole, once and for all, would now enjoy and exploit a structural advantage over the Latin American "periphery." He reads the grammar of imperialism, and he dramatizes how the U.S. domination of the weaker economies in Our America (and its political and social superstructures) was to ensure the extraction of economic rewards— what Andre Gunder Frank calls the "development of underdevelopment."[22]

As a handbook describing the codes of imperialism, "Nuestra América" not only analyzes the overdetermined causes but points out strategies for resistance to "Yankee" domination. Martí believed that the first step for governing "our republics" is a thorough knowledge of the diverse elements that make up the Americas as a continent, for "the able governor in Our America is not the one who knows how to govern the Germans or the French; he must know the elements that compose his own country; and how to bring them together, using methods and institutions originating within the country" (86). Secondly, he contended that Our America must refrain from rewriting its American narratives of government, according to paradigms not their own—with laws, constitutions, discourses, and systems taken from totally different cultural contexts: "A decree by Hamilton does not halt the plainsman's horse" (86). Leaders from Our America would have to take into account the popular indigenous elements contained within each culture and recognize their inherent value. As Philip Foner suggests in his study of Martí, because Our America had not taken these elements into account, or rather because, like its neighbor to the north, it had destroyed the cultures of the First Americans, Our America had suffered and would continue to suffer from despotism, tyranny, and authoritarianism.[23]

In rejecting the European university for the American, Martí, like many of our contemporary cultural critics, believed that one of the principal sites of contention was to be at the institutional site of the University: "The European university must yield to the American university. The history of America, from the Incas to the present, must be taught letter perfect, even if the Argonauts of Greece is never taught. Our own Greece is preferable to the Greece which is not ours" (88). What is at stake in Martí's cultural studies view of the University are competing political and intellectual visions. What should count as knowledge and critical thought in the education of our hemisphere's future generations? How can we prepare students to enter the multicultural world of the future? In negating European and North American colonial and imperial rule (the imposition of the European institutional nondiscursive practices over the American), "Nuestra América" also anticipates Caliban's revolutionary overturning of Prospero's disciplinary techniques of mind control, repression, and anxiety in January 1959, namely, in the Cuban Revolution.

Put plainly, for all its rhetorical significance, its expressive emphasis, its tropical melodic variety, and its delicate use of repetition and balance, the real power behind Martí's discourse is not in its grammatical play but in its historical challenge to U.S. imperialism. Against the Eurocentric reading of American history and the canon ("our own Greece is preferable to the Greece which is not ours"), "Nuestra América," like "The American Scholar," privileges an indigenous American cultural practice. For Martí, political discourse and what he called *versos sencillos* (simple verses) had to be written "*en mi propia sangre*" ("in my own blood"), not in "*tinta de académicos*" ("academic ink"). What is significant for our new American literary history, then, is the lesson Martí teaches us about the real historical, cultural, and geopolitical differences between "Our America" and "the America which is not ours." Martí warns us that two distinct peoples, which language and psychology has set poles apart from each other, inhabit the same hemisphere. Martí's America spoke mainly in Spanish, worshipped non-Protestant gods, and struggled against the political and economic realities of U.S. empire.[24]

It would indeed be an understatement to remark that Martí has had a profound influence on the course of Cuban-Marxist oppositional thinking in the twentieth century. Although one Marxist-Leninist critic, Juan Marinello, has chastised Martí for being a romantic idealist, most Cuban Marxists (including Fidel Castro) acknowledge their revolutionary ties to the political, aesthetic, and social philosophy of Martí.[25] Others, like Roberto Fernández Retamar, director of Cuba's Center for José Martí Studies, and editor of the Cuban journal, *Casa de las Américas,* however, have had to insist that they are not rewriting Martí as a Marxist revolutionary, which he was not. In his numerous studies of Martí, Fernández Retamar has illuminated the ties between Martí's oppositional criticism of North American culture, and the Cuban-Marxist ideology of resistance to U.S. empire as a way of life. What is essential in Fernández Retamar's interpretation of Martí's work can be summarized in the following manner: Martí took the first necessary step toward ending Cuba's "periphery" status in the American continent by advocating the solidarity of all the indigenous peoples of Our America. By April 1960, Che Guevara was able to state about Cuba, with biting irony and self-mockery: "Sometimes we even thought it was rather pompous to refer to Cuba as if it were the center of the universe. Nonetheless, it was true or almost true. If someone doubted the revolution's importance he should read the newspaper. . . . Man, we're strong and dangerous. We have poisoned the American environment and threatened the sweet democracy of Trujillo and Somoza. . . . Oh it is so great and comfortable to belong to such a strong world power as dangerous as Cuba."[26] Only after the Cuban Revolution in 1959, did the United States's "institutional practices" begin to invest aggressively in "Latin American Studies." For instance, according to Roberto González Echevarría, "the financing of literary journals had a crucial bearing on the creation [and reception] of the new Latin American literature of the sixties."[27] I would add that it also certainly had an ideological bearing on how we imported an "idealist" literary aesthetic into our U.S. universities, for the importation of typically colonial writers such as Jorge Luis Borges rendered Latin American radicalism safe for the so-called Free World.

Fernández Retamar's *Casa de las Américas* and the *Nueva Narrativa*: Rethinking Literary History from the Other Side

> What is our history, what is our culture, if not the history and culture of Caliban?
> —Roberto Fernández Retamar, *Caliban*

> In Latin America those most receptive to Marxist thought have not been the proletarians but rather students, professors, journalists, professionals, and artists. In particular, Marxism has gained a great deal of respectability by its acceptance by outstanding literary figures such as Jorge Amado, Julio Cortázar, Gabriel García Márquez, and Pablo Neruda.
> —Sheldon B. Liss, *Marxist Thought in Latin America*

> Last June in La Habana with theater people from Uruguay, Nicaragüa, Mexico, El Salvador, Colombia, we walked many nights, El Malecon. Rum. Poetry. The full moon. Old women walking their dogs at 4 a.m., safe. . . . To breathe in 'el primer territorio libre de América.'
> —Ntozake Shange, "Palabras y Balas"

> Cuba is a peculiarly emotional issue in the United States.
> —Wayne S. Smith, *The Closest of Enemies*

This section, dealing with my Foucauldian motifs of power, genealogy, and history, has its origins in my attempts elsewhere to write a brief history of the new Latin American narrative and its profound influence on postmodernist, ethnic American literatures.[28] In the process, however, it became clear to me that the discourses of these new American writers were themselves historically situated acts understandable, in the last instance, only as events within larger networks of discursive and nondiscursive practices in the American hemisphere, at the height of what Ernest Mandel calls "late capitalism."[29] It became apparent, moreover, that there was no way to grasp the past and present social and cultural role of the new narrative in the Americas except by trying to see it as situated within an intense, heated quarrel between North American imperialism, on the one hand, and a new (Cuban) Latin American Marxist resistance to U.S. empire, on the other.

In my previous section on Martí's "Nuestra América," I tried to illustrate Martí's historically positioned critique of U.S. empire as a way of life. I only suggested some of Martí's interrelationships in an attempt to indicate part of his critical legacy to Our American discourse. In the limited genealogy that I will now reconstruct, Roberto Fernández Retamar becomes central to an oppositional American literary history precisely because his work makes clear that the Latin American *nueva narrativa*, literary history, and intellectual power are specifically situated historical practices enacted within a set of hostile relations in the American hemisphere. Focusing on the tensions between "Nuestra América" and "el Occidente," then, permits us to look at American cultures anew. My main concern here is with the role of the committed artists and critical intellectuals associated with Fernández Retamar's literary organization and journal—*Casa de las Américas*. Fernández Retamar has produced perhaps the most powerful model of oppositional critical practice in Our America since Martí's. In large part, Fernández Retamar's project results from his organic relationship to Fidel Castro and Che Guevara's practice of new Latin American Marxism, which, in turn, explains his passionate desire for solidarity and social change in the Americas as a continent.

Fernández Retamar is an oppositional figure who has learned many of the lessons of the anti-imperialist efforts of Martí, Che Guevara, and Fidel Castro. But, as González Echevarría states, "To read him is to discover not the bilious ideologue that some imagine, but a searching, groping essayist with an academic bent, who is far from being a doctrinaire Marxist-Leninist."[30] As I see it, he is important to the history of modern criticism, to the new American literary history, and to comparative cultural studies precisely because in numerous books and essays—such as *Caliban,* "Nuestra América y Occidente," and "Algunos usos de civilización y barbarie"—the question of the intellectual-writer in a postcolonial context emerges as the central issue in contemporary critical practice in the Americas.

Caliban, "Nuestra América y Occidente," and "Algunos usos de civilización y barbarie" are all intimately engaged with the problematics of Latin American history—how it has had to serve the economic, political, and cultural "barbarism" of the West. In this regard, Fernández Retamar is, on the one hand, dialectically overturning Marx's and Engels's use of the term "barbarian" in *The Communist Manifesto* (1848): "Just as [the bourgeoisie] has made the country dependent on towns, so it has made barbarian and semibarbarian countries dependent on civilized ones, nations of peasants on nations of bourgeois. . . ."[31] On the other, he is subverting Domingo Faustino Sarmiento's idealist vision of an epic struggle between "civilization" and "barbarism" in Argentina. In his highly influential *Facundo Quiroga: civilization and barbarism* (1845), Sarmiento equated all that was wrong with the marginalized and the periphery—the gauchos and the pampas.[32] Again, I think González Echevarría is correct when he writes that "Though there is a progressive loss of specificity with respect to literature . . . [in his essays in *Casa de las Américas*] one finds a greater ideological and methodological coherence."[33] It is precisely this "ideological" coherence in Fernández Retamar's work that I would now like to examine.

Like Edward Said's oppositional criticism in *Orientalism*, Fernández Retamar negates what he sees as an insidious "Prosperean" and "Occidental" ruling culture of anxiety and mind control in Our America. Put more forcefully, he deconstructs these hierarchical terms, empties them out, and reveals their hegemonic function to oppress those who are excluded from their domains—or, to exclude those who are other. Fernández Retamar's deconstruction, defined in this light, is the inversion of hierarchies and systems, the overthrow of entrenched authority in the West, and the reversal of the subjugated "concepts" in the hierarchies.

In "Nuestra América y Occidente," for example, Fernández Retamar suggests that we should recatalogue the organizing term, "Discovery of America" in our historical textbooks in terms of what it in fact really was: "El Desastre." He says that:

> A lo largo de la historia, hay numerosos casos de encuentro de dos comunidades y sojuzgamiente de una por otro. El hecho ha sido llamarse de muy diversas maneras: a menudo, recibe el nombre de invasión o migración o establecimiento. Pero la llegada de lo paleocidentales a estas tierra, llegada que podria llevar distintos nombres (por ejemplo, El Desastre), ha sido reiterdamente llamada descubrimiento, "*El Descubrimiento.*"

> (The encounter of two communities, and the subjection of one by the other, has been known throughout history by many names: invasion, migration, or foundation. But the arrival of the paleo-western European on these shores, an event which could have been variously designated (e.g., The Disaster), has been repeatedly referred to as a discovery, "*The Discovery*".)[34]

From the very beginning of European versions of history in Our America, Fernández Retamar continues, "Los hombres, las culturas de estas tierras, pasan así a ser cosificados, dejan de ser sujetos de la historia para ser 'descubiertos' por el Hombre, como el paisaje, la flora y la fauna" ("Thus are the people and cultures of these lands reified—ceasing to be subjects of history. Rather, they are "discovered," like landscape, flora and fauna, by Man") (359). In other words, Fernández Retamar shows us how Western culture depersonalizes the First American as subject, and, in the process, falsifies Our American historical experience. Like E. L. Doctorow's reading of metahistory in "False Documents" (1983), Fernández Retamar examines how history is explicitly connected with "the power of the regime," self-interest, and falsity.[35] Fernández Retamar's criticism recognizes the political materiality of culture. He does not merely turn "Our American culture" into a literary myth, but as a Cuban Marxist he describes how culture is related to the idea of hegemony.[36] In this light, "Western culture," for Fernández Retamar, is not only a literary sign but also a social structure and concept that must be negated.

Suffice it to say that Fernández Retamar's Cuban experiences of colonialism and dependency account for his negative attitude toward what he sees in Our America as a fairly monolithic "Occidental" culture. As is clear from his many references to Césaire and Fanon in his *Casa de las Américas* essays, Fernández Retamar has been influenced by their "studies of resistance"—their strong anticolonial discourses.

In his autobiographical "pamphlet" *Caliban,* for example, his description of the colonial hegemony of Western culture in Our America is scandalous, powerful, and moving:

> The white population of the United States (diverse, but of common European origin) exterminated the aboriginal population and thrust the black people aside, thereby affording itself homogeneity in spite of diversity, and offering a coherent model which its Nazi disciples attempted to apply even to other European conglomerates—an unforgivable sin that led some members of the bourgeoisie to stigmatize in Hitler what they applauded as a healthy diversion in Westerns and Tarzan films. Those movies proposed to the world—and even to those of us who are kin to the communities under attack and who rejoiced in their evocation of their own extermination—the monstrous racial criteria which has accompanied the United States from its beginnings to the genocide in Indochina.[37]

Given Fernández Retamar's strong sense of Western culture's oppression (it is even dramatized for him in the westerns and Tarzan films he saw as a young boy in Cuba), it is not surprising to find him, like Martí, advocating an alliance of Third World American politics: all Americans, including "el indio autóctono" and "el negro indígena importado" are engaged in a hostile struggle between "Nuestra América" and "el Occidente." Broadly conceived, then, Fernández Retamar's discourse is about the role of Third World American intellectuals and writers in a postcolonial world—how intellectuals and writers in their work in and on culture choose either to involve or not to involve themselves in the political work of social change and cultural critique. As he suggests in his allegorical *Caliban,* intellectuals (Ariels) have a choice to make: either they can side with Prospero (the Occidental metropole) and help him or her to fortify ruling culture and hegemony, or he/she can side with Caliban, "our symbol," and help him/her to resist, limit, and alter domination in the Americas.[38]

Since my primary concern here is less with Fernández Retamar's literary theory, and more with his leadership in the Casa de las Américas' literary organizations, let me now turn to his intellectual work as editor and publisher, and discuss how the new narratives and poetics produced by some Latin American and ethnic North American writers are inscribed within the discourses and institutions based in Havana.

Each year for almost thirty years, writers, professors, and intellectuals from across the Americas are invited to Havana to judge Latin America's premier literary prize, the Casa de las Américas Award, what Steve Hellman, a recent judge of the Cuban prize, called "the Cuban Pulitzer."[39] The Casa de las Américas prize, since its inception in 1960, has been judged by brilliant writers, such as Alejo Carpentier, Julio Cortázar, Carlos Fuentes, Allen Ginsberg, and most recently by Gabriel García Márquez, and has been awarded to outstanding writers from Our America, including Roque Dalton (El Salvador), Austin Clarke (Barbados), Edward Kamu Brathwaite (Barbados), Reina María Rodríguez (Cuba), Rigoberta Menchú (Guatemala), and the Chicano novelist Rolando Hinojosa (United States).

Perhaps, for our purposes, the most significant cultural conversation between Cuba and the U.S. occurred when, in 1976, Hinojosa was awarded the prestigious award for his novel, *Klail City y sus alrededores* (*Klail City and Its Environs*), a chronicle of U.S. and Mexican border hostility. Hinojosa's novel became an immediate international success. Almost overnight, Hinojosa's ethnopoetic American subject, his mythical Belken County, Texas, in general, and Klail City, Texas, in particular, became required reading not only for intellectuals in Our America, but also for leftist intellectuals in East Germany, Spain, France, Italy, and England.[40]

Klail City y sus alrededores was praised by Carlos Onetti (Uruguay), Domingo Miliani (Venezuela), Lisandro Otero (Cuba), and Lincoln Silva (Paraguay) for its postmodernist dialectical forms and content; its artistic use of the revolutionary avant-garde form, the collage; its folkloric Texan-Mexican motifs (such as the *decimia* and the *corrido*); and its startling multiplicity of sociopoetic dialogues. No longer could Chicano narrative be seen by U.S. literary critics as an anomalous North American discourse—a product of a marginalized tradition. Instead, Chicano narrative, through Hinojosa's novel, had joined the lofty tradition of the *nueva narrativa* exemplified by the works of Gabriel García Márquez, Carlos Fuentes, Guillermo Cabrera Infante, and Isabel Allende.

Why is this moment significant in radically altering the course of American literary history? Here I want to suggest that because of Fernández Retamar's leadership in helping to include Chicano narratives within the Latin American *nueva narrativa* in general and the Cuban-Marxist literary canon in particular, American literary history can no longer be written by separating the ethnic groups (even Yankees and WASPs, according to Werner Sollors, are ethnic!) that produced the literatures. The dominant assumption behind this kind of American literary history is that North American writers have little in common except their so-called national "ethnic roots." As Werner Sollors tells us in his study of American literature, *Beyond Ethnicity: Consent and Descent in American Culture* (1986), "The published results of this procedure [of separating the American ethnic groups] are the readers and compendiums made up of random essays on groups of ethnic writers who have little in common . . . meanwhile, obvious and important literary and cultural connections are obfuscated."[41]

I propose, then, that we take the Casa de las Américas's cultural conversations between Cuba and the U.S. as a possible model for a broader, oppositional American literary history. If we are to begin mapping out this new American literature, I believe that we would have to start by examining what the new narratives by such Latin American writers as Gabriel García Márquez (who helped found Prensa Latina in Havana after the Cuban Revolution in 1959), Carlos Fuentes (who initially supported the Cuban Revolution by completing his novel about the Mexican Revolution, *La muerte de Artemio Cruz,* at the home of Alejo Carpentier in Havana in May 1960), Julio Cortázar, and Isabel Allende have in common with ethnic North American works, produced by U.S.

writers such as Rolando Hinojosa and Ntozake Shange, whose radical ethnopoetics have been dialectically validated by the Casa de las Américas. To be sure, all of the aforementioned Third World American writers are rewriting American history from a subversive "Calibanic" typology, in opposition to the U.S. ruling "center."[42]

I am therefore in agreement with Sollors that, if anything, our new American literary history "ought to *increase* our understanding of the cultural interplays and contacts among writers of different [national] backgrounds, the cultural mergers and secessions that took place in [the] America[s], all of which can be accomplished only if the categorization of writers as members of [national] ethnic groups is understood to be a very partial, temporal, and insufficient characterization at best" (15).

Recast in this light, American literatures can only be understood as part of the larger debates and confrontations between "Our America" and the "other America," which is not ours. Whether they know it or not, writers, teachers, critics, and literary historians participate in this rhetorical war. Suffice it to say that Cuban-Marxist intellectuals, at least since 1960, have known this to be the case. Fernández Retamar, in particular, has attempted to develop a new terminology that goes beyond a North American and Latin American "idealist" criticism, for Casa de las Américas was born in the very struggle between American imperialism, on the one hand, and Latin American Marxism, on the other.

To understand how far-ranging Fernández Retamar's editorial leadership in Casa has evolved, I will introduce one more dialogue between writers from across the Americas which took place in June 1981 in Havana: namely, El primer Encuentro de teatristas Latino-Americanos y del Caribe, sponsored by Casa de las Américas. In her "Diario Nicaragüense" (1982), Ntozake Shange informs us how American playwrights from Colombia, Mexico, Brazil, El Salvador, New York, and San José, California—including the U.S. writers Ronnie Davis, of the Amigos del Teatro de los Estados Unidos; Miriam Colón, of the Puerto Rican Travelling Theater; and Adrián Vargas, of the Teatro de la Gente— talked of theater, "palabras y balas. Poesia & dying," and how they performed their "teatros" in Cuban factories at 2 A.M.[43] It should not be surprising that one of Casa's most sought-after Afro-American writers is Ntozake Shange. She is singled out by the Cubans, perhaps, because she best reflects the new African consciousness in the Americas: "I write in English, French, & Spanish," she tells us, "cuz my consciousness' mingle all New World African experiences."[44] What is especially attractive to Cuban audiences in Shange's work is this: in her "choreopoems" and new narratives she reveals in Third World American images the inner nature of racism, sexism, and exploitation in the colonized Americas. Her Afro-American discourse thus mediates a powerful contact between at least four cultures in the Americas: African, English, Spanish, and French.

This cultural mediation is illustrated spatially and graphically in "Bocas: A Daughter's Geography," where Shange dramatizes an alternative map of the world, and a strong critique of patriarchy:

> i have a daughter/mozambique
> i have a son/angola
> our twins
> salvador & johannesburg/cannot speak
> but we fight the same old men/in the world. . . .
>
> i have a daughter/la habana
> i have a son/guyana
> our twins
> santiago & brixton/cannot speak
> the same language
> yet we fight the same old men.[45]

What I find powerful and moving in Shange's feminist ethnopoetics is her vision of cultural critique. As in most of her work, Shange envisions a new sort of geographical space altogether, in which new kinds of social and sexual relations denied by the older classical American literatures might flourish. Shange's geography is thus always a sociopoetic geography, and places act in her discourse as "ciphers" for alternative visions of social existence in the Americas. For as Russell A. Berman suggests, in a different context, "Geographical designations, even the apparently most objective, are never neutral. Names, distances, and directions not only locate points but also establish conceptualizations of power relations. The nomenclature of space functions as political medium."[46] From this point of view, Shange's "Bocas: A Daughter's Geography" allegorizes for us the persistence of an antithetical geographical space in the New World. Her archeology of Our America uncovers many layers of New World identity in opposition to the Occidental tradition which tries constantly to project its structures outward, creating and recreating its North-South dichotomy in order to render the South as "Other" and victim.

I suggest, then, that for the purposes of investigating the literary history of the Americas and of analyzing New World group formation and geographical space in totality, we may be better served in the long run by the oppositional vocabulary of Martí's "Nuestra América" and Fernández Retamar's negative dialectical, "Calibanic" typology of the self than by the separatist, formalist baggage that idealist readings from both North and Latin America contain.

This schematic reconstruction of the Casa de las Américas will not only negate North American parochial versions of literary history; it will also subvert traditional models of contemporary Latin American literary history. Let me use the institutional history of the Latin American *nueva narrativa* to illustrate what I mean. Traditional histories of the "new writing" in Latin America usually recount the genealogy of the new fiction from Borges to García Márquez and Cabrera Infante, but fail to adequately explain why those narratives came to dominate in the Americas.[47] For example, Emir Rodríguez Monegal skillfully shows that, although Latin American poetry (as practiced by Pablo Neruda, Octavio Paz, and César Vallejo) was the leading force during the avant-garde in Latin America, the new narrative produced in the 1940s by Borges and in the early 1950s by Carpentier soon rose to international prominence. According to Rodríguez Monegal, it was the new fiction "that projected Latin American literature onto the global stage."[48]

When a group of European and U.S. publishers awarded the first Formentor Prize *ex aequo* to Samuel Beckett and Jorge Luis Borges in 1961 (Rodríguez Monegal's symbolic starting date for the rise of the *nueva narrative* in Latin America), Our American literature was finally given its rightful place in the sun. Borges's *Ficciones* (1941) was immediately translated into various languages and, according to Rodríguez Monegal, "aroused general interest" in the totality of the Latin American new fiction that Borges "so brilliantly represented" (686). Traditional accounts of the Latin American new narrative thus give a prominent place to the *ficciones* of Borges in Latin American literary studies. (As a parenthetical aside, I would remind the reader that the North American novelist John Barth, among many others, has likewise dedicated enthusiastic essays to Borges's work.)[49] Because of Borges, Rodríguez Monegal concludes, "The new Latin American novel was no longer the exclusive province of specialists but was recognized and discussed all over the world" (687).

Rodríguez Monegal's otherwise lucid and insightful literary analysis, however, does not grant Casa de las Américas—the institutional organization of Fernández Retamar—its full share in determining the final political shape and influence of the new narrative in the Americas. In supplementing Rodríguez Monegal's "idealist" reading of Latin American literary history, I would suggest that we ought to read the literary history of the *nueva narrativa* in terms of an oppositional, rhetorical, hermeneutic model: in this view, textual facts are, in the words of Steven Mailloux, "never prior to or independent of the hermeneutic activity of readers and critics."[50] Against Rodríguez Monegal's incomplete view of the *nueva narrativa,* then, I would submit an alternative reading of its literary history in terms of a historical set of topics, arguments, tropes, and ideologies that determine how discourses are established as meaningful—in other words, through socially symbolic, rhetorical exchanges between "Our America" and "the other America, which is not ours." As Mailloux contends, "[we] should provide histories of how particular theoretical and critical discourses have evolved" (629).

If anything, my rhetorical hermeneutic model is conceived as part of a Calibanic practice, an intervention in cultural politics; for the emergence of the new narratives by Cortázar, García Márquez, Fuentes, Allende, and others in Latin America, and by Rolando Hinojosa and Ntozake Shange in the U.S. are themselves part of a global social and cultural struggle which had reached its zenith at the end of the 1950s: the ascendancy of the American typology of Caliban, the negative of the master-slave relationship, over its bourgeois white supremacist counterpart, Prospero. What Castro and Che initiated in their negation of Prospero (and the subsequent subversion of U.S. seignorial "rights" in Our America prohibiting "outside" intervention in the "American" hemisphere) was completed at the discursive level by García Márquez and his Third World American heirs. In the words of the North American novelist Robert Coover, the *nueva narrativa* from Latin America "was [thus] for a moment the region's headiest and most dangerous export."[51]

The Dialectics of Ideology and Utopia

> The interpretation of our reality through patterns not our own serves only to make us ever more unknown, ever less free, ever more solitary.
> —Gabriel García Márquez, "The Solitude of Latin America"

I want to end my discussion by providing one final example of how literary and mass cultural texts participate in the historical conflicts and

RONALD REAGAN'S WORLD

cultural debates between "Our America" and "the America which is not ours." I use the term "text" in the broad sense to include a political cartoon in the *Washington Post* and Gabriel García Márquez's 1982 Nobel Prize address.

"Ronald Reagan's World"—a political cartoon depiction of the right-wing conception of Russia's "apocalyptic military involvement" in Latin America in general, and Nicaragua in particular, through its "surrogate," Cuba—illustrates the kind of "exaggerated tale" every U.S. president since Dwight D. Eisenhower has used against Castro's socialist government: hemispheric subversion. Cuba is seen as a synecdochic agent for the Soviet Union, fomenting revolution in almost every country in the Americas. Since it took office in January 1981, the Reagan administration charged Havana with providing arms, training "terrorists," and giving political direction to the revolutionaries in El Salvador and Nicaragua. "Ronald Reagan's World" is but another socially symbolic text dramatizing the hostile conflicts that Martí mapped out for us in "Nuestra América." It is the essential U.S. world view reifying "Contras" as "freedom fighters," even as it supported an ideologically right-wing dictator, Pinochet, in Chile.

This globalized view of ideological war in the Americas, depicted schematically in the *Washington Post* cartoon, is precisely the position that García Márquez chose to attack in his 1982 Nobel Prize address, "The Solitude of Latin America." As is well known, García Márquez wanted his address "to be a political speech presented as literature."[52] Almost as if to dispel Reagan's negative ideological view of Latin America, García Márquez negates North American and European narrative versions of a Soviet Union–inspired revolution in Our America by countering that:

> Latin America neither wants, nor has any reason, to be a pawn without a will of its own; nor is it merely wishful thinking that its quest for independence and originality should become a Western aspiration. . . . Why is the originality so readily granted us in literature so mistrustfully denied us in our different attempts at social change? Why think that the social justice sought by progressive Europeans for their own countries cannot be a goal for Latin America, with different methods and for dissimilar conditions. No: the unmeasurable violence and pain of our history are the result of age-old inequities and untold bitterness, and not a conspiracy plotted 3,000 leagues from our homes. But so many European leaders and thinkers have thought so, with the childishness of old-timers who have forgotten the fruitful excesses of their youths as if it were impossible to live at the mercy of the two great masters of the world. This, my friends, is the very scale of our solitude.[53]

Almost as if to deconstruct his earlier negative dialectical hermeneutic in *One Hundred Years of Solitude* (1967) (where "races condemned to one hundred years of solitude did not have a second opportunity on earth"),[54] García Márquez replies to Western leaders' "interpretations of our reality through patterns not our own" by asserting a more positive position: namely, his "utopian" side of the hermeneutic dialectic. He tells us that it is not too late to undertake the creation of a "new and leveling utopia of life where no one can decide the form of another person's death" (1). As any reader of his fiction knows, the utopian view represented in "The Solitude of Latin America" is much more optimistic than any yet depicted in his literature. His Nobel Prize address offers in fact a profound affirmation of the essentially humanistic imagination in Latin American socialism: "In spite of this, to oppression, plundering and abandonment, we respond with life. Neither floods nor plagues nor famine nor cataclysm nor even the eternal wars throughout centuries and centuries have managed to reduce the tenacious advantage of life over death" (1).

Although García Márquez begins his speech playfully by referring to the magical and exaggerated visions inspired by the "discovery" of the New World (El Dorado, the fountain of eternal youth, or the indigenous giant of Patagonia who, when shown a mirror for the first time, "lost his sense, overwhelmed by his fear of his own image" [1]), he ends his address by describing a Frankfurt School, Marxist ideology of hope, a vision diametrically opposed to Ronald Reagan's vision, where "races condemned to one hundred years of solitude will have at last and forever a second opportunity on earth" (1).

By presenting this limited genealogy of American discourse from José Martí and Roberto Fernández Retamar to Gabriel García Márquez, Rolando Hinojosa, and Ntozake Shange, I am not arguing that institutional accounts are the only significant narratives for understanding what the literatures of the Americas have in common. But I am suggesting that what they have in common, whether the writers consciously or unconsciously know it, are their often hostile artistic ideological and utopian responses to the larger, sociopolitical forces in the American hemisphere.

Antonio Benítez-Rojo

The Repeating Island*

In recent decades we have begun to see a clearer outline to the profile of a group of American nations whose colonial experiences and languages have been different, but which share certain undeniable features. I mean the countries usually called "Caribbean" or "of the Caribbean basin." This designation might serve a foreign purpose—the great powers' need to recodify the world's territory better to know, to dominate it—as well as a local one, self-referential, directed toward fixing the furtive image of collective Being. Whatever its motive, this urge to systematize the region's political, economic, social, and anthropological dynamics is a very recent thing. For it is certain that the Caribbean basin, although it includes the first American lands to be explored, conquered, and colonized by Europe, is still, especially in the discourse of the social sciences, one of the least known regions of the modern world.

The main obstacles to any global study of Caribbean societies, insular or continental, are exactly those things that scholars usually adduce to define the area: its fragmentation; its instability; its reciprocal isolation; its uprootedness; its cultural heterogeneity; its lack of historiography and historical continuity; its contingency and impermanence; its syncretism, and so on. This unexpected mix of obstacles and properties is not, of course, mere happenstance. What happens is that postindustrial society navigates the Caribbean with judgments and intentions which are like those of Columbus; that is, it lands scientists, investors, and technologists (the new discoverers), who come to apply the dogmas and methods that have served them well where they came from, and who

*Translated from Spanish by James Maraniss. Originally published in the *New England Review and Breadloaf Quarterly* 7 (1985).

cannot see that these refer only to realities back home. So they get into the habit of defining the Caribbean in terms of its resistance to the different methodologies summoned to investigate it. This is not to say that the definitions we read here and there of pan-Caribbean society are false or useless. I would say, to the contrary, that they are potentially as productive as the first reading of a book, in which, as Barthes said, the reader inevitably reads himself. I think, nevertheless, that the time has come for postindustrial society to start rereading the Caribbean, that is, to do the kind of reading in which every text begins to reveal its own textuality.

This second reading is not going to be easy at all. The Caribbean space—remember—is saturated with messages sent out in five European languages (Spanish, English, French, Dutch, and Portuguese), not counting aboriginal languages or the different *Créole* tongues that erode Prospero's discourse from the canebrake to the urban marketplace. Further, the spectrum of Caribbean codes is so varied and dense that it holds the region suspended in a soup of signs. It has been said many times that the Caribbean is the union of the diverse, and maybe that is true. In any case, my own rereading has taken me along different paths, and I can no longer arrive at such admirably precise reductions.

In this (today's) rereading, I propose, for example, to start with something concrete and easily demonstrated, a geographical "fact": that the Antilles are an island bridge connecting, in "another way," North to South America. This geographical accident gives the entire area, including its continental foci, the character of an archipelago, that is, a discontinuous conjunction (of what?): empty spaces, unstrung voices, ligaments, sutures, voyages of signification. This archipelago, like others, can be seen as an island that "repeats" itself. I have drawn attention to the word "repeats" because I want to give it the unsettled meaning with which it appears in poststructuralist discourse, where all repetition brings necessarily a difference and a deferral. Which one, then, would be the repeating island, Jamaica, Aruba, Puerto Rico, Miami, Haiti, Recife? Certainly none of the ones that we know. That original, that island at the center, is as impossible to reach as the hypothetical Antillis that reappeared time and again, always fleetingly, in the cosmographers' charts. This is again because the Caribbean is a meta-archipelago (an exalted quality that Hellas and Malay possessed), and as a meta-archipelago it has the virtue of having neither a boundary nor a center. Thus the Caribbean flows outward past the limits of its own Sea with a vengeance, and its Ultima Thule may be found on the outskirts of

Bombay, near the low and murmuring shores of Gambia, in a Cantonese tavern of circa 1850, at a Balinese temple, in an old Bristol pub, in a commercial warehouse in Bordeaux at the time of Colbert, in a windmill beside the Zuider Zee, at a discotheque in a barrio of Manhattan, in the existential *saudade* of a Portuguese lyric. But what is it that repeats? Tropisms, in series: let's say a dancing flourish, a deep improvisatory sense, a taste for certain foods (great streams of rice, plantain, bean, pepper, yucca), polyrhythmic expression, intermarriage, syncretic forms, a high level of popular culture, ways of approaching and avoiding the Western world (remember that, as Malaparte said, the Volga is born in Europe), the socioeconomic experience of the plantation, in short, parallelisms here and there, contradictions here and there.

Too much has already been written about all this. The Caribbean is this and much more. What I've said so far is not enough to make it a meta-archipelago or anything of the kind. But the Caribbean really is something quite sophisticated and accomplished: the last of the meta-archipelagoes. If you need a visual explanation, a picture of what the Caribbean is, I would suggest the Milky Way, that flux of transformative plasma whirling narrowly on the dome of our globe, drawing there an "other" map that changes with each passing instant, where objects are born to light while others disappear into the vault of darkness; production, interchange, consumption, machine (these are words that come to mind).

There is nothing marvelous in this, or even poetic, as will be seen. A few paragraphs back, when I proposed a rereading of the Caribbean, I suggested as a point of departure the unargued fact that the Antilles are an island bridge connecting, "in another way," South with North America; that is, a machine that links the narrative of the search for El Dorado with the narrative of the finding of El Dorado; or if you like, the discourse of utopia with the discourse of history; or even, the language of desire with the language of power. I made a point of the phrase "in another way" because if we were to take the Central American ligament as our connection between continents, the result would be much less fruitful and would not suit the purposes of this study. That connection gains objective importance only on maps concerned with our current situation seen as geography, geopolitics, military strategy, and finance. These are maps of the pragmatic type which we all know and carry within us, and which therefore give us a first reading of the world. The words "other way" are the signs of my intention to give meaning to this text as an object of rereading, of an "other" reading. In my reading, the link that really counts is the one made by the Caribbean machine, whose flux, whose noise, whose presence, covers the map of world history's contingencies, through the great changes in economic discourse to the vast collisions of races and cultures.

Let's be realistic, let's be skeptical at least: the Atlantic is the Atlantic (with all its port cities) because it was once engendered by the copulation of Europe—that insatiable solar bull—with the Caribbean archipelago; the Atlantic is today the Atlantic (the space of capitalism) because Europe, in its mercantilist laboratory, conceived the project of inseminating the Caribbean womb with the seed of Africa, and even of Asia; the Atlantic is today the Atlantic (NATO, European Economic Community, and so on) because it was the painfully delivered child of the Caribbean, whose vagina was stretched between continental clamps, between the *encomienda* of Indians and the slaveholding plantation, between the servitude of the coolie and the discrimination toward the *criollo,* between commercial monopoly and piracy, between fortress and surrender; all Europe pulling on the forceps to help at the birth of the Atlantic: Columbus, Cabral, Cortez, de Soto, Hawkins, Drake, Hein, Rodney, Surcouf. . . . After the blood and saltwater spurts, quickly sew up torn flesh and apply the antiseptic tinctures, the gauze and surgical plaster; then the febrile wait through the forming of a scar: suppurating, always suppurating.

Without intending to, I have drifted toward the accusatory and militant rhetoric of my first writings about the Caribbean. It won't happen again. At any rate, to put an end to the matter, it must be agreed that before there was a Caribbean Sea the Atlantic lacked even a name.

Its having given birth, however, to such a favored ocean, with its coasts and everything, is not the only reason that the Caribbean is a meta-archipelago. There are other reasons of equal weight. For example, it is possible to defend successfully the hypothesis that without deliveries from the Caribbean womb Western capital accumulation would not have been sufficient to effect a move, within a little more than two centuries, from the so-called Mercantilist Revolution to the Industrial Revolution. In fact, the history of the Caribbean is one of the main strands in the history of capitalism, and vice versa. This conclusion may be called polemical, and perhaps it is. Here is surely not the place to argue the issue, but there's always room for some observations.

Let's look:

The machine that Christopher Columbus hammered into shape in Hispaniola was a kind of *bricolage,* something like a medieval vacuum cleaner. The flow of Nature in the island was interrupted by the suction of an iron mouth, taken thence through a transatlantic tube to be deposited and redistributed in Spain. When I speak of Nature in the island, I do so in integral terms: Indians and their handicrafts, nuggets of gold and samples of other minerals, native species of plants and animals, and also some words like *tabaco, canoa, hamaca,* and so on. All this struck the Spanish court as meager and tepid (especially the words), so that nobody (except Columbus) had any illusions about the New World. A machine of the same model (think of a forge with its sparkling clangor and combustion), with an extra bolt here and a bellows over there, was installed in Puerto Rico, in Jamaica, in Cuba, and in a few miserable settlements on terra firma. At the time of the great conquests—the fall of the upland civilizations of the Aztecs, the Incas, and the Chibchas—Columbus's machine was quickly remodeled and, carried on Indians' backs over the sierras, set into motion in a half-dozen new places. It's possible to fix the date when this machine began working. It happened in the spring of 1523, when Cortez, manipulating the levers and pedals, smelted down a part of the treasure of Tenochtitlán and selected a smattering of deluxe objects to be sent through the transatlantic tube. But this prototype was so defective that the transporting machine—the tubing—became irreparably damaged some ten leagues from Cape San Vicente in Portugal. French privateers captured two of the three inadequate caravels that carried the treasure to Spain, and Emperor Charles V lost his whole share (20 percent) of that year's Mexican revenue. This couldn't be allowed to happen again. The machine had to be perfected.

I think I ought to clarify at this point that when I speak of a machine I am talking about the machine of machines, the machine machine machine machine; which is to say that every machine is a conjunction of machines coupled together, and each one of these interrupts the flow of the previous one; it will be said rightly that one can picture any machine alternatively in terms of flow and interruption. Such a notion is fundamental to our rereading of the Caribbean, for it will permit us to pass on to an even more fundamental one.

In subsequent years the Spaniards introduced major technological changes and surprising elaborations. This was so much the case that, by around 1565, Columbus's small and rudimentary machine had evolved into the Grandest Machine on Earth. This is absolutely certain. It's proven by statistics: in the first century of Spanish colonization this machine yielded more than one-third of all the gold produced in the whole world during those years. The machine produced not only gold, but also silver, emeralds, diamonds, topaz, pearls, and more. The quantity of molten silver that fell in droplets from that enormous shelf was such that the haughtiest families of Potosí, after dining, tossed their silver service out the window along with the leftover food. These fabulous deliveries of precious metals were the result of various innovations: those of installing an excellent system of timetables; creating an auxiliary hauling system (the mule train); using wind energy and marine currents to speed up production; implanting a costly system of security and control; building a system of pumping stations and warehouses; but, above all, establishing the system called *la flota,* the fleet. Without the fleet system the Spaniards would not have been able to hoard within the walls of Seville any more gold or silver than they could fit into their pockets. We know who thought up this extraordinary system (machine coupled to machine coupled to machine, etc.): Pedro Menéndez de Avilés, a cruel Asturian of genius. If this man, or someone else, had not invented the fleet system, the Caribbean would still be there, but it might not be a meta-archipelago.

Menéndez de Avilés's machine was complex in the extreme and quite beyond the reach of any nation but Spain. It was a machine made up of a naval machine, a military machine, a territorial machine, a geopolitical machine, a bureaucratic machine, a commercial machine, that is, an entire huge assemblage of machines which there is no point in continuing to name. The only thing that matters here is that it was a Caribbean machine; a machine installed in the Caribbean Sea and coupled to the Atlantic and the Pacific. This machine was set in motion after 1566, although it had been tested in a trial run in 1562. In that year Menéndez de Avilés, commanding forty-nine sailing ships (including six galleons outfitted for war), set off from Spain with the dream of stanching the leaks of gold and silver caused by shipwrecks and pirate or privateer attacks. His plan was this: in the future, all navigation between the West Indies and Seville (the only port allowed transatlantic trade) would be undertaken in convoys consisting of cargo ships, warships, and light reconnaissance craft; the cargoes of gold and silver were to be boarded only on given dates and in only a few Caribbean ports (Cartagena, Nombre de Dios, San Juan de Ullúa, and some other secondary ones); forts would be built and garrisons stationed not only at these ports but also at those defending the entrances to the Caribbean (San Juan de Puerto Rico, Santo Domingo, Santiago de Cuba, the eastern coast of Florida, and especially Havana); all of these ports would be bases for squadrons of coast guard and patrol ships, whose mission would be to keep the Caribbean waters clean of pirates, privateers, and smugglers, while at the same time providing rescue service to convoys in trouble. (The plan was approved.)

Generally the name *flota* (fleet) is given to the convoys that twice a year entered the Caribbean to come back to Seville with the great riches of America. But this is not entirely correct. The fleet system was itself a machine of ports, anchorages, sea walls, lookouts, fortresses, garrisons, militias, shipyards, storehouses, depots, offices, workshops, hospitals, inns, taverns, plazas, churches, palaces, streets, and roads that led to the mining ports of the Pacific along a sleeve of mule trains laid out over the isthmus of Panama. It was a system knowingly articulated to suit the Caribbean's geography, and its machines were geared to be able to take greatest advantage of the energy of the Gulf Stream and the region's trade winds. The fleet system created all of the cities of the Spanish Caribbean and it made them, for better or for worse, what they are today, Havana in particular. It was there that both fleets (those of Cartagena and Veracruz) joined to form an imposing convoy of more than a hundred ships to begin the return voyage together. In 1565 Pedro Menéndez de Avilés, after indifferently slaughtering five hundred Huguenots who had settled in Florida, finished his network of fortified cities with the founding of St. Augustine.

As we speak in our astonishment of the inexhaustible richness of the Mexican and Peruvian mines, we should think of them as machines joined to other machines; we should see them in terms of production (flow and interruption). Such mining machines, by themselves, would not have been much help in accumulating European capital. Without the Caribbean machine (from Columbus's prototype to the working model of Menéndez de Avilés), Europeans would have been in the absurd position of the gambler who hits the jackpot at the slot machine but who has no hat in which to catch his winnings.

There was another Caribbean machine, infinitely more useful and productive than the fleet machine. This machine, this extraordinary machine, still exists today. It is called the plantation.

Its prototypes were born in the Near East, just after the time of the Crusades, and moved toward the West. In the fifteenth century the Portuguese installed their own model in the Cape Verde Islands and on Madeira, with astonishing success. There were certain entrepreneurs— like the Jew Cristóbal de Ponte and the *Sharif* of Berbery—who tried to construct machines of this family in the Canaries and on the Moroccan coast, but the venture was too big for any single man. It turned out that an entire kingdom, a mercantilist monarchy, would be needed to get the big machine going with its gears, its wheels, and its mills. I want to insist that Europeans finally controlled the construction, maintenance, technology, and proliferation of the plantation machines, especially those that produced sugar. (This family of machines almost always makes cane sugar, coffee, cacao, cotton, indigo, tea, bananas, pineapples, fibers, and other goods whose cultivation is impossible or too expensive in the temperate zones.)

So much has already been written about all this that it is not worth the effort even to sketch out the incredible and dolorous history of this machine. Still, something must be said, if just a few things. For one: the singular feature of this machine is that it produced no fewer than ten million African slaves and thousands of coolies (from India, China, and Malaysia). All this, however, is but little: the plantation machines turned out mercantile capitalism, industrial capitalism, African under-development, Caribbean population; they produced imperialism, wars, colonial blocs, rebellions, repressions, sugar islands, alliances, interventions, banana republics, dictatorships, revolutions, and even totalitarian socialism.

You will say that this catalogue is unnecessary, that the whole subject is already too well known. But how is one to establish firmly that the Caribbean is not just a sea or a group of islands divided by different languages and by the categories Greater and Lesser Antilles, Windward Islands, and Leeward Islands? Finally, how is one to establish for all time that the Caribbean is a meta-archipelago? If this idea has stayed in sight, there is no reason to keep on leafing through the yellow pages of the history books, telephone directories that allow communication through time and space but never do give us the certainty of "presence." Let us talk then of the Caribbean that we can see, touch, smell, hear, taste; the Caribbean of the senses, the Caribbean of sentiment and presentiment.

I can isolate with frightening exactitude—like the hero of Sartre's novel—the moment at which I reached the age of reason. It was a stunning October afternoon, years ago, when the atomization of the meta-archipelago under the dread umbrella of nuclear catastrophe seemed imminent. The children of Havana, at least in my neighborhood, had been evacuated; a grave silence fell over the streets and the sea. While the state bureaucracy searched for news off the shortwave or hid behind official speeches and communiqués, two old black women passed "in a certain kind of way" beneath my balcony. I cannot describe this "certain kind of way"; I will say only that there was a kind of ancient and golden powder between their gnarled legs, a scent of basil and mint in their dress, a domestic wisdom, almost culinary, in their gesture and their gay chatter. I knew at once that there would be no apocalypse. The swords and the archangels and the beasts and the trumpets and the breaking of the last seal were not going to come, for the simple reason that the Caribbean is not an apocalyptic world; it is not a phallic world in pursuit of the vertical desires of ejaculation and castration. The notion of the apocalypse does not exist within the culture of the Caribbean. The notions of crime and punishment, of your money or your life, of *patria o muerte,* have nothing to do with Caribbean culture; these are Western propositions (remember Malaparte again) which the Caribbean adopts only in terms of declamation, or rather, in terms of a first reading. The so-called "October crisis" or "missile crisis" was not won by JFK or by NK or much less by FC (men of state always wind up abbreviated in these great events); it was won by the Caribbean, together with the loss that any win implies. If this had happened, let's say, in Berlin, children there would now be discovering hand tools and learning to make fire with sticks. The plantation of rockets sown in Cuba was a Russian machine; but neither the sea nor the rivers were. Let me clarify this.

The culture of archipelagoes is not terrestrial, as are almost all cultures: it is fluvial and marine. We are dealing here with a culture of bearings, not of routes; of approximations, not of exactitudes. Here the world of straight lines and angles (the wedge, the inclined plane, the intersection) does not dominate; here rules the fluid world of the curving line. The culture of meta-archipelagoes is an eternal return, a detour without destination or milepost, a roundabout that leads nowhere but back home; it is a feedback machine, as is the sea, the wind, the Milky Way, the novel, the natural world, the food chain, the sonata. It will be said that in that case Hellas does not meet our canon for meta-archipelagoes. But yes, it meets it and defines it. What has happened is that Western thought has kept on thinking of itself as the diachronic repetition on an ancient polemic. I am referring to the repressive machine made up of the binary opposition, Aristotle *versus* Plato. Greek thought has been subjected to such sleight of hand that Plato's version of Socrates has been accepted as the limit of the tolerable, while the glowing constellation of ideas that made up the Greek heaven has been ignored or distorted. This magnificent firmament has been reduced almost as if we were to erase every star in the sky but Castor and Pollux. Certainly Greek thought was much more than this philosophical duel organized before the birth of Christ, and it is not necessary to pursue the matter because the proofs are everywhere you look. And anyway we are speaking here of the Caribbean. Then, how can we describe the culture of the Caribbean in any way other than by calling it a feedback machine? Nobody has to rack his or her brains to come up with an answer; it is in the public domain. If I were to have to put it in one word I would say *performance*. But performance not only in terms of scenic interpretation and the execution of a ritual, but also as a style, something like a combination of what the Americans call performance and the English call a "good show."

And yet there's "something more."

It is surely that "something more," that "certain kind of way" in which those two old black women walked when they conjured away the apocalypse, that brings us back in contact with the primal gnostic or mythic ooze of the non-"scientific" civilizations that contributed to the formation of Caribbean culture. Of course, this too has been written about, although I think in an inadequate and superficial way. There was a time in which I believed that the codebook to reading the Caribbean was the plantation. I thought then that the source of our syncretic cultural forms must be sought in the violent interplay of European, African, and Asian elements within the plantation machine. Today, without discarding this hypothesis, I must say that my attention is directed toward syncretic machines that are more distant, remote even, toward machines that are found in the subsoils of America, Africa, Asia, Europe.

Certainly, in order to reread the Caribbean we have to visit the sources from which the widely various elements that contributed to its cultural system flowed. We must do this because as soon as we succeed in establishing and identifying as separate any of the signifiers that make up the syncretic object under analysis, those signifiers begin to shift radically. Let us take as an example a syncretic object that has been well studied, the cult of *la Virgen de la Caridad del Cobre* (still followed by many Cubans). If we were to analyze this cult—presuming that it hasn't been done before—we would necessarily come upon a date (1605) and a place (El Cobre, near Santiago de Cuba: i.e., within the spatiotemporal frame where the cult was first articulated upon three sources of meaning: one of aboriginal origin [the Taíno deity Atabey or Atabex], one from Europe [the manifestation of the Virgin Mary in the Spanish form of *Nuestra Señora de Guía Madre de Dios de Illescas*] and, finally, another from Africa [the Yoruba *oricha* Oshun]). For many anthropologists the history of this cult would begin or end here, and of course they would give reasons to explain this arbitrary break in the chain of signifiers. They would say that the people who today inhabit the Antilles are "new," that is to say that their previous condition of having been Europeans, Africans, and Asians should not count; they would say that with the disappearance of the Antillean aborigine during the first century of colonization these islands were left unconnected to the Indo-American mechanisms, and thus there remained a "new" space for "new" men to create a "new" society and, with it, a "new" culture that can no longer be taken as an extension of those that brought the "new" inhabitants. This is apparently a structuralist approach, systemic if you like, since that which created the "new" men of the Antilles was nothing more nor less than a whole family of "new" systems. I will go along with this systemic approach, but only insofar as it offers a first reading of the Caribbean (a reading as necessary as the first step in a long journey). I want to say, though, that now that we have taken this path of revisitation, we have to keep shifting the signifiers that inform the syncretic cult of the *Virgen de la Caridad del Cobre*.

The first surprise that the triptych Atabey–Nuestra Señora–Oshun presents us—we have to keep pretending that nothing has been said about this—is that it is not "original" but rather "originating." In fact Atabey is a syncretic object in itself, one whose meanings deliver to us another meaning that is somewhat unforeseen: Orehu, mother of waters to the Arawaks of Guyana. This voyage of signification is a heady one for more than one reason. In the first place it involves the grand epic of the Arawaks: the meticulous settlement of each island until arrival in Cuba, the connecting of machine to machine until the "other" connection was established between both subcontinental masses (such was the extraordinary feat of the Arawaks of Amazonia). It involves also the no less grand epic of the Caribs: the Arawak islands as objects of Carib desire; the construction of large canoes, preparations for war, raids on the coastal islands, ravishing the women, victory feasts. Then the invasion stage: the killing of the Arawaks; the glorious cannibalism of men and of words, carib, calib, cannibal, and Caliban; finally, the Sea of the Caribs, from Guyana to the Virgin Islands, the sea that isolated the Arawaks (*taínos*) from the Greater Antilles, that cut the connection with the South American coast but not the continuity of cultural flow: Atabey–Orehu, the flux of meanings that crossed the spatiotemporal barrier of the Caribbean to continue linking Cuba with the Orinoco and Amazon basins; Atabey–Orehu, progenitor of the Supreme Being of the *taínos,* protector of feminine ebbs and flows, of the great mysteries of the blood that women experience, and there, at the other end of the

Antillean arc, the Great Mother of Waters, the immediacy of the matriarchy, the beginning of the cultivation of the yucca.

There is something enormously old and powerful in this, I know; a contradictory vertigo which there is no reason to interrupt, and so we reach the point at which the image of Our Lady venerated in El Cobre is also a syncretic object produced by two quite distinct images of the Virgin Mary, which were to wind up in the hands of the chiefs of Cueíba and Macaca, and which were adored simultaneously as Atabey and as Nuestra Señora (this last in the form of an amulet). Imagine for a moment these chiefs' perplexity when they saw for the first time what no *taíno* had seen before: the image, in color, of the Mother of the Supreme Being, the lone progenitor of Yucahu Bagua Maorocoti, who now turned out to be the mother of the God of those bearded, yucca-colored men, she who, according to them, protected them from death and injury in war. *Ave Maria,* these Indians would learn to say as they worshipped their Atabey, who at one time had been Orehu, and before that the Great Arawak Mother. *Ave Maria,* Francisco Sánchez de Moya, a sixteenth-century Spanish captain, would surely say when he received the commission and the order to start copper foundries in the town of El Prado. *Ave Maria,* he would say once again when he wrapped the image of Nuestra Señora de Illescas, of whom he was a devotee, among his shirts. *Ave Maria,* he would repeat on the day he placed it upon the humble altar in the solitary hermitage of El Cobre to be adored by those poor Indians who worked in the mines. But the image of Nuestra Señora de Illescas is itself another syncretic object. The chain of signifiers now takes us across the Renaissance to the Middle Ages. It leads us to Byzantium, the unique, where among all kinds of heresies and practices the cult of the Virgin Mary was born (a cult unforeseen by the Doctors of the Church). There in Byzantium, among the splendors of its icons and mosaics, a likeness of the Virgin Mary and her Child may have been plundered by some crusading and voracious knight, or acquired by a seller of relics, or copied on the retina of some pious pilgrim. At any rate the cult of the Virgin filtered surreptitiously into Europe. Surely it would not have gone very far on its own, but this happened at the beginning of the twelfth century, the legendary epoch of the troubadours and of *amour courtois,* when Woman ceased to be Eve, the dirty and damned seducer of Adam and ally of the Serpent. She was washed, perfumed, and sumptuously dressed to suit the scope of her new image: the Lady. Then the cult of Our Lady spread like fire through gunpowder, and one fine day it arrived at Illescas, a few miles away from Toledo.

Ave Maria, the slaves at the El Prado mines repeated aloud, and quickly, in an undertone that the priest could not hear, they added: *Oshun Yeye.* For that miraculous altar image was for them one of the most conspicuous *orichas* of the Yoruba pantheon: Oshun Yeye Moro, the perfumed whore; Oshun Kayode, the gay dancer; Oshun Ana, the lover of the drum; Oshun Akuara, she who mixes love potions; Oshun Ede, the *grande dame*; Oshun Fumike, she who gives chilren to sterile women; Oshun Funke, the wise one; Oshun Kole-Kole, the wicked sorceress.

Oshun as a syncretic object is as dizzying as her honeyed dance and yellow bandanas. She is traditionally the Lady of the Rivers, but some of her avatars relate her to the bays and the seashores. In any case, she is the Goddess of Love and of Feminine Flows. Her most prized objects are amber, coral, and yellow metals; her favorite food is honey. At times she shows herself to be insensitive, and she can even become nasty and treacherous; in these darker apparitions we also see her as an old carrion-eating witch and as the *oricha* of death.

This doubleness of Oshun makes us think at once of the contradictions of Aphrodite. Both goddesses, one as much as the other, are at once "luminous" and "dark"; they reign over a place where men find both pleasure and death, love and hate, voluptuosity and betrayal. Both goddesses came from the sea, and inhabit the marine, fluvial, and vaginal tides; both seduce gods and men, and both protect cosmetics and prostitution.

The correspondences between the Greek and Yoruba pantheons have been noted but they have not been explained. How to explain, say, the unusual parallel of Hermes and Elegua (also Legba and Echu)? Both are "the travelers," the "messengers of the gods," the "keepers of the gates"; both were adored in the form of phallic stone figures, both protect crossroads, highway, and commerce, and both can show themselves in the figure of a man with a cane who rests his body's weight on one foot alone. Both sponsor the start of any activity, make transactions smooth, and are the only ones to pass through the terrible spaces that mediate the Supreme Being and the gods, the gods and humans, the living and the dead. Both, finally, appear as naughty, mendacious children, or as tricky and lascivious old men; both are the "givers of discourse," alpha and omega of all trials, of all changes. For this reason, in Yoruba rituals, Elegua eats and dances first. He is *número uno*, like Hermes.

In the same way, Africa and Aphrodite have more in common than the Greek root that unites their names; there is a flow of marine foam that connects two civilizations "in another way."

The cult of the *Virgen de la Caridad del Cobre* can be read as a Cuban syncretic cult, but it can also be reread as a meta-archipelagic text, a metamachine of marine flowings which connects the Orinoco to the Hellespont, the Niger to the Bahamian Channel, Olympus to a street in Kingston.

The peoples of the sea, or better, the Peoples of the Sea, are all one. Their culture, in essence, is the same. If I were to have to put it in one word—and I already have—I would say "performance" and I would add: "something more"; if I could add again another word, it would be this: rhythm.

Nature is a continuum which humans interrupt with the most varied rhythms. Each rhythm is itself a flux cut through by other rhythms, and we can pursue fluxes upon rhythms endlessly. Well then, the culture of the Peoples of the Sea is a flux interrupted by rhythms which, unlike those produced by nuclear warheads, attempt to reconstruct, reproduce, or reinterpret the unity of Nature in terms of performance and "something more." As this unity is not only paradoxical but also impossible, the cultural discourse of the Peoples of the Sea is the "repetition" of a ritual in the course of which one can come to intuit that although, after all, there is a unity in Nature, that unity is also impossible. In this discourse there is no room for Hamlet's doubt, which refers only to a first reading of the world. Here we are reaching toward a point where something is and is not at the same time, at which one experiences oneself as if one were Nature. Here there is no desire (only the will to exist), there is no contradiction, no repression, no time and space; we are in free orbit, with a higher form of freedom.

All machines have their master codes, and the codebook to the cultural machine of the Peoples of the Sea is made up of a network of subcodes holding together cosmogonies, mythic bestiaries, remote pharmacopoeias, oracles, profound ceremonies, and the mysteries and alchemies of humanity. One of these subcodes may lead us into the labyrinth of Minos, another to the Tower of Babel, another to the garden of the unicorn, another to the first harvest or the first musical instrument. The keys to this vast hermeneutical system give us an "other" wisdom that runs next to and erodes the mortar of postindustrial society. I need hardly say that all the nations of the world were at one time Peoples of the Sea. What interests me is to establish that the peoples of the Caribbean remain so today.

What kind of performance then is particularly Caribbean? Is it dance? Music? Actually, neither of the two by itself. What is specific to Caribbean culture resides in its attempt to rewrite Nature in terms of rhythm. Here's an example: Let us suppose that we beat upon a drum and set its skin to vibrating. Let us suppose that this sound stretches until it forms something like a salami. Well, here comes the interruptive action of the Caribbean machine; it starts slicing pieces of sound in an unforeseen, improbable, and finally impossible way.

To anyone interested in the way machines function, I ought to say that the Caribbean machine is not a Deleuze & Guattari model. The specifications of that model are clear and final: here is a flow machine; we hook up an interrupting machine, to which another interrupting machine is then connected, making the previous interrupter appear to be in motion. We are dealing with a system of relative machines. The Caribbean machine, on the other hand, is flow and interruption at once; it is an absolute machine, a metamachine, which cannot be diagrammed and whose user's manual may be found scattered among its own network of codes. It is a machine very different from those we've been discussing up to now. In any event, the notion of polyrhythm (rhythms cut through by other rhythms which are cut by still other rhythms)—if it takes us to the point at which the central rhythm is displaced by other rhythms in such a way as to make it fix a center no longer, then to transcend into a state of flux—may fairly define the type of performance that characterizes the Caribbean cultural machine. This is to say that rhythm, in the Caribbean, precedes music, even percussion. It is something already there, something to which percussion may be joined at a given moment—a kind of sacred zone or *mandala* which can be reached, for example, by a battery of *batá* drums.

It would be a mistake, though, to reduce the rhythm of the Caribbean to a polyrhythmic percussion system like that of the *batá* drums. The Caribbean rhythm is in fact a metarhythm which can be arrived at through any system of signs, whether it be dance, music, language, text, or body language. One begins to walk and all of a sudden he realizes that he is walking "well," that is, not just with his feet, but also with other parts of his body; each muscle moves with its own rhythm, absolutely comfortable, which nonetheless adjusts admirably to the rhythm of his steps. All right, there's nothing particularly special about this yet, nothing that we could call "Caribbean"; we've simply taken up the conventional notion of polyrhythm, which presupposed a central rhythm (footsteps). It's possible (though it doesn't happen very often) that a person might feel that he wants to walk "better," and to that end he sets all his muscles into their "optimal" rhythms. This will cause many of them to cease following the rhythm of the footsteps, and then he begins to walk with his whole body, that is, to walk "in a certain kind of way." The center has been decentered, and now it moves from muscle to muscle, stopping here and there, lighting intermittently, like a firefly, each of the body's rhythmic centers. Here we can say that the conventional machine has coupled with the Caribbean machine.

Of course the process that I just described is no more than a mediocre example. I have not mentioned one of the most important dynamics working toward the decentering of the polyrhythmic system: the very complex phenomenon usually called improvisation. Without it one could never arrive at the optimal rhythm for each particular muscle; one has to give them freedom to look around at their own risk. Thus, before a person can walk "in a certain kind of way," his entire body must pass through an improvisational stage.

This theme is nowhere near exhausted, but we have to keep moving. I know that there must be doubts and questions at this point, and I will try to anticipate a few. Someone might ask, for example, what the use is of walking "in a certain kind of way." In fact, there's not much use in it; not even dancing "in a certain kind of way" is of much use in terms of industrial production. A jazz improvisation (jazz being a kind of music that dwells within the Caribbean orbit) which achieves a decentering of the canon by which a piece has been interpreted previously is hardly useful, either. The improvisation can be taped by a record company, but the product is a recording, not the improvisation, which is linked indissolubly with a space and time that cannot be reproduced. Of course the company in question will try to persuade us that it is not selling us a phantom. And this company or another will try to convince us that if we acquire certain audio components we will be able to hear the phantom improvisation better than the improvisation itself. Which is not necessarily false, of course. The deception lies in maintaining that "listening" is the only sense touched by improvisation. In fact, improvisation, if it has reached the level of "a certain kind of way," has penetrated all of the percipient spaces of those present, and it is precisely this "totality" that leads them to perceive the impossible unity, the absent locus, the center that has taken off and yet is still there, dominating and dominated by the soloist's performance. It is this "totality" that leads those present to another "totality": that of rhythm-flux, but not that of the rhythms and fluxes that belong to industrial production, to computers, to psychoanalysis, to synchronicity and diachronicity. The only useful thing about dancing or playing an instrument "in a certain kind of way" lies in the attempt to move an audience into a realm where the tensions of binary opposition are inoperative.

It will be objected that the property of displacing centers without displacing them is not exclusive to Caribbean culture. Oriental cultures reach something similar through meditation, to give one example. True, but in Caribbean culture an audience is needed, and in this it is unique. The Caribbean performance, which includes the ordinary act of walking, does not turn upon the performer, rather it is directed toward the "other"; it is an attempt to seduce the "other," mediated through the performer's wish to set himself up as the "other's" object of desire. Perhaps this is why the most natural forms of Caribbean cultural expression are dance and popular music; perhaps this is why people of the Caribbean become stars in the spectacular sports (baseball, boxing, cricket, and so on) rather than in the more chaste ones (swimming) where the arena is less visible or where the rules are more constraining (shooting, fencing, riding, tennis, and so on).

Boxing is a sport detested by many, but I ask you to think for a moment about its tremendous performance possibilities: the boxers' dance in the ring, their bouncing off the ropes, the elegant jab and sidestep, the flourish of the *bolo* punch and the uppercut, the implicit rhythm in all of their gesticulation, the theatricality (facial expressions and taunting shouts), the hero-villain role-swapping from one round to the next, the performances of the supporting players (referee, cornermen, doctor, judges, the announcer in his tuxedo, the cut man, the bell man), and all of this in a perfectly illumined space, filled with silks and colors, with blood, photographers, shouts and whistles, dramatic knockdowns, a crowd on its feet, cheering. It's no surprise that people of the Caribbean should be good boxers, and also, of course, good dancers, good walkers, good singers, good musicians, in short, good improvisers, good performers, and finally, good writers.

I know you will say that writing is an art as solitary, as quiet, and as ardent as a prayer. Not true. Literature is without a doubt one of the most spectacular media in the world. This is because it is a system of texts, and there is nothing as spectacular as a text. Remember that what an author writes, at a typewriter, by hand, or on a word processor, is not a text, but rather something previous and qualitatively different: a pre-text. For a pre-text to transform itself into a text, certain stages, certain requisites (which I won't list for reasons of space and argument) must be gone through. I will content myself by saying that the text is born when it is read by the "other," the reader. From that moment on the text establishes itself as an infinite act of double seduction. With each reading the reader seduces the text, transforms it, makes it his or her own; with each reading the text seduces the reader, transforming, making him or her its own. If this double seduction reaches the intensity of "a certain kind of way," both the text and the reader will transcend their respective centers without transcending them. This possible impossibility has been studied philosophically, epistemologically, through the discourse of poststructuralism. But poststructuralist discourse corresponds to postindustrial discourse, while the Caribbean discourse is prestructuralist and preindustrial, and to make matters worse it is a nondiscursive discourse. I mean to say by this that the area of "a certain kind of way" is taken by poststructuralist thought as an episteme, while intuitive Caribbean discourse takes it to contain the limits of Being.

A French reader can seduce the text of *Cien años de soledad,* but he can't be seduced by it "in a certain kind of way." I mean that the French reader's seductive capacity—that of Lévi-Strauss, Barthes, Lacan, Foucault, Derrida, Deleuze, Guattari, Lyotard (taking the text here as a feminine object)—is so great that *Cien años de soledad* would quickly fall into these consummate reader-lovers' arms, knowing beforehand that it was going to be possessed in a rich and memorable way. It would also know ahead of time that its *affaire* would not be more than an intense adventure, without perspective, since the seductive arts would deploy too early or too late to move the hearts of these experienced lovers. In truth, the only people who can be seduced "in a certain kind of way" are the people of the Caribbean, or if you like, the Peoples of the Sea. This explains why Gabriel García Márquez, the caretaker of *Cien años de soledad,* was put forward by the Caribbean to receive the Nobel Prize and why he is regarded as a permanent candidate for the presidency of his country. The entire Caribbean was seduced by this novel.

A non-Caribbean reader will enjoy the text of *Cien años de soledad,* but he cannot be transformed by it "in a certain kind of way." I mean to say that this novel is there to be seen by postindustrial society; to a Caribbean person, however, reading it is a transcendental experience, an experience of Being.

One might ask here how we can even begin to talk about Caribbean literature when its very existence is doubtful. This question, of course, has to do with the issue of multilingualism, which apparently divides the literature of the Caribbean irreparably. But I would answer with another question: is it any more correct to think of *Cien años de soledad* as a work of Spanish literature, or the work of Césaire as an achievement of French poetry, or Machado de Assis as a Portuguese writer, or V. S. Naipaul as an immigrant English writer? Of course the answer would be a strong no. Then the assertion becomes: there is no Caribbean literature, there are only literatures written in the anglophone, francophone, and other language blocs within the Caribbean. I agree with this proposition. Only in terms of a first reading, of course. Beneath the *árbol, arbre, tree* lies the same island that keeps "repeating" itself all the way to its arrival as a meta-archipelago. There is no center or circumference; there are tropisms, common patterns highlighted differently and then gradually assimilated into African, European, Indo-American, and Asian contexts until they have reached the point at which none of them can be differentiated.

What is a good example of this passage beyond Ultima Thule? The field of literature is always full of conflict (narrow nationalism, passion, human weakness); my example will not be a literary author but an author of ideas: Martin Luther King. This man was a North American without ceasing to be Caribbean, or the other way around. His African ancestry, the texture of his humanism, the ancient wisdom in his words, his improvisatory nature, his cordially high tone, his ability to seduce and be seduced, and above all, his vehement status as a "dreamer" (*I have a dream . . .*) and performer, all make up the Caribbean element of a man who is unquestionably idiosyncratic in North America. Martin Luther King occupies and fills the space in which Caribbean thought (L'Ouverture, Bolívar, Martí, Garvey) meets North American black discourse; that space can also be filled by the blues.

It is sterile and senseless to try to confine the Caribbean to a given geographical area. There are writers born in the middle of the Caribbean Sea who are not Caribbean in their writing; there are others born in New York who are. Nevertheless there are different kinds of manifestations, and they occur most often along an axis that runs from the mouth of the Amazon to the Mississippi delta, and whose breadth takes in the northern coast of South and Central America (as far as Veracruz), the old Arawak-Carib bridge, and some imperfectly integrated areas of the United States, where vestiges of Spanish and French colonization persist (Key West, Louisiana), or in the Old South (the plantation), or in certain cities with heavy Caribbean populations (Miami, New York).

The time has come to speak of the common forms taken by the multilinguistic literature of the Caribbean. With regard to this, I think that the Caribbean text's most characteristic movement tends, paradoxically, away from the text, to project itself outside of its own nature as text, to move it into music and into myth. In either case we're dealing with "a machine for the suppression of time." The attempt to avoid the net of intertextuality in order to join with nondiscursive or transhistorical systems must always, of course, end in failure. A text is finally a text, and will be so *ad infinitum,* no matter how much it may try to be something else. This failed attempt at flight, however, leaves its mark on the surface of the text, not as a sign of frustrated escape but rather as a sign of the will to keep trying to break loose. We might say that Caribbean texts are "fugitive" by nature. So it is that the Caribbean *bildungsroman* does not end with a graduation ceremony and a nostalgic farewell to apprenticeship. Nor does a Caribbean text's dramatic structure usually end with the phallic orgasm of a climax. If we look at the most representative Caribbean texts we see that the discourse of "content" is erased by forms that are nondiscursive, circular if you like, which finally come forth as the only vehicles able to lead the reader (and the text) to the plenitude of Being and non-Being, of the here and now together with the oblivious and absent. And so the final page of the text becomes the beginning.

I think that this literary system's tendency to flight comes from the working of African components in the cultural interplay. African cultures can be taken, as belonging to Peoples of the Sea, to be nondiscursive systems if we understand the discursive as a diachronic or metonymic axis. Or we could say that the cultures of the Peoples of the Sea are discursive, but that their discourse runs along a metaphoric axis; that is, these are essentially "poetic" cultures. All of this, though, pertains to a first reading of the Caribbean text. A second reading would have to detain us among the rhythms (myth, music) of Caribbean literature. Here, necessarily, we will meet two great rhythmic systems: Africa and Europe. Certainly there are Asian and autochthonous rhythms, but in morphological terms and in a general way we can align these rhythms with the African ones. In the end, we're talking about the rhythms of the Peoples of the Sea. The polyrhythmic system that these two kinds of rhythms inform has been described and analyzed in the most divergent ways and through the most varied disciplines, and I do not want to attempt to do the same here. Let us take up some of those studies' findings, though. For example: European rhythms try to command a center, and basically articulate themselves in a binary fashion (the rhythm of footsteps, of marching, of territorialization). This is the narrative of desire, of knowledge, of power. The rhythms of the Peoples of the Sea attempt to go nowhere, and if they were to try to go somewhere they would float toward the pleasurable condition of "totality," which finally is nowhere. There is an apparently irreconcilable contradiction between these two kinds of rhythms. However, at the moment that the contradiction is established, a possible reconciliation appears: the syncretic rhythm, the *mestizo* rhythm, the mulatto text. Such a rhythm, such a text, is not real; it is a *mirage*. In reality, neither the culture nor the literature of the Caribbean are *mestizo*, of mixed blood. They cannot be so because such a mixture is impossible, if by it we mean the condition of having reached a kind of "unity" or "totality." The promise of *mestizaje*, its solution, did not originate in Africa or with any other People of the Sea. We're dealing here with a positivist and logocentric argument, an argument that sees the biological, economic, social, and cultural "whitening" of the Caribbean black as a series of steps toward "progress," thus legitimating conquest, slavery, colonization, and dependence. In fact, this *mestizaje* is a concentration of conflicts, an exacerbation brought about by the closeness and density of the Caribbean situation. Then, at a given moment, the binary syncretism Europe-Africa explodes and scatters its entrails all around: here is Caribbean literature. This literature should not be seen as anything but a system of texts in intense conflict with themselves. The Caribbean poem, story, and novel are projects conceived to shore up not the effects of an explosion or crisis in universal values, but rather of their own explosion, their own void, their *black hole,* which "repeats" endlessly through the Caribbean space.

And so Caribbean literature is the expression of innumerable conflicts: of the black who studied in Paris; of the white who believes in the Yoruba *orichas* or in the voodoo *loas*; of the black who wants to return to Africa after so many centuries; of the mulatto who wants to be white; of the white man who does not want his child to marry a black; of the white man who loves a mulatto woman; of the black woman who loves a white man; of the black man who despises the mulatto; of the rich black and the poor white; of the white who claims that race does not exist—but why go on? If I wanted to, I could cite titles of poems and novels in the place of this conflictive enumeration, since everything listed (and much more) has been covered by Caribbean authors. You see that we are dealing here with an impossible society where contradictions of sex and class are reinforced, or rather, sent spinning out of control, by racial conflict. The impossibility of assuming even the color of one's own skin can only be assuaged by the possibility of reaching a plenitude of Being, the *aleph* about which I have been speaking so much. The most viable systems to approach it are those articulated in the area of the Afro-European religious cult, in music, song, dance, and myth—certainly not in writing. Hence the Caribbean text that proposes to transcend its own fragmentation must go to these systems to find forms that speak intuitively in the reader's metalanguage. This sort of metarhythm passes now and again through the net thrown out by the West: the language of the colonizer which, with its deafening binary march, will always try to subdue the forms that are untainted by meaning, or only partly so, as happens in myth.

I think that these formal models come mainly from African cultures, which is not to exclude Asian, Indo-American, and even European presences. But if the structure of the myth is African, its theme is unquestionably Caribbean. In fact, if we were able to reduce those themes to something like a metatheme, we would soon find ourselves face-to-face with an archetype. Not, of course, a Jungian archetype; however, I have always believed in an archetype of "liberation" that places us in conflict with any form of oppression (sexual, racial, economic, political, and so on). I also believe in an archetype of "totality," which I would define as the sum of scientific knowledge plus the great metaphor of tradition, that is, the sphere of poetic knowledge. Perhaps we are dealing with a single archetype that projects itself into every Caribbean myth. If that were so, I would say that there is in our myths, more or less explicitly, a desire to reach some place free of tension, through the search for "totality."

As to the rest, the Caribbean text shows the specific features of Caribbean culture. It is, without a doubt, a consummate performer, a daring improviser. This text, in its most authentic form, can be seen in terms of the *carnaval,* the Caribbean celebration that brings together all of its semiotic systems (music, song, dance, myth, language, dress, food, body expression, and so on). There is something strongly feminine in this extraordinary *fiesta*: its flux, its diffuse sensuality, its generative force, its capacity to nourish and conserve (juices, spring, pollen, feedback, rivers, Milky Way—these are words that come to stay). Think of the dancing flourishes, the rhythms of the *conga,* the *samba,* the hoods, the masks, the men dressed and painted as women, the bottles of rum, the sweets, the confetti and colored streamers, the hubbub, the carousal, the trumpeting, the flirting, the jealousy, the razor that draws blood, death, life, reality in forward and reverse, baroque contesting the hyperbolic, irony rivalling the *pastiche,* torrents of people who flood the streets, the night lit up like an endless dream, the figure of a centipede that comes together and then breaks up as it winds and stretches with the rhythm, always the rhythm: People of the Sea.

José Piedra

Through Blues

I

BUT SCRIPT-WRITERS WHO KNOW BETTER
WOULD HARDLY WRITE IT IN THE SCRIPT—
—Langston Hughes, "IS IT TRUE"

Musical language is not exempt from the scourge of alphabetic writing; most Westerners think of musical sounds as either distorted variants of complete words or rhythmic patterns of isolated letters—such as the scales arbitrarily labeled with monosyllabic "nonsense" as *do, re, mi, fa, sol, la, ti,* or with alphabetic "sense" as *a, b, c, d, e, f, g.* These linguistic renderings of sound struggle with a notion of logic based on rules of writing—what Langston Hughes problematizes as "THE SCRIPT" in the epigraph above.[1]

Given the pervasiveness of writing, literary critics can easily assert that musical language has fallen below literate standards, or demand that it be translated into a language that can be approached critically as if it were recorded in letters. If these expectations are already placed on music written according to sounds that approximate the master languages, the situation is even worse for music that is left unwritten, as it is for the type of writing that a commanding audience chiefly appreciates for its "musical" rather than its "logical" qualities. Signifying systems that appear to be based more on rhythm than on meaning remain baffling to traditionalist, Western-trained critics who might consider them linguistic disguises for illiterate and illogical communication. The disguised values, in fact, can be neither translated into "grammatical" writing nor reduced to a "logical" reading, much less to conventional forms of "critical" judgment.

The attempt to define the "logic" of the unwritten has nourished the modern study of signs and challenged the predominantly *literate* field of semiotics. My present effort is much more modest: to identify a particular pattern of thought based on the forced articulation of "musical" values within a literary language. The forced articulation in question is responsible for the inscription of a significant set of Hispano- and Anglo-African means of expression in the Americas. This effort also requires some review of the notion of signification applied by the Western-dominated master discourse to the forms of expression that it considers marginal.

In spite of their translation into letters or discourse, values that are marginal to writing, such as musical ones, only appear to accept the compromise of literary, or simply literate, logic. Critics would have to interpret the extent of the compromise in order to assess the "original" logic. This approach mirrors a notion present in Hughes's aesthetics. For Hughes, defenders of marginal values become scriptwriters even though they resent "THE SCRIPT," which they use as a means to store unwritable experiences—of notions as well as of sounds, voices, and motions—that could then be released in a "critical" performance. In the best of circumstances, interpreters read writing as a script for performance. For example, a mere change of inflection or a chosen break in phrasing is capable of altering meaning, representing an otherwise hidden voice or message, or otherwise suggesting the existence of a "logic of performance" beyond a "logic of reading."

In reference to the logic of performance with which I identify Hughes's aesthetics, an old-fashioned word such as "logic" is applied in its broader interpretation as a pattern of thought, stretching the core notion of *logos,* or rational principle, from a single commanding model of logic to the widest possible range of critical performances. Since there would likely be as many performances as there are active interpreters, one could argue that the application of the logic of performance to a written script leads to "contradictions." Yet the effect is no different than comparatively reviewing the cumulative interpretations actors give to a dramatic role. Such contradictions also nourish the Western notion of logic, in which case they would likely be called "paradoxes." Furthermore, Western "modernity" elevates paradoxes to a stylistic peak and exploits misscripted records as poetic licenses that are ostensibly permitted for the sake of artistic self-expression.

In attempting to define the forms of expression adopted by neo-African logic, I intend to consider its similarities and differences with respect to the so-called Western tradition, which still acts as the master code in most academic circles. I am referring to the post-Aristotelian heritage, which is built on the notion of linking propositional sequences. I shall review such a heritage through the perspective of different interpretations which lie at the humanist core of twentieth-century Western modernity: the formalist (fable, subject, defamiliarization), Saussurean (signifier, signified, and signification), and musical models (theme, variation, and resolution). According to this lingering propositional vocabulary, order can be emblematized by letters that represent each step of a progression geared to complete and justify itself as a "logical" statement. However, there is always a built-in critical "unknown" in each of these propositional sequences, and it might, at any moment, upset its predicted pattern. I am referring to an element of guessing, leading to multiple options and, in turn, to interpretive decisions chosen by given critics to fit their existential circumstances. This final step in the signifying process implies a paradoxically *personal,* and implicitly biased, experience of "neutral" logic. The process leads to "(intuitive) perception" in the Aristotelian legacy, to "(re)familiarization" according to the formalist, to "(counter)signification" in a Saussurean vein, as well as to the sort of "performance" that liberates musical "sense." Likewise, in the "modern" language of science the culmination of many a propositional sequence is to find the actual value of the X-variable in a formulaic equation. In spite of its signifying a "neutral" or "universal" value, this X *means* something different to everyone.

In the neo-African logic of performance that I consider here, the value of the textual unknown emerges mostly from the musical projection of the script. Due to the West's linguistic prejudices, this form of active projection provides a relief for marginal individuals and values whose ill-fitting inscription can only expect to be embraced by logical strictures through paratextual performances. Black music presumably transcends "first-rate" logic through a "second-rate" language of rhythm. Such a critically perceived weakness is, in fact, a strength. Rhythm serves as a disguise for (or subtle guide to) the X-factor of Afro-American textuality. It was identified as such by Ishmael Reed in his novel *Mumbo Jumbo* (appropriately titled after a "black" language of riddle) and adopted by Houston A. Baker, Jr., as the crucial unknown of black signification.[2] This factor finds a Cuban parallel in the perception of an "unknown voice" which is to be released through this island's ubiquitous *son* or translated as the axial center of the *Anaforuana* Afro-Cuban ritual writing.[3]

The X-factor is born from a textual script corrected, completed, liberated, or simply acted out by writers, performers, and critics. Whereas in traditionally scripted logic, an X-factor concludes and justifies a propositional sequence, in performance logic the X-factor reopens the cycle, or questions the validity, of a given logical sequence. Thus, the X-factor emerges as the residual or converging factor resulting after alternative readings have contradicted or canceled each other out. Instead of embracing a Western propositional sequence of the type "A leads to B leads to C, and maybe to X," the neo-African logic of performance pinpoints, from a given perspective, the interception of as many offshoots of interpretation as possible: "A intercepts B intercepts C in point X."

I consider that neither the logic of reading nor that of performance ever acts alone in either a Western-style text or an African-style script. My proposed critical perspective assumes that the logic of either text or script, reading or performance, is ultimately the responsibility of a subject who imposes him- or herself onto the object of signification. The vehicle of such an imposition is "interpretation," which is always relatively active. The interpreting subject in question acts as a Heideggerian Being inasmuch as he or she does not embody either a singular referent or a specific state of mind but rather impersonates the very process of becoming or acting a text or script. As we shall see from my subsequent analysis of several texts, the neo-African connection with Heideggerian notions is far from gratuitous. The connection is historical or, at least, a historical coincidence that serves me well as a basis for my comparative study.

In neo-African aesthetics born of colonial interventions, the writing of the critical Self and the performance of the proverbial Other cross in a middle ground. The textual scripts in which their paths cross yield an image of split referentiality and misscripted textuality. Neither the Self nor its Other ever become One in the referential world—that is, in the mimetic reality projected by a single literary perspective. They become One only momentarily in the limited rhetorical space provided by the textual script. In turn, critical "performers" provide the liberating experience of re-creating or expanding on such a coincidental union. Therefore the process of signification that I am studying is not a matter of determining the logical sequence of a referent destined to become a "Being-in-the-World," that is, a Being whose "being" is the result of the sequential process of a logical act.[4] The neo-African referent in question is a "Being-through-the-Text" or, better yet, a being that exploits its Eurocentric misscripting. Instead, the neo-African interpretative agent tends to rely on the accumulation of signification around the coincidental X-factor of the textual script.

Not only the cross-referential X-factor of signification (Reed and Baker) or the unknown voice (Guillén) but also the "textualization" of thought patterns (which I have named "Being-through-the-Text") have ample roots in traditional African concepts of axial inscription.[5] Among them are the visual representations of the Yoruba mythology of the crossroads, Kongo cosmological crosses, and Calabar *nsibidi* cross-writing, as well as its offspring in the Afro-Americas, such as the Haitian *vevé* and the Cuban *Anaforuana,* both of which project onto an axial setting elements from the different African sources previously mentioned. The X-factor also finds a "performed" counterpart in Cuba: the inscription of an *Anaforuana* X on the surface of the silent drum of woman's power (the *sesê*).[6] In each of these cases the interpretative options are either superimposed over or paired against the traditional logic of writing, as well as that of oral and musical communication—including even the semiotics of silent gestures.

In the neo-African world, traditional African "variants" defend themselves against the "master model" with which they have strategically allied themselves, in a wide range of forms: from discreet *parodic* signification (X as disguise) to aggressive *counter*signification (X as display). These traditional African notions find parallels in the ongoing relativization of logic that characterizes twentieth-century Western thought. They also reach into the seemingly sacred domain of scientific "certainty," from the "unknown" element in mathematical expression (X as disguise) to the mapping of points onto an orthogonal system of coordinates (X as display).

I have chosen as critical objects two forms of expression that, although musically very different, emerge as parallel historical and rhetorical expressions of a neo-African logic of performance: the North American blues and the Cuban *son.* Both have suffered from a literate prejudice that considers their lyrics as mere clusters of distorted words or rhythmic sounds. But the blues and the *son* thrive on the simultaneous, contradictory playing of more than one "chord"—perceived as either string, beat, voice, language, or meaning. This is what Langston Hughes praises as a "SCRATCHY SOUND" and is called in the vocabulary of the Afro-Cuban tradition *fragayar*—a "raspy" playing of the sacred surface of the *ekwue* or *bonko* drum that offers a ritual alternative to the silent writing/ playing of the *sesé* drum.[7] These sounds do not have a clear or fixed source, quality, or notation, nor do they follow a predictable order or furnish an exact meaning. Upon comparing them to their notations, they appear to be born of "splits" in traditional "written-down" notes, or to be "hidden" concentrically or to "swing" rhythmically between several of these notes at once. This willful dissonance is not exclusive to music; it can also occur in other textual or critical systems accused of being merely musical. The uninitiated perceive these systems to rely on a relative or faulty pattern of written logic.

Western logic's prejudices against unscriptable values influence the linking of them to pathological behavior. Even the Western names of "blues" and "*son*," as well as their traditional Western interpretations, conjure an image of linguistic and behavioral impropriety. Toward the turn of the century, at the time of the public surfacing of the blues, the name was already associated with a mildly pathological sadness that the mainstream attributed to the marginal.[8] This translated into a linguistic irregularity: the color blue became the grammatically improper "blues" that musically released the "blue moods" of the culturally and linguistically dispossessed. The blues's expression of dispossession has been largely taken for granted, except when exploited for commercial purposes.

Some Latin American writers have discreetly objected to the literary fate of the blues as a song of existential and linguistic dispossession. This is particularly true in Cuban literature. In the 1920s we have Alejo Carpentier's "reinscription" of the blues according to its predicted origin as a song of mourning by enslaved workers in his grammatically titled "Blue."[9] In the 1980s there is Gustavo Pérez Firmat's "Carolina Blues," which deals with the malaise of an exile living in the midst of conflicting codes, commercial images, and artificially induced moods.[10] Pérez Firmat offers a tongue-in-cheek medical cure for his Carolina-Cuban blues. Both of these Cuban writers embrace the philosophy of blues through the *son*'s form, but this is no guarantee of their awareness and admission of formal influences from Africa. Cuban culture tends to disguise African notions as its own, often overlooking contributing heritages other than the European. Critics such as Octavio Paz often intend to reassure us by stating that the Afro-Hispanic "poetic modality," dating back to the seventeenth century, reveals positive social concerns as well as negative aesthetic prejudices.[11] Paz makes a special mention in this regard of the poem "North Carolina Blues," by his fellow Mexican writer Xavier Villaurrutia, but instead of focusing on the merits of this poem or the lack thereof, he only mentions Villaurrutia's fear of "folklorism"— presumably a poor substitute for autochthonous logic.[12]

In its subsequent commercial adaptation as an Anglo-American genre for an international audience, the blues emphasized the incurable irregularities of logic and moody longings suggested by its name. Meanwhile, for the Afro-Americans of the United States who "lived" them, blues themes continued to center on the struggle of individuals against what was deemed "deviations" and "failures" by a master code: the past memories, present dissatisfaction, or unrealizable hopes of displaced marginals. To this day, in spite of its commercialization, the blues has continued to yield rich textual possibilities not normally accounted for by literate logic and classical Western performances. These unusual qualities also are apparent in the history, theory, and practice of the Afro-Hispanic American *son*.

At about the same time of the commercial success of the blues, the *son* achieved parallel notoriety in the Spanish-speaking Caribbean basin. *El son* as notion and music was born with an ungrammatical aura. This song of self is roughly translatable as "the they are" or "he they are," as if being through a form that is not, at least singularly, ours. No wonder Argeliers León rebaptized *el son* as *lo son,* the grammatically neutral form of being—an emphatic form of "they are" which is grammatically applicable to all and/or to none.[13] Both the Cuban acceptance of this linguistic misnomer and the occasional critical attempt to correct it presumably signal a deeper identity crisis: the *son* as an improper behavioral connection between Selves and Others—viewed as insiders and outsiders to a culture. In its literary context, this presumed form of being-through-others is twofold. It means that illiterate marginals express themselves through literate means. It also suggests a complementary act: marginals who are slaves of letters mold the written logic of the master code into a Creole language of compromise that is, folklorically as well as logically speaking, a rhythmic and meaningful countercode.

My comparative study of the blues and the *son* divides into two parts. First, I discuss the historical development of the *son*'s logic of performance as a systematic relativization of signification, subversively paired against traditional and modern notions of Western logic. Second, I compare the parallel development of the blues with what we have learned of the *son,* and how each has adopted and adapted traditional African and modern Western notions of signification. In so doing, I propose a journey to the common linguistic roots of the ontological *salsa* (sauce) of the *son* and, by extension, of the *soul* of the blues.

II

Na-na-nanita, Nana,
las dos negritas en una cama.
Duerme, blanquita, que viene el Coco
y se lleva los niños que duermen poco.

(Ma-Ma-Mammy dear, Mammy,
the little black notes are two to a bed.
Sleep on, little white note, for Bogeyman
comes to grab children who sleep little.)
　　—Cuban jingle

In Cuba, prejudice has been part of an agenda poorly hidden in the very fabric of written discourse. This is illustrated by the above jingle that serves as an epigraph, which was naïvely sung on this island circa 1950 by children learning the values of black as opposed to white notes in the proto-European "Kindergarten Musical Hubert de Blanck." In spite of its Eurocentric perspective, this jingle attaches a singular importance to the threat of the *Coco* (or *Koko*), a Kongo-derived challenger of significa-tion equivalent to the Bogeyman. The jingle shares with Afro-Cuban lyrics hidden musical values, as well as social prejudices, within an alien-ating written discourse. The jingle reveals that when musical notes are given numerical values, black or quarter notes are assigned half the value of white or half notes; we also might become aware that the two quarter notes have to sleep two to a bed, ostensibly because they are too poor for each to occupy its own. Moreover, the jingle also suggests, perhaps ironically, that the white note should continue to sleep (dreaming a self-validation dream?). It might as well, for it cannot do anything against the visit of the black Bogeyman who lurks in the hidden corners of a textual night, ready to shock the white notes into awareness. The drama between the dreams of power of white notes and a black envoy of aware-ness, or, for that matter, between white writing and black unwriting, frames the present approach to the *son*.

Throughout its history, the legendary literature of the *son* has survived and thrived amidst prejudice and adaptation through a few geographical and linguistic exiles—in Africa, Haiti, Cuba, and even the international market. In the process, it has developed a subversive strategy of onto-logical differentiation against all sorts of aggressions by written logic and the textual models of the Spanish literate establishment. The *son* has remained loyal to its remote, nonliterate source: the Dogon *sò*. *Son* and *sò* are core principles of Cuban and Dogon ontologies respectively. The evolution from the latter to the former likely involved the mediation of Afro-Haitian culture and language, which from the onset of the revo-lution of the slaves went into exile to the eastern tip of Cuba.

For the traditional Dogon, the utterance of sound "inside" of oneself or the formation of words "outside" of oneself constitute two stages of being through the process of naming, in thought and in speech. In fact, the word *sò* means both the "sound" and the "word" through which individuals claim their essence.[14] It also approximates the Franco-Haitian and Afro-Cuban pronunciations and meanings of the word *son,* jointly suggesting "sound," "son," and "[they] are." Moreover, *sò* is likely to be the source for the Anglo-African "soul," a Guillén-like "unknown voice." In any case, it is a form of signification that marks us from the inside out as different. In each of these situations, the ontological search and its expression are hindered by the very nature of the linguistic system of discourse that each of these expressions of human experience is forced to assume.

The negative effect of certain indirect types of discourse on the clarity of direct communication was already observed by the Dogon, for whom such a discourse (be it oral or written) promotes the "distortion of words, riddled matter."[15] Instead of a discourse attached to a literate or literary topic, the Dogon propose to express and make public their notion of Being as a process whereby individuals "find themselves" in the *áduno-sò* ("the word of the world")—that is, their "Being-in-the-World."[16] They seek the kind of "word" that reflects a textual system that, like most notions of the "world," is constantly being challenged by the evolving consent of a given community.

The history of the *son* in Cuba is obscured by literate systems and literary discourse just as the *sò* is for the Dogon. The African background of the *son* enriches and subverts the traditional logic of its own "Spanish" lyrics. Among the most significant examples of just such a subversion are: the oldest known Cuban literary fragment, the reputedly sixteenth-century "Son de la Ma Teodora" ("*Son* of the Ma Teodora"); the ostensibly nineteenth-century traditional *son,* "Son de la loma" ("*Son* of the Moun-tain"), associated with Miguel Matamoros's early twentieth-century in-terpretation; the more recent narrative interpretation of the "Son de la loma," Severo Sarduy's *De donde son los cantantes (Where Singers Are From)*; and, finally, perhaps the most abstract of traditional renderings of the *son,* Ñico Saquito's "Oye mis son" ("Listen to My *Son*").[17]

In the evolution of the *son* there are always three propositions whose precarious balance brings forth a fourth element of critical decision. Briefly, the four elements which I intend to elaborate throughout this essay are: *Mamá, Monte, Coco,* and the *Sò* itself—the Word personified as *áduno-sò,* a discursive "Being-" not directly "in-the-World" but rather "through-the-Text." In fact, it is feasible that the other three elements derived as well from a Dogon/Kongo context as they contributed to the notion of *Sò* in the African and, subsequently, the Afro-American settings. Thus, according to African (mostly Dogon and/or Kongo) sources: *mama* means "thought," *muntu* (from where I believe derives *monte*) implies a people's symbol for the "world" or "community," and *koko* (the phonetic version of *coco*) means "neck"—referring to the most superficial organ for uttering the Word, as well as to a threatening figure that often appears to children in the guise of a monkey.[18] The meaningfulness of such an act/system is determined by agreement from the community (Muntu) as to what thoughts (Mama) become palatable as they pass through the channel of voicing, the rhetorical neck (*Coco*). Whether we agree or not with all the details of the transposition of Dogon/Kongo notions to the Cuban *son* does not change the validity of considering this form of expression as an ontological effort involving sound at some level in the process of expressive utterance: from thought, through silence, to voicing/wording. The fact remains that the notions alluded to, or at least their names, appear often as "characters" in the lyrics and that criticism seems to have treated them as innocent bystanders from a neglected or misunderstood heritage.

The Mother is an intellectual and physical source as well as a goal of inspiration and invocation that appears as Nana, Mammy, or Nanny as well as Ma, Mama, or Mamá: a predominantly female principle signifying reassurance and defensive disguise. It also refers to the placement of the voice in words ("A" element of propositional logic, fable, signifier, or theme). The Monte represents the Afro-Hispanic space of identification as a sacred meeting place in the Wild, either an elevation or a clearing that is roughly equivalent to the "Muntu" of the Kongo culture and the "Down Home" of the Anglo-Africans.[19] It is also the displacement of the voice beyond words ("B" element of propositional logic, subject, signified, or variation). The Coco is a predominantly male, challenging figure of signification and of offensive display better known in semiotic terms as the "Signifying Monkey"; it encompasses a long line of African countersignifying tricksters, ranging from the Bogeyman to a series of Afro-Cuban counterparts that hide in natural "breaks" and textual "loopholes."[20] It is also the displacement of the voice through interpretation ("C" element of propositional logic, defamiliarization, signification, or resolution). The Text itself actually presents the surface for the projection of a critical Being whose existence or lack thereof either comes to be grammatically trapped, takes rhetorical refuge, or awaits the right outlet of signification while strategically entrenched in words. This Being-through-the-Text is evident in African traditions—notably, the Dogon and the Kongo—as well as existentialist Western circles—especially Heidegger—as a process that eludes any given image but rather reveals itself circumstantially in the "performance" of words. It is also the replacement of the voice for a personalized enigma (X, critical intervention, countersignification, existential interpretation).

In comparing the system of the *son* with post-Aristotelian, formalist, Saussurean, and Heideggerian patterns of logic, I emphasize that they all share at least one element that points beyond its graphic renderings. Thus it should not be essentially disruptive to Western thinking to acknowledge the possibility of connecting that fourth unscriptable element of logic to a nonliterate realm. The unresolved question of whether we think in words or not should not deter us from allowing the existence of other, musical, forms of logic. A historical review of Afro-Cuban discourse will illustrate alternative systems of communication that are compatible with Western patterns of thought.

In the "Son de la Ma Teodora," the rhetorical ambiguity of being through the *son* centers on a Mammy figure and the space of the Monte. The Ma herself dominates the refrain: "¿Dónde está la Ma Teodora?" ("Where is the Ma Teodora?"), whereby she is addressed as either being always absent, remembered as having been present, or invoked as forever performing in the nearby unnamed Wild. In any case she is beckoned by an anonymous caller as a personal martyr of music and sex rather than in her secret role as social champion of meaning and justice. Meanwhile, she "hides" defensively, along with her secrets, in a timeless space: a Monte, which is not just a linguistic trap but also a natural haven projected as a rhetorical disguise and an undefinable existential trench from which she defends herself in absentia. In this sense, Ma Teodora is neither here (actually *in* the compromised Euro-Cuban text) nor there (symbolically in her uncompromised Afro-Cuban Monte) but on the edge of a performance-like interpretation.

Documented Cuban history contributes to the Ma's ambiguous and ubiquitous presence; she is the first black performer to have been officially recognized by the Spanish colonial government in the New World. She was paid to make music and act out her black Cubanness—this questionable commodification overshadows not only her contribution but also the history of public display of the black culture of the Americas. Seduction, either sexual or commercial, becomes the Ma's reason for being. In spite of her paid services to the colonial establishment, her memory lives only through a Text in which she is but the seductive ghost of a performer. It is up to historians and critics to doom or to rescue her Being-through-the-Text.

The lyrics of Matamoros's "Son de la loma" attempt to solve the dilemma of literate compromise and signifying challenge that so far propose to taint ontological search with rhetorical disguise or commercial display. The circumstantial solution offered by this *son* is an eminently ironic fusion of the two. The "*son*(g)" raises the leading question it proposes to answer: "Mamá, yo quiero saber de dónde son los cantantes" ("Mother, I want to know where singers come from"). The question is most difficult to answer, as it represents a quest for the original source of a voice which is veiled in alien literary terms. The quest is also part of an even more alienating material journey: from the mountains to the plains and from obscurity in the easternmost province of Cuba to a projected commercial success in the capital. The lyrics express this ambiguous sense of propriety and property, being and becoming somebody as well as successful—in short, "earning" a place in the national discourse.

Implicitly or explicitly, all the national characters of the *son* are present in "Son de la loma": Mamá, Coco, Monte, and Sò or Being-through-the-Text. Like the Mammy in the mnemonic jingle used as an epigraph to this section, or the Ma of the earliest Cuban literary fragment, Matamoros's lyrics center on a rhetorical Mamá or Mother who knows the singers' origin—and thus defines their present and presence and controls their future and absence. The singers are from mountains and wild plains that provide the geographical limits of "her" Monte in its double connotation of sacred elevation and ritual forest. Within the perimeters of neo-African culture, this is the home/country space for thought under the secret control of women (representing the marginals) and the overt discursive domination of men (representing the mainstream). Likewise, this space can be present as a bed for the uneven sharing of musical values (in the jingle of the epigraph) and as an unnamed Wild (in Ma

Teodora's poem). The Coco, who emerged already as a superficial channel and as a parodic, monkey-like challenger of signification, is here
disguised in the mechanics of interpretation. The image of the neo-
African Being-through-the-Text remains trapped in the narrator's perspective: a naive testimony in the search for a rhetorical image and a
textual voice not blinded or strangled by traditional recording.

In Severo Sarduy's *De donde son los cantantes,* the intellectual and material reach of the *son* is humorously "performed" in the first section
entitled *"Curriculum Cubense."*[21] This is a "pig-Latin" title in which
"Cubense" refers to "Cuba" and to "cube," at the critical core of tripartite associations leading to a fourth dimension of Being "textually"
Cuban. The section centers on the scene of the "Self-Service" that takes
place in an automat cafeteria. According to Enrico Mario Santí's essay
on Sarduy's writings, this first section of the novel presents a parodic
allegorization of Heidegger's ontological "Fourfold" [*das Geviert*]: earth,
heaven, man, and gods.[22] Sarduy contrasts this Heideggerian "Fourfold"
to the four "facets" of being Cuban. I propose a further comparison:
Mother-earth, heavenly-Wild, Bogey-man, and the gods of textual signification themselves. These facets do not attempt to be pure or station-
ary; on the contrary, they alternate throughout the three parts of the
body of the novel as preponderantly Chinese, African, and Spanish variations on the relative theme of a controversial Cuban perspective. These
are the main cultural and/or racial options in the background of every
Cuban; literarily, as well as literally, Sarduy represents them all.

At any level of interpretation, the fourth element in Sarduy's textual
scheme is always the most contested: authority, authorship, critical finality, and, ultimately, meaningful death and critical resuscitation of a
godly and ghostly White Being that rules over the Cuban Being. This
fourth element appears as a diluted (self-)critical presence that frames
the text. The novel opens with a section on the "Curriculum Cubense,"
a model for Being Cuban that ironically bypasses the preponderance of
the vernacular Castilian status in search of a pig-Latin source. It includes
the scene at the Self-Service which is based on a parody of U.S. illusions
of choice in the midst of authoritarian consumerism. The novel concludes
with the academic sarcasm of a "Note" that yields a map of critical
reading leading to a sardonic statement of rhetorical justice: *excusatio
propter infirmitatem* (literally "excuse on account of infirmity"), translated
by the author as "incapacidad ante el tema a tratar" ("unpreparedness
at facing the task [of writing]"). Thereby Sarduy excused his text for
making parodic attempts to image and voice, *à la* Heidegger, a global

space, a critical paradise, the human race, and a ghostly inquisitor steeped in written contradictions. Sarduy's text barely keeps in balance the mock-Heideggerian and hyper-Cuban models of existential behavior.

The *son*'s logic of performance emerges as the core model of Sarduyean signification: the essence of original thought (Mamá or Mother) provided by the complementary characters of Auxilio and Socorro (literally two ways of asking for help and understanding, perhaps "Aid" and "Relief") that fuse into Dolores Rondón (literally, "Big Painful Turnaround"—the macabre Mother figure of dependency, sexual submission, and death combined?). The ritual place (Monte or Muntu) is in the Self-Service. The semiotic principle of challenge (Coco or Signifying Monkey) is exemplified by Mortal, who is a Spanish Christ-like figure. Finally, there is a critical Being-through-the-Text as an ever-present absence; this is fragmentarily personified by the apparitions of the character Pelona, or "Baldy": *Gran Pelona* ("Grand Baldy") also referred to as *Pelona innombrable* ("unnamable Baldy") and as the act of returning to *Nada pelona* ("bald Nothingness").[23] To a Cuban reader, these names connect with the glans and with hitting the jackpot, as well as with the will of a god and the certainty of death. Furthermore, taking the logic of performance to an extreme, Sarduy renders his own text as a target of consumption: food for thought (his idiosyncratically modern and personal view of identity as a chance-like form of nourishment—Muntu as "Manna"). The Self-Service cafeteria offers characters and readers the possibility of selecting and consuming from the text whatever pleases them. However, all textual participants must *pay* for what they consume; they sign their "X" and assign their own price for Being-through-the-Text.

Finally, the lyrics of Ñico Saquito's *son* "Oye mis son" synthesize the core of being through a questionable cultural package handled by alien codes and market forces. The expression of its logic of performance pivots around the interpretation of the refrain "Son de los que son y no son" ("They are [*son*] of the kind that [who] are [*son*] and are not [*son*]). *Son* is here not only a musical clue but also a form of the verb "to be," which proposes to divide the "are's" [*los que son*] and the "are not's" [*los que no son*]. This *son* is what it is not as much as what it purports to be and whatever mediates between this pendulum of extremes. Each instance of the word *son* is the same and yet different according to its "placement" in the four-part structure of the text and within the relative perspective of each textual participant. As was the case in the previous examples, the critic has to break the deadlock in both symbolic and material signification.

Saquito's *son* also reveals its pattern of thought to be a pendular infrastructure that is associated with metaphysical relativism and physical relativity; meaning is whatever mediates between rhythmic variations among the signposts of signification. Words in the *son* depict idiosyncratic characters, ritual spaces, and critical perspectives in constant swing. We could say the same of Ma Teodora's relationship with her text, Matamoros's trajectory of the *son,* or Sarduy's general approach to writing. This quality of calculated ambivalence, along with the steps and characters themselves of the *son,* appear in the blues. This is compactly sketched in a line by Little Brother Montgomery: "The first time I met the blues, Mama, they came walking through the woods"—in which the Mother principle is invoked in a wooded Wild whence emerges a challenge of signification personified by the apparition of the character of Blues-in-the-Text. The same can be said of the relativization of words, which leads to a pendular swing that subverts the very notion of sequence at the core of Western inscription.

III

I don't dare start thinking in the morning.
I don't dare start thinking in the morning.
If I thought thoughts in bed, them thoughts would bust my head—
So I don't dare start thinking in the morning.
—Langston Hughes, "Blues at Dawn"

Langston Hughes's "blues" often subvert literate logic. In the present example, the reader seems forced into illiterate thinking after experiencing a parody of the traditional "A, B, C, X" of textual sequencing. The parody of logic goes something like this: A is equal to B and does not "logically" lead to C, which in fact appears to be rather a negation than a resolution of its two hesitant premises ("I don't dare. . . .").[24] Furthermore, the X-factor reinstates the hesitant premises simply by virtue of a most idiosyncratic conjunction: "So" (*Sò?*). It is easier to describe the blues by what it is not vis-à-vis traditional logic; yet by now we should be aware that this is a critical strategy and not a critical deficiency. In fact, these blues lines illustrate the dilemma of reducing one system into another, as they encourage the projection of thought beyond the limits of writing: thinking of thinking as the undoing of the written image of thinking. The logical sequence of the written image has a paralyzing effect on signification. Thus the stage is set for a "relativistic" critical appreciation of the relativity of blues performance.

I propose that the poetics of the blues and the *son* share in the questioning of rhetorical authority that is attached to and endorsed by each stage of the evolving notion of a Western master code. Modernists are as likely as traditionalists to accuse marginal patterns of thought of nonsensical illiteracy. In the paternalistic language of modernity, nonliterate systems could be deemed as inferior attempts at relativism. Moreover, I frame my approach to the blues with the unlikely aid of two Hispanic champions of marginal relativism: the Cuban Juan Marinello and the Spaniard José Ortega y Gasset.

Most innovators, whether from the mainstream or the margins, speak "through a language that is alien," as Marinello put it.[25] Thus, they resent the very linguistic limitations of their respective disciplines—still modeled after a heritage of postpositivistic science, postsyllogistic philosophy, and postcolonial rhetoric. Meanwhile, Afro-Americans involved in the Harlem Renaissance seem to be making the opposite claim, such as is evidenced in James Weldon Johnson's statement that "the language of Harlem is not alien."[26] In fact, whether they are Europeans speaking from the shaken premises of a mainstream struggling to emerge from positivism, syllogism, and ethnocentrism, Cubans defending their own marginality while posing as liberal European intellectuals, or Afro-Americans speaking from a marginal culture targeted for discovery by intellectual or financial impresarios, they all share a parallel sense of alienation toward a decadent rhetorical empire searching for alternative solutions to logocentrism. The end result is to make one's own an alien master code—as Johnson would have it, and Marinello would undoubtedly agree.

Thinkers raised in alienating linguistic circumstances tend to identify with a Heideggerian notion of Being subject to an unfinished process of recording. This existential performance and recording process are the result of existential compromises: where one and one's adopted code are coming from, what one and one's code are going through, and where and what one and one's code are moving toward. In other words, self-image and textual identity are subject to ever-changing perspectives in perception and interpretation—writing as if one were playing, so to speak, on more than one "chord" at once. This form of performance (identified by Langston Hughes) relates to the linguistic application not just of relativism but also of relativity. Ortega y Gasset puts it succinctly: "The theory of Einstein is a marvelous proof of the harmonious multiplicity of all points of view."[27] He used the scientific revolution endorsing "harmonious multiplicity" as the basis for a philosophy he loosely named "perspectivism"—implying simultaneous perspectives. The Spanish philosopher then proceeds to give a simplified example of the kind of thought pattern that links Einstein's relativity and his own philosophical perspectivism and offers his own compromise as the basis for a "new" form of logic to explain the "common sense" of the illiterate masses: "According to the theory of relativity, the event A, which from the mundane point of view precedes the event B in time, will, from another place . . . seem to succeed B."[28]

According to the pendular explanation often invoked by popularizers of the theory of relativity, point A and point B can actually seem to be the same, or point A might not be point A from another perspective, experience, or circumstance. Every time, person, and place in reference to which a point is set will give it a different interpretation regardless of their being expressed in the same or in different terms. This pendular rendering of uncertainty, on which are based significant developments in scientific language (from Galileo to Einstein), strengthens the notion of a logic of performance. Regardless of Ortega y Gasset's elitist attitude as an enforcer of the new logic of perspectivism, his participation in the diversification of European thought helped pave the way for the validation of nonliterate patterns of thought.

As the measurement of reality comes to be at odds with a single perception, scientists and humanists argue new applications for the pendular perception. The misunderstood notion of a pendular critical perception is likely what moves Sarduy and other writers of marginal values to take dramatic steps to establish an explicit relationship between what is concealed in the signs of which they avail themselves and what they and their signs could conceivably reveal given the right critical circumstances. That is, writers like Sarduy establish a parallel between the signification of impersonal, logical, or authorial conformance and that of personal, metalogical, or critical performance. I am referring, for example, to Sarduy's Self-Service and "Note," which extend *critically* the textual body of *De donde son los cantantes*. This form of built-in critical notation reinforces my belief in the writer's treatment of his text as a script for performance.

Ishmael Reed introduces this notion of authorial conformance and critical performance in his blues-inspired novel *Mumbo Jumbo* as the X-factor of black expression, whose "words were [still are] unprintable but its tune irresistible."[29] This self-consciously ironic treatment of rhythmic nonsense (illustrated by the very title of his novel) resembles that of Sarduy's novel in its requirement for a *built-in* critical vocabulary. As in Sarduy's case, Reed signals the deficiencies of a language based on the logic of "THE SCRIPT" and launches instead his own exhaustive search for the "unscripted" and presumably "original" version of writing—in his case, a voiced pattern of a thought before it was subjected to the prejudicial treatment of literate logic. After this is accomplished, what is left is what should be considered worth preserving in print. In Reed's case this includes the existential meaning beyond the worded and commercializable image of the voice of tradition, a task for which he involves similar characters to those traditional to the *son*. For example, the character of the Mother is implicitly central in *Mumbo Jumbo*, a Creolized version of Bantu roots: *ma* (Mother [thought or origin]) *-gio* ("trouble") *-mbo* ("to release"). The same can be said of the challenging principle of signification and the identifying space for being oneself, as the word for "black nonsense" actually derives from "trouble- releasing- mother/ thought," where "trouble" suggests the perils of signification and "mother" can refer to country, language, roots, or any other form of placing identity. Not surprisingly, these same roots in Afro-Cuban culture yield the concept of *Mayombe,* a Bantu-derived ritual language to speak with nature and with ancestors, as well as the Afro-Brazilian "woman-chastising" society of the *Mumban-Jumban*.[30]

According to Houston Baker, Reed's X-factor names the "anonymous (nameless) voice issuing from the black (w)hole" [should we say womb?] of a Being that lies both within and beyond the words of the harmonious sphere of the master code.[31] This X also stands for the basic "cross" principle of Afro-Cuban writing (be it derived from the Yoruba, Calabar, Dogon, or Kongo cultures). This crossroads of Being-through-the-Text is a familiar image in Sarduy's work and the four-part logic of the *son* in general, as will also become evident in our study of Langston Hughes's "blues logic"—a term coined by Houston Baker.

The X-factor is at once the most decisive and most deceiving fourth element in the ordering systems of each of these forms of expression. This fourth element appears to stress an accomplished dispersal, when in fact it should be taken to signify a dynamic core of signification: whatever (or whoever) remains after the fullest possible, and thus most contradictory, performance of THE SCRIPT. In forms of expression that do not abide by the illusion of permanency, writing signifies a fated dispersion (or crossing out) of a Being in at least four directions at once. Criticism in tune with the peculiarities of these forms of expression would attempt the reconstruction of a given role of such a Being dispersed (crossed out) in the Text—through any of the traditional neo-African characters, for instance, the Mother figure.

To add to the poetical connections between blues and *son,* I will turn to three of Langston Hughes's poems from his book *ASK YOUR MAMA.* This work is suggestive of a musical montage in which the traditional folk melody and lyrics of the "Hesitation Blues" constitute a leitmotif, as stated in the introduction.[32] A "secondary" column of words that parallels the "main" text is made of "literate" renderings of this blues and other "complementary" melodies and lyrics (European, Afro-American, and even Afro-Arabic) interwoven with other comments that act as stage directions (tempo, orchestration, solos, choral participation, muting, special modulation, and improvisation of sounds). Unlike the main text which is written in capital letters, the secondary parallel text is written either in "normal" script or in smaller capitals. In addition, the book includes a prose section at the end (reminiscent of Sarduy's "Note"). This is the "LINER NOTES," which address the circumstantial, and therefore critical, implications of each poem "For the Poetically Unhep" (84).

Limiting myself to the main text, the vocabulary of relativity and relativism begins with the opening poem, which is titled (aptly for my present purposes) "CULTURAL EXCHANGE":

IN THE
IN THE QUARTER
IN THE QUARTER OF THE NEGROES
WHERE THE DOORS ARE DOORS OF PAPER
DUST OF DINGY ATOMS
BLOWS A SCRATCHY SOUND.
(3)

The statement represents an atomic breakthrough (either as implosion or as explosion of meaning) awaiting in a script ready for performance. The slow build-up of variants, practically word by word, relates the image of atomic break in terms of a pendular motion—a common practice in modern calculus. The resolution of the pendulum might seem contrary to expectations: a personal awareness of one's relative perspective on natural phenomena. The text provides an approximative script, that is, one that does not attempt to image a logical whole but a literate (w)hole composed of particles of signification—as if they had been shadowed in letters by an impending, concurrent, or past performance. Thus, the scripting of the blues (or of the *son*) is a literate rite of passage, which in Hughes's own words leads beyond "DOORS OF PAPER" swinging open to a "DUST OF DINGY ATOMS," blown (or barely "scripted") by "A SCRATCHY SOUND."

The atomic swing toward the "unscripted" is made much more evident in other poems, such as in "ODE TO DINAH":

> IN THE QUARTER OF THE NEGROES
> WHERE THE PENDULUM IS SWINGING
> TO THE SHADOW OF THE BLUES
> EVEN WHEN YOU'RE WINNING
> THERE IS NO WAY NOT TO LOSE.
> (31)

For Hughes, words elude the uncertainty of musical "SHADOWS" swinging in the "QUARTER OF THE NEGROES." For the marginal, even "THE SCRIPT" of relativity remains either an echo chamber of someone else's values or a ghetto of repressed voices. Both images imply rhythmic dismemberment of meaning in the QUARTER OF THE NE-GROES. Thus the negro quarter becomes both a nominal refuge and a ghetto of signification, as well as a verbal sign and a space of social dismemberment. The potentially implosive or explosive situation is further compounded by the claustrophobic use of the double negative "NO WAY NOT TO LOSE." After critical unscrambling, this phrase becomes grammatically "proper" as a "way to lose"—the endorsement of this agonic option in signification matches the essence of poetic "unconcealment" shared by Heidegger and Saquito.

All terms of Hughes's main text are recorded in capital letters, presumably in order that rhetorical differences imposed by a dominant literate logic dissolve in the sameness of the letters that name them in print. Difference will thus be far more dependent on qualities of sound associated with music, as if the text were made of homonymal words (or values) requiring verbalization or musicalization in order for the individual to choose a meaning. The reading is disconcerting because there seem to be no privileged perspectives, formal or contextual markers indicating who, what, when, where is naming and/or being named. The words themselves also speak of this forced egalitarian perspective that is only capable of knowing by admitting language's own predisposition to be based on contradictions and musical projections.

Although neither I nor Hughes himself would advocate that *ASK YOUR MAMA* is a collection of traditional blues, one can still argue that this book is based on a blues logic of performance built against the grain of literate prejudice. A blues provides the performance leitmotif for a scripted collage of Afro-American values. The poems also include thematic remarks that allude to literate prejudice, which are reminiscent of parallel Cuban themes. These include revolutionary images of surrogate nurturing ("BLACK CHILDREN HAVE WHITE MAMIES" [8]) and a Monte, ritual Wild or Down Home, built for and against whites ("THE JUNGLE OF WHITE DANGER" [27]). The text also challenges literate logic, stretching meaning to the crossroads of signification, such as in the passage:

TO THE FARTHEREST CORNERS SOMETIME
OF THE NOW KNOWN WORLD
UNDECIPHERED AND UNLETTERED
UNCODIFIED UNPARSED
IN TONGUES UNANALYZED UNECHOED
UNTAKEN DOWN ON TAPE—
(55)

Blues-inspired performance logic defies even the recording technique that gives some twentieth-century listeners the sense that they are experiencing music as it is, beyond literate translation or any other mediating interference—a music that is Being-through-the-Text in spite of rhetorical restriction. In fact, the progress of recording methods seems to detract from the actual experience as much as literate language does. Musical experiences of that sort are subjected to performances that can never be duplicated; they thrive on their circumstantial uniqueness. Hughes completes the quoted stanza with a sour note on even the most "genuine" commercial efforts to capture for posterity Afro-American voices on tape:

NOT EVEN FOLKWAYS CAPTURED
BY MOE ASCH OR ALAN LOMAX
NOT YET ON SAFARI.
(55)

These three lines introduce what is perhaps the most eloquent obstacle to the literary assimilation of Afro-American musically expressed difference. In Hughes's poem "HORN OF PLENTY," a list of performers, impresarios, and theatrical acts are woven into a grammatical fabric that includes dollar and cent signs as punctuation marks. These signs point toward a tacit danger, already suggested in Matamoros's "Son de la loma": the commercialization of the black voices' Being-through-the-Text. The very same performance that adds a modern and black notion of logic to twentieth-century Western discourse could also condemn marginals to becoming paid illiterate performers of literate logic. In other words, a form of commodification almost unavoidably accompanies the mainstreaming of marginals' expression: the theatrical performance of difference before a paying audience that is (af)fluent in the language of the master code. Viewed in this light, the "QUARTER" of the recurring phrase "IN THE QUARTER OF THE NEGROES" signals a figment and a fragment of both an ontological and a monetary space and value.

IV

> Hay una voz distinta de la que siempre oímos
> un golpe que no suena, vibra raramente
> dentro de nosotros mismos.
>
> (There is a voice different from the one we usually hear
> a silent beat, that quivers unusually
> within our own selves.)
> —Nicolás Guillén, "La voz desconocida"

For the study of the *son* and the blues, I have proposed a four-part system of signification encompassing rhythms as well as meanings, logical steps as well as legendary characters. I have even suggested the link in their paralogical signification, illustrated by Hughes's "SCRATCHY VOICE" and the Cuban *fragayar*—sketched in Guillén's epigraph[33] as an unusual inner quivering. I have attempted to illustrate how this systematic approach, as well as the pendular notions of signification, willfully deviate from more traditional Western forms of recording—at once coinciding with Western notions of modernity and with African traditions. As we have seen, the recording and unscrambling, layering and unlayering, of neo-African signification in Western writing does not only respond to rhythmically expressed meaning and a second-rate view of relativity likely confused with ambivalence and nonsense. The blues and the *son* fit into a common tradition of *sò*, interpreted as the "inner word," "implicit meaning," "unknown voice," "sound," or "soul" of the Self through a text that is actually a script for performance. The *sò* eventually releases its X-factor of signification in the performance logic and critical vocabulary of transatlantic African culture(s). Perhaps no cultures other than those of the Americas express themselves so consistently through languages that are not their own and define Selfhood according to differences that lie so strategically hidden within the performance of alienating languages.

Doris Sommer

Plagiarized Authenticity:
Sarmiento's Cooper and Others

Poor Cora! Why must James Fenimore Cooper kill her off in *The Last of the Mohicans* (1826)? After lingering so long on her heroism, generosity, resourcefulness, and sheer ethical strength (not to speak of the physical attractions that fix Cooper on Cora) her death seems entirely undeserved. And poor us. Why make Cora so admirable only to deny us the continuing fantasy of possessing, or of being, her? This is especially distressing in a romance, or sentimental novel, which should typically unite hero and heroine after making them overcome apparently insurmountable odds.

One of the problems is that she is not the heroine at all. Nor, much less, is the Mohican Uncas her hero. Cora is a woman marked by a racially crossed past that would have compromised the clear order Cooper wanted for America. And this is precisely why, tragically, he has to kill her off: to stop us short in our sentimental sidetracks, and to leave us only the legitimate lovers who must command our lasting sympathy. They are childlike Alice, Cora's half sister, and her dashing English suitor, Major Heyward.

I should confess right away that my responses to Cooper, romantic heartbreak alternating with practical resignation, are marked by my own past as a reader of Cooper's Latin American heirs. They reread and rewrote him, either to defend Cora's death as a necessary sacrifice or to redeem her as America's more colorful and more convincing heroine. Given the inevitable years and books that have intervened between Cooper and me, I cannot help but read him through these writers, just as Jorge Luis Borges read *Don Quixote* through Pierre Menard's rewriting. Like Menard in Borges's story, the Latin Americans produced contemporary texts with each rereading of Cooper. Borges tells us that

"Cervantes' text and Menard's are verbally identical, but the second is almost infinitely richer. (More ambiguous, his detractors will say, but ambiguity is richness.)"[1] When Cervantes wrote, for example, that history is the mother of truth, he was merely a "lay genius" offering rhetorical praise for history. But when Menard writes it, Borges finds that "the idea is astounding. Menard, a contemporary of William James, does not define history as an inquiry into reality but as its origin. Historical truth, for him, is not what has happened; it is what we judge to have happened." Borges comes to understand that this brilliant updating of the text should not be surprising, because Menard had taught him that,

> "Thinking, analyzing, inventing . . . are not anomalous acts; they are the normal respiration of the intelligence." . . . Menard (perhaps without wanting to) has enriched, by means of a new technique, the halting and rudimentary art of reading: . . . that of the deliberate anachronism and the erroneous attribution. This technique, whose applications are infinite, prompts us to go through the *Odyssey* as if it were posterior to the *Aeneid*. . . . This technique fills the most placid works with adventure.[2]

Why not, then, read Cooper through the Latin American writers who read him? Each reading is original, because none really is, since the very pretense of originality is mocked by the endless success(ion) of rereadings. Originality is precisely what is unstable, that which decomposes and recomposes itself with every reading. Menard's lesson is that even if we *could* succeed in bracketing all the texts that have come between Cooper and us we would be fetishizing his novel by assuming that "thinking, analyzing, inventing" are discrete activities. And worse, perhaps, we would miss a series of "adventurous" Latin American revisions.[3]

Cooper himself might well have objected to these exploits when it came to exploiting *The Last of the Mohicans*. All such liberties would surely confound his foundational project, a book that became America's "gymnasium of the heart" according to a century and a half of autobiographical testimony by "politicians, businessmen, and soldiers—but also those who became her historians, preachers, writers."[4] To be fair, few nation-builders would have welcomed other writers to tinker with their constructions. Nor could they have appreciated the controlling charm of Walt Whitman's injunction to "stray from me," a liberating gesture that of course insures a paradoxical obedience by granting the right to disobey: "yet who can stray from me?"[5] And Cooper seems particularly defensive about his founding text for America: tampering was tantamount to meddling with Providence, because Cooper's pretext for writing was (to defend) God's own creation, the pristine and natural lines of America. It denounces no traces of writing, but reveals a perfect creation that a spiritual elite may inherit. More true certainly than "cowardly" written histories, whose absent authors avoid criticism (35),[6] and truer even than the Bible, in which God's intentions are colored by fallible human language (107), America's Wilderness is His transparent writing. When David Gamut misses Hawk-eye's reference to the only book worth reading, the scout explains,

> "'Tis open before your eyes, . . . and he who owns it is not a niggard of its use. I have heard it said that there are men who read in books to convince themselves there is a God. I know not but man may so deform his works in the settlements, as to leave that which is so clear in the wilderness a matter of doubt among traders and priests. If any such there be, and he will follow me from sun to sun, through the windings of the forest, he shall see enough to teach him that he is a fool, and that the greatest of his folly lies in striving to rise to the level of One he can never equal, be it in goodness, or be it in power" (138).

Yet, the very novel he gives us to read shows that Cooper is his own Menard, taking timeless nature as a pretense for adventurous historical embellishments. If God has already written, who is man to overwrite the creation until nature spells civilization? This contradiction certainly seems to nag Cooper as he reduces the divine work to writerly raw material. Only the author's forbearance, and the Puritans' mission to make God's signs visible, can hope to resolve it. Cooper seems alive to the problem and makes visible efforts at writing an extension of Nature, thus to provide his heroes with a legitimating prehistory. But extending, interpreting, writing, inevitably produce supplements. And in Cooper they convert an alleged static plenitude into the animated project of endless rewritings.

The *ways* in which Latin Americans rewrote Cooper assume a reason *why* they gave him so much attention. Why did they? Domingo Faustino Sarmiento (1811–1888) gives more than a clue. Probably the foremost author of the Argentine nation as journalist, ideologue, general, and president, Sarmiento provided an argument for Cooper's usefulness to other national authors which practically set off a Coopermania among them. His reasons were evidently powerful enough to make Sarmiento refer in great detail to Cooper's novels at the beginning of *Facundo: Civilización y barbarie* (1845), translated as *Life in the Argentine Republic in the Days of the Tyrants*.[7] Something about Cooper's writing warrants the Argentine's review of several scenes from *The Last of the Mohicans* and from *The Prairie* (1827) in order to launch his own book, a book that seems to have little to do with fiction and less to do with North America. Or was that something, perhaps, Cooper's emblematic value among European readers as *the* American writer of his day? These admirably civilized readers admired Cooper—and this is Sarmiento's argument—because he had developed a formula for writing about America that took advantage of her originality, and that should therefore be taken as a model of New World writing. It amounted to removing "la escena de sus descripciones fuera del círculo ocupado por los plantadores, al límite entre la vida bárbara y la civilizada, al teatro de la guerra en que las razas indígenas y la raza sajona están combatiendo por la posesión del terreno" ("the scene of the events he described from the settled portion of the country to the borderland between civilized life and that of the savage, the theater of war for the possession of the soil waged against each other, by the native tribes and the Saxon race").[8]

The Double Cross: Racial and Gender Crossings Crossed Out

This is one hint that Sarmiento understood Cooper's sign for the natural, legitimate hero and heroine as, rather, a lack of sign, a pristine blankness in the original sense of whiteness, that leaves fair Alice and Heyward unblemished.[9] Unlike Cora, whose dark hair and dignified manner denote a complicated history, and Uncas, whose race is marked by his savage coloring, no mark or trace of a compromising past, no "cross" of blood, burdens Alice or Heyward. They not only survive more colorful Cora and Uncas, but also, presumably, prosper and populate the innocent and benign America. Inheriting her by virtue of a mutual love that bears no crosses of the past, they set out together, he to inscribe himself on, and she to be inscribed along with, an equally untraced Wilderness.

The heroine of the piece is, then, also America, both mother and consort to the founding white fathers. By the same token, seen from its flip side, women can offer the legitimate ground for society only if they seem unmarked and nonhistorical, as America appeared to the settlers who called her a Wilderness. Rhetorical figures like the "virgin forest" and her "bosom" are so standard here that one may miss the vanishing act of a language that vaporizes woman by substitution. Cooper's romance gives a domestic cast to what has been called America's pastoral dream, and helps to relieve some ambiguity or guilt over the white man's conquest of a Virgin Land.[10] What could be more legitimate than courting and winning a virgin? If man's penetration threatened to destroy the Wilderness, certainly this was not true once conquest was figured as mutual love. Or was it? The domestic conquest of women was not entirely benign, as we see from Cora's case. How could it be when, for apparently ethical and historical reasons, women should be inert terrain for human activity?[11] Those who can serve do not act. And those who cannot serve are eliminated.

Reducing the female to a blank page, the better to bear man's inscription, means that Cora will not do. Her flaw is not only a racial slippage, but also a certain gender indeterminacy evident in her manly dignity (119). Similarly, Uncas is victim to this founding romance not only because he threatens to complicate Cora's racial crossings, but also because his masculinity has room for the grace and sensitivity associated with women. Both characters cross over the rigid racial and sexual divides, although readers have more often noted Cooper's defense of racial purity than his simultaneous policing of gender boundaries. Misgivings about miscegenation spill over into misogyny. I do not mean to ignore the pained ambiguity that one senses each time this exterminating angel waxes critical of pure whites, or each time Cooper prefers women with histories. I merely want to underline the pain, the cathartic sacrifice of social impurities, that became necessary if the nation was to be established in the clearest possible terms.

From reading Michel Foucault, one might imagine that Cooper's defense of racial and gender purity is consistent with an eighteenth-century "map" or "grid" of knowledge. Foucault understands the classical *episteme* to posit a universal plenitude, every part of which fits neatly into a table of categories; any spillovers from one category to the other were simply errors, or symptoms of the temporary limits of human knowledge. Science, in one form or another, was taxonomic. Yet Cooper either shows that this view of the eighteenth century is unnecessarily static, or that he is caught between a classical affirmation of knowledge and the daring nineteenth-century pursuit of new categories. Taxonomies, Foucault continues, were giving way to histories, and attention shifted from static parts to unstable organisms, changeable combinations that disturbed and finally dismantled the meticulous grids of classical knowledge.[12] Charles Brockden Brown was already dabbling with crossovers in *Arthur Mervyn* (1799), where the hero's marriage to a Portuguese-Jewish widow makes social order seem possible through inclusion rather than elimination.[13] But he worried along with Cooper about the appropriateness of certain mixes for America. Various Europeans might combine, as they do in Cooper's *The Pioneers* (1823), but cautiously.

In the more defensive *Mohicans* written three years later, both Sarmiento and his straying Latin American readers would find an endorsement of their alternative assumptions about order and progress. On the one (Sarmentine) hand, each of the characters in the novel can be located on a stable graph of utility in: language (French being inferior to English, for instance); musicality and religiosity (David Gamut's excess in contrast to Iroquois paucity); domestic practices (the cooking Mohicans and the raw-eating Iroquois); and gender (Alice's ideally infantile femininity, Heyward's masculinity, and the confused categories of Cora and Uncas). These hierarchies function more to establish a grid of values than to motivate the novel. Motivation comes precisely from a commitment to keep the categories pure against the disturbances in gender and, more conspicuously perhaps, against racial amalgamations. It is bad enough to be an Indian or even a Frenchman, but much worse to be a mixture that upsets the neat rungs of the racial ladder. That is why Hawk-eye keeps insisting, rather defensively, that he is a man without a cross (of blood); but Chingachgook, too, is bound to call himself "an unmixed man" (37).[14] As for Cora, her tragedy is announced by the fact that she is the product of a leaky grid of blood. Her blood was so rich that it "seemed ready to burst its bounds" (21). It stains her, makes her literally uncategorizable—that is, an epistemological error.[15] Heyward agrees that this is "unfortunate" because even though there is no blame in Cora, there is a blemish that "obscures" her worth (308). By contrast, Alice is pure, named for truth itself and for the mother who sacrificed her youth to remain true to Munro.

But on the other (romantic novelists') hand, Cooper's novel seems ready to explode the Classical prison house of knowledge by way of its most vital and most admirable characters. Through them, America and the nineteenth century practically promise to be the place and time for new possibilities and unplotted histories. If America is different from Europe, as Cooper's and Sarmiento's nationalism must insist that she is, surely her children must subject Old World categories to a new re-flexivity and to new combinations. How could it be otherwise, if instead of the historicized Nature of Europe, America was a Wilderness, an unknown and surprising land? Therefore, along with their map of civilization, Cooper and Sarmiento give us guides to the unknown, a scout named Hawk-eye and an entire class of *mestizo* Argentine pathfinders. And alongside this quintessentially "American" character whose rustic nobility dares to straddle social categories, we get a combination of "masculine" dignity and "feminine" sensuality in Cora.

We do not get them for long, however, as Sarmiento is quick to recognize. Cooper introduces these anomalous figures as if to pledge that America can be original by providing the space for differences, variations, and crossings. But then he recoils from them, almost as if they were monsters, misfits. If Hawk-eye seems redeemable inside the grid-work of a classical reading because, unlike the gauchos, he is a man without a cross, he is finally as doomed as they are by Cooper's obsessive social neatness. Hawk-eye disturbs the ideal hierarchies that Sarmiento and his Cooper have in mind, because neither birth nor language can measure his worth. And Cooper leaves the scout behind as surely as his characters leave their crossover identities after the carnival-like masquerade of the final rescue scenes. Chingachgook can no more remain a beaver than Heyward can be a buffoon or Alice an Indian. And Cora, already exposed as impersonating a white maiden, can hardly remain the beloved of a Mohican. At her funeral Munro asks Hawk-eye to comfort the mourners with the promise that "the time shall not be distant when we may assemble around [God's] throne without distinction of sex, or rank, or color." The more "natural" man objects: "To tell them this . . . would be to tell them that the snows come not in the winter" (411). To be beautiful, vital, virtuous, and resourceful was not enough for Cora; rather, it was too much for any woman.

Some readers weep along with the Indian maids. Sarmiento may have wept too, but with the grateful cathartic tears that felt the profound injustice, but also the "necessity," of what had already become a policy of Indian removal or genocide in both the U.S. and in Argentina. For Sarmiento, Cooper's dedication to progress made the sacrifice inevitable. Surely Cooper could not have been serious about imagining that America was already the rational and uncorrupted given order of things. Instead, she was clearly available for men to impose clarity and rationality. Apparently loyal to the eighteenth-century *episteme,* Cooper seemed to defend the purity of her Wilderness, just as he insisted on the transparent simplicity of his virginal heroine. But what he really wants, in Sarmiento's reading, is to defend the nature of society, for inchoate Nature to embrace Civilization. This reader is untroubled by the possible paradox of loving the Wilderness to death,[16] or by the related paradox of loving virgins like Alice. Love a virgin and she stops being one; inhabit the pristine Wilderness of America and you have civilized it. The violation of the purity that seems to legitimize America may be a problem for some North American readers, but it was precisely what Sarmiento wanted: to engender civilized settlers who would conquer the still overpowering Land.

He had no pretense of preserving the virginity or totality of America; quite the contrary. Empty spaces were the problem itself: "Its own extent is the evil from which the Argentine Republic suffers."[17] The country's demographic and discursive nature was an emptiness that "se le insinúa en las entrañas" ("threatened to invade her entrails"),[18] and that invited man's writing and the supplement they could produce together. That meant, of course, bodies to populate the Pampa and modern systems of production and exchange. But Sarmiento's immediate supplement was, in fact, his native overwriting of "exotic" texts, travelogues, and voyagers' accounts that provided the only Pampa he knew.[19] As for the danger that objections to Nature could be construed as blasphemy, Sarmiento arrogantly quips, "Debiéramos *quejarnos ante la Providencia* y pedirle que rectifique la configuración de la tierra" ("We should lodge a *complaint against Providence* and ask it to correct the land's configuration").[20] (Mann's pious mistranslation reads: "This would be to complain of Providence and call upon it to alter physical outlines.")[21] Sarmiento and his Cooper then proceeded to take Providence in hand; he resents the awe-inspiring Land, so immense and empty that it was uncontrollable.[22] The indistinct horizon on an endless Pampa may inspire the American sublime and may be a source of national pride—as in Sarmiento's reverie about the American subject whose gaze "sinks into that shifting, hazy, undefined horizon, the further it withdraws from him, the more it fascinates and confuses him, and plunges him in contemplation and doubt. . . ."[23] But that same obdurate landscape defeats reason and industriousness.

More specifically, it mocks him in the figure of an overwhelming tease, a taunting and tempting virgin who doesn't quite have the shape of a woman because no one has yet been able to make a woman of her. Unlike Cooper's Wilderness, Argentina's Pampa is chaste only in the most technical sense. Demanding to be admired in her natural wild and shapeless state, the Land lies ready for the man who dares to make her productive. She "flaunts her smooth, infinite, downy[24] brow without frontiers, without any landmarks; it's the very image of the sea on land, . . . the land still waiting for the command to bring forth every herb yielding seed after its kind."[25] The American sublime may well be that conflicted response to the combination of responsibility and inadequacy, the duty to intervene and the helplessness before an enormous hermetic body. In any case, Sarmiento is saying that Argentina needs the manageable, recognizably demarcated body that a modern subject could love, because his real passion was for progress.

That is why the Land's unproductive consorts, Indians and gauchos so indolently at peace in unredeemed Nature, had to be erased from the national project. They were racially unfit, in Sarmiento's protopositivist language, for associative behavior.[26] Learning about European positivism in Latin America was like learning that people spoke in prose. As in Europe, positivism was a habit of thought that had developed from certain disappointments with revolutionary idealism. Very broadly, positivism in Latin America is an often eclectic tradition that combines a reverence for positive or "scientific" (empirical) data along with the assumption that the emerging social sciences should take the physical sciences, mostly biology, as their models. Social ills were duly diagnosed and remedies were prescribed. Herbert Spencer's organicism was especially popular and coordinated with a Comtian schema of the progressive stages of history.[27] Since growth meant modernization and Europeanization, the more extreme ideologues advocated a combined policy of white immigration and Indian or black removal, while others settled for redeeming the "primitive" races through miscegenation and ideological whitening. Cooper's nineteenth-century Latin American readers either defended Sarmiento's categorical position or, as we will see below, developed a more conciliatory and romantic one.

Self-Authorized Disciples

The book that Sarmiento wrote to follow (from) his praise for Cooper's novels seems dutifully to follow the master's lead. In *Facundo*, Sarmiento was in fact writing America through her racial and cultural conflicts, and he produced what is probably the widest read and the most influential of any book Cooper may have inspired. Yet my point here will be that Sarmiento's endorsement of Cooper is quite subtle, even paradoxically self-advancing. By establishing Cooper's America as a model for Argentina, Sarmiento will hardly sacrifice his own particularity or his country's; Sarmiento is far too cunning an author simply to subordinate either himself or the nation he hopes to lead to another's authority. He was in the habit of giving strong readings or, as Sylvia Molloy astutely points out, translating others' work, an operation she shows was related to plagiarism.[28] I will be suggesting that in the case of his Cooper, and in multiple cases from *Recuerdos de provincia* (*Provincial Memoirs*, 1850), Sarmiento's apparently deferential gesture and his respectful naming of masters and models is merely a strategic distancing. It constitutes the second move in a maneuver that works like a boomerang, ultimately circling back with the spoils of borrowed authority. The first step, logically, is to wield the rhetorical boomerang, assume full control, announce the pursuit, and predict the prize.

Everyone who reads Spanish-American literature, history, or politics knows what Sarmiento is pursuing in *Facundo*. He practically tells us what the prize is in the book's subtitle, *Civilization and Barbarism*. This opposition constructs a normative difference between what Argentina should be and what it now is, between productive control and desultory excess, a difference that amounts to a program for accomplishing one by eliminating the other. Sarmiento reviles Argentina's present excess as unproductive waste. He does so repeatedly and passionately every time he mentions a gaucho who butchers a cow just to eat its tongue, or a regional *caudillo* like Facundo Quiroga who sacrifices whole armies to his personal glory and scores of women to his lust.

Yet excess is precisely what characterizes Sarmiento's writing in this exorbitant text, half fiction, half biography, half political history, half manifesto, a generically immoderate book that obviously adds up to much more than one.[29] He is writing inside what he might have called the American idiom, as well as against it, writing *in* conflict as well as *about* it. Sarmiento is founding a peculiarly American political rhetoric by resisting, simultaneously, his anarchic environment and the unnatural constraints of European genres that would distinguish between poetry and politics and that keep missing the specificity of American life.[30] *Facundo* spills over standard generic categories, and even seems to be written out of Sarmiento's writerly control; it reads like a feverish product of an inspiration that never condescended to an editing job. On rereading the very title, we may notice that the equivalence introduced by the colon makes both opposing terms of the subtitle curiously apposite to the name Facundo.[31] The explosive rhetorical pressure keeps threatening to blow up (in both senses of exaggerating and destroying) his initial dichotomy of civilization vs. barbarism, and the ones that follow from it: the future vs. the past; Europeans vs. Indians; settlers vs. nomads; and, generally, deliberation vs. passion. These oppositions tend to cross out/into one another until Sarmiento himself admits how useless it may be to keep them straight. One notorious example is his treatment of the "savage" dictator Rosas, who is credited with having accomplished the national unity that his civilized Unitarian antagonists only dreamed of. Their improvement on Rosas would certainly not be to level his top-down style, but to replace him at the top with a more legitimately elite leadership.[32] Far from wanting to destroy the work of this authentically Argentine "barbarian" (just because some defensively dichotomous definition would make barbarians incapable of real work), Sarmiento wanted to appropriate it, in the same way that he wanted to appropriate whatever was salvageable in Argentina's special character. Her originality, after all, was the justification for Independence and for the patriotism that Sarmiento must attribute to himself in order to win support for his own leadership.

His paean to that originality comes early on, long before his treatment of Rosas, and even before the bulk of the book where he sketches out the figure of the national tyrant in Facundo's minor regional lines. It comes in the first section, after Sarmiento rushes his reader through the vast, empty expanse of the country left barren by nomadic gauchos and Indians, an emptiness that mutely invites him to write. Chapter two is where Sarmiento pauses at his own dichotomy as he stops, with some pride, to consider the "Originalidad y Caracteres Argentinos. El Rastreador. El Baqueano. El Gaucho malo. El Cantor." This early double-take about laudable Argentine peculiarities in Sarmiento's apparently single-minded campaign for civilization is, as I said, itself a peculiarly Sarmentine move. He shows his American self to have non-European tastes, values, structures of feeling. Different from Europeans on the one hand and from native nomads on the other, Americans are also extensions of both; they are culturally doubled and different from themselves, a violent excess. Therefore, a truly American literature would necessarily be unorthodox by European standards; it would attend to "escenas tan peculiares, tan fuera del círculo de ideas en que se ha educado el espíritu europeo, porque los resortes dramáticos se vuelven desconocidos fuera del país donde se tornan los usos sorprendentes y originales los caracteres" ("scenes so peculiar, so characteristic, and so far outside the circle of ideas in which the European mind has been educated, that their dramatic relations would be unrecognized machinery outside the country that developed these surprising customs and original characters").[33]

Those inimitable Argentine characters occupy Sarmiento in this second chapter, where his legitimacy as a specifically Argentine leader must be established. And yet Sarmiento's literary model for describing the indigenous drama and the extravagant actors is, as I have already said, the North American Cooper. How strange that Sarmiento should refer to a foreigner precisely when he is celebrating that which is most homespun and characteristic. It is as if the difference between domestic self and imported other did not matter when it came to marketing his national political identity. One explanation Sarmiento offers is that he senses the stirrings of a local, properly American aesthetic in Cooper's work, a barbarous aesthetic of the sublime (probably taken more from travels in the U.S., like Chateaubriand's, than from Cooper)[34] that was both deferential to and contemptuous of Europe. "The natural peculiarities of any region give rise to customs and practices of a corresponding peculiarity, so that where the same circumstances reappear, we find the same means of controlling them invented by different nations."[35] But to offer this explanation, Sarmiento has had to tailor Cooper to fit Argentina; he purposefully ignores the differences in terrain among Cooper's novels, which by Sarmiento's own deterministic logic (roughly, geography is destiny) should have mattered. Whereas Cooper's Wilderness is a womb-like enclosure in *The Last of the Mohicans*, *The Prairie* shows a blinding expanse. It is this expansive landscape that Sarmiento chooses to universalize for America. "To arouse the poetic sense . . . we need the sight of beauty, of terrible power, of immensity of extent, of something vague and incomprehensible. . . . Hence it follows that the disposition and nature of the Argentine [and North American?] people are poetic. How can such feelings fail to exist, when a black storm-cloud rises, no one knows whence, in the midst of a calm, pleasant afternoon, and spreads over the sky before a word can be uttered?"[36]

It is very possible that Sarmiento's apparently eccentric national identity—seemingly mirrored through Cooper's America—was programmatic for a man who wanted to modernize his country through "Europeanization" or "North Americanization." What interests me here is less the degree to which Sarmiento may be borrowing from Cooper's originality than the way he manages to invert the terms and perhaps even the implied debts. He manages through a double-dealing logic that begins by announcing programmatic oppositions between civilization and barbarism, then proceeds to defer to a model of writing about American oppositions, a model endorsed, significantly, by a European (exoticizing) standard that allegedly glorifies the Land. She had resisted domesticating inscriptions, for Cooper as much as for Sarmiento, because "Mr. Right" and his writing tool had not yet come along. To whose authority would the virtuous, or stubborn, Land yield? Whom would she allow to inscribe his name, to produce a landmark? Certainly not the Indians. They had had their chance and were obviously unequal to the challenge, mostly because they had been cast as nomads in the discourse of America ever since the sixteenth-century settlement of Roanoke and Shakespeare's *The Tempest*. And since civilization meant stable settlements for the Europeans, the Indians were practically synonymous with barbarism. From the European "discovery" through the period of imperialist rivalries and internal conquests, the Americas were named and renamed after the fathers who fought on and over her. Cooper traces one such history of conflict over what is now called Lake George. The Jesuits had given it the "title of lake 'du Saint Sacrement.' The less zealous English thought they conferred a sufficient honor on its unsullied fountains when they bestowed the name of their reigning prince," both having blotted out the "original appellation of 'Horican.'" (12).

If Cooper was indeed convincing himself that America was worthy of love because she was pristine and untouched by history, it must have been to establish her legitimacy as wife. To acknowledge her former consorts might have been to cast doubt on the permanence of her current ones. Cooper, in fact, manages with one hand to write the Land's "erotic" prehistory with the Indians and the French, and to erase it with the other. Like Alice, whose family history leaves no mark of experience, the landscape around Lake George remains a Wilderness because it shows no trace of rivalries and intrigues. These became the history of her suitors, but not hers. "Forts were erected at the different points that commanded the facilities of the route, and were taken and retaken, razed and rebuilt, as victory alighted on the hostile banners" (13). Perhaps her innocence, her wildness, allowed her to resist their efforts to brand her.[37] In any case, the traces of successive inscriptions would have been problematic for Cooper if he hoped to convince us that the Wilderness was pure and virginal. The Father may be willing to share his Virgin child with a worthy husband, so that they might be fruitful and multiply. But her chastity and the transparency of her language cannot survive the marriage.

With far less show of guilt or nostalgia, Sarmiento performs a similar *ninguneo*, the "nobody-ing" of a threatening somebody.[38] Calling the

Indians and the *mestizo* gauchos "American Bedouins" in *Facundo*[39] is enough to eliminate them from history, since "there can be no progress without permanent possession of the soil, or without cities . . ."[40] This would be embarrassing enough for today's readers if nomadism really canceled "conjugal" rights to the Land. After all, the Old Testament promised Land to the patriarchs and the prophets, so dear to the Puritan settlers and so inspiring to Sarmiento.[41] Their nomadic life was the only spiritual safeguard in a world of decadent settlements. But recent work shows that the North American Indians he gleefully saw exterminated were not invariably nomadic. In fact, the Algonkin word for the Land known now by the pristine name of "Virginia" meant "densely populated." Algonkins typically lived in towns, to which the English settlers would flee periodically when their own resources failed them.[42] The obviously winning suitors are the Europeans, the ones who know how to write on smooth surfaces. Sarmiento does not mince words, because he casts himself here as none other than Mr. Right, writing an epic of (pro)creation; and he can attribute no less to his putative model, Cooper.

The third step in Sarmiento's roundabout rhetorical trajectory is, then, to close up the distance between imported models and local manufacture. His Cooper evidently supported the extreme racist position that backed Sarmiento against some critics at home.[43] If he had paused to consider that Cooper's struggle for the Land probably had as much to do with his own rearguard defense of "feudal" rights in New York State (besieged by the antirent legislation of the democratizing "masses") as with Monroe's Indian removal policy formulated in 1824, Sarmiento might have admired him even more.[44] It was as easy for the Argentine as for the New Yorker to conflate the "anarchic" landless classes with "savages." Unfortunately for Cooper, the "masses" were winning some ground, while the more obliging Indians continued to lose it. Jane Tompkins underlines how typical Cooper's guilt-ridden celebration of that loss was in those years. "Between the War of 1812 and the Civil War, Americans wrote seventy-three novels dealing with Indian-white relations. . . . With few exceptions, the white hero and heroine marry at the end, the bad . . . Indians are killed, and the good Indian either dies, or dies out. . . ."[45] These blood-purging novels lament the sacrifice, as Sarmiento apparently laments it in the second chapter of *Facundo,* but not so loudly that readers could miss the barely muffled gasp of relief.

Sarmiento's Cooper is uncannily close to a Marxist Cooper, like the one Lukács remembers through Gorky, one who bids a mournful but necessary farewell to the primitive world that capitalism replaces.[46]

Neither Lukács nor Sarmiento could afford to worry themselves over Cooper's possibly ambivalent position between classical, clearly defined signs and romantic evolutionism.[47] Sarmiento "knew" that Cooper was a modern man dedicated to progress and change. And he also "knew" that progress depended on keeping the signs clear; it depended on distinguishing Indian from white and male from female, so that in the battle for America the best man would win. His Cooper was not only tidying up the sloppy signs that exceeded ideal categories. He was also setting the American record straight by clearing up the space that previous settlers had scribbled on, before the Ideal English writers appeared. So, unlike the average North American reader and the Latin American novelists who would follow, Sarmiento doesn't allow sentimentality to distract him. He assures us that genocide is the necessary condition for progress; and he affirms that this is the deepest and the most significant message of Cooper's novels.

And right after he establishes Cooper as the model for literary and military exploits that Argentina would do well to imitate, Sarmiento makes the fourth and final move in his magisterially circular (or twisted) logic. He boldly questions the master's own originality by noting that Cooper's "descripciones de usos y costumbres . . . paracen *plagiadas* de la pampa" ("descriptions of practices and customs . . . seem plagiarized from the Pampa").[48] Notice that he says "plagiarized," not inspired, or suggested, or even copied. What could Sarmiento possibly have meant with that word? Is he simply telling us that the North American experience is notably similar to that of South America? If that were the case, then why not point out the reverse relationship and say that the South shows similarities with the North? This would maintain the chronological (and ontological) order between Cooper's text and Sarmiento's commentary, between center and periphery. In other words, why not say that the Pampa seems like a copy of the Prairie? After all, it is rather obvious from the very fact of his references to Cooper—not to mention his national catching-up projects—that the U.S. provided the model for Argentina, and not the other way around. Of course his comment could pass for an offhand or ironic way of emphasizing the similarities and thus establishing the possibility that Argentina could develop just like the U.S. did. It might pass for levity, perhaps, if it were not for the nature of the details from Cooper's novels that Sarmiento finds so appropriate(able), and that immediately precede the remark about plagiarism. Those details, which I mentioned as the measure of Sarmiento's admiration for Cooper and which we should consider now, are some significantly predictable scenes for the Argentine reader:

When I came to the passage in Cooper's *The Last of the Mohicans,* where Hawkeye and Uncas lose the trail of the Mingos in a brook, I said to myself: "They will dam up the brook." When the trapper in *The Prairie* waits in irresolute anxiety while the fire is threatening him and his companions, an Argentine would have recommended the same plan which the trapper finally proposes—that of clearing a space for immediate protection, and setting a new fire, so as to be able to retire upon the ground over which it had passed beyond the reach of the approaching flames. . . .

When the fugitives in *The Prairie* arrive at a river, and Cooper describes the mysterious way in which the Pawnee gathers together the buffalo's hide, "He is making a *pelota,*" said I to myself. "It is a pity there is no woman to tow it," for among us it is the women who tow *pelotas* across rivers with lassos held between their teeth. The way in which a buffalo's head is roasted in the desert is the same which we use for cooking a cow's head or a loin of veal. I omit many other facts which prove the truth that analogies in the soil bring with them analogous customs, resources, and expedients. This explains our finding in Cooper's works accounts of practices and customs which seem plagiarized from the pampa. . . .[49]

Sarmiento can tell, before Cooper tells him, how the most characteristically American characters will (or, in the case of the Pawnees, should) behave. This sustained display of foreknowledge has a peculiar effect: it suggests that the real Cooper was (and maybe is) Sarmiento himself, especially if the redundancy of publishing what the Argentine public already knew could have occurred to him. Sarmiento practically boasts of having anticipated many of Cooper's pages before he read them. And one can just imagine how he read, almost preparing textual ambushes and traps for poor Cooper, to see if the revered American author could get out of his own tight spots with the right American solutions.

Perhaps already sensitive to his reputation as an inveterate braggart, Sarmiento slyly evades any renewed imputations of arrogance by removing himself from the comparison with Cooper. Sarmiento was not, he implies, competing with or, much less, improving on Cooper. Cooper's copying was not of Sarmiento at all, but of the Pampa, since the plagiarism which he attributes to Cooper is not of a particular text, or even of the Pampa's foremost interpreter, Sarmiento himself. It is having deliberately imitated the Land, God's creation, the divine Text that Cooper says he respects. And Sarmiento's attribution of a divine inspiration for Cooper's plagiarism is even more crafty than the calculated modesty of avoiding a comparison. It safeguards the model's value as an American artist. If Cooper, plagiarist that he was, were not also valuable as the honorably mimetic portrait-maker of American reality, he would be no good to Sarmiento as a point of departure or as a mentor.

Sarmiento's double-take here is to reduce the stature of his model and to keep him as a model at the same time. It responds to a characteristic double-bind for some national authors in Latin America; that is, a certain reticence to share authority, even with the models who bestow it on their disciples and who, therefore, must be respected as legitimate. In Sarmiento's exemplary case, Cooper is as much an opportunity to improve on the model as to improve himself. If it were not for Cooper's success, and for the success of the country he helped to found, what foundation would Sarmiento have for writing America? On the other hand, if Sarmiento let himself become a simple copy of Cooper, or if the Pampa were an imitation of the Prairie, where could his own authority come from, and where the very sovereignty of his country? The military strategist in Sarmiento surely understood that the best defense is sometimes an offensive move. So, in a tactic designed to free himself and his country from the ignominious charge of being mere copies (which he was more than willing to acknowledge in his arguments for modernization in this same book), Sarmiento fires the first shot at Cooper. Of course, he aims to do very little damage, because without his opponent as counterpart, without the mirror that would reflect back a legitimate American name, Sarmiento could not have hoped to make a name for himself.

What does he hope to accomplish, then, by sowing a seed of doubt about the North American model's originality, suggesting that it might be the copy of his own imitation of Argentina? He hopes, I am suggesting, to harvest an irrefutable originality that is well rooted in a stable landscape of precursors. And Sarmiento's desire for unquestionable authority is so great, that instead of simply cannibalizing Cooper's text as a subtext, as a pre-text of his own work (a consumption that would make conspicuous the model's priority), Sarmiento prefers to toy with it, as if time and linearity were illusory, and as if a reader could be the greatest authority of someone else's text.

This displacement or metaleptic inversion between text and commentary, between master and disciple, will repeat itself in *Recuerdos de provincia,* where at one revealing point Sarmiento makes the paradigmatically circular and self-serving assertion that "A mi progenie me sucedo yo" ("to my progeny I am my own successor").[50] In general, the book's self-reflexive logic, twisted always to reflect well on its author, needs to propose a revalorization of plagiarism. It does this quite explicitly through mention of Deacon Funes, about whom Sarmiento writes, "he has been burdened too long with the charge of plagiarism, which for me turns into something far from a reproach, but rather a sure sign of merit,"[51] the merit of erudition and good taste. This indulgence bordering on enthusiasm for plagiarists frees Sarmiento from any qualms about plagiarizing his own biography from Benjamin Franklin's. "No other book has done me as much good as this one. . . . I felt I was Franklin," he says, immediately to ask himself rhetorically and a bit defensively, "and why not? I was very poor, just like he was, a diligent student like he was." That is, a veritable "Franklincito" before discovering his own person in someone else's book. A little later he adds, "prodding myself on and following his footsteps, I could one day become as accomplished . . . and make a name for myself in American literature and politics."[52] Sarmiento's staged adulation here is probably meant to dramatize his endorsement of Franklin's book for Argentine schoolboys. In general, Sarmiento instructs us in one of the appendices—which lists some of his publications and promises others—that "Biography is the most original kind of book that South America can produce in our times, and the best material we can offer history." It is the genre, according to him, to which *Facundo* and *Recuerdos* belong, both being personal stories about exemplary persons.

But Sarmiento's celebration of Franklin's achievements may also serve to provide a measure for the celebrant's even greater success. He must already have felt the satisfaction of surpassing Franklin, both in terms of literary accomplishments and of the brilliant political career that these very *Recuerdos* helped to assure. While he was writing them, as a kind of narrative curriculum vitae or political self-portrait,[53] he was also circulating a photographic portrait with the caption, "Sarmiento, future president of Argentina."[54] If his cautiously respectful diminution of Franklin seems a daring appropriation, Sarmiento had anticipated it in his lines about Cooper; and he had also gone arguably further in an earlier chapter of the *Recuerdos*. It is the one dedicated to Domingo de Oro as the "model and archetype of the future Argentine."[55] But this future model is past history for the prophetic Sarmiento who declares, "De Oro's life is proof of the way I understood his rare eloquence."[56] How do we disentangle the subject from his representation here? How do we know where priority resides? In the prophecy, or in the proof?

This tactical inversion will already be familiar to us through Pierre Menard's work. If it seems a bit anachronistic to read Sarmiento via

Borges, it is at least a strategy that both teach us. It would be almost perverse to miss reading Sarmiento as Cooper's and Franklin's and de Oro's Menard. If we had attempted respectfully to stabilize some of his sources as Cooper's novels, Franklin's biography, and de Oro's life we would have been mistaking "thinking, analyzing, inventing" as discrete activities. And if we care to be even more anachronistic, we could mention that Jean Baudrillard makes a similar observation about production in the "postmodern" world, an observation which should have little relevance for a nineteenth-century writer who found that his country was already behind the times. Alleging that Western culture used to be or to feel itself more solidly grounded, Baudrillard complains that all we can produce today are simulacra, copies of models that are themselves unauthentic. Even what we call reality is nothing more than a series of fictitious constructions, neither more nor less genuine than their "re-presentations."[57]

Baudrillard begins his meditation with a gesture that has evidently become stylish in French philosophy. He begins with a Borgesian parable, that of the cartographers who are so determined to make a scientifically exact representation of reality that they produce a map as big as the empire. He starts with Borges in order to promptly discard the model, condescendingly charging that Borges's irony depends on a naive notion of the Real, on an empire that precedes the map.[58] Baudrillard thus reads without mentioning Borges's proverbial circularity, the textual whirlwind that blows away any pretense of stable originality and that is so notorious among his French fans. Whether or not this reading does justice to Borges's thought, one must agree that Baudrillard's is a strategic reading (in the same way that Sarmiento strategically misreads Cooper). It would be rather out of character for the theorist of simulation and of the failure of referentiality to refer respectfully to the authority who gave him the base for theorizing. Baudrillard evidently opted for intellectual orphanhood, perhaps in order to dramatize (not to say represent) his own theme: the impossibility of lineage and of the relationship between origin and following. If everything is (and all of us are) unauthentic, it would be absurd to follow in anyone's footsteps.

But it was not absurd for Sarmiento, who preferred another option. I say option, because I imagine in my necessarily Menardian reading that he had several to choose from. One was to resign himself to renouncing originality, with the same ironic and haughty modesty that Baudrillard and Borges no doubt affected. Another was to assume absolute, practically divine originality, as Sarmiento does in *Mi defensa*

(1843) and, by an apparent rhetorical slip as he does once in *Recuerdos*. "When I had finished this work (a book on pedagogy), I could say in my rejoicing that I had produced something worthy: *et vidi quod esset bonum*. Then I applauded myself."[59] A third option was what I am calling the boomerang effect: to attribute originality and the authority it implies to someone else, so that they may be snatched out of the model's hands in a lightning game of "now you see it, now you don't." If the strategy Sarmiento used with Cooper is characteristic, it follows from the subsequent uses he made of Funes, Franklin, de Oro, and others that he clearly preferred this last choice. He proposes models, cuts them down to manageable superable size, and glories in their presumed (or explicit) approval, even when they have doubtful credentials. The chapter on de Oro, for example, criticizes the model's misdirected shrewdness which results in clearing the political obstacles to Rosas's victory. Yet the chapter ends by quoting in its entirety a letter of recommendation that de Oro had sent the author.

Sarmiento distances himself from his models only enough to outdistance them, so as not to dismiss either them or their offer of legitimacy. The ambiguity is really ingenious here for someone who may have "known" history to be a fiction, a simulacrum. If he did, it was always as an opportune fiction for the writer who dared to invent it. Sarmiento succeeds in attributing to himself the authority and the privilege of a foundational thinker. At the same time his claim to legitimacy is based on implied approval by an established origin, an origin established by the very fact that he considers it a model. *Facundo,* after all, had something to do with Cooper's exemplary status among Latin Americans who admired, imitated, and adopted him as the first among (North) American narrators.

Pierre Menard's Coopers

Menardian readers that they were, though, Latin American novelists followed neither the foreign model nor the Argentine purveyor too closely, unless of course, following Sarmiento means learning a Whitmanian step that strays enough to find comparably opportune uses for Cooper. These are the national authors, in the same multivalent sense that describes Sarmiento, who occupy me in *Foundational Fictions,* so that short mentions may suffice here as I consider the (perhaps imagined) repercussions of Sarmiento's praise for Cooper.[60] As novelists they were generally bound to challenge Sarmiento's assumptions about the didactic and socially constructive potential of exemplary single lives.[61] Writing novels was already a statement about the collective or coupling nature of nation-building. If one of the main goals of Argentina's national program was to populate the deserted Pampa, if for the modernizing bourgeois culture that South America's elites were trying to adopt sexual desire had indeed become what Foucault characterized as "the explanation for everything," heroic biographies would hardly be (re)productive enough.[62] Typically, the novelists presumed to "correct" Cooper, or at least to read him correctly. Most knew, for instance, that the author of *The Last of the Mohicans* really preferred (or should have preferred) Cora as America's archetypal mother. Rather than keep America racially pure, a "Latin Americanized" and romantic Cooper was warning his compatriots that their country's hope for peace and progress should not be sacrificed to an ideal of purity as anachronistic and self-destructive as military heroism. National consolidation needed the reconciliation of differences, not their exclusion. The hegemonic project of the dominant class had to win the support of other interests for a (usually) liberal national project that would benefit them all, just as the hero of romance won the heroine through love and practical concern for her well-being.[63] A white elite, often in the large port cities, had to convince everyone— from landholders and miners to the indigenous, black, and mulatto masses—that liberal leadership would bridge traditionally antagonistic races and regions in a new prosperity.

In political practice, Argentines were evidently far less jealous husbands than was Cooper. In *Foundational Fictions* I show that jurisprudent Juan Bautista Alberdi recognized his own national shortcomings and made a virtue of the necessity to share his patrimony with foreigners— to import Anglo-Saxon studs in order to develop a superior and manageable breed, one might say in the cattle-breeding logic that prevailed. Sexual love would do the rest, once Argentina's army of desirable women conquered the white would-be conquerors. But Cooper, convinced of his own superiority, had seen no advantage to amalgamation. After all, he *is* the Anglo-Saxon Prince Charming whom the swarthier Argentines want.

Is it possible that the erotic or fairy tale rhetoric that I am attributing to the political theorist Alberdi comes from contemporary Latin American novels rather than from his own juridical discourse? Is it also possible that I have been reading Sarmiento's Cooper as an advocate for enlightened inscription, or the civilizing kiss, through this same literary tangle of romance and nation-building? Perhaps Sarmiento was insensible to the love story between the Land and the men who would make her prosper. The drama of seduction may be superfluous to a man accustomed to command. If I am caught in a rhetorical jumble, it owes as much to a tradition of Latin American writing as to my belated reading. Sarmiento became the pre-text for so many other Pierre Menards in Latin America. Nevertheless, to defend this possibly misplaced "romantic" reading of Sarmiento, I should point out that he practically invents the term "*romancista*" for Cooper, which Mann variously translates as "romancer" and "novelist."[64] The difference between these terms is a tradition in Anglo-American criticism, romance referring to broadly allegorical (male) adventures or histories, and novels being sentimental (female) tales of everyday life.[65] But in Spanish this difference makes little sense, since the word "romance" had already slipped away from its traditional literary sense of ballad and meant what it means now: a love story. This is how Sarmiento uses it in a sarcastic remark about Facundo's abuse of his girlfriend, "No es éste un lindo romance?" ("Isn't this a fine romance?").[66] I choose, then, to read Sarmiento's epithet as acknowledging the erotic core in Cooper's work.

The national novelists certainly read it as erotic. Their Cooper allegorized Sarmiento's pseudoscientific rhetoric about civilization and barbarism—white settlers tackling the Pampa—into a story of requited love. Therefore, the ideal national marriages were often projected in romances between whites and Indians (the title characters of José de Alencar's Brazilian *O guaraní* [1857] and *Iracema* [1865] are examples), or *mestizas* inspired no doubt from Chateaubriand's *Atala* (such as Manuel de Jesús Galván's Doña Mencía in *Enriquillo* [Dominican Republic, 1882] and Marisela in *Doña Bárbara* [Venezuela, 1929] by Rómulo Gallegos). The ideal of *mestizaje,* so pejoratively translated into English as miscegenation, was based in the reality of mixed races to which different virtues and failings were ascribed, and which had to be amalgamated in some countries if anything like national unity was to be produced. Unity, in positivist rhetoric, was not so much a political or economic concept as it was biological. José Vasconcelos gave probably the most famous and utopian formulation in *Raza cósmica* (1925), written when the postrevolutionary Indian masses forced themselves into any consideration of Mexican nationalism and progress. But as early as Simón Bolívar's famous discourse at Angostura, Latin Americans have at least rhetorically assumed a racially mixed identity. "It is impossible to correctly determine," said the Liberator, "to which human family we belong. . . . Born all of the same mother, our fathers [are] of different origins and blood."[67]

Only an atypical novel like Jorge Isaacs's *María* (Colombia, 1867), his swan song for the slavocracy, could afford to revive Cooper-like pessimism about *mestizaje*. Like double-crossed Cora, the originally Jewish María was born in the West Indies (Jamaica), and though perfectly innocent and admirable, she too bears a blemish of racial difference. It is a Jewish stain, and serves as a sign for the more troubling differences between blacks and whites. As in *Enriquillo* and in *O guaraní,* the real threat that darkens a plantation society becomes unspeakable to Isaacs. Instead, he seems to be saying that no amalgamation, however innocent and sincere, can be productive in the aristocratic society he yearns for.[68] Although more programmatic, perhaps, Uruguay's *Tabaré* (1888), by Juan Zorrilla de San Martín, is atypical too for its sacrifice of racial difference in the person of the *mestizo* hero. The blue-eyed Indian is as out of place in either white or native society as was Cooper's tragic, culturally *mestiza* Ruth, the captive of *The Wept of Wish-Ton-Wish* (1829). Most Latin American writers by far, however, tended to be programmatic in a more synthetic way. When the lovers in romance are both white, they probably come from mutually hostile areas, as in José Mármol's *Amalia* (1851), where the hero is a Buenos Aires boy and his heroine a childless young widow from the rival center of Tucumán. Far from being put off by his heroine's past, as an unassimilated Cooper might have been, Mármol admitted that Argentina had an unproductive history that national romance would cure. And Alberto Blest Gana's *Martín Rivas* (1862) joins the son of a bankrupted mining entrepreneur in the north of Chile to the daughter of the usurer in Santiago who had acquired the mine. The hero finally convinces Santiago's bankers that getting together would be mutually satisfying, at the same time that Chile's elite sectors were making political and financial deals. Where racial and regional differences keep lovers apart, as in Cuba's abolitionist novels, *Francisco* (1839) by Anselmo Suárez y Romero, *Cecilia Valdés* (1839, 1882) by Cirilo Villaverde, and *Sab* (1841) by Gertrudis Gómez de Avellaneda, the blame for personal and national tragedy falls on archaic and un-American habits of social ordering. The implied or explicit program for change saves these novels from the ruthlessness of Sarmiento's Cooper and from the pessimism of Isaacs's tragedy. This is not to say that racism and economic partiality ceased to exist among the novelists. To see prejudice at work, one has only to observe that Indian and *mestiza* lovers appear in books like *O guaraní* and *Enriquillo* so that blacks can disappear, or that *Amalia*'s Tucumán remains a background producer for the trade decisions made in Buenos Aires. Hegemony, after all, is not an egalitarian project, but one that legitimizes the leadership of one social sector by winning the consent of others. Romance had, therefore, to give a loving cast to national unity, not necessarily to equalize the lovers.

The Latin Americans must have been relieved to see that Cora Munro was redeemed at home after the defensive nervousness about gender- and race-coding relaxes; that is, after the man's work is done and the West is won. She comes back to be celebrated in the late and "decadent" period of dime novels. Cooper himself paved the way by freeing at least one legitimate heroine, Ellen Wade in *The Prairie* (1827), from the noble birth that confers inhuman paralysis on his women,[69] and especially in "self-reliant" Mabel Dunham of *The Pathfinder* (1840). In fact, Cooper's dime-novel writing Menards of the North became fond of celebrating half-breed heroines and even of displacing the traditional genteel heroes with savage women protagonists. The great difference from South America is that the mass industry of Western novels, starting with Beadles's literary industry in 1858, was less an enterprise to establish an American consciousness and national project than to mine that earlier effort in order to supply the growing market for sensationalism. The Amazon cum heroine of the end of the century, according to Henry Nash Smith, is one exemplary innovation that marks the decay of dime Westerns which learned to pander to an American public hungry for ever more gratuitous adventure.[70] But if we read more sympathetically, these un-genteel heroines encode the return of the repressed Cora. Cooper may have been compelled to doom her because she was too able and too full of surprises for the benighted hero's taste. Her self-motivation complicated his rights to motivate her, and by extension to manipulate the Land. But for his Menards to the South, Cooper may also have preferred her. In that case, his novel is a tragedy, along the lines of Isaacs's *María* and Cuba's heartrending antislavery novels. To prove the tradition's profound preference for Cora they could point to her domestic line of descendants: the straight-shooting, hard-drinking Calamity Janes who get their men one way or another.

I am suggesting, perhaps provocatively, that gender-crossing is as endemic to foundational romances in Latin America as are racial and regional crossings. Even in a late, defensive, "populist" romance such as *Doña Bárbara,* written when men were men and women women, again the apparently ideal hero has a paradoxical lesson to learn from women. He has to fall helplessly in love with the right one in order to maintain his masterly control.

These romancers understood why Cooper had to make impressionable Heyward, rather than the ideally male Hawk-eye, a founding father.

They also felt the tragedy of sacrificing as graceful and sensitive a man as Uncas, whom Alencar revives to be the hero of *O guaraní*. Some readers, including Sarmiento, may have thought that Cooper's ideal America was based on precise gender and racial categories, but Latin American romancers recognized the unproductive distance that ideal opposites have to maintain in order to stay pure. If a lover at all, Hawk-eye is in love with the equally pure Wilderness, which is as sublimely simple as Alice, or with impassive Chingachgook, D. H. Lawrence's choice. In fact, their mutual affection is most convincing if we consider the two men bound together through their equal respect, rather than their erotic love, for Nature. Their very chaste version of homosocial desire[71] takes the form of a *ménage à trois* where nobody really violates anybody else. Nobody makes children either. This categorical purity is one reason why Natty must shun Judith Hutter in *The Deerslayer* (1841). What other readers have called his chastity is also his pride in being a "man without a cross," as free of feminized, domestic inclinations as he is of Indian blood. North American readers may be concerned with what appears to be the unresolvable dual allegiance to civilization and to barbarism that plays itself out through Hawk-eye's contradictions. He of course betrays Chingachgook by acting as scout for the other men, those who "civilize" the wilderness, marry virgins, and turn them into mothers. But the Cooper whom Latin American romancers read calmly kissed Hawk-eye's ideal and obsolete masculinity good-bye, just as they had turned their backs, during this peaceful moment, on heroic Bolívar and San Martín.

Their impressive chain of reading and writing Cooper surely began from a particular text. But after Sarmiento's playful remark about plagiarism, after noting that it is he who makes Cooper a landmark in South American literature, we should wonder whose text is originary. Is it Cooper's, or is it Sarmiento's appropriation? Is it the father who makes the son, or is it because of the son that the father recognizes himself as such? With this simile, I want to suggest the Oedipal character of this inversion between model and commentator, aligning it therefore with a strategy that Carlos Altamirano and Beatriz Sarlo have identified so convincingly in *Recuerdos de provincia*. I am referring to Sarmiento's repeated denial of his paternal lineage, and of his father's personal importance. The son seems to have engendered himself upon the body and the genealogy of his mother, whose identity is sometimes and purposefully confused with that of the motherland. The superfluous father is infantilized, or feminized (which amounts to the same thing), so that Sarmiento can replace him in the familial text.[72]

Yet despite a possible parallel between his father and Cooper, or any other model in *Recuerdos,* Sarmiento's rivalry with adoptive mentors allowed for something different from denial, something that must have been an inspiration for other national authors. It allowed him to subordinate the master, gently and without eliminating him, so as not to lose the legitimacy of the master's approval that Sarmiento attributes to himself. This difference (which Tulio Halperin Donghi also suggested when he contrasted the self-creation of *Mi defensa* with the respect for lineage in *Recuerdos*)[73] suggests a pattern for the strategy that I have been trailing here. It may be parallel to parricide, but it is cunningly restrained. I mean Sarmiento's practice of making plagiarism count for the most efficient originality by inverting the priority between model and revision.

Happily for authorized imitators like Sarmiento, and for their Menardian readers, imitation often surpasses the model,[74] even as it constitutes the model as such. It is, to sum up, doubly foundational: first by establishing the origin, and second by improving on it. And if this displacement tends to throw all pretension of originality in doubt, the liberating side of doubt for latecomers to writing and to history is that it leaves unresolved the question of priority between master and pupil. Sarmiento turns out to be a proto-Borgesian priest who unites the two with a Möbius ring for which inside and outside, origin and trajectory, are only illusions of perspective. After this marriage, it would be rather mean-spirited to remind Cooper of his distance from Argentina, as mean-spirited as reminding Sarmiento of his debts as a disciple.

Enrico Mario Santí

The Accidental Tourist:
Walt Whitman in Latin America

For Roberto Esquenazi-Mayo

The American poets are to enclose old and new, for America is the race of races. Of them a bard is to be commensurate with a people. To him the other continents arrive as contributions.
—Walt Whitman, 1855 Preface to *Leaves of Grass*

But because we live not in a continent but in islands, so terribly isolated, we know so little of each other that we don't even hate one another. . . .   —Octavio Paz, "¿América es un continente?"

Does this Aleph exist in the heart of a stone? Did I see it there in the cellar when I saw all things, and have I now forgotten it? Our minds are porous and forgetfulness seeps in . . .
—Jorge Luis Borges, "The Aleph"

I

In 1943, amidst a year ridden by crisis—personal, political, and poetic—Octavio Paz wrote a proposal to the John Simon Guggenheim Memorial Foundation for one of its year-long research fellowships. Paz's proposal called for a study of "America and its Poetic Expression," by which he meant poetry in both North and South, Anglo and Latin America, and taking at face value the Foundation's stated criteria for "strengthening interamerican cultural relations and fostering greater continental intelligence." In that study, which set out to answer one single question: "Do the Americas have a common soul?," Paz sought to isolate, in the history of Western hemispheric poetry, "those traits that single it out, give it an original native profile, accent, and direction," though not so much, he warned, in order to show "the forms in which that poetry has crystallized" as "to find in its language the history of a sensibility." While surveying the span of continental poetry from Sor Juana and Emily Dickinson to Alfonso Reyes and Robert Frost, the proposal did single out three names—Poe, Darío, and Whitman—as varied cases divided into two distinct tendencies: one (Poe's and Darío's) universal or cosmopolitan, the other (Whitman's) a native strain expressing a "burgeoning American soul." Indeed, Whitman's name punctuated Paz's entire proposal, and although Paz never did complete (mercifully, perhaps) that study and instead spent his fellowship year at Berkeley working on his own verse, his proposal does stand as a significant document in the history of what one could call, for lack of a better name, the Whitman question in Spanish America.[1]

That Whitman, rather than Poe or Darío, was the focus of Paz's proposal was confirmed several years later, in the first edition of *The Bow and the Lyre* (1956), Paz's treatise on "the poem, poetic revelation, poetry, and history." He included a special appendix entitled "Whitman, American Poet" that, without alluding to his earlier project, appears to distill it. In it Paz argued (against Borges, whose name, except by inference, went unmentioned) that Whitman's "mask—the poet of democracy—is something more than a mask: it is his true face," while also defining Whitman's Americanism in terms of its utopian character. "America dreams itself in Whitman because America itself was dream, pure creation." And concluded: "Before and after Whitman we have had other poetic dreams. All of them—be the dreamer named Poe or Darío, Melville or Dickinson—are really attempts to escape from the American nightmare."[2]

Paz's gradual fraying away of this Americanist question, so to speak, in a sense anticipates the course of his better-known quest after Mexican identity—one of the central themes of his early thought and a subject which his essays of the 1930s and 1940s take up only to abandon it later in *The Labyrinth of Solitude* (1950). In both cases, "the history of an [American] sensibility" is gradually subsumed under conceptual or imaginary constructs (Solitude, Utopia) well beyond the mirages of nationalism or geography. But Paz's two-stepped approach reveals something more than just the gradual embodiment of Whitman as the focus of that particular question. It dramatizes the tensions and complications attendant to Whitman's reception in Latin America. The narrative of that reception, whose first chapter Fernando Alegría wrote over thirty years ago in his *Walt Whitman en Hispanoamérica* (1954), ought certainly to include not just the bare facts of Whitman's fortunes, but also those repressed elements, internal polemics, and open misunderstandings that make up its significance—a story that Doris Sommer, in a recent essay on Whitman, has rightly called "The Contest for a Legitimate American Poetry."[3] This essay departs from Sommer's by insisting on the significance of the bibliographical details of such a story. With it, however, I share a concern for the role played by the Imaginary (in its loose Lacanian sense of the constitutive role of fantasy) and modify it further as a narrative of Error—a kind of "experiment in international living" redolent with late arrivals and near misses.

By a perhaps uncanny coincidence, Paz chose to spend his fellowship year at the University of California at Berkeley, precisely where Eugene Bolton, then Professor of History in its faculty, had for some time advocated his controversial views about a "Greater America" (also known as the "Bolton Theory") toward the concept of a hemispheric rather than a culturally determined historiography. ("Do the Americas Have a Common History?"—the English title of Edmundo O'Gorman's trenchant critique of the Bolton Theory—is of course the source of the title of our own volume.)[4] To be sure, Paz does not mention Bolton in the Guggenheim proposal (or anywhere else, for that matter), even though the conceptual basis of his argument at times sounds uncannily like an application of the Bolton Theory to literary history. That resemblance itself is uncanny enough, in fact, since barely two years before writing his Guggenheim proposal, in 1941, Paz had gone so far as to question, in a revealing early essay, the very continental status of America. Remarking wistfully that "because we live not in a continent but in islands, so terribly isolated, we know so little of each other that we don't even hate one another," Paz in fact broached the possibility that the Americas might not, after all, have a common history—or literature, for that matter.[5] Neither does the 1956 appendix to *The Bow and the Lyre* make any mention of Alegría's study of Whitman's reception in Latin America, even though the latter had also been published in Mexico two years before. Alegría, in turn, could not have known about Paz's unpublished Guggenheim proposal, though in a stranger turn he does not mention Bolton either. Stranger, that is, because in 1944 Alegría, like Paz, was himself living at Berkeley and studying with Professor Arturo Torres-Rioseco, a fellow Chilean under whose mentorship (I suspect) Alegría first undertook his research on Whitman and who, in the 1920s, had produced, as Alegría himself notes (373–77), what at the time were some of the best Spanish translations of Whitman.

Bolton's theory, Paz's proposal, Alegría's study, even the criteria for the Guggenheim Fellowship Program, all share of course one immediate common source: the Pan-Americanist ideology of the Roosevelt era. This was the period (the 1930s and 1940s) in U.S. history marked by the "Good Neighbor" policy as a result of its entry into World War II and its efforts to secure reliable allies to the South. Whitman, the American Poet of Democracy, thus became a convenient emblem of this ideology, and it is not by accident that his cult in Latin America reaches its apex then. These were the years when Henry Seidel Canby, a noted Whitman scholar, addressed an annual meeting of specialists on Latin American literature in order to ask, on the subject of Whitman, "Who Speaks for New World Democracy?" An echo of Canby's rhetorical question can still be heard in Alegría's quite literal introduction to *Walt Whitman en Hispanoamérica,* where, adopting Canby's motto as his own, he describes the Roosevelt era as "the heroic years of the war against fascism" and his own study, implicitly, as his contribution to U.S. foreign policy toward Latin America—comparative literature as a kind of academic Good Neighbor. But just as the Latin American cult of Whitman precedes by a good many years the Good Neighbor policy, so the omissions one notes in both Paz and Alegría cannot simply be dismissed as accidents of a given political moment. Paz's transparent allusion to Borges's well-known reading of "the other Whitman"—the latter's view that Whitman's creation of his heroic persona compensated for his banal real life—has a greater and, in a sense, more significant antecedent in the wholesale omission of Pablo Neruda from his Guggenheim proposal. Neruda had by then produced much of the Americanist verse that he was later to gather together in *Canto general* (1950) but Paz had publicly and violently broken with him barely a year before.[6] Paz's repression of Neruda's name, his critique of Borges, as well as the other instances we will have occasion to note in Borges, Neruda, and Alegría are all part of this commonly shared contest or *conquest* of Whitman—a contest or conquest of wills over the most accurate appropriation of the American bard's legacy. "La tradición no se hereda, se conquista" ("Tradition is conquered, not simply inherited"), one of Paz's fighting maxims during the forties, could itself be viewed as the motto of that conquest.

II

The Whitman cult is international, of course, not just Latin American. And it is a poetic myth of modernity in general, not just of the United

States in particular. Why Whitman, one might ask? To begin with, Whitman stands at the crossroads of modern literary history; both a belated romantic and the premonition of the avant-garde, Whitman is the Janus-figure of that history. To this temporal duality corresponds its rhetorical convenience, for Whitman's poetry incarnates what lately has been called the romantic subject; only that subject too dissolves conveniently into the impersonality of either pantheist or populist ideologies. Seemingly the poet for all seasons, Whitman fulfills Emerson's ideal project for "The Poet" and thereby dazzles equally symbolists like Vielé-Griffin, Martí, and Darío; inspires alike Pound the imagist, Marinetti the futurist, Becher the expressionist, and Claudel the neo-Thomist, not to mention the postmodern Borges and Neruda. Like the cowboy storming across *Leaves of Grass,* Whitman rides astride the last two centuries, but the dust that storm unsettles often prevents us from tracing its tracks.

In the specific case of Latin America that crossroads is situated at a stage somewhere between *modernismo* (Hispanic symbolism) and modernity, a kind of twilight zone that reveals the flux of our literary history. Often linked to post- or anti-*modernismo*—an alleged reaction on the part of late nineteenth-century poets to a decadent French influence—Whitman actually forms part of the very mythology of *modernismo,* a truism understood from Paz's remark that "the *modernistas* did not want to be French; they wanted to be modern." As discovered by *modernistas* like Martí, Darío, and Lugones, Whitman became yet another emblem of modernity, one of the missing portraits in Darío's gallery of *Los raros.* This initial cult of Whitman, then, did not mean the denial of *modernismo* but was rather one of its phases: a different, critical, and I would add *political*—in the sense of a rhetorically powerful interpretation—phase whose real culprit was not France but Spain, or at least a certain empty rhetorical Spanish tradition. It is this critical or political use of Whitman in the initial phase of its Latin American cult that explains, I believe, his emblematic use in some of the early texts of *modernismo*—Martí's 1887 chronicle, for example, or Darío's plodding sonnet in *Azul . . .* (1888).[7] The *modernistas* invoke rather than imitate Whitman. In their works Whitman tends to be a *theme* rather than a stylistic or rhetorical model, even in particularly hostile instances like Darío's haughty dismissal ("The rest is yours, Democrat Walt Whitman . . .") at the end of the "Preliminary Words" of his *Prosas profanas* (1896). Later, during the first decades of the century, the Whitman theme would be gradually replaced by his persona as it seduced Latin American bards into adopting it as a full-blown rhetorical model. And by the time they did accept it, that persona became fused with yet another, perhaps unlikely, kindred spirit by the name of Nietzsche.

About Nietzsche's presence I shall have more to say later. For the moment we should underscore the collapse of the distinction between the emblematic and rhetorical uses of Whitman in most critical discussions about his influence in Latin America. That collapse, one of critical distance, was soon noted by Borges in a sharp 1929 essay where he remarked that those who write about Whitman incur two fallacies, one of which was the confusion of the poet and his persona, while the other was "the senseless adoption of the style and vocabulary of his poems, that is, the same surprising phenomenon that aims to be explained."[8] Borges's remark may appear to underscore an isolated critical problem but it actually has roots in Latin American historical life. When José Enrique Rodó, in his review (later to be the preface to the second edition) of *Prosas profanas,* reports to have heard that Darío was not "el poeta de América," he must have said so regretting that Darío was not in fact Whitman, or at least not yet. Shortly thereafter Darío would write his ode "A Roosevelt," which he was to include in *Cantos de vida y esperanza* (1907)—a book he dedicated to Rodó—in which he explicitly invoked "el verso de Walt Whitman" in order to address the bellicose American president. By then, of course, Darío and other *modernistas,* like the Uruguayan Alvaro Armando Vasseur, had gradually begun to internalize Whitman's prose and rhetoric, and it could be said that by invoking "el verso de Walt Whitman" Darío marked Whitman's passage from theme to persona. But despite the blank verse Darío adopted as a Whitman password in his ode, what his persona expressed in that particular poem was not so much Whitman's proverbial eroticism or democratic chant as a turgid anti-imperialist speech echoing Old Testament prophecy.

Indeed, Darío's equivocal gesture could be taken as emblematic of the erratic relationship between Latin American poets and Whitman; it appears to be constituted by the disparity between what Whitman actually was and wrote and what they *imagined* he was and wrote. *Whitmanism,* that is, writes not so much *from* a Whitman point of view as *about* him. Such an erratic relationship, in turn, depends on a political paradox: it wishes to borrow Whitman's mask from North America as the rhetorical shield of Latin America *against* North American imperialism. Whitman thus became rhetorically useful and even politically expedient, but that expediency was no less subject to bad faith. While that bad faith may be explained as one more version of the paradox with which all of (Latin) American culture is fraught—being an American

Self through the language of the European Other—the Whitman model in particular may yet turn out to be the most dramatic instance of that general cultural paradox.

Whitman had in fact come to poets like Darío and Vasseur indirectly since they could not read him in the original English; they relied on foreign sources, mostly France, where, as Betsy Erkkila has recently shown, Whitman had an immense impact.[9] Alegría himself showed, in turn, that idealized French biographies of the "Good Gray Poet," like Léon Bazalgette's popular *Walt Whitman: L'Homme et son oeuvre* (1908), inform much of the notes and summaries of Whitman's Latin American reception beyond Martí's early chronicle. In two long and heavily documented chapters (15–150), Alegría took pains to show the recurrence of a Whitman myth in Spanish-American discussions of his life. Yet curiously missing from Alegría's chapters was any discussion about the effect that such an idealized perception of Whitman's biography might have had on the actual creation of Whitmanian personae among Latin American poets. That is, Alegría's study on the reception of Whitman in Spanish America failed to articulate precisely the most crucial question of that entire subject: the relationship between the prevalence of a certain Whitman myth and actual writing, and thereby to show the connection between the Latin American poet as *reader* of a foreign influence and as interpreter and *recoder* of that same influence. This failure is revealingly dramatized in Alegría's placement of his chapter on the Spanish translations of Whitman at the end rather than at the beginning of his study, thus obviating the possible (con)sequential use of those translations by the poets discussed in earlier chapters. This is only one of many missed opportunities in Alegría's otherwise useful account of the Whitman cult in Latin America, a fact which further reinforces my view that it too forms part of the cult and as such participates in what Borges called the "senseless adoption" of a rhetoric blinded by the very object of study.

My point is that far from the pious Pan-American chorus for which Alegría and others have argued, the production of a Whitman question in Latin America constitutes a revealing instance of an alienated colonial discourse, in the sense of a body of information filtered through the language of an Other—in this case, idealized (and foreign) biographies as well as translations twice-removed from the original. And since the only thing that counts within such a discourse is what the subjects *imagine* their object to be (hence the crucial role of a Whitman Imaginary, so to speak), the actual discourse appears contaminated by features that are structurally similar to (when not radically different from) those proper to the object—what biologists, using a structural term, have called iso-morphic traits, as in Darío's Old Testament speech derived from "el verso de Walt Whitman." The end result is a literally *rhapsodic* text: that is, not so much ecstatic in content (though Whitmanism shows that, too) as heterogeneous in form, constituted by a porous, fractious lan-guage that magnifies its otherness in what Mikhail Bakhtin would call an instance of the *carnivalesque*.[10]

The point seems worth making especially in cases like Vasseur's, in whom the roles of Whitmanian poet and Whitman translator converged, and whose work as both poet and translator (as Alegría himself took pains to show) lies at the origin of much of the Whitman cult in Latin America.[11] It is thus hardly surprising that a good portion of Alegría's chapter on the Spanish translations of Whitman (349–396) should be devoted to a detailed technical critique of Vasseur's contribution—what Alegría took to be Vasseur's truncated and often "incorrect" readings of Whitman's English, his "excessive liberties" in reinterpreting Whitman's poems for a Hispanic audience. Alegría's critique may have been tech-nically accurate but it was certainly misguided for the purposes of a reception study. Among other things, Vasseur did his translations not from English as Alegría claims (Vasseur did not know it), but from Italian translations as early as 1881. Vasseur himself acknowledged this fact in his 1951 preface to the sixth edition of his *Poemas: Walt Whitman* (a text missing from Alegría's otherwise extensive bibliography), and it is suggested in the use of Italian epigraphs of Whitman verses for the different sections of his Whitmanian *Cantos augurales* (1904), of which Alegría did take note.[12] Working thus at twice-remove from the original (and it would of course be instructive further to collate Vasseur's text with his Italian sources), Vasseur was free to turn his translation into a loose *versión* (his word) in which he *rewrote* Whitman according to his own idea of a *certain* Whitmanian voice or persona equally as valid as (and potentially more interesting than) the one at work in his own *Cantos augurales* (1904).

Far from Alegría's view that Vasseur's "translations" were defective or aberrant because they did not render faithfully Whitman's English original, I find them to be the most apposite. These "unfaithful" ver-sions of Whitman, foundation-texts of his Latin American cult, confirm the alienated, second-order quality of such a discourse. I suspect that much of what sounded particularly un-Whitmanian to Alegría's ears was due to Vasseur's professed admiration for Nietzsche, as a Zarathustrian title like *Cantos augurales* suggests, and the contamination of his style with Whitman's. Indeed, Vasseur's debt to José Enrique Rodó's influential *Ariel* (1900)—whose verse version he may even have intended in his own work (Rodó, in addition, was also from Uruguay)—cannot be discounted. And yet Nietzsche's peculiarly strident, egocentric rhetoric permeates so much of Vasseur's style (in both his own poems and his Whitman versions) that it could be said his was a truly Nietzschean mode of writing, or *écriture*. Such a contamination would not be unusual, after all. The affinity between Whitman and Nietzsche, twin postromantic heroic figures, is a virtual cliché of late nineteenth-century intellectual and cultural history, to the point that an early essay by Borges described Nietzsche's theory of the Superman in revealing terms: "Nietzsche wanted to be Walt Whitman, he wanted minutely to fall in love with his own destiny."[13] Vasseur himself, in the preface to the Whitman versions that Alegría cites in his own study (151–54), expounded at length on the parallels between the two writers, twin "supermen" in Vasseur's heady vision.

I suggest that virtually all the distortions and misunderstandings that Alegría points out in Vasseur—particularly the latter's suppression of Whitman's borrowings from phrenology, the general secular tone of his Whitman versions, and the "neoclassical residue" (285) that he finds in the poetry—can be explained by Nietzsche's tacit yet powerful presence in Vasseur's versions or in his Italian sources. In our own discursive terms, Nietzsche represents an isomorphic trait with respect to Whitman that contributed greatly to a poetics of post-*modernismo*, particularly a new concept of the poet (or of a poetic persona such as D'Annunzio in Italy), whose dramatic traits would be Whitman's American utopianism and Nietzsche's plea for the Superman. Within the peculiar economy of that discourse, Nietzsche serves one special purpose: to hold in check, without necessarily canceling, Whitman's religious tone. For as a historian of these two figures puts it: "Whitman's joy envisages a transfigured rather than a perfected human nature. It is the joy of the Oversoul, not of Damocles. In contrast, Nietzsche's joy is wholly mundane and derives solely from Zarathustra's service to life."[14]

Nietzschean joy, then, and not simply Whitmanian Democracy, provides the explanation for such Latin American titles of post-*modernismo* as Vasseur's *Cantos del Nuevo Mundo,* Sabat Ercasty's *Pantheos,* and Neruda's *El hondero entusiasta,* even though such books would be simply inconceivable without Whitman. And it was Nietzsche (influenced by Italian bravura) who was the tacit if raucous voice that Latin American readers overheard in Vasseur's "defective" Whitman versions. In an insightful though vitriolic essay of 1929, Borges attributed that voice exclusively to a "French connection" that turned each budding Latin American Whitman into what Borges ridiculed as an "insistent Hugo." Be the connection French or German, however, its existence suggests that the study of Whitman's presence in Latin America includes as well the manner and extent to which his followers may have repressed his figure, a repression consonant perhaps with the privileged cultural paradox that Whitman represents. Whitman, following Emerson, urged self-reliance for the American: to celebrate not History or Nature, but Oneself. But the legacy of that urging has been equivocal, if not outrightly anxious and repressive. To boast, as Whitman had, of having "an American Bard at last" meant that the search for that bard was at last over. "Of them, a bard is to be commensurate with a people," claimed the first preface to *Leaves of Grass* of that one lucky fellow to be echoed later by his followers North and South. But how can one sing oneself simply within a tradition of self-singers? In North American poetry such anxiety surfaces in what Harold Bloom has called "the American Sublime," the simultaneous desire for and resistance to influence that riddles the works of Dickinson, Crane, Frost, and Stevens.[15] We have no name for the Latin American equivalent of Bloom's term, but I suspect that it is somewhat different from its Anglo counterpart. To this difference, if indeed there should be one, I now turn my attention in the exemplary instances of Neruda and Borges.

III

Both Neruda and Borges first read Whitman in their teens. Like Vasseur, both discovered him through indirect sources; both imitated his poetry in their early verse; and both rejected Whitman soon thereafter, only to recover him in later years through other creative means. In Neruda's work, Whitman became the Continental American voice; in Borges's, one more embodiment of the idea of Literature. In keeping with the general intent of this essay, I bring Neruda and Borges together in this context partly to oppose the commonplace view that Whitman influenced both poets differently though still simply and directly, as in a Pan-Americanist rapture. I propose instead a less sentimental version of what I take to be their complicated kinship. And it is for this reason that my reading of these two poets concentrates on texts that perhaps may appear marginal or at least eccentric in relation to the canon usually invoked for the opposite purpose.[16]

Neruda once wrote that he learned of Whitman as early as 1919, at the age of fifteen, but it was actually in 1923, at eighteen, that he published a review of Torres-Rioseco's 1922 translations.[17] The review itself was instructive in its contradictions. Writing as "Sachka"—one of his several pre-Neruda pen names—he praised Whitman and his Chilean translator yet objected to the former's example. Whitman had a vital, energetic message well enough, but that vital energy was itself damaging: "Lost words," Sachka thus admonished. "Each poet will sing whatever he wishes without caring about Whitman's hygienic precepts." That admonishment in itself amounts to an early restatement of Bloom's "American Sublime"—influence both sought and repressed—and becomes all the more telling when compared to a second review, published barely a week later, of the poetry of Carlos Sabat Ercasty, another Uruguayan bard, which praised his poetry effusively yet suppressed that gesture altogether.[18] A dedicated Whitman follower (Alegría cheerfully calls him an "apostle of his message" [291]), Sabat Ercasty knew of course the Whitman versions of Vasseur, his countryman and contemporary; Sachka's sycophantic review, in turn, demonstrates the extent to which he took in the influence he resisted in Whitman. Within two years the conflict reached a crisis, as soon as Neruda published *Crepusculario* (1923), his first book of poems, and began writing, in the seductive Sabat Ercasty mode, a second book that years later would be published under the title of *El hondero entusiasta* (*The Ardent Slingsman,* 1933).

Neruda suppressed publication of this book for ten years, well after acquiring just fame for the more mature poetry of *Residencia en la tierra* (*Residence on Earth,* 1933). When he did publish *El hondero entusiasta,* however, the preface contained several admissions: Sabat Ercasty's influence had in fact led him to suppress the book; the published book contained only a portion of the original poems (thus suggesting that the poems he did suppress made such influence even more evident); and the published book was merely "the document of an excessive and burning youth." In a telling retrospective piece written thirty years after this preface, Neruda explained further that Sabat Ercasty's influence was part of a broader and lifelong "cyclical ambition" in his own poetry. He revealed also that at the time he wrote the poems of *El hondero entusiasta* he had even corresponded with Sabat Ercasty and that, upon acknowledging receipt of some of Neruda's poems, Sabat Ercasty had confirmed his own influence on Neruda. The shock of recognition thus led Neruda not only to withhold publication but to repress completely the Sabat Ercasty model in his work. Instead, he turned to paring his style— "reduje estilísticamente, de una manera deliberada, mi expresión" ("I reduced stylistically, and deliberately, my expression")—which resulted in *Veinte poemas de amor y una canción desesperada* (*Twenty Love Poems and a Song of Despair*, 1924), a work that, while removed from the lifelong project of a "poesía aglomerativa" ("cumulative poetry"), did succeed in making a name for him for the first time in his career as a poet.[19]

Neruda's "cyclical ambition" of a "cumulative poetry" was nothing less than his elliptical naming of the Whitman model. And it was by repressing rather than giving in to it—as forebears like Vasseur, Sabat Ercasty, and many a poetaster collected in Alegría's study had done— that he achieved his *first* distinctive voice, that of the melancholy lover of the *Veinte poemas*. That the Whitman model should so thoroughly have informed as well Neruda's *most* distinctive voice in the years to come— the militant prophet of works like *Canto general* (we are working, let us recall, with the poet's *imaginary* relationship to Whitman)—demonstrates the persistence of that model in the constitution, the very institutional signature, of his poetic voice. Nowhere does Neruda approach Whitman more than in the latter book, though less so for the peculiar way in which the by-then Communist Neruda piously thematized his relationship to Whitman—particularly in the socialist-realist section titled "Que despierte el leñador" ("Let the Rail Splitter Awake")—than for the analogy the entire book assumes. Like *Leaves of Grass,* as I have shown elsewhere, *Canto general* is a modern, secular analogy of the Sacred Book, an encyclopedia of American Nature and Culture in the tradition that Brotherston has called "the Great Song of America" and that embodies most closely Neruda's "cyclical ambition."[20] For this reason, I agree with Alegría's statement that Neruda ultimately turned out to be less Whitman's disciple than his heir—someone who digested Whitman and then went on to write his own verse. But I could not agree with Alegría less than when he contends, in the course of making the same statement (317–18), that there were no traces of Whitman in *El hondero entusiasta,* or even in *Tentativa del hombre infinito* (*Venture of the Infinite Man,* 1925), Neruda's long avant-garde poem, and that it was only in *Residencia en la tierra* that one can begin to find such traces. Neruda's relationship to Whitman was far more complex. In the case of the first book, Sabat Ercasty's imprint is enough to suggest otherwise; and the second one happens to be the one book where, by Neruda's own admission in the same retrospective piece, his "cyclical ambition" resurfaced (even if unsuccessfully) for the first time since receiving Sabat Ercasty's honest letter.

Borges's struggles with the Whitman model parallel closely Neruda's own even as they show a more violent rebellion against the model's meaning. Borges, not unlike Neruda and Vasseur, read Whitman through sources other than English. Borges, however, did know English, but the Whitman he read in German in 1917 was filtered through his contact with the German expressionists, for whom Whitman was a modernist hero of their own. In his "Autobiographical Essay" (1970), he reported:

> It was also in Geneva that I first met Walt Whitman, through a German translation by Johannes Schlaf ("Als ich in Alabama meinen Morgengang machte"—"As I have walk'd in Alabama my morning walk"). Of course, I was struck by the absurdity of reading an American poet in German, so I ordered a copy of *Leaves of Grass* from London. . . . For a time I thought of Whitman not only as a great poet but as the *only* poet. In fact, I thought all poets the world over had merely led up to Whitman until 1855, and that not to imitate him was a proof of ignorance. This feeling had already come over me with Carlyle's prose, which is now unbearable to me, and with the poetry of Swinburne. These were phases I went through. Later on, I was to go through similar experiences of being overwhelmed by some particular writer.[21]

Borges imposes his peculiar stamp while acknowledging the second-order nature of his reception. For the young Borges, Whitman was no less than Literature incarnate, the first in a gallery of heroes—like Carlyle, Cansinos-Assens, and Macedonio Fernández—that throughout his work he would either choose personally or analyze impersonally as exemplary figures in the achievement of a literary destiny. Unlike the other heroes, though, Whitman was the only model the young Borges went on to imitate faithfully in his early poems, a fact whose anxiety he acknowledges implicitly by pointing to its "overwhelming" nature. That this was an internal disturbance and not just a superficial fancy for Whitman's poetic technique, is confirmed in Borges's own description of one of these early poems, "Himno del mar" ("Hymn of/to the Sea") where he admits that there "I tried my hardest to be Walt Whitman."[22] What it means to *be* Walt Whitman, and not simply to imitate him, is in fact the key to understanding Borges's troubled kinship—much as to *be* and not just imitate Cervantes would be the key to understanding the plight of a struggling writer like Pierre Menard. Borges offers, in other words, a *metaphysical* solution to the Whitmanian paradox and thereby a precarious solution to his disturbing legacy—in Latin America or elsewhere. Yet in order to see clearly through the implications of what it means to *be* Walt Whitman, we must differentiate it from two other alternatives.

One obvious way to *be* Walt Whitman would of course have been to translate Whitman, something that Borges would eventually do in his 1969 partial translation of *Leaves of Grass*. By translating an author's work, the translator takes the place of that particular author. The result, however, is both short-lived and imperfect, for regardless of the sympathy between translator and author, the otherness of the translating enterprise (as Walter Benjamin sadly discovered) is always inherent. An echo of such melancholy is heard in Borges's preface to his *Leaves of Grass* translation where, forty years after his first attempts at the same task (and so, presumably, after that many years of translating Whitman), he still described it as "oscillating between personal interpretation and resigned rigor."[23] Yet a second way to *be* Whitman in practice was to identify and to write like the prodigious persona staged in *Leaves of Grass,* much as the early Borges does in poems like "Himno del mar," "Insomnio," or "Guardia Roja." And yet to be that self-idolatrous, romantic character meant also, in turn, to be fundamentally at odds with the modernist project for aesthetic impersonality that Borges would undertake even while writing these same early poems. The conflict, which in some ways is parallel to Neruda's own early ambivalence, soon became evident and resolved itself in the following fashion.

Shortly after returning to Buenos Aires in the early 1920s, Borges attacked outright the growing Whitman cult in Argentina (and by extension in Latin America) as a symptom of a romantic holdover that contemporary art should identify and eradicate. This militantly modernist position—whose implicit butt may have been Leopoldo Lugones, an Argentine *modernista* whom the *ultraístas* disparaged—appears in his essay "La nadería de la personalidad" ("The Bagatelle of Personality," 1925)[24] where Borges argues (following Schopenhauer) that since the self is an illusion, then self and world cannot simply be coextensive, as the Whitman followers simply assumed. Thus focusing on the fallacy that "to want to express oneself should mean the same thing as to want to express all life" (91), Borges remarked that "[Whitman] thought it was enough to enumerate the names of things so that we would immediately find out how unique and surprising they all are" (91) and concluded, in a sweep of his unique neobaroque prose, that "la egolatría romántica y el vocinglero individualismo van así desbaratando las artes" ("Romantic egomania and raucous individualism are thus destroying the arts") (93). Borges's real target, both then and later (as we will yet see), was not so much Whitman as his faithful epigones—including Lugones, chief of the Argentine *modernistas*—whom Borges then proceeds to caricature at length in the same essay. Yet it remains significant that Whitmanism should have been the explicit butt against which Borges defined his modernist poetics, a fact that suggests not only the prevalence of the cult but also the young Borges's personal stake in opposing and repressing it.

By then Borges himself had gone through the modernist mill of *ultraísmo*—the Hispanic synthesis of futurism and imagism—in Spain, where he lived during two separate periods in the late 1910s and early 1920s. If *ultraísmo* was a cult of the impersonal image—"agudezas imprevistas y maravillas verbales" ("unforeseen wit and verbal marvels" [91]), as Borges calls it in the same essay—Whitmanism meant an opposite cult of the self that was no longer operative, a paradoxical "new anachronism" so *démodé* that even his fellow Argentines could not recognize it as unfashionable. Repressing Whitman—which for the young Borges meant repressing an "overwhelming" passion and an earlier self—had already been the way to effect the self-discipline that had made possible imagistic poems redolent with "agudezas imprevistas" like those of *Fervor de Buenos Aires*. With Neruda's *Crepusculario*, Borges's first published book of poems shared the publication date of 1923 by when both poets were sharing as well a common repression—less Whitman than Whitmanism, or at least the Whitman *within them both*. Unlike Borges the militant *ultraísta*, Neruda the budding lover had shied away from the cult of the image in *Crepusculario* and his other early works— in reaction, most likely, to Vicente Huidobro's *creacionismo*, the peculiar version of imagism concocted by this contemporary fellow Chilean. Thus Neruda's later repression of Whitman/Sabat Ercasty had meant a self-imposed reduction of his own style; Borges's repression, by contrast, was done in the name of (or as a consequence of) a more radical change in style and poetics, a different concept of poetry altogether that questioned, in effect, the very basis of the Whitman cult.

That Borges meant to attack the cult rather than Whitman became sharply clear four years later (1929), in the first of his two classic essays on the subject, where he draws the distinction. Borges argues that since fascination for Europe—rather than continental communication, unity, or solidarity—is what binds all Americans together, and since Paris (the only part of Europe Latin Americans care about) cares only for the politics of literature, so our Whitman cult in particular reflects all those prejudices. "El asombro, con todo, labró una falseada imagen de Whitman: la de un varón meramente saludador y mundial, un insistente Hugo inferido desconsideradamente a los hombres por reiterada vez" ("Amazement, despite all, created a false image of Whitman: that of a merely saluting and worldly male, an insistent Hugo inconsiderately inferred to men time and again").[25] That is, our so-called (Latin/North) American Whitman myth is actually a peculiarly French misreading that has resulted in petrifying that sprightly American voice into a plodding institution—certainly as plodding as the last clause of the latter quotation makes it sound. To counter this myth Borges provides, in the same essay, his own translations of several passages from *Leaves of Grass* that for him demonstrate Whitman's contrary "trembling and sufficient laconic quality," his "denial of all intellectual schemes and appreciation for the primary senses"—a discrete poetics sounding close to the very *ultraísmo* that Borges was still advocating in those years. For Borges, then, Whitman was ultimately an impersonal rather than a self-proclaiming romantic poet, a heroic persona that compensated for a shy self but whose ultimate goal, consonant with his celebration of Democracy, was to identify with everyone. "With impetuous humility," writes Borges in the second of his two essays on Whitman, "he wants to resemble all men."[26] By so doing, however, Whitman succeeded in being not Himself, as romantic heroes—from those of Byron to Valery (124)—had done, but No One.

Truly to *be* Walt Whitman, then, meant neither to translate nor to imitate his work. Whereas translation reinforces rather than dispels otherness, imitation, in turn, would have meant incurring the very French myth Borges had denounced earlier. Borges's fascination for Whitman did not exclude the knowledge that to imitate him would have meant sounding like Neruda, or at least the Neruda of *Canto general*. There Neruda had wanted to sound like Whitman: "Al oeste de Colorado River / hay un sitio que amo" ("West of the Colorado River / there's a place I love"), as the speaker of "Que despierte el leñador" says turgidly. In this he would have been no different from many a Whitman follower, American or otherwise. "Numerous are those who have imitated, with degrees of success [con éxito diverso], Whitman's intonation," writes Borges, tongue-in-cheek, in the preface to his translation; he then proceeds to enumerate, Whitman-like and with perverse vengeance, their names in a catalog: "Sandburg, Lee Masters, Maiakovski, Neruda . . ." (173). Borges's solution—the third way to *be* Walt Whitman—was therefore to elude *directly* the totalizing ambition (cyclical or otherwise) shared equally by all these American poets through the imitation of Whitman and to realize, instead, that the way to Walt Whitman, "semi-divine hero of *Leaves of Grass*," was through Walt*er* Whitman, "man of letters," or as the preface to his translation puts it, "modest journalist from Long Island" (172), who wanted to be the other self but could not.

Where Borges essayed most fully this third way to *be* Walt Whitman was neither in an essay nor in a poem—though a late text like "Camden 1892," which re-creates Whitman's last moments, can certainly be read this way—but in "The Aleph" (1949), one of his most enigmatic short stories. For who, after all, is Carlos Argentino Daneri, the rambling poetaster of this tale, if not that self-conscious [Latin] American, Whitmanesque bard whose life ambition is to write an encyclopedic poem titled (no less than) "The Earth," which "consisted of a description of the planet" lacking "no amount of picturesque digression and bold apostrophes," and the "Argentine sections" of which ultimately attain the dubious "Second National Prize for Literature"? To Daneri's arrogance Borges opposes the uncertainty of "Borges," timid admirer of the beautiful (and late) Beatriz Viterbo, who literally stumbles upon literary totalization in a cluttered basement of Buenos Aires. The "Borges" of this story, an aspiring writer in his own right, is Borges's own self-projection of Walter Whitman, "modest journalist from Long Island," stripped here of any heroic persona. He is the proverbial banal "I" of the parable "Borges and I," the Borgesian passive reader.

The paradox on which the story turns is thus obvious: the totalization all poets seek—and the Whitman cult would be but one version—obtains from accidents with the lowly and banal and not, as Daneri thinks, from a deliberate and self-conscious pursuit of the monumental. While Daneri—whose name, like Beatriz Viterbo's, as Rodríguez Monegal showed, conceals a parody of Dante—seeks to be Walt Whitman (like Dante, a totalizing poet), he succeeds only in achieving what even Walter Whitman had rejected as a writing method: "Urdir laboriosamente una oda o tal vez una alegoría no desprovista de interjecciones vocativas y de letras mayúsculas" ("Sedulously to plot an ode or perhaps an allegory not devoid of vocative interjections and capital letters") says Borges in his preface.[27] "Borges," still pining after the late and unfaithful Beatriz, uncertain about his own literary talent and humiliated by Daneri's insufferable arrogance, stumbles into being Walt Whitman and creating, in his confessional text, a totalizing allegory. Daneri, sedulously at work on "The Earth" for several years, mistakes literal prolixity for literary totalization and celebrates the abstract while pretending to write about the concrete world. "Borges," on the other hand, in his personal and oblique elegy to Madame Viterbo, catches a glimpse of the universe (including a capsule summary of Daneri's "The Earth") while pretending to offer a personal confession. Daneri tries to sing like Walt Whitman but fails; "Borges" cries like himself and thereby succeeds in *being* Whitman, that is, in being everyone, which is to say, No One: ". . . I saw in the drawer of a writing table (and the handwriting made me tremble) unbelievable, obscene, detailed letters, which Beatriz had written to Carlos Argentino; I saw a monument I worshipped in the Chacarita cemetery; I saw the rotted dust and bones that had once been Beatriz Viterbo . . ." (27–28). "Beatriz Viterbo," wrote the real Borges years later, as if pointing to the one central issue of this text, beyond all literary implications, whether Dante's or Whitman's, "really existed and I was very much and hopelessly in love with her. I wrote my story after her death" (264).[28]

IV

Is "The Aleph" a parody of *Canto general*? Such a reading would not be farfetched. We know, of course, that Borges wrote "The Aleph" at the peak of Perón's rule, its Hebrew title (which is also that of the book where the story is included) a dare to the anti-Semitic climate of the regime. Under Perón, the entire Borges household suffered penury and humiliation, even as Borges himself continued to write and publish freely. The story thus contains a veiled satire not only of the Whitman cult but of the vulgarity determined by Peronist literary tastes. Neruda, by contrast, prospered under Perón even as his fellow Communists were persecuted by the Argentine police, an irony that did not escape Borges when, years after *Canto general* had been published, he complained that in the book's section on Latin American dictators (section 5, "La arena traicionada") Neruda had conveniently skipped over Perón, possibly to obtain favor in a pending lawsuit in Buenos Aires.[29]

It matters little of course that Borges's story should have been published a year before Neruda's book: news of Neruda's project of a poem of continental proportions was known at least since the early 1940s. It is more likely, however, that what appears to be a direct parody may be merely an effect of Borges's satire of the Whitman cult. The point of that satire is to identify the object of the cult as the desire for totalization—what could otherwise be called an anxiety of literary legitimacy or, perhaps, the contest for encyclopedic form—and to demonstrate instead the undeliberate, accidental nature of such status. Its lesson runs along proverbial Borgesian lines: at no time do we reach the Other more than when we decide to be ourselves. Thus imitating Whitman in literature bears the same error as imitating our peers in real life: we thereby succeed not in being the Other but in alienating ourselves, becoming a mere abstraction, like Daneri's impersonal "Earth." Only in being oneself, and in resigning ourselves to being No One, do we succeed in being the Other and thereby everyone else. The shortest distance between the Self and the Other, Borges seems to say, is not a straight line but a slip.

Borges's reading of the Whitman cult is also a reading of its history, a history of hidden (and, as we have seen, not-so-hidden) polemics, confrontations, and misunderstandings. Much, of course, remains to be said about that history, not the least of which is the relative lack of discussion in most studies (including this one) of Whitman's fortunes in the Luso-Brazilian world. Far from being a poet of heroic vitalism, Whitman for many of these poets—beginning, perhaps, with Sousândrade, the pen name for the nineteenth-century Brazilian Joaquim de Sousa Andrade (1833–1902), author of *O Inferno de Wall Street*—was a poet of death, a writer of elegies and of nihilist allegories like "The Sleepers." With time we have learned to view the Latin American version of the Whitman cult as one of several overarching cultural myths—like the Monroe Doctrine, the Hispanism once advocated by Franco's Spain, or the oas—that historically have meant to compensate for the fragmentation and isolation of (Latin/Anglo) American societies. But just as the political versions of such myths have been shown to quell pluralism for the sake of a united front, so the workings of the Whitman reception in Latin America show a different story. It is the story of a dependent discourse whose production shows both the heterogeneity of its origins and the denial of a synthetic product. What purports to be the result of simple, direct influence is actually a rhapsodic production of contradictory, often erratic effects. And because its unsynthesized elements cannot cohere into a sum or unity, as neither text nor ideology, its discourse remains polemical and thus open to further transformation and change— a further *translation,* in effect, into multiple languages and perspectives. To acknowledge the erratic, accidental nature of that history does not lessen the values that spurred it originally, as our sentimental historians will in all likelihood complain. It merely restates the question on a more realistic basis.[30]

Appendix

During the summer of 1989, as I was finishing the final draft of this essay, I had the privilege of visiting Santiago de Chile and of consulting the two preserved libraries of Pablo Neruda. These libraries are located in a special collection of the library of the University of Chile and at Neruda's last Santiago residence, known as "La Chascona" (Fernando Márquez de la Plata 0192). While the former collects Neruda's books until 1954, the year he donated them as a collection to the University of Chile, the latter houses those he collected since then, and which he owned at the time of his death in 1973. Following is a list of the Whitmaniana in both collections. I must add that the actual cataloging was done for me. While doing research in the former collection I was fortunate to meet Ms. Selena Millares, a graduate student working on a thesis about Neruda's literary sources at Madrid's Universidad Complutense, who proceeded to inform me that because the collection catalogue was very incomplete she had undertaken all the listings under Whitman and would allow me to copy them. In addition, Ana María Díaz Grez, of the Pablo Neruda Foundation, kindly allowed me to copy the relevant entries of the Chascona collection. My thanks to both of these ladies for their many kindnesses. Accidents do happen . . .

At the University of Chile

Leaves of Grass. Boston: Thayer and Eldridge, 1860–1861.
Leaves of Grass. New York: D. Appleton and Co., 1919.
Leaves of Grass, Including Sands at Seventy, Good Bye My Fancy, Old Age Echoes, and A Backward Glance O'er Travel'd Roads. Boston: Small, Maynard and Co., 1899.
Poems of Walt Whitman (Leaves of Grass). New York: T. Y. Crowell and Co., 1902.
Paul Famati, *Walt Whitman, Une étude, un choix de poemes*. Paris: Seghers, 1950.

At La Chascona [entries 71–98 of Library Catalog]

Leaves of Grass. New York: Doubleday, Doran and Company, 1940.
Specimen Days & Collect. Philadelphia: Rees Welsh and Co., 1882–1883. [2 copies]
Leaves of Grass. Philadelphia: David McKay, 1884.
Leaves of Grass. London and New York: D. Appleton and Co., 1911.
November Boughs. Philadelphia: David McKay, 1888.

An Exhibition of the Works of Walt Whitman. Detroit, Detroit Public Library, 1955.

An Exhibition of the Works of Walt Whitman. New York City, Mrs. Frank Julian, 1939.

The Gathering of the Forces. 2 vols. New York and London: G. P. Putnam's Sons, 1920.

Pictures. New York: June House, 1927.

After All, Not to Create Only. Boston: Roberts Brothers, 1871.

Autobiographia. New York: Charles L. Webster & Co., 1892.

Complete Prose. New York and London: D. Appleton and Co., 1910.

Good-Bye My Fancy. Philadelphia: David McKay, 1891.

Leaves of Grass. Philadelphia: David McKay, 1900.

The Tenderest Lover. New York: Delacorte Press, 1970.

Catalogue of an Exhibition. London: American Library, 1954.

Walt Whitman in Europe Today. Detroit: Wayne State University Press, 1972. [2 copies]

Leaves of Grass. Washington, D.C.: Library of Congress, 1972.

Complete Prose and Works. Philadelphia: David McKay, 1892.

Walt Whitman Review. Vol. 18, no. 1 (1972). [Ottawa, Wayne State University Press].

Franklin Evans. New York: Random House, 1929.

Democratic Vistas and Other Papers. London: Walter Scott, 1888.

Poems. London: Chatto and Windus, 1892.

Leaves of Grass. 3rd ed. Boston: Thayer and Eldridge, 1860–1861.

Poems. London: Reviews Office, Masterpiece Library, 1895.

Walt Whitman Catalog. Washington, D.C.: Library of Congress, 1955.

A Whitman Portrait. Woodcuts by Antonio Frasconi. New York: Spiral Press, 1960.

Eduardo González

American Theriomorphia: The Presence of *Mulatez* in Cirilo Villaverde and Beyond

MULO, 'macho,' 1042. From lat. MULUS . . . Deriv. *Mula* . . . *Mulato*, 1525 . . . 'young macho,' by comparison with the hybrid engendering of the mulatto and the mule; *mulata*, 1602 . . .

TEZ, 1470, 'color and terseness of the surface of things, and principally of the epidermis and the human visage.' A word peculiar of Castilian and Portuguese. Probably from the reduction of *aptez* to *atez*, 'perfección, robustness,' derived from lat. APTUS, 'perfect,' 'appropriate,' and later on 'robust,' 'healthy.'
—J. Corominas, *Breve diccionario etimológico*

Pariahs and Priests

Several years ago I traveled on Greyhound from New England to Indiana to attend a rite of passage. Besides the necessary clothes, a toothbrush, and Fredric Jameson's *The Prison House of Language,* the only heavy piece I carried was my freshly typed dissertation bound in black. The driver (he was brown) who assumed command in Philadelphia, and who was to steer our transient lives only up to Toledo, was asked a question regarding St. Louis as a point of passage along someone's trip to California. Thrice he stood firm and rather unhelpful in answering: "Lady, this goes to Toledo and points West!" Obviously, he was neither Hermes the Psychopomp nor an imperial agent; his map was defined by his salary, as mine was by the vague anxieties that litter the academic realm. It must have been beyond Toledo that I fell asleep resting my head on the shoulder of a massive brown woman; when I got up at Indianapolis, she told me not to forget my hat. A few years later this

177

same appendage—bought at an army surplus store—prompted some revelers to call me "rabbi" as I left an elevator at a Holiday Inn in wintry Syracuse, where I had gone to read a paper on Carpentier's "Viaje a la semilla." If I indulge in these colorless memories it is to underscore a point about the intended meaning of *beyond* in my title: that it should imply being away from home but in a new home; being homeless but reasonably happy; discovering home as it may be found, as much within the old as in the new.

"It's not a house, it's a home!" pleads a voice in a Bob Dylan song, referring to a brothel and addressing none other than Jesus himself, the incarnate pilgrim whom every house should welcome as a brother and not just as a client. Indeed, the homeless seek more than shelter, for they are as tired of carrying a makeshift home on their backs as they are of being offered sanctuary by the institutions of charity. A spiritual lesson on exile emerges from their wretched situation: home is always built; whether or not it is covered by a roof, it dwells in the heart and rises outward; home is the only furnishing that must survive wandering. In a comic and stoic sense, exiles should resemble turtles: no matter where they move, a portable, horny canopy should cover them from neck to tail. Likewise, resembling those ancient Chinese turtles known for their hieroglyphic shells, a literature of exile (which consists mostly of read-ings and recognitions) runs the risk of being surveyed from above by alien eyes; a literature that should remain a pariah among gentiles may fall one way or the other in the hands of priests. Regardless of other distinctions, in certain exile situations pariahs and priests stand apart from each other by the style and substance of their approach to amal-gamation: priests are likely to impress their hosts by devising cults based on scriptures and murals; but pariahs, quite romantically, want to scare and seduce them, so they arrive at the party with the old or the native copied on their skin, and with the mixed ink of the new still fresh from the tattoo parlor, where it needled itself into shape in front of a smoking mirror. In this sense at least, our pariah exiles seem like pagans who had to leave home without a chance to regret it, and who flaunt on themselves and others their double birth.

Having said enough about *beyond,* I should simply add that it stands for a condition of the *here* and *now,* and that it *works* or takes effect mainly as it may inspire us into awareness of the sacred and the erotic. Yes, like Coriolanus's *elsewhere, beyond* lies beyond politics and wars; it is rather the crib where the political unconscious must have first hallucinated and dreamed. But, beware: *beyond* is anecdotic, not surreal. Two places in

Freud's text need revision in order to adjust us to this old-fashioned site, the *here* and *now* surveyed in exile. In "The Uncanny," the tourist (Freud himself) wanders into a maze-like ghetto of prostitutes, their painted faces framed on windows; he keeps returning to the same spot until regaining the piazza, free from "any further voyages of discovery."[1] Neither epiphanic nor in any real sense demonic, Freud's encounter with the unsavory and vulgar—his slip into remote but neighborly temptation—wraps theory in the garments of biography. But for the one in exile, the biographic as such may not ring a personal note as authentically experienced and recalled as Freud's; the exile's biographic *topoi* have a harder time finding an actual place in ancestral life wherein to dwell: for the exile, every trace of personal memory is already ancestral; he suffers from a Jungian complex. At its best, the exile's biographic spot may lie between any former native habitat or encounter still within reach of his remembrance and some piece of reading; in this case, perhaps a fragment from Herodotus (with a hint of Borges) about a sacred temple or something about sacred prostitution (now it is Georges Bataille who comes to mind) that must have been read after leaving home for good (the hungry nostalgia of having known old Havana while reading Bataille is the spark that sets off biography in this instance). As a pariah, the exile does not know how to separate biography from allegory; Walter Benjamin transformed this pedestrian inability into migratory essays worthy of Montaigne.

The other element from Freud belongs to the much exploited and reworked (by Lacan, Derrida, and so on) *fort/da* game in *Beyond the Pleasure Principle*: the child lies adrift in the crib, the mother comes and goes, a toy spool has been left behind by her, only to be transformed into a (here-now-and-then-gone-and-here-again) mobile idol of captivity (or perhaps into the prelude to a Pythagorean siesta). But for the exile of the here and now, little Moses may find himself as if by miracle out of the crib, as the mother comes to him on the cool floor, and beholds him right under the suspended spool, unharmed by theory, gone to sleep in tiny hardness.

The Kitchen as Ghetto

While living in the sugar mill enclave where I grew up, I often ate in the kitchen, where one of my three living mothers cooked, killed chickens, drank an occasional beer (with sugar), and taught me how to play cards. She was brown with a hint of Chinese in her cheekbones. All I have to say about Cuban *mulatez* is curiously tempered by her vivid presence in my mind, and only as such does it become worthy of being something more than sheer fiction. She knew about Cecilia Valdés, I am certain, only through the overture and songs of Gonzalo Roig's sugary operetta, whose most famous lines ("yo soy Cecilia, Cecilia Valdés") represent our best "Call me Ishmael." How many among well-educated Cubans had read Cirilo Villaverde's novel remains a matter of guessing; the essence of its plot was all that mattered: a white master had a daughter with a light-colored *mulata,* the girl ended up seduced and rejected by her white half brother, who was then killed on the way to his wedding by her frustrated suitor, another mulatto. Even if known by many, the rest of the novel—with its copious account of Cuban society in the 1830s—would probably have nurtured in most readers sentimental visions of colonial life.

As an object of serious study, *Cecilia* found a salient place in the roster of antislavery novels written in Cuba during the nineteenth century. From such a vantage point, it can inspire comparison with any number of abolitionist works and, of course, with *Uncle Tom's Cabin,* with which it has little in common besides its program to expose and condemn slavery. The dominant tendency in *Cecilia* studies has taught us how to appreciate Villaverde's avowed realism, just as much as it has played down or deplored his reliance on romantic melodrama and the incest machinery behind it. If it were up to most critics I know, the whole business of incest would play a minor role in our reflections on the novel, or at least one in which the essentially white ghost of incest would be exposed and punctured, for it may represent just a boogeyman nagging the master's conscience with a measure of intoxicating masochism.[2] What these critics find in *Cecilia* is what they are best trained to explore: evidence of Cuban social and economic history during the age in which the colony approached its first war of independence and acquired everlasting racial tones enslaving and decimating broken nations of African blacks. Under the influence of more or less orthodox Marxism, the best informed critics of *Cecilia* hold in suspicion or rule out most theoretical constructs of the speculative sort. Homegrown materialism weeds out any hybrid forms of interpretation, of mythic or psychoanalytic origin. The argument that such approaches—with their own specular rapport with romantic ideology—should have heuristic value in confronting Villaverde's haunted sensibility would be dismissed by Marxists as being abstruse and in itself ideological. For what is at stake in such criticism is nothing less than the liberation of the novelist from the vestigial hindrances of plot and character stereotyping that he learned, in his own peculiar way, while reading Scott, Cooper, and Manzoni (Villaverde produced but never published a translation of *David Copperfield*). What emerges from such an isolationist project is a rehabilitated *Cecilia Valdés o, la Loma del Angel,* acting as the founding text of Cuban realism and historical fiction. The novel's *mulata* protagonist and her rich iconography play a marginal and controlled role in such readings; she becomes a poor sister to Clio, and her fiction is seen sustaining mature interest only if it gives historical testimony above any dalliance with myth.

Such an emphasis on social realism can result in extinguishing the ritual fires in *Cecilia* and obscuring the novel's kinship with ancient forms of melodrama, in which the protagonist remains luxuriously central while playing the role of sacrificial victim. No matter how morally objectionable such a sacrificial covenant with passion might be, its prestige (and the stormy effects of a truly ironic rapport with religious performance) are likely to outlast milder forms of social drama. Restored to the center of dramatic strife, Cecilia would bring back excess, embarrassment, and turbulence; elements whose consensual sublimation most realistic formulas tend to promote. Since it cannot in the end be arrested, sublimation boils down to a question of deferral, of how long it may be held off.

Not far from being Nietzsche's hot *mulata* (he called her his "sirocco incarnate"), Lou Andreas-Salomé wrote the epigraph for what could serve as our understanding of *mulatez* lifted in sublimation: "to sublimate (she says) is to bury an impulse in part and substitute another as different as is resurrection from the grave, the tabooed and the highest values— the sub- and the super-human—are mutually dependent, in fact covertly equivalent, and the grandest transmutations befall those objects or instincts most reviled, which then, when their hour strikes, ride the golden coach like that cloacal heroine Cinderella to a dignity and glory far exceeding their once worthier sisters."[3] The charm and power of this view of sublimation resides in the minor spectacle of folk characters rising and falling. Andreas-Salomé might have agreed that folklore and myth are peculiarly enchanting forms of sublimation in a preanalytic sort of way; and I would press the issue of adopting such older means (like folktale and myth) in order to reenchant the Cuban cult of the *mulata* besides (but not too far away from) its erotic and sexist cant. A vernacular Cuban version of Cinderella would not name its heroine *la Cenicienta* but instead *la Tiznada:* in place of ashes, it would have *smut, grime, soot,* as attributes of the sister who all but spends her whole life in the kitchen.

Mulatto Cynegetics

It took me a while to understand why I disliked and found absurd the word *mulatto,* while at the same time finding useful and caressing the words *mulato* and *mulata.* The extra *t* distracted me into false details: was it that creeping, unfamiliar *r*-sound, as when Mrs. Tulliver thanks God for not putting in her family Maggie's hue: "no more nor a brown skin as makes her look like a mulatter"?[4] But my enthralled reading of *The Mill on the Floss* could only confuse the issue of an ambivalence toward *mulatto* soon running into decent dread. The answer was plain and un-literary: I had known, played, and dealt intimately with—and had in fact slept for years next to—people who gladly accepted the name *mulato* in coy and picaresque fashion. Quite besides the erotic cult of the *mulata* I had lived with and loved common beings of that description. On the other hand, American English and polite manners in this country had taught me slowly but surely to regard *all* people of color [*gente de color*] as black. And then, reading deeper into black culture in this country, I thought I learned another, far more interesting fact: the unencumbered richness of hues and colors that blacks have created throughout their history in order to pinpoint their own amalgamation with nonblacks. Racial polemics and white racism prevent this essentially erotic and play-ful impulse—to name hues and verbally flavor them—from breaking into the open.[5]

As far as I know, Freud left no thoughts of great consequence on the matter of race mixture, but one may venture a guess on the matter in reference to his greatest speculation on reproduction and the survival of organisms. In *Beyond the Pleasure Principle,* the fate of *thanatos* is to unravel and destroy the binding impulses of *eros*; rather than disruptive, sexual-ity's aim is seen as life-enhancing. It is hard to imagine a better example of Freud's dualistic norm than the one offered by a race or ethnic group that controls or prevents its own reproductive mixture with other such groups, and which most often would enforce cross-racial taboos on cho-sen (and tacitly on all) females of its own kind. In Freud's grand scheme the distinction between primitive, unicellular, asexual organisms and more developed or sexually reproductive ones plays a dominant role; in this regard, sexual reproduction would seem to imply an inherent ten-dency to procreate mixtures and to insure adaptation through the pro-liferation of somatic differences. Finally, it should not pass unnoticed that, in harboring eggs, the female within sexual reproduction might bring into Freud's biologistic fantasy an archaic tendency on the part of the organism's regressive capabilities to forgo sexual reproduction in favor of self-induced engendering. Were sex to disappear in its present bisexual form, the last race to vanish before the onset of a universe of mothers would be that made up of connected males—of all colors. A close reading of a racist paranoiac like the Southerner Tom Dixon would tend to confirm that behind the specter of miscegenation lies the threat of male extinction and the incestuous horror of excessive masculine dependence on female ovulation.

In this regard, the racist mytheme derived from mule infertility opens the manual of what I should like to call the art of chasing mulattoes, or the cynegetics so lavishly bestowed on their hybrid breed by friends and foes alike. The motifs of the chase and its taxonomy are of central concern in Mark Twain's *Pudd'nhead Wilson* and Faulkner's *Light in August,* regarded by many as the best novels on black-white crossbreeding in American culture.

In Twain's satire, the cryptic fault opened by the mere arrival of children of mixed race runs parallel to their fingerprinting by amateur detective Wilson. It is as if the two milk-brothers belonged more to dactylography than to their breast-mother, with the novel technique of fingerprinting playing the role of an asexual foster parent. One may recall how the *daktuloi,* or Dactyls of Mount Ida in Crete, represent fingertip versions of the Couretes, the ephebic *kouroi* or young men who in various myths undergo initiation, most often in a grand cynegetic affair like the one involving the hunt of the Calydonian boar.[6] Detective Wilson is far from being a sensualist, and therefore lacks one of the features that could qualify him as a racist technician of the flesh and its birthmarks; his business consists in locating minuscule and mintlike traces of difference, so he might not heed the obvious nostalgia that mythic fingertips could feel for the navel, the old *omphalos.* Wilson's addiction to folklore is of the satirical sort, so instead of noting that our primal parents might not have sported a navel, he is quick to remind us of one of their principal advantages: "that they escaped teething." It seems clear that, at least in his *Calendar,* Wilson regards myth and religious folklore with the appetite of a debunking heretic: "Adam was but human. . . . He did not want the apple for the apple's sake; he wanted it only because it was forbidden. The mistake was in not forbidding the Serpent; then he would have eaten the Serpent."[7] Where this leaves Eve is not clear, although Wilson's sense of cannibal instincts in Adam suggests forms of totemic sex between the primal pair worthy of Géza Róheim's psychoanalytic ethnography.[8] Besides Wilson's humor, the lack of a navel (rather than the exemption from teething) has been regarded as a sign of purity in Adam and Eve and their motherless engendering. In his "La creación y P. H. Gosse," Borges begins by reminding us of such a belief,[9] as when Sir Thomas Browne writes: "The man without a Navel yet lives in me" or when Joyce mentions Heva in *Ulysses*: "naked Eve. She had no navel. Gaze. Belly without blemish, bulging big, a buckler of taut vellum, no, whiteheaped corn, orient and immortal, standing from everlasting to everlasting. Womb of sin."[10] Not being a courthouse gnostic, Wilson does not commit the excess of linking the minted identity that he can reveal in the fingertips with the *omphalos,* its inherent place at the center of the garden, its cordlike ties with the mother, and the fanciful notion of her fingers having possibly fashioned that mark in her sons. For it might have been at the navel of some lost garden that the milk-brothers could have found a way to preserve their preracial resemblance as twins, and where they might have kept themselves free from the mythic need of one of them being a criminal. But the hunt exists in order to turn fingers into weapons and brothers into predators and prey. Wilson is the God of the hunt and the labyrinth, he can read the cynegetics of the hands' tenfold name grooved on each finger.

Faulkner's Joe Christmas fits into this mythic framework like a thumb with no print, a sure sign of not having (or ever being) a father. He becomes the object of a chase, a theriomorphic being, and a god of the wild; his tragic and at times grotesquely comic dumbness in human intercourse may suggest that Joe is sacredly sterile. He is more blank than either white or black; Joe is anything but a mulatto: he excels in resembling *no one* in particular, while mulattoes are chased by a culture in which they are forced to resemble someone. Mulattoes are pushed into a racial either/or beyond the boundaries of the properly white. But Faulkner places Joe's tragic presence inside the souls of white folks. In killing only whites, Joe kills that part of himself that whites hate most: themselves. With Joe Christmas, the chase of the mulatto reaches an ontological impasse before the mirror of incest and suicide.

Hamlet and the Sacred Mule

The negro is the human donkey. You can train him, but you can't make of him a horse. Mate him with a horse, you lose the horse, and get a large donkey called a mule, incapable of preserving his species.

—Tom Dixon, *The Leopard Spots*

Ese seguro paso del mulo en el abismo
suele confundirse con los pintados guantes de lo estéril.
(The mule's steady step over the abyss
begs confusion with the painted gloves of sterility.)
    —José Lezama Lima, "Rapsodia para el mulo"

Tom Dixon confuses the blend of black and white with male sterility; and behind his view of blacks as donkeys one can feel him being struck by the fantasy that all blacks are or should be male (one wonders if Dixon ever had a dream in which all men were black, including himself). On his part, Lezama Lima pays poetic homage to the mule, who climbs over the abyss like a beast burdened with sacredness. Such are the extremes of theriomorphia: a formula linking breeder and beast through maleness stands next to a visionary poem in which a beast tremulously climbs the ladder of sacredness. At the very least, the theriomorphic imagination involves two possible acts: the latent crossbreeding of the master with his male beast, and the poet's sublime grasp of transcendent form. The male homoerotic aspect of theriomorphia harks back to those primary processes that were so dear to Melanie Klein, who regarded fantasies as their typical manifestation. In psychoanalytic language, theriomorphia involves the narcissism of the poet, as he shapes forms in his imagination, and the paranoia of the breeder, as he copulates with some ultimate shape of punishing phallicism.[11] Theriomorphia includes two central characters: a narcissist and a masochist. So reduced, the man-animal bonding between metamorphosis and racial mixture can indeed imply that the poet sublimates twice: he lifts breeding into voice and vision, and he transforms the aberrant desire to copulate with himself in beastly form into multiple uplifted figures in his unbound imagination. Such might be the case, in a blunt speculative sense.

In any event, the question of *mulatez* enters history and biography embedded in a racist complex whose deepest sources in fantasy are difficult to fathom without practicing a form of parasitic and erotic racism. In literary fictions, racial mixture and incest go hand in hand; their kinship forces the interpreter into the role of son or Oedipal detective, who repeats in analytic language the destruction of paternal maleness (in both father and son) and the desperate foreclosure of the mother's love already witnessed in the plot. The case of Melville's Pierre Glendinning seems exemplary: from the vast figure of the grandfather (who was "a great lover of horses" and who liked to breed himself into them) comes the delirious assumption of incest in his male grandchild, impotently in love with his dark half sister. In the ruins of narcissistic enthusiasm and pantheistic rhetoric lie both the Glendinning family and Pierre's extinct life as an artist.[12]

Before addressing the place of women in this scenario, I should review it as follows: mulatto theriomorphia is *sexist* (colored by sex) and *homoerotic* (it recognizes in sex the exclusive rule of one gender); the actions of its imaginary characters include the poet's implied but sublimated fusion with the breeder's hated and enviable potency, and the poet's incestuous and hateful kinship with the master's beastly management of reproduction. These ambivalent mergers and intermixtures would also include the woman (she too might be an artist, a *soul*) and her conception of a similar fantasy of rampant maleness; a maleness dominant in what should be (but almost never is) her own untramelled approach to fe-male *mulatez*. Reflected in the mirror of *mulatez,* the *womansheartist* (to echo Faulkner's savage use of "womanshenegro" in *Light in August*) can play several roles: she may cast herself specularly as her own sexual adversary, or as her potential fe-male lover, and also she might engage in the male-exclusive revelry of phallic theriomorphia. Phallocentric? Yes, for, as *mulatas* well know, Phaedra has always been the most feared goddess in the plantation.

Even before reading Reinaldo Arenas's *Graveyard of the Angels,* I thought that Villaverde's understanding of *mulatez* gave direct access to a full theriomorphic scenario. Arenas's satirical reading confirmed my sense of the *daimonic,* of the pagan element in *Cecilia* and the need to translate it in terms of certain outlandish forms of romantic transcendentalism, wholly lacking on the surface of Cuban prose fiction perhaps until Lezama Lima's orphic digressions. When Martín Morúa Delgado deplores the absence in *Cecilia* of "un personaje simpático," or of someone "truly understanding," he might be unwittingly calling for a strong representative of romantic self-love and of the self's own pantheistic beauty. Most critics think that Morúa Delgado's readings of *Cecilia* are resentful and naive, but these critics are mainly interested in building Cuban literature around Villaverde's maturing and belated revisions and expansions of the novel and the purging of his own romantic sensibility; they want Villaverde as a full-fledged social realist.[13] Morúa Delgado rejects what he sees as Villaverde's imprisonment in moralistic romanticism; he wants a more naturalistic novelist, or the kind of writer capable of creating *Sofía,* which became his own answer to the question of the mulatto in *Cecilia.* Unlike Morúa Delgado, I look for evidence of a genuine romantic crisis which Villaverde never quite managed to re-create in his fiction. What I deplore is the absence in Cuba of the artistic and religious ferment that informs the writings of Hawthorne and Melville. (No one has yet explained why Carpentier should have used an epigraph from a Melville letter to Hawthorne near the end of *La consagración de la primavera* (*The Rites of Spring*); the possibility that Carpentier might have felt a void in Cuba's lack of transcendentalist and romantic anxieties should be explored.) Cuban culture in the 1830s and 1840s experienced crisis in resisting colonial despotism and in dealing with the political economy of slavery. In religious matters nothing took place at the time but a shuffling of scholastic formulas. One gets the feeling that our writers were on the run, and that, like a certain fellow in Kierkegaard, just as they were about to be born, they climbed back into the womb nagged by the feeling of having forgotten something. Some of them, like Plácido, were put to death in barbaric fashion; others, like Heredia, Villaverde, and eventually Martí, fled into exile. There was little opportunity in Cuba to create and then to revise and assault an agonistic sense of national consciousness, one freed from harsh political demands; nor was there a well-established philistine class, with its fiction, poems, and temples, capable of driving some imaginations into the sort of domestic alienation from which Hawthorne and Melville began writing. (The epigraph quoted by Carpentier expresses just such alienation; I will quote it only in Spanish in order to preserve its freshness and current urgency in Cuban terms: "¿Cuándo acabaremos de acontecer? Mientras nos quede algo por hacer, nada hemos hecho.") In the end, to appreciate a writer like Villaverde within and without his national boundaries, we ought to imagine him at least in part as a woman writer. In dedicating *Cecilia* from exile to Cuban women, he hoped that they represented those persons most eager to read such a book; but he thought that they should form a group, rather than just a collection of much-worshipped individuals who nonetheless remained an unfulfilled and hidden community.

The absence of a person of sympathy (perhaps a woman) noted by Morúa Delgado should be reinterpreted as the apparent lack of answerable pathos, or of the crucial romantic element of centeredness in *Cecilia*. The invention of such a center of personal depth in Villaverde's melodrama requires a dramatic strategy. The lure of strong feelings that turns sympathy into a call to come inside and to partake of the person's inner turmoil should take effect, paradoxically, as a denial of depth, as an affirmation that the melodramatic unconscious lies outside each major character, and that the soul is on stage, on parade. A drama (or a film) becomes imaginable when based on the notion that one literary work can serve as the concrete unconscious of another. For instance, Melville's Pierre Glendinning could become the full archetype of Leonardo Gamboa, or perhaps his melodramatic antitype. Leonardo's shallowness and frivolity make a travesty of incest; he remains his mother's surrogate, her ambassador to a land of romance whose very existence she denies. But, in assessing this relationship in *Cecilia,* one should think of Pierre, whose ardor to become a writer and to purge evil from his family overwhelms the very notion of any sexual decorum: if incest did not exist, Pierre would invent it. For him, incest represents an artifice, a climate that one can dare to create until it breaks loose and wrecks havoc in the manor. This suicidal assumption is what Pierre's archetype as a ruined artist reveals to Gamboa's indolent sexuality. Critics are both right and wrong when they see an idealist distraction in *Cecilia*'s preoccupation with incest. They are right in seeing its seductiveness, its tokenism of darkness, and its descent from the religion of poets in love with themselves. But the critics are wrong when they fail to see in incest a mode of defense against impersonality and against the absence of an organic community, inside and outside the family. It is fitting then that mulattoes should crop up at the heart of incest fear, but not as their presence is commonly understood. Mulattoes in novels like *Cecilia* should have no part of incest; to begin with, they have all but been deserted by their fathers, and in order to fall into incest, as conceived in these novels, one must have a father. This much might be learned from Pierre: it does not matter whether or not your dark half sister is your father's daughter; in her alluring hues, she incarnates the mother, the *womanity,* the universal and yet particular human being in whom we are all by turn engendered. And Pierre sees in this woman as transcendent object a sort of maleness transfigured, a mishmash that haunts every self-conscious mulatto as well as everyone who, like Pierre, would translate *mulatez,* rather accurately, as *maleness* sublime.

Leonardo Gamboa's dubious sister signifies among other things the real and symbolic exclusion of black and mulatto males from the engendering of *mulatez.* Cecilia is a *sister* by virtue of her nonblack breeder; she is a *daughter* by virtue of her rank within a genealogy of breeding mothers in whom the regressive force of blackness continues to implant sex and predatory mating. These mothers and daughters have something truly sororal about them, as if they represented the elementary structures of the harem. Consider these words: "My great-grandmama told my grandmama the part she lived through that my grandmama didn't live through and my grandmama told me what they all lived through and my mama told me what they all lived through and were suppose to pass it down like that from generation to generation so we'd never forget."[14] The female voice of *mulatez* speaks here in a way not found and yet implicit in *Cecilia*. Actually, this utterance of single-gender lineage can become an instance of reunion, if and when someone like Cecilia Valdés meets a mother like María de Regla, the breast-feeder who sets in motion the daughter-relation in the plot; she also speaks about the dispersal of children and of brothers and sisters in the wake of a rupture in black kinship. Through María de Regla's presence, the two severed sisters in the novel come face to face: Cecilia and her look-alike Adela Gamboa, Leonardo's youngest sister. Sisterhood remains split as long as the father retains his power over these women and keeps them as perennial daughters, whom he one day might seduce. In the role of specular sisters, Cecilia and Adela look at themselves in a mirror held by their father. As their resemblance shifts from portrait into action, their father's features change registers: an allegory of mythic sisterhood replaces any realistic emphasis on the mere facts of crossbreeding.

Adela's portrait at the Gamboa dinner table enhances the father's coinage of her: "There was between father and daughter something more than what is generally regarded as a family resemblance; the same physiognomic expression, the same spirit in her carriage, impressed on her face the seal of her progeny."[15] A second affinity is soon noted between Adela and her father's only son: an *ángel,* a love messenger binds them together; they would love each other like "the most celebrated lovers ever known," if they were not "hermanos carnales" (57). Leonardo inhabits a love triangle drawn by the father and his two daughters. But we should listen to Nemesia, Cecilia's mulatto understudy, who tells her brother José Dolores Pimienta, who is Cecilia's frustrated suitor, that the Gamboa "father and son are in love with Cecilia up to the tip of their hair" (94). Nemesia's words are well-founded: with the Gamboa pair, breeding comes like a one-man tribe in which a single male plays both father and son. In this regard, Leonardo's rapacious loneliness (his being an only son and his lack of a brother) has its own tribal resonance. His mother sends him to Cecilia as to a whore; she knows better than to think of incest regarding this matter; she is in her own ways a better father than her husband. With her blessings, Leonardo enjoys something of the forbidden mother in Cecilia. What arouses the avenging angel in José Dolores Pimienta is the cynical and exclusive use of the *mulata,* as both mother and daughter, on the part of the conspiring white predators; that is why Pimienta plays the Oedipus role that Leonardo has the luxury of avoiding, as long as he can continue to trick Cecilia behind his and her father's back; a father who neither of them really has beyond the rhetoric of breeding. With his vanity nourished by a paternalistic mother and his manhood sought after by one of the father's madwoman creations, Leonardo Gamboa is killed by the excluded mulatto who, unlike him, cannot afford to regard females as objects of leisure; his murder at the hands of Pimienta includes the death of the father as a parasite of the paternal order.

Euripides in Havana

As a matter of theme and technique, incest had already been tried by Villaverde before he undertook writing the first version of *Cecilia*. But he never quite made it out of stories like "El ave muerta" ("The Dead Bird") (1837). Reading it, one struggles with Villaverde to corner incest and to let it fly over the churchyard wall; one tries in vain to awake the brother and the sister as they become narcoleptic; as such, their spiritual ruin turns into a replica of the writer's own failure to produce a successful story. The relative artistic success of the final 1882 *Cecilia* can be attributed to Villaverde's escape from a similar plot and to his attainment of a broad vision of Cuban society. It can equally be said, however, that in his youthful exploitation of romantic themes he failed to translate inspired incest into a theme nimble enough to animate an entire novel. Maybe *Cecilia* was held for too long in the hands of its slowly maturing author, far too long after what might have been its romantic release point.

A partial view of a more romantic *Cecilia* can be obtained by imagining a movie version of it. With a big budget, I would add New Orleans and Rome to the Cuban locations, using as decor George Washington Cable's *The Grandissimes* and Hawthorne's *The Marble Faun*. Imagined in its bare essentials, the film could begin at the dinner table, with a close-up study of resemblances focused on Adela and her father, in preparation to a flashback about the birth of Cecilia, the internment of her mother, and the young nymph's street-urchin life in Havana. This flashback would be narrated from inside a jail cell by José Dolores Pimienta, the closest thing to my protagonist, who would be played by Terence Trent D'Arby, somewhat disfigured by makeup, and cast also, in shameful splendor, in the role of Cecilia as a teenager. In my film, the elder Gamboa will be colored olive brown; he should possess the strong genius of an upstart mulatto, acquired as if by mimicry in his dealings with *negreros*; but in his visits to various octoroon women, he will resemble a properly white Victorian gentleman. Leonardo should be like his mother, both being white and incongruous, speaking and acting like a yuppie couple on holiday from Miami. Finally, Cecilia's grandmother, María de Regla, and Dolores Santa Cruz should be strictly barred from taking any part in the action; they would live in Rome, where the director comes to interview them at intervals that should create a certain choral tone, with the old but quite spirited women risking offhand, nostalgic, but bawdy comments on the entire story.

My present surmise comes to rest on two scenes. Adela is getting down from a carriage, when the snake-bitten Pimienta pulls her hair loose and creates a bronze maiden. Frightened and confused, Adela will dream that, sometime in the near future, a young, beautiful brown woman whom she seems to know by the name of Cecilia finds herself in the same situation. Instead of the unknown man who took away her shell comb, however, it is Leonardo, who in the company of his fiancé looks just like Adela herself, as he gets insulted by this other Cecilia, who somehow seems to look like not only Adela and Isabel but Leonardo as well! As the dream unfolds and gets scary, the insulting maiden begins to look like a harpy, uncannily resembling the dreamer herself, although crude and awesome, like a black Medusa.

My film is becoming too much like a mere dream. Also, I do not know yet how to get to New Orleans, and the trick of bringing that city to Havana seems too literary, in the worst postmodernist style. So I may have to settle for a soap, being content with seeing the same drama changing somewhat with each serial, or from movie to movie. There could always be surprises in this method. For instance, in *The Grandissimes*, Cecilia could become a neo-African princess named Palmyre Philosophe; she would descend from "high Latin ancestry" and be colored with "Jaloff African" tints, and have a "barbaric and magnetic beauty," and be endowed with "mental acuteness, conversational adroitness, concealed cunning, and noiseless but visible strength of will," and have, finally, "that rarest of gifts in one of her tincture, the purity of true womanhood."[16] But this threatens to become a museum piece unless it travels the road of myth. So, as "a little quadroon slave-mate," Palmyre may grow up as the sole playmate of the fair Aurore Nancanou. They are sisters, just like, in a certain way, Cecilia and Adela are, in spite of everything else. But wait, Palmyre and Aurore get separated (for "Aurore had to become a lady and her playmate a lady's maid; but not *her* maid, because the maid had become, of the two, the ruling spirit").

This is just how Adela and Cecilia might separate in order to become heraldic sisters with a third presence ruling over them, the same force of female sacredness that causes Palmyre to be rushed away from Aurore. . . .

Euripides is blamed for inventing melodrama. Perhaps plays like his seriocomic *Ion* should serve as mediators between the unfinished romanticism of *Cecilia* and the mythic coloration of *The Grandissimes*. I think of *Ion* because of the richness of its treatment of Athenian beliefs in racial purity and all the tough questions of birthright, because of its earnest interest in the suffering of women, and because of its ironic reverence for mothers.[17] Besides, *Ion* includes the story of Pallas's slaying of her playmate, the Gorgon, in which I see an archaic instance of the specular themes that inform the relationship among females discussed thus far. Palmyre Philosophe could easily embody Pallas's wisdom and masculinity plus the Gorgon's threat to each of these endowments; but she may also represent the tragic sublation, the simultaneous adoption and banishment of the killing female by the domestic and xenophobic rules of kinship. Thus, Palmyre gives, as Euripides seems to have intended, an ironic view of mythic recognition and, in our terms, of a certain romantic covenant with archaic religion as the ultimate social unconscious. Recessive and gorgonic, Palmyre turns sisterhood into a mirror of surrounding cruelties; the Gorgon becomes an effect rather than just a personified character as she fades into a trauma and then flashes into sudden view and becomes archaic only by virtue of her blunt and at times horrifying recurrence. The Gorgon happens: upon being captured and tortured, a fugitive slave kills himself by swallowing his tongue. Villaverde's close-up description of the black face (eyes bulging out, warrior scars running from eyelids to chin, teeth filed, jaws clenched withholding tongue inside the throat) evokes a bizarre quotation of the Gorgon's apotropaic display; the unseen tongue, swallowed rather than hanging, transfers the grotesque ornamental value of the Gorgon into unspeakable wretchedness. It might seem frivolous to plaster the iconography of a magic toy on a scene of witnessed suffering (Villaverde actually saw what he narrates); but that is precisely the point. At the most graphic moment of its testimonial realism, *Cecilia* comes out of the novelistic frame; and to pretend that nowadays the slave's face would be available to most readers outside of their film memories and expectations, I find ridiculous. After all, films of whatever genre tend to survive within memory in expressionistic fragments, much like myths do in Euripides' melodramatic repertoire.

The idea of the modern Faun . . . loses all the poetry and beauty which the Author fancied in it, and becomes nothing better than a grotesque absurdity, if we bring it into the actual light of day. He had hoped to mystify this anomalous creature between the Real and the Fantastic, in such a manner that the reader's sympathies might be excited to a certain pleasurable degree, without impelling him to ask how Cuvier would have classified poor Donatello, or to insist upon being told, in so many words, whether he had furry ears or no. As respects all who ask such questions, the book is to that extent, a failure.

—Nathaniel Hawthorne (to a reader), *The Marble Faun;*
The Centenary Edition

In the absence of Calvinism and of any subsequent awakenings, the romantic sublime in Cuba could only grow by internalizing and purging other codes, other disciplines of the self not directly influenced by a powerful current of religious egoism.[18] The approach to the sublime in Cuba, as in Villaverde's case, led to the exorcism of the demons of race. Carpentier approached it from the other end, or by celebrating what he once called our *"fecundos mestizajes."* He included his own version of *Cecilia* in Cuba's greatest work of romantic apprenticeship and disenchantment, *El siglo de las luces (Explosion in the Cathedral)*. Like Melville's *Pierre*, Esteban represents Leonardo Gamboa's antitype and, in purely fictional terms, he is Leonardo's precursor. Esteban is the son of a gross merchant, a primitive accumulator who might have died while having sex with a mulatta. In Sofía, Esteban found his incestuous horizons, his literature, and the template of revolt against despotism (those who read *El siglo* as a companion piece to Castro's revolution are only kidding themselves). Esteban is learning to be Stendhal, but he is not quite there yet. At the end of *El siglo,* he seems to have fallen from the pages of one of Ann Radcliffe's romances and into a private diary in which he cannibalizes Chateaubriand's incestuous American pastorals with all the greed of a cultural pariah. Earlier, he relives on a Caribbean beach a Jungian version of Wordsworth's unrevised *Prelude*; and in fact, Esteban and the pilgrim protagonist of that poem visit revolutionary Paris almost at the same time: the main difference in their subsequent political disenchantment lies in Esteban's slow ascent to an ascetic form of eroticism warmed by the savage feminism of mother Sofía.

Had they survived the third of May, 1808, in the turbulent Madrid of Goya, Esteban and Sofía, in their wanderings through Europe, might have run into the young, hauntingly dark and charismatic Simón Bolívar. Esteban would have had to prevent Sofía from running away with this new and improved version of Victor Hughes. Perhaps escaping from him, they would have moved to Italy, and with a stolen treasure bought a villa in the heart of Etruria. I think that their next avatar, or the only way for them to return to America without leaving Europe, is found in late Hawthorne; for it is with him that the theme of transcendental incest reaches a peculiar impasse, in a shift from the myths of poets and revolutionaries to those fashioned by a cultural elite.

In a recent study of *The Marble Faun,* Richard Brodhead argues that Hawthorne wrote it "in full awareness of the contemporary reorganization of the literary sphere"; thus, Hilda becomes "the exponent of the canonical attitude, the attitude that identifies art with an exclusive group of transcendent makers."[19] Earlier in his career, Hawthorne's artist types worked somewhat like pariahs, at the margins of community; like Hester, they were branded with the stigma of sacred pollution. But, in Brodhead's view, Hilda "imagines, in extraordinary precise detail [a counterpart of Hester's eroticism of embroidery?], the mid-nineteenth-century development in which the freshly segregated sphere of secular high art became sacralized, made a new locus for the sacred" (74). Through Hilda, "Hawthorne reads the advent of a canonical model of art as one phase of a more general objectification of authority in his culture, the artistic yield of a process whose products also include the intensification of the superego's abstracting legalism and the compulsory etherialization of erotic life" (75). These are high charges against those who, as cultural tourists, became beacons of moral reference and deserted a hazardous encounter with the spirit of place, or with the sublime and uncanny.

By means of its archeological obsessions with mythic mixtures and the primal breeding of an aristocratic family, *The Marble Faun* elevates the theme of miscegenation to the artistic context of the *Kulturroman* and its inherent cosmopolitanism. A Southern plantation is brought to the ancient navel of Etruria at Monte Beni, but well within reach of Rome. On the other side of Brodhead's view of the elite, I see a portrait of an upper-crust group of unfulfilled bohemians, a troupe of future celebrities and entertainers, of filmmakers. There is a strong hint of publicity, of the search for the right angle and exposure, as if these characters were making a documentary or a television drama on the life of Gibson, for instance, with his "colored Venuses," so pruriently tainted or "stained" with "tobacco juice"; or his Cleopatra, with "full, Nubian lips," inspected and almost professorially flavored by Kenyon. And then of course we have Miriam to contend with: the padded mystery of a celebrity, "the offspring of a Southern American planter," with "the one burning drop of African blood" that drove her into exile. Allegory has a hard time finding unpolluted luster in Rome, where everything exudes a measure of lust; it is no wonder that Hilda has moved up into a tower.

It should be remembered that with the 1860 publication of his romance in Germany, under the title of *The Transformation,* Hawthorne became one of the first American authors to "weave daguerreotypy into his fiction."[20] Since photolithography had not yet been developed, the two volumes were sold with an optional set of original photographs pasted at places deemed appropriate along the narrative. The photograph of Praxiteles' Faun stands out as a kind of unique photogenic object ideal for the delights of theriomorphia; all the generic amalgams in the textures of *The Marble Faun* find quiet resolution in this simple study of ephebic beauty. Seeing it, one can better appreciate the exertions of the allegorical work ethic evident in Hawthorne's descriptions of paintings. The spiritual sweating implied in the enhancement of such artwork evokes the combustive aura generated by lovers during sex. But the painted scene concerns the mixture of eroticism and race. With her own history of amalgamation, Miriam is about to ruin the beatitude of Guido's Archangel subduing Satan: "Just fancy," she tells Kenyon, "a smoke-blackened, fiery-eyed demon, bestriding that nice young angel, clutching his white throat with one of his hinder claws; and giving a triumphant whisk of his scaly tail, with a poisonous dart at the end of it!" This is, she concludes, "what they risk, poor souls, who do battle with Michael's enemy."[21] Such a blasting of Guido's balanced forces creates pollution by mixture; Miriam's fantasy of a painting that she dreads to actually copy may imply that her own mixture of the angelic and the demonic puts her, by turn, in both of the contending and heavily eroticized positions that she awakens in the painting. I see Miriam and Donatello in a transparency: holding them up like a slide, I can see the teenage Cecilia, her theriomorphic image split in two from a vanishing point. On one retina is Donatello, on the other Miriam; and on the retina's target either Praxiteles' Faun or Cecilia herself.

Amid the pastoral accretions of Monte Beni, two bachelors sojourn as they delay what could never be a single wedding. Miriam enters the scene in the role of intruder already patented by the predatory Model when he haunted her and Donatello. She complains to Kenyon about his curious abrogation of Donatello's interest in her: "You are taking him from me . . . and putting yourself, and all manner of living interest, into the place that I ought to fill" (284–85). Kenyon abides, perhaps fearing that the scene could turn into one of Miriam's hideous mental paintings: he does not "pretend to be the guide that Donatello needs"; he is a man, "and between man and man, there is always an insuperable gulf. They can never quite grasp each other's hands; and therefore man never derives any intimate help, any heart-sustenance, from his brother man, but from woman—his mother, his sister, or his wife" (285). I ask: what sort of masochism has taken possession of Kenyon? If his words are meant as premarital wisdom, they border on the perverse. For, in proving that she is fit to marry Donatello, Miriam has had to involve him (and herself) in the violent and contaminating ordeal that should prove that she can become a chaste bride, by showing that she was never a criminal on the occasion of her own outrage—that of being raped by her father. Yet the proof of female innocence obtained by Donatello, the murderous manner in which he grasps and releases it, and the need to have Miriam's vision ravished by the sight of his liberating crime, make her more than ever a suspect in the former perpetration of her own defilement. Here, reenacting the crime means blaming its victim. In not being able (in masochistic fashion) to see this shameful transfer of guilt onto a daughter, Kenyon becomes an impotent sadist toward women, and a potent ally of those females in whose invulnerable chasteness eroticism has died. There is then a dire need for the Etruscan sanctuary in which perennial bachelors (like Kenyon) and ancestral love-objects (like Donatello) can sublimate their sensuousness while embowered in a rustic landscape of immense pictorial femininity, a virtual womb of projected eroticism forbidden to men.

In one of her many celebrations of what she called *protonarcissism,* Lou Andreas Salomé once noted "that huge, simple fact that there is nothing to which we are not native."[22] It seems to me that Hawthorne loved and feared this crude form of pantheism, and that in writing *The Marble Faun,* he found no cure for this ambiguity; if anything, his pantheistic horizons are reached through exhaustion and the wreckage of romance. In *Concierto barroco,* Carpentier took a Cuban African named Filemón all the way to the Venice of Longhi and Vivaldi; I cannot see why Cecilia should not, in similar fashion, migrate to the Rome of Miriam and Donatello, and into a carnival in which she could even play Baubo with all the cunning of a black Athena. I surely would like to find some traces of her there, if I ever reach Rome. I would avoid the Faun out of a certain romantic fear; or as if, upon seeing it, I could suddenly feel very old, incapable of finishing all my readings. But I would go in search of a narrow alley like those in Havana's old colonial center; and there, in front of some suitable effigy, I would utter some words of prayer to our Lady of the Anal Sublime. I would say something in little Italian, like: "Io sono Cecilia, Cecilia Valdés . . ."

John T. Irwin

Mysteries We Reread, Mysteries of Rereading: Poe, Borges, and the Analytic Detective Story; Also Lacan, Derrida, and Johnson*

I

Let me start with a simpleminded question: How does one write analytic detective fiction as high art when the genre's basic structure, its central narrative mechanism, seems to discourage the unlimited rereading associated with serious writing? That is, if the point of an analytic detective story is the deductive solution of a mystery, how does the writer keep the achievement of that solution from exhausting the reader's interest in the story? How does he write a work that can be reread by people other than those with poor memories? I use the term "analytic detective fiction" here to distinguish the genre invented by Poe in the Dupin tales of the 1840s from stories whose main character is a detective but whose main concern is not analysis but adventure, stories whose true genre is less detective fiction than quest romance, as one of the masters of the adventure mode, Raymond Chandler, implicitly acknowledged when he gave the name Mallory to an early prototype of his detective Philip Marlowe.

For Chandler, the private investigator simply represents a plausible form of modern knight-errant. In his essay "The Simple Art of Murder," he says that a detective story is the detective's "adventure in search of a hidden truth, and it would be no adventure if it did not happen to a

*A shorter version of this essay was delivered at the annual meeting of the Poe Studies Association in 1981 at the kind invitation of Kent Ljungquist and Ben Fisher. The essay is part of a book entitled *The Mystery to a Solution: Poe, Borges, and the Analytic Detective Story* presently being completed.

man fit for adventure."[1] The emphasis in Chandler's remarks, as in his fiction, is on the detective's character and his adventures, with the revelation of a hidden truth simply serving as a device to illuminate the former and motivate the latter. But in the pure analytic detective story the matter is otherwise. As a character, Dupin is as thin as the paper he's printed on. As for his adventures, they amount to little more than reading newspaper accounts of the crime and talking with the prefect of police and the narrator in the privacy of his apartment. What gives the analytic detective genre its special appeal is that quality which the Goncourt brothers noted on first reading Poe. In an 1856 journal entry they described Poe's stories as "a new literary world" bearing "signs of the literature of the twentieth century—love giving place to deductions . . . the interest of the story moved from the heart to the head . . . from the drama to the solution."[2] Precisely because it is a genre that grows out of an interest in deductions and solutions rather than in love and drama, the analytic detective story shows little interest in character, managing at best to produce caricatures—those monsters of idiosyncrasy from Holmes to Poirot. In its purest form it puts all its eggs in the basket of plot, and a specialized kind of plot at that. The problem is that this basket seems to be one that can be emptied in a single reading.

Related to this difficulty is another. If the writer does his work properly, if he succeeds in building up a sense of the mysterious, of some dark secret or intricately knotted problem, then he has to face the fact that there simply exists no hidden truth or guilty knowledge whose revelation will not seem anticlimactic compared to an antecedent sense of mystery and the infinite speculative possibilities it permits. Borges, one of the contemporary masters of the analytic detective story, acknowledges this difficulty in his tale "Ibn Hakkan al-Bokhari, Dead in His Labyrinth." He says that one of his characters, "steeped in detective stories, thought that the solution of a mystery is always less impressive than the mystery itself."[3] But if in the analytic detective story the solution is always in some sense an anticlimax that in dissipating the mystery exhausts the story's interest for us, an interest in speculative reasoning which the mystery empowers, then how does one write this kind of story as a serious, that is, rereadable, literary form? How does one both present the analytic solution of a mystery and at the same time conserve the sense of the mysterious on which analysis thrives?

Given the predictable economy of a critical essay, I think the reader is safe in assuming that if I didn't consider Poe's Dupin stories to be, on the one hand, archetypes of analytic detective fiction, and on the other, serious literary works that demand and repay rereading, there would be no reason for my evoking at this length the apparent incompatibility of these modes and thus the writer's problem in reconciling them. All of which brings me to the task of uncrumpling that much crumpled thing, "The Purloined Letter," to consider the way that this problem of a mystery with a repeatable solution, a solution that conserves (because it endlessly refigures) the sense of the mysterious, lies at the very origin of the analytic detective story.

II

My approach to "The Purloined Letter" will be along what has recently become a well-worn path. I want to look briefly at three readings of the story that form a cumulative series of interpretations, each successive reading commenting both on the story and on the previous reading(s) in the series. They are Jacques Lacan's "Seminar on 'The Purloined Letter'" (1957), Jacques Derrida's "The Purveyor of Truth" (1975), and Barbara Johnson's "The Frame of Reference: Poe, Lacan, Derrida" (1978). Each of these essays presents a lengthy, complex argument in which "The Purloined Letter" is treated as a pretext, which is to say, read as a parable of the act of analysis. However, I am not so much interested in following the convolutions of their individual arguments as in isolating a thread that runs through all three, a clue to conduct us through labyrinthine passages. That thread is the position that each essay takes on what we might call the numerical/geometrical structure of the story.

Let us begin with Lacan. He says that the story consists of "two scenes, the first of which we shall straightway designate the primal scene, and by no means inadvertently, since the second may be considered its repetition."[4] The first or primal scene takes place in "the royal *boudoir*" (41), the second scene in "the Minister's office" (42). According to Lacan, each of these scenes has a triangular structure: each is composed of "three logical moments . . . structuring three glances, borne by three subjects, incarnated each time by different characters":

> The first is a glance that sees nothing: the King and the police.
>
> The second, a glance which sees that the first sees nothing and deludes itself as to the secrecy of what it hides: the Queen, then the Minister.
>
> The third sees that the first two glances leave what should be

hidden exposed to whomever would seize it: the Minister, and finally Dupin. (44)

Thus in the royal boudoir, the King does not see the incriminating letter which the Queen in her haste has hidden in the open, leaving it with its address uppermost in plain sight on a table. And the Queen, seeing that the King does not see the letter, mistakes his blindness for the letter's concealment, thus leaving herself vulnerable to the Minister who sees both the King's glance and the Queen's and realizes that the letter can be seized before the Queen's very eyes precisely because she dare not do anything to attract the King's attention to it. Similarly in the second scene, at the Minister's residence, the letter, having been turned inside out and readdressed in a female hand, is once again hidden in plain sight in a card rack on the mantelpiece. And this time the police, who have searched the Minister's quarters repeatedly without noticing the letter, represent that first glance which sees nothing; the Minister, who mistakes the blindness of the police for the concealment of the letter, represents the second glance; and Dupin represents the third glance that sees what the first two miss, that the letter hidden in the open is his for the taking. The figure who participates in both these triangular scenes is the Minister, and his shifting from the position of the third glance in the initial scene to that of the second glance in its repetition exhibits the special vulnerability to self-delusion, to a blind spot, which the possession of the letter conveys.

Consider, now, Derrida's critique of this reading, keeping in mind that in his essay "The Purveyor of Truth" Derrida is motivated less by an interest in Poe or "The Purloined Letter" than by a desire to score points off Lacan. As Johnson points out, Derrida, in a lengthy footnote to his book *Positions,* sketches the argument that will become "The Purveyor of Truth" and cites in this context Lacan's multiple "*acts of aggression*" against him since the publication of *De la grammatologie* in *Critique* in 1965.[5] Obviously, Derrida takes the case of "The Purloined Letter" for one of the same reasons that Dupin did—the Minister once did Dupin "an evil turn" (Poe, 3:993) at Vienna, and Dupin sees the affair of the letter as an opportunity to get even. The wit of Derrida's essay lies in the way that it uses Lacan's reading of "The Purloined Letter" against itself, for if Lacan believes that with his interpretation of the story he has, as it were, gained possession of Poe's "Purloined Letter," has made its meaning his own, then Derrida will show him that the possession of that letter, as Lacan himself pointed out, brings with it a blind spot. In his essay Derrida sets out to repeat the encounter between Dupin and the Minister with himself in the role of Dupin and Lacan in the role of the Minister.

Derrida attacks Lacan's reading of the story on a variety of points, but the one that concerns us has to do with Lacan's notion of the triangular structure of each of the two scenes in the tale. Derrida agrees that the story consists of two scenes, but not the two on which Lacan focuses. He points out that the scene in the royal boudoir and the subsequent scene at the Minister's residence are two narrated scenes within the framing artifice of the story, but that the story itself consists of two scenes of narration—the first scene being the Prefect's initial visit to Dupin during which the Prefect recounts the events in the royal boudoir, and the second scene being the Prefect's subsequent visit during which Dupin recounts the events at the Minister's residence. While the narrators of the two *narrated scenes* in the royal boudoir and at the Minister's residence are respectively the Prefect and Dupin, the narrator of the two *scenes of narration* at Dupin's lodgings is Dupin's unnamed companion. Thus, according to Derrida, Lacan reduces the four-sided structure of the scene of narration—what Derrida calls "the scene of writing"—to the three-sided structure of the narrated scene "by overlooking the narrator's position, the narrator's involvement in the content of what he seems to be recounting."[6] In ignoring the presence of the narrator of "The Purloined Letter," Lacan cuts "a fourth side" out of the narrated figure "to leave merely triangles" (54). And he does this, says Derrida, precisely because as a psychoanalyst, Lacan projects upon Poe's story the structure of the Oedipal triangle in his desire to read "The Purloined Letter" as an allegory of psychoanalysis or *"an allegory of the signifier"* (Johnson, 115).

Now since in his critique of Lacan's interpretation of "The Purloined Letter" Derrida aims to get even with Lacan by being one up on him, and since Lacan in his reading of the numerical structure of the tale has already played the numbers one, two, and three (the tale is composed of two scenes, the second of which, by repeating the triangular structure of the first, creates a sameness or oneness between the two), then being one up on Lacan means playing the next open number (four); and that is what Derrida does in arguing that the structure of the scenes is not triangular but quadrangular. However, whether Derrida arrives at this quadrangular structure by adding one to three or by doubling two is a problematic point, a point on which Johnson focuses in her critique of Lacan's and Derrida's readings of the tale's numerical structure.

As Johnson notes, Derrida objects to the triangular structure which Lacan sees in the repeated scenes because this structure, derived from the Oedipal triangle, represents in Derrida's opinion a characteristic psychoanalytic attempt to dismiss or absorb the uncanny effects of doubling, a doubling which Derrida maintains is everywhere present in the tale. Doubling tends, of course, to be a standard element of the analytic detective story, in that the usual method of apprehending the criminal involves the detective's doubling the criminal's thought processes so as to anticipate his next move and end up one jump ahead of him. And, of course, the number associated with doubling is usually four rather than two, for what we refer to as doubling is almost always splitting and doubling. Which is to say, the figure of the double externally duplicates an internal division in the protagonist's self (but with the master/slave polarity of that division characteristically reversed), so that doubling tends to be a structure of four halves problematically balanced across the inner/outer limit of the self rather than a structure of two separate, opposing wholes. Thus in the first Dupin story, "The Murders in the Rue Morgue," the narrator says that while observing Dupin in the exercise of his "peculiar analytic ability," he entertained "the fancy of a double Dupin—the creative and the resolvent" in accordance with "the old philosophy of the Bi-Part Soul" (2:533). And in "The Purloined Letter" the Minister, as both poet and mathematician, is represented as having this same dual intellectual power. In matching wits with the Minister, Dupin first doubles the Minister's thought processes—a mental operation that Dupin illustrates by telling the story of the schoolboy who always won at the game of even and odd—and he then replays, or temporally doubles, the scene in which the Minister originally seized the letter, but with himself now in the Minister's role, thus shifting the Minister into the role played by the Queen in the original event and evoking the destabilizing "reversal-into-the-opposite" inherent in doubling.

As Johnson notes, Derrida thinks that "the problem with psychoanalytical triangularity . . . is not that it contains the wrong number of terms, but that it presupposes the possibility of a successful dialectical mediation and harmonious normalization, or *Aufhebung,* of desire. The three terms in the Oedipal triad enter into an opposition whose resolution resembles the synthetic moment of a Hegelian dialectic" (122). But that synthetic moment, that successful dialectical mediation of desire, is precisely what the uncanny destabilizing effect of doubling constantly subverts: in the Oedipal triangle each of the three positions functions as one pole of a mutually constitutive opposition with one of the other positions and thus each position is subject to being reversed into its opposite. There exists in the Oedipal triangle, then, no privileged position that is above or outside the uncanny effects of doubling, no exempt, objective position from which to mediate or regularize the subjective interaction of the other two positions.

As with Derrida's reading of Lacan, the wit of Johnson's reading of Derrida lies in the way that she doubles Derrida's own insights back upon themselves to make them problematic. Thus in dealing with Derrida's attempt to be one up on Lacan by playing the number four to Lacan's three, Johnson assimilates their opposed readings of the numerical structure of the tale to the game of even and odd, the game which Dupin proposed as an illustration of the way that one doubles the thought processes of an opponent in order to be one jump ahead of him. Derrida opts for a quadrangular structure, that is, he plays the even number four, in order to evoke the uncanniness, the oddness of doubling; while Lacan opts for a triangular structure by playing the odd number three, in order to enforce the regularizing or normalizing effect of the dialectical triad. In this game of even and odd, Derrida and Lacan end up as reciprocal opposites, as specular doubles of one another: Derrida asserts the oddness of evenness, while Lacan affirms the evenness of oddness. Given the destabilizing reversal-into-the-opposite inherent in doubling, Johnson sees the opposition between Derrida's and Lacan's interpretations as an "oscillation" between the former's "unequivocal statements of undecidability" and the latter's "ambiguous assertions of decidability" (146).

As to Johnson's own position on "The Purloined Letter," her reading of Lacan and Derrida is meant to free her from having to take a position on the numerical structure of the tale, or more exactly, to free her from having to take a *numerical* position on that structure. She does not intend, for example, to play the next open number (five); for since she has reduced Lacan's and Derrida's readings of the numerical structure of the story to the specular game of even and odd, there exist only two numerical positions that one can take on that structure—even and odd—and these, Johnson contends, have already been played by Derrida and Lacan without any clear conclusion. Johnson's strategy is to call into question the whole concern with numbers. At one point she asks, "But can what is at stake here really be reduced to a mere numbers game?"; and a bit later she answers, "Clearly, in these questions, the very notion of a number becomes problematic, and the argument on the basis of numbers can no longer be read literally" (121). As Johnson sees it, taking a position on the numerical structure of the tale means, for Lacan and Derrida, taking a numerical position, choosing a number, but that means playing the game of even and odd, the game of trying to be one up on a specular, antithetical double. And playing that game means endlessly repeating the structure of "The Purloined Letter" in which being one up inevitably leads to being one down. For if the structure created by the repeated scenes in the tale involves doubling the thought processes of one's opponent in order to use his own methods against him—as Dupin does with the Minister, as Derrida does with Lacan, and as Johnson does with Derrida—then the very method by which one outwits one's opponent in order to come out one up on him is the same method that will be employed against oneself by the next player in the game, the next interpreter in the series, in order to leave the preceding interpreter one down.

Is it possible, then, to interpret "The Purloined Letter" without duplicating in the interpretive act that reversal-into-the-opposite inherent in the mechanism of seizing the letter as that mechanism is described in the tale? Is it possible to generate an insight without a blind spot in it, a flaw that allows the insight subsequently to be turned against itself? Clearly, the desire for such an invulnerable insight is at work in Johnson's essay and accounts for the sometimes disconcerting level of self-consciousness which she tries to maintain regarding her own methodological stance, her own critical assumptions. For Johnson the refusal to take a numerical position on the structure of the tale—to play the next open number—is an effort to avoid the game of numerical one-upmanship which will simply turn into an oscillation between even and odd running to infinity. But is it possible for Johnson to avoid becoming involved in this numbers game simply by refusing to choose a specific number with which to characterize the geometrical/numerical structure of the tale? Doesn't the very form of her essay—as a critique of Derrida's critique of Lacan's reading of "The Purloined Letter"—involve her in the numbers game?

In situating her essay as the third in a series of three critical readings, Johnson places herself in that third position which, in the structure governing the wandering of the purloined letter, is not only the position of maximum insight, but also the position in which the observer is subject to mistaking his insight concerning the subjective interaction of the other two glances for an objective viewpoint above such interaction. And indeed, how are we to describe the relationship between Johnson's interpretation and those of Lacan and Derrida? Are they linked in a triangular structure in which Lacan and Derrida face off as antithetical doubles, while Johnson, by refusing to become involved in the game of even and odd, occupies a position of "successful dialectical mediation" above them, a Hegelian synthesis of their positions? Or are they involved in a quadrangular structure in which Lacan and Derrida are reciprocal halves of one pole of a mutually constitutive opposition (that is, the pole of trying to be one up on a specular double), while Johnson occupies the other pole of this opposition by doubling back Lacan's and Derrida's methods against them in order to avoid this game of one up? Indeed, Johnson's final comment on her own methodology invokes the image of Derrida's quadrangular frame: ". . . my own theoretical 'frame of reference' is precisely, to a very large extent, the writings of Lacan and Derrida. The frame is thus framed again by part of its content; the sender again receives his own message backward from the receiver" (146).

Johnson's essay is at odds with itself, as she is the first to acknowledge. Indeed, it is precisely her strategy to present the opposed aspects of her essay—its explicit refusal to take a numerical position on the structure of the tale coupled with its implicit assumption of a numerical position in representing its own relationship to the two earlier critical essays, a numerical position that reinscribes the question of a triangular versus a quadrangular structure present in the tale—as an aporia, as a trope of undecidability not unlike the one which Paul de Man describes in the passage Johnson uses as the epigraph to her book *The Critical Difference,* the book whose final chapter is her essay on Derrida and Lacan.

In that epigraph de Man evokes the aporia between grammar and rhetoric by citing as an example the case in which Edith Bunker asks her husband Archie if he wants his bowling shoes laced over or laced under—to which the irascible Archie replies, "What's the difference?" In terms of grammar Archie's reply asks for the difference between two alternatives, but in terms of rhetoric his reply means "Whatever the difference is, it's not important enough to make a difference to me." De Man remarks, "The same grammatical pattern engenders two meanings that are mutually exclusive: the literal meaning asks for the concept (difference) whose existence is denied by the figurative meaning" (Johnson, v). It is in this same vein that Johnson at the end of her essay, after having described the opposition between Derrida's and Lacan's positions as "the oscillation between unequivocal statements of undecidability and ambiguous assertions of decidability," concludes, "'undecidability' can no more be used as the last word than 'destination.' . . . The 'undeterminable' is not opposed to the determinable; 'dissemination' is not opposed to repetition. If we could be sure of the difference between the determinable and the undeterminable, the undeterminable would be comprehended within the determinable. What is undecidable is whether a thing is decidable or not" (146).

Now what are we to make of these words? By which I mean not just what do these words say grammatically but what do they convey rhetorically, for what purpose are they being said in this context. I think the key lies in Johnson's statement that "'Undecidability' can no more be used as a last word than 'destination.'" At the point she says this, Johnson is nearing her own destination, the end of her essay, and is faced with the formal requirement of saying a last word and thus with the question of whether a last word can be said in the oft-renewed critical discussion of "The Purloined Letter." Having to say a last word, she says in effect, "The last word is that there is no last word."

This type of statement which says one thing grammatically and means its opposite rhetorically occurs again and again in her essay. As we noted, it is the strategy at work when Johnson simultaneously refuses to take a numerical position on the structure of the tale and implicitly assumes a numerical position in relation to the two earlier critical readings which her own essay retrospectively groups into a series along with itself. It is at work again when she turns Derrida's insights on doubling back upon themselves to tell Derrida that it is impossible to be one up on his specular double Lacan, for though what she says on a grammatical level is that it is impossible to be one up in such an encounter, the rhetorical effect of her statement is to leave her one up on her specular double Derrida. And this strategy is at work once again when she decisively concludes, "What is undecidable is whether a thing is decidable or not."

These instances of an aporia between grammar and rhetoric occur in statements that are in one way or another self-reflexive, statements that are themselves included in the class of things to which they refer. A simple example of such a self-including statement would be the sentence "All statements containing seven words are false." Precisely because the sentence is itself a statement made up of seven words, we are faced with a paradox: if this statement is true, it is false, and if it is false, it is true. Similarly, in an aporia between grammar and rhetoric we are faced, as de Man notes, with a single grammatical pattern that engenders two mutually exclusive meanings. By reason of the fact that they include themselves in the class of things to which they refer, these statements double back upon themselves and exhibit that uncanny reversal-into-the-opposite inherent in doubling.

One thinks in this connection of Russell's paradox. Distinguishing between two kinds of classes (those which do not include themselves as members and those which do), Russell calls the first class "normal" and the second "non-normal," and he then doubles back upon itself this distinction between nonself-including and self-including classes by asking whether *the class of all normal classes* is a normal or a non-normal class. By definition *the class of all normal classes* includes within itself all normal classes. Consequently, if it is itself a normal class, it must be included in itself. But self-inclusion is the distinguishing characteristic of a non-normal class. *The class of all "normal classes"* is, then, a concept whose form and content are at odds: on the one hand, the concept involves a formal notion of *class* as absolutely inclusive (that is, as ultimately self-inclusive) that is contradicted, on the other hand, by the content, by the specific definition of the *"classes"* which the former is to include completely within itself. As a result, the class of all normal classes is normal only if it is non-normal, and non-normal only if it is normal. Part of the infinite fascination of paradoxes of self-inclusion is, of course, that they seem to reflect in the facing mirrors of language and logic the mysterious nature of self-consciousness as that which seeks to include wholly within itself an exact representation of that which by its very essence cannot wholly include itself.

At the very start of her essay Johnson sets the tone for all the self-including statements that are to follow when she remarks that in Poe's tale, Lacan's reading, and Derrida's critique, "it is the *act of analysis* which seems to occupy the center of the discursive stage, and the *act of analysis of the act of analysis* which in some way disrupts that centrality. In the resulting asymmetrical, abyssal structure, no analysis—including this one—can intervene without transforming and repeating other elements in the sequence, which is thus not a stable sequence, but which nevertheless produces certain regular effects" (110). The key phrase, of course, is "no analysis—including this one." It has about it the brisk American quality of Mark Twain's "No general statement is worth a damn—including this one"—a general statement worth a damn only if general statements are not worth a damn. The very fact that Johnson makes an analytic statement that includes itself (an analysis of her own analysis) in the sentence immediately following her statement that it is the act of analysis of the act of analysis that skews analysis in Poe, Lacan, and Derrida is her way of announcing her strategy at the start. It is not that Johnson will do anything different in her essay from what Lacan and Derrida have done in theirs. Indeed, it is not clear that she thinks that anything different can be done at this point inasmuch as Lacan and Derrida have already replayed the structure of the tale in a critical register by acting out the game of even and odd in their opposing positions. What will be different in her version is that these positions will be repeated with a complete awareness of their implications, a total critical self-consciousness that aims to create an insight without a blind spot; for what is at issue here is not so much whether one's critical argument is logically true or false, or one's reading of the tale perceptive or dull, but whether one's interpretive stance is methodologically self-aware or methodologically naive.

In its translation from fiction to criticism, the project of analyzing the act of analysis becomes in effect the program of being infinitely self-conscious about self-consciousness. Or put another way, if the structure that we find in "The Purloined Letter" involves doubling an opponent's thought processes in order to turn his own methods against him, then the only defense against having the same strategy repeated against oneself by the next player is to produce an insight or take a position that is already self-consciously doubled back upon itself, as is the case with the type of self-including statement that says one thing grammatically but conveys its opposite rhetorically. For a position that knowingly includes itself and its opposite seems to leave no ground on which it can be undermined.

III

The commitment to an increasingly self-conscious analytic posture that animates this cumulative series of interpretations produces at last a kind of intellectual vertigo, a not uncharacteristic side effect of thought about thought—the rational animal turning in circles to catch itself by a tale it doesn't have. And certainly no one enjoyed creating this vertiginous effect more than did Poe, an effect that he imaged as dizziness at the edge of a vortex or on the brink of a precipice. That the giddy, self-dissolving effect of thought about thought—what Johnson calls the "asymmetrical, abyssal structure" of analyzing the act of analysis— forms the continuing theme of the Dupin stories is announced in the opening sentence of the first tale, "The Murders in the Rue Morgue." The story begins with the narrator's lengthy prefatory remarks on the nature of the analytical power, remarks that conclude by presenting the detective story as a "commentary upon the propositions just advanced"

(2:531). But those prefatory remarks start with this curious proposition: "The mental features discoursed of as the analytical are, in themselves, but little susceptible of analysis" (2:527). Now inasmuch as this statement initiates the narrator's own brief analysis of the analytical power, it is self-reflexive: as an analytic statement about the nonsusceptibility of analysis to being analyzed, the statement is included in the class of things to which it refers, but what the statement says in effect is that analytic statements cannot wholly include themselves. In analyzing the act of analysis, self-conscious thought doubles back upon itself to discover that it cannot absolutely coincide with itself.

This insight about the nature of thought is, of course, at least as old in our tradition as the philosophies of Zeno and Parmenides and as new as Gödel's proof and Borges's (and Carroll's and Royce's) map of natural size. It is the paradoxical insight that if one considers the act of thinking and the content of thought as two distinguishable things—as it seems one must in dealing with self-consciousness, with thought that is able to represent itself to itself, able to take itself as its own object—then the attempt to analyze the act of analysis, to include wholly the act of thinking within the content of thought, will be a progression of the order $n + 1$ to infinity. Which is to say that there will always be one more step needed in order to make the act of thinking coincide with the content of thought.

Since the self-including gesture of analyzing the act of analysis involves a doubling back in which self-consciousness, attempting to be absolutely even with itself, finds that it is originally and essentially at odds with itself, it is not surprising that Dupin, in illustrating the way that one doubles the thought processes of an opponent, gives as an example "the game of 'even and odd'" (3:984). In this game "one player holds in his hand a number" of marbles "and demands of another whether that number is even or odd. If the guess is right, the guesser wins one; if wrong, he loses one" (3:984). Dupin then tells the story of an eight-year-old boy who was so good at this guessing game that he won all the marbles at his school. The boy's "mode of reasoning" involved "an identification of the reasoner's intellect with that of his opponent" (3:984), and this doubling of the opponent's thought processes was achieved by a physical doubling of his appearance. The boy explained to Dupin: "I fashion the expression of my face, as accurately as possible, in accordance with the expression" of the opponent "and then wait to see what thoughts or sentiments arise in my mind or heart, as if to match or correspond with the expression" (3:984–85). The narrator comments that "the identification of the reasoner's intellect with that of his opponent, depends, . . . upon the accuracy with which the opponent's intellect is admeasured" (3:985); and Dupin, agreeing with this observation, adds that "the Prefect and his cohort fail so frequently, first, by default of this identification, and, secondly, by ill-admeasurement, or rather through non-admeasurement, of the intellect with which they are engaged. They consider only their *own* ideas of ingenuity; and, in searching for anything hidden, advert only to the modes in which *they* would have hidden it . . . but when the cunning of the individual felon is diverse in character from their own, the felon foils them, of course. This always happens when it is above their own, and very usually when it is below. They have no variation of principle in their investigations" (3:985).

Now what is going on here? Dupin cannot be the close reasoner that he is reputed to be and not realize that what he has just said undermines his use of the game of even and odd as an illustration of the way one doubles the thought processes of an opponent in order to be one up on him. First of all, if "the identification of the reasoner's intellect with that of his opponent, depends, . . . upon the accuracy with which the opponent's intellect is admeasured," then it cannot be that the Prefect and his men fail, "first, by default of this identification, and, secondly, by ill-admeasurement, or . . . non-admeasurement," for if the identification follows from admeasurement, the Prefect's first failure would have to be in admeasuring the opponent's intellect. And if the reason that the Prefect and his men fail so frequently in this admeasurement is that "they consider only their *own* ideas of ingenuity," that they are unable to imagine or conceive of the workings of a mind "diverse in character from their own" (always the case when the level of the mind is above their own and usually the case when it is below), then is there anything that occurs in the rest of Poe's tale that would lead us to believe this observation of Dupin's about the reason for the Prefect's failure? Which is to say, if the Prefect and his men can only catch felons whose minds are similar to their own and if what they need in this case is the ability to imagine the workings of a mind radically different from their own, then does Dupin's method of outwitting the Minister provide us with any evidence that this ability to imagine a mind radically different from one's own really exists? In fact, isn't all of the tale's emphasis on the resemblance between Dupin and the Minister, on their possessing the same dual creative/resolvent power, part of a plot line in which Dupin outwits the Minister only because their minds are so much alike? Isn't it precisely because the Minister has hidden the letter at his residence in the same way that the Queen hid it in the royal boudoir—by turning it over and leaving it out in the open—that Dupin already knows where to look for the letter when he visits the Minister? And doesn't Dupin recover the letter by replaying the same scenario by which the Minister originally stole it?

Isn't all this simply a device to make us realize that it is impossible to imagine or conceive of a mind whose workings are radically different from one's own? We don't have any direct access to another's thoughts. Our ideas of the workings of another person's mind may be derived from what that person says or does or tells us he is thinking, but our ideas of another's mind are still *our* ideas, a projection that we make of another mind's otherness to one's own based on the only immediate experience that one's mind has of psychic otherness, the self's original otherness to itself, that difference that constitutes personal identity. In his story "Morella" (1835), Poe quotes Locke's definition of personal identity as "the sameness of a rational being" (2:226). But one immediately thinks, "Sameness as opposed to what?" For in differential terms, it makes no sense to speak of the rational being's continuing sameness with itself unless there is also a sense in which the rational being is continually different from itself. In "Morella" Poe says, "Since by person we understand an intelligent essence having reason, and since there is a consciousness which always accompanies thinking, it is this consciousness which makes every one to be that which he calls 'himself'— thereby distinguishing him from other beings that think, and giving him his personal identity" (2:226). It is this difference of thought from itself—which Poe evokes here as the difference between thinking and "a consciousness which always accompanies thinking"—that enables the rational being to recognize its sameness with itself and thus recognize its difference from others, distinguish itself "from other beings that think." It is precisely because the self's thought of another mind's otherness to it reflects the otherness of thought to itself that the effort to imagine the thought processes of an opponent produces a specular, antithetical double of the self, the self's own projection of psychic difference. And consequently, for all that "The Purloined Letter" purports to be about the way in which one effects "an identification of the reasoner's intellect with that of his opponent," it is in fact about that psychic difference which permits thought to be identified with itself, that difference which constitutes self-identity but which prevents thought from ever absolutely coinciding with itself, indeed, which constitutes self-identity precisely *because* it prevents thought from being absolutely even with itself. And it is this difference, this condition of self-conscious thought's being originally and essentially at odds with itself, that Poe evokes at the very start of the Dupin stories when he says that the "mental features discoursed of as the analytical are, in themselves, but little susceptible of analysis."

As is often the case in his fiction, Poe, using the picture language of radicals, emblematizes this latent meaning on the level of etymology, a level to which he explicitly directs our attention in "The Purloined Letter" when he has Dupin, in arguing against those who equate analysis with algebra, remark, "If a term is of any importance—if words derive any value from applicability—then 'analysis' conveys 'algebra' about as much as, in Latin, '*ambitus*' implies 'ambition,' '*religio*,' 'religion,' or '*homines honesti*,' a set of *honorable* men" (3:987). Since in each of these examples an English word has a meaning different from that of its Latin root, the inference seems clear: in "The Purloined Letter," "if a term is of any importance," we should submit that term to philological analysis to see if the root from which it derives has different or additional meanings compared to its English form, meanings that might alter, reverse, or deepen the significance of the passages in which these words appear.

Let me apply this principle suggested by Dupin's remark to two interlocking pairs of words in the tale. On his first visit, the Prefect introduces the affair of the letter like this: "The fact is, the business is *very* simple indeed, and I make no doubt that we can manage it sufficiently well ourselves; but then I thought Dupin would like to hear the details of it, because it is so excessively *odd*." To which Dupin replies, "Simple and odd" (3:975). Dupin's emphatic repetition of the words is meant to fix them in our minds so that later when he describes the game of even and odd, we hear the echo and link the pairs. And to make sure that we don't miss the connection, Dupin, immediately after mentioning the game of even and odd, says, "This game is simple" (3:984).

Simple, even, odd—what are their roots? The word "simple" comes from the Latin *simplex*, meaning "single," "unmixed," "uncompounded."[7] The word "even" derives from the Anglo-Saxon *efne*, meaning "flat," "level," and ultimately from the Indo-European base *im-nos-, meaning "what is the same," and containing the adverbial base *im-, meaning "just like" (503). The word "odd" derives from the Old Norse *oddi*, meaning a "point of land, triangle, hence (from the third angle) odd number" (1017). Three words and at the root of each a number—simple, single, *one*; even, things just alike, *two*; odd, a triangular point of land, *three*. And these three words are grouped into two pairs—simple/odd, even/odd—that contain, as it were, four syntactic places between them which the three words fill by having one of the words repeated. The doubling of the word "odd" links the two pairs; it gives them their element of sameness, evoking that condition of being at odds with itself, that difference with itself, which constitutes the sameness of a rational being (a condition of being at odds with itself that is most clearly perceived when thought tries to be absolutely even with itself). The three words—both through their meanings and through the way that they are paired and linked—are an emblem of the numerical structure that governs the tale, which is to say, of the numerical steps or geometrical patterns that self-consciousness goes through in trying to analyze itself.

Dupin says that the game of even and odd is simple, and throughout the Dupin stories Poe associates simplicity with the highest, purest form of ratiocination. It is in this vein that Dupin suggests to the Prefect on his first visit that "the very simplicity" of the affair of the letter constitutes its oddness: "Perhaps the mystery is a little *too* plain. A little *too* self-evident" (3:975). And later Dupin says that the Minister, in hiding the letter, "would be driven, as a matter of course, to *simplicity*, if not deliberately induced to it as a matter of choice" (3:989). As in that "game of puzzles . . . played upon a map" (3:989), the Minister would choose a hiding place that would "escape observation by dint of being excessively obvious," relying on the fact that "the intellect suffers to pass unnoticed those considerations which are too obtrusively and too palpably self-evident" (3:990). But what is that simple thing whose very simplicity makes it so odd, that thing which is so mysterious because so obvious, hiding out in the open "immediately beneath the nose of the whole world" (3:990)? What but self-consciousness, that condition of being at odds with itself that constitutes the sameness, the singleness, the simplicity of a rational being?

By definition a number is odd if when the number is divided by two, there is a remainder of one. And by that definition the first odd number is three. In that simple game of even and odd in which self-consciousness analyzes itself, the question inevitably arises as to whether, when the mind's desire to be absolutely even with itself is divided into the mind's essential condition of being at odds with itself, the one that is always left over is the same as the number one that precedes two, the same as that mythic, original, undivided unity prior to all paring/pairing. Or put another way, when the mind tries to make the act of thinking coincide absolutely with the content of thought only to find that there is always one more step needed to achieve this coincidence, is the infinite progression that results simply the mirror image, the antithetical double, of a Zenonian infinite regression which, by dividing a quantity in half, then dividing the half in half, then dividing the quarter in half and so on to infinity, seeks a lower limit, a part that cannot be halved again, a thing so small that, being indivisible, it represents an undivided unity, an original one? Poe is too good both as philosopher and philologist not to know that the simple thing that is self-consciousness could never be as simple as that. Indeed, if the mind were ever able to make the act of thinking and the content of thought coincide absolutely so that there was no difference between them, then self-consciousness, that self-identity constituted by thought's difference from itself, would simply go out like a light. Such an undifferentiated one would be indistinguishable from zero. Though the root of the word "simple," the Latin *simplex,* means "single," "unmixed," "uncompounded," the roots of the word *simplex*—the Latin words *semel,* meaning "once," "a single time," and *plico,* meaning "to fold, fold together"[8]—make it clear that to be unmixed or uncompounded does not mean to be undifferentiated. For in the picture language of these radicals we can see that a thing which is single-fold— like a sheet of paper, a letter—is something that in being folded a single time is doubled back upon itself. That the image of self-consciousness as a *simple* fold doubling an inscribed surface back on itself was in Poe's mind when he plotted the folding/refolding of the purloined letter can be inferred from an 1845 poem on folding money called "Epigram For Wall Street" attributed to him:

> I'll tell you a plan for gaining wealth,
>> Better than banking, trade or leases—
> Take a bank note and fold it up,
>> And then you will find your money in *creases!*
> This wonderful plan, without danger or loss,
>> Keeps your cash in your hands, where nothing can trouble it;
> And every time that you fold it across,
>> 'Tis as plain as the light of the day that you *double* it! (1:378)

The infinite progression implicit in the analysis of the act of analysis is evoked at the end of "The Purloined Letter" with the revelation of Dupin's revenge on the Minister, for this attempt by a mastermind to get even with his specular double clearly serves as a figure of the analytic mind's attempt at mastery, its attempt to be absolutely even with itself. Knowing that the Minister "would feel some curiosity in regard to the identity of the person who had outwitted him" (3:993), Dupin leaves him a clue by substituting for the purloined letter one containing a quotation from Crébillon's *Atrée* copied out in Dupin's own handwriting, a hand with which the Minister "is well acquainted" (3:993). In signing his deed, Dupin marks it as revenge, which is to say, he insures that the Minister will interpret his actions not simply as the paid intervention of a gifted amateur sleuth or a duel of wits between two of the cleverest men in Paris, but as a repayment for the evil turn which the Minister did Dupin at Vienna. For I take it that the satisfaction of revenge requires—except in those cases where it is carried out on a substitute—a moment of revelation in which the object of revenge learns by whom and for what he is being paid back, a point that Poe underlines by having Dupin choose his quotation-signature from just such a revelatory moment in an eighteenth-century revenger's tragedy. And yet from what we know of the Minister it is inconceivable that once he learned of Dupin's revenge he would let the matter rest there—and equally inconceivable that his double would not know this. For though it might seem that with Dupin's revenge the score between them is even at one apiece (one bad turn at Vienna repaid by one bad turn at Paris), if the Minister allows Dupin's trick to go unanswered, then Dupin will have had the last turn; and, as proverbial wisdom assures us, the last word or the last laugh is not just one word or one laugh like any other. The power to say the last word or have the last laugh, the power to bring a series of reciprocal actions to an end, like the power to originate, involves the notion of a one that is simultaneously more than one. Consequently, we are left with the paradoxical situation in which Dupin's outwitting of the Minister will constitute an evening of the score between them at one apiece only if the Minister *does not* allow Dupin's trick to end the series, does not allow it to be that one last turn which in its finality is always more than one. It is not so much that one bad turn deserves another as that one bad turn demands another if it is to be experienced as simply one turn. All of which emphasizes the mutually constitutive contradictoriness of seeking *to get even* with a specular double *by being one up on him*.

In using the affair of the letter to even an old score, Dupin gives up his "objective" fourth position as an apparently disinterested observer of the triangular structure of King, Queen, and Minister described by the Prefect, in order to insert himself for personal reasons into the third position of an analogous triangle in which the police and the Minister occupy respectively the first and second positions. Similarly, in describing this triangular structure in which Dupin shifts the Minister from the third to the second position, Lacan would himself appear to occupy an "objective" fourth position as a disinterested observer outside the triangle. Yet to a supposedly more objective observer of Lacan's position such as Derrida, Lacan's description is not disinterested at all, but simply a psychoanalyst's imposition of the structure of the Oedipal triangle on a double story. This imposition, though seemingly made from an objective fourth position outside the triangle, has the effect of inserting Lacan into the third position of a triangle in which the psychoanalyst's "objective" unmasking of the personal motive that lies behind Dupin's "disinterested" involvement in the affair of the letter shifts Dupin into the second position and his double the Minister into the first. Or so says Derrida from a fourth position outside Lacan's triangle, a fourth position that will itself be shifted in turn.

This mechanism by which the shifting from the third to the second position within the triangle is extended (as a supposedly more objective point of view is assumed from which to observe the subjective triangle), and thus becomes the shifting from a fourth position outside the triangle to the third position within it, evokes the infinite regression that, in this quest for absolute self-consciousness, accompanies infinite progression as its shadow image. For while the progressive series moves in one direction in its flight from subjective involvement, in its termless search for an absolutely objective point of view from which to examine the self, it only exists *as a series* because of the regressive movement of consciousness, because of the retrospective gaze that keeps all the earlier terms of the series in view so that they are perceived as related, as serial in character. Thus the mental step that one takes in order to separate the self from itself, to distinguish absolutely the observer from the observed, is always a backward step, a step in the opposite direction from the one in which we are looking.

IV

In the sardonic name of simplicity let me add one more, final (or else one, more final) element to this discussion. So far we have looked at three analytic readings of "The Purloined Letter" by Lacan, Derrida, and Johnson, and then gone back to consider Poe's own self-conscious thematizing within the story of the numerical/geometrical structure enacted in its interpretation. I would now like to look at a literary reading of Poe's tale that antedates the earliest of the three analyses we have considered by some fifteen years: the reading that Borges gives of "The Purloined Letter" when he rewrites its numerical/geometrical structure in his own detective story, "Death and the Compass" (1942).

In the story's opening paragraph Borges explicitly links the tale to Poe's Dupin stories, remarking that his detective Erik Lönnrot "thought of himself as a pure logician, a kind of Auguste Dupin" (65). "Death and the Compass" concerns a series of murders. All the obvious clues suggest that the number in the series will be three, but all the less than obvious clues—the kind that police inspector Treviranus would miss, but Erik Lönnrot wouldn't—suggest that the number of murders will be four. We learn at the end of the story that the series of crimes has been planned by Lönnrot's archenemy, the criminal Red Scharlach, who, seeking to lure Lönnrot unawares to his own destruction, has counted on the fact that the detective would solve the arcane clues which Inspector Treviranus missed and that Lönnrot's intellectual pride would blind him into thinking that because he was one jump ahead of the police, he was one jump ahead of the criminal as well. In effect Borges reworks the triangular structure from "The Purloined Letter." He has Scharlach create a situation in which Lönnrot's apparent solution to the crimes constitutes that second glance whose observation of blindness in the first glance (Treviranus's apparent misreading of the clues) becomes itself a blind spot in the observer by convincing him that he sees everything. In the meantime Scharlach occupies the position of the third glance (hidden at the fourth point of the compass), seeing the blindness of the first glance, the blind spot in the second, and the fact that the object he seeks—Lönnrot's life—is his for the taking.

Lönnrot and Scharlach are, of course, doubles of one another, as their names indicate. In a note to the English translation of the tale Borges says, "The end syllable of Lönnrot means red in German, and Red Scharlach is also translatable, in German, as Red Scarlet" (269). Elsewhere Borges tells us that Lönnrot is Swedish, but neglects to add that in Swedish the word *lönn* is a prefix meaning "secret," "hidden," or "illicit." Thus Lönnrot, *the secret red,* pursues and is pursued by his double, Red Scharlach (Red Scarlet), *the doubly red.*

Scharlach's motive is revenge. In their final confrontation, Scharlach reminds Lönnrot that three years earlier the detective had arrested Scharlach's brother in a gambling dive and that in the ensuing shootout Scharlach had escaped, as he says, with "a cop's bullet in my guts" (75). In hiding, delirious with fever for nine days and nights, "I swore," says

Scharlach, "by the god who looks with two faces and by all the gods of fever and of mirrors that I would weave a maze around the man who sent my brother to prison" (76). I take it that this elaborate revenge on "a kind of Auguste Dupin" for the arrest of a brother is an allusion to the fact that in "The Purloined Letter" the Minister D ———— has a brother with whom he is sometimes confused because they "both have attained reputation in letters" (3:986). Since Dupin gets even with the Minister, are we to see Scharlach's revenge on Lönnrot as an attempt to even the score for that earlier revenge on a brother criminal?

The maze that Scharlach weaves around the detective begins with the murder of Rabbi Marcel Yarmolinsky on the third of December at a hotel in the north of the city. Yarmolinsky is a Talmudic scholar, and among his effects the police find "a treatise . . . on the Tetragrammaton" and a sheet of paper in his typewriter bearing the words "*The first letter of the Name has been uttered*" (67). The second murder occurs on the night of January third in the west of the city. The victim, Daniel Simon Azevedo, is found lying on the doorstep of a paint store beneath "the shop's conventional red and yellow diamond shapes" (68–69). Chalked across the diamond shapes are the words "*The second letter of the Name has been uttered*" (69). The third murder occurs on the night of February third in the east of the city. The victim, whose name is either Gryphius or Ginzberg, telephones Treviranus offering to give him information about the murders of Yarmolinsky and Azevedo, but the call is interrupted by the arrival of two men who forcibly remove Gryphius-Ginzberg from the sailors' tavern where he has been staying. It is Carnival time and the two men are wearing harlequin "costumes of red, green, and yellow lozenges" (70). Tracing the interrupted phone call, Treviranus arrives at the tavern to find scrawled on a market slate in front "*The last letter of the Name has been uttered*," and in Gryphius-Ginzberg's room "a star-shaped spatter of blood" and "a 1739 edition of Leusden's *Philologus Hebraeo-Graecus*" with the following passage underlined: "the Jewish day begins at sundown and ends the following sundown" (71). On the night of March first Treviranus receives a sealed envelope containing "a letter signed by one 'Baruch Spinoza'" (72) and a map of the city. The letter writer predicts that on the third of March there will not be a fourth murder because the locations of the three previous crimes in the north, west, and east form "the perfect sides of an equilateral and mystical triangle" (72), as demonstrated by a triangle drawn in red ink on the map.

Appropriately, the letter predicting that only three men will be killed is sent to Treviranus, the first two syllables of whose name recall the Latin words for "three" and "man"—*tres* and *vir.* The Inspector's name probably alludes as well to the *tresviri capitales,* a group of three magistrates who "exercised general control over the city police" in republican Rome. According to the eleventh edition of the *Encyclopaedia Britannica,* "Caesar increased their number to four, but Augustus reverted to three. In imperial times most of their functions passed into the hands of the *praefectus vigilum*"[9]—an etymological-historical link between Borges's Treviranus and Poe's Prefect. Not to mention the fact (which Borges must have noticed) that the emperor who restored the number of the *tresviri capitales* from four to the original three also gave his name to the detective C. (César) Auguste Dupin. In "An Autobiographical Essay" (1970), Borges reports that he used part of the proceeds from a literary prize he received in 1929 to acquire "a secondhand set of the Eleventh Edition of the *Encyclopaedia Britannica*" (233), by no means an insignificant detail in the life of a writer obsessed with the image of the encyclopaedia, a writer who says that some of his earliest memories are of "the steel engravings in *Chambers's Encyclopaedia* and in the *Britannica*" in his father's library (209).

It is worth noting that in the eleventh edition of the *Britannica* the entry for *tresviri* occurs on the page facing the entry for Gottfried Reinhold Treviranus (1776–1837), a German naturalist. Not unpredictably, Inspector Treviranus's first words in the story point to the numerical image that lies at the Latin root of his name: " 'We needn't lose any time here looking for three-legged cats,' Treviranus said, brandishing an imperious cigar. 'Everyone knows the Tetrarch of Galilee owns the world's finest sapphires. Somebody out to steal them probably found his way in here by mistake. Yarmolinsky woke up and the thief was forced to kill him' " (66). The only historical Tetrarch of Galilee, as the entry for *tetrarch* in the *Britannica* informs us, was Herod Antipas—the Herod of the gospels—whose reign (4 B.C.–A.D. 39) began under the emperorship of Augustus Caesar (hence Treviranus's "imperious cigar") and bracketed the life of Christ. At the death of Herod the Great in 4 B.C., his realm was divided among his three sons: half went to Archelaus, with the title ethnarch; a quarter to Philip, with the title tetrarch; and a quarter to Herod Antipas, with the same title. As with Treviranus's initial image of a four-legged animal with only three legs, his reference to the Tetrarch of Galilee—with its historical resonance of a quadripartite realm divided among three people by doubling the portion of one of them—evokes the numerical structure that governs the tale. That Borges intends the historical allusion (and intends for us not to miss it) seems clear from an exchange between Lönnrot and the editor of a Yiddish newspaper at the scene of Yarmolinsky's murder: " 'Maybe this crime belongs to the history of Jewish superstitions,' Lönnrot grumbled. 'Like Christianity,' the editor from the *Judische Zeitung* made bold to add" (67). Need I add that the entry for *tetrarch* in the eleventh edition of the *Britannica* occurs on the page facing the entry for *Tetragrammaton*.

Treviranus sends the map with the red triangle and the letter suggesting that the number of murders will be three to Lönnrot who now has, he believes, the final clue needed to capture the murderer. Since the letters in the Tetragrammaton are four rather than three, since the Jewish day begins at sundown so that the three murders were committed not on the third but the fourth day of each month, and since in both the second and third murders a diamond shape is prominently displayed, Lönnrot concludes that the series of murders is not threefold but fourfold and that the shape which the locations of the crimes describe on the map is not a triangle but a diamond. Using a pair of dividers and a compass, Lönnrot pinpoints the location of the planned fourth murder in the south of the city, "the deserted villa Triste-le-Roy" (73); and he arrives there well in advance, so he thinks, of the murderer to catch him in the act.

But, of course, at the villa of Triste-le-Roy—a building of intricate doublings, a kind of House of Usher designed by Zeno the Eleatic—Scharlach is already lying in wait and easily captures Lönnrot. Completing his triumph, Scharlach explains the maze to his prisoner. "The first term of the series came to me by pure chance," says Scharlach. He and some of his associates—among them Daniel Azevedo, the second victim—had planned to commit a jewel robbery at the hotel where Rabbi Yarmolinsky was staying. Double-crossing his friends, Azevedo tried to commit the robbery a day early, got into Yarmolinsky's room by mistake, and killed the rabbi when he tried to ring for help. From the newspaper accounts of the crime, Scharlach learned that Lönnrot was seeking the key to Yarmolinsky's death in the rabbi's writings, and so he planned the series of murders to encourage Lönnrot's belief that Yarmolinsky had been sacrificed by a group of Hasidic Jews in search of the secret and unutterable Name of God, a ruse to keep Lönnrot looking in the wrong direction while being led to his own destruction. Appropriately, the second victim was the double-crosser Azevedo, while the third murder was simply a ruse with Scharlach himself doubling as the victim Gryphius-Ginzberg.

Borges gives us a clue to the type of cabalistic design on which Scharlach's labyrinth is based when he tells us that among the books written by Yarmolinsky and found in his room at the time of his death there was "a *Study of the Philosophy of Robert Fludd*" (67), the seventeenth-century English physician and Christian cabalist whose work on geomancy ("a method of divination by means of marking the earth with a pointed stick" [Poe, 2:420]) Poe had included a century earlier in his catalogue of Roderick Usher's favorite reading (Poe, 2:409). In Fludd's major work, *Utriusque cosmi majoris scilicet et minoris metaphysica, physica atque technica historia* (1617–1619), we find the following diagram illustrating the mirror-image relationship between God and the universe:[10]

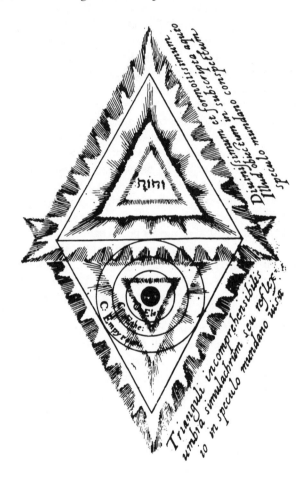

At the center of the upper triangle (whose angles represent the three persons of the Trinity) is the Tetragrammaton, and along one side a Latin legend which reads: "That most divine and beautiful counterpart visible below in the flowing image of the universe" (83). In the lower triangle are "the three regions of the universe—empyreal, ethereal, and elemental" which correspond to "the triangular form of the trinitarian deity," and along one side of this is the Latin legend: "A shadow, likeness, or reflection of the insubstantial triangle visible in the image of the universe," the lower triangle being "a projection of an idea" in the divine mind and thus a mirror image of the deity (83–84). Surrounding both triangles is a flamelike effulgence suggesting at once the radiant nature of this Platonic projection or emanation, the symbolic character of the deity as fire or pure light (i.e., as mind), and the traditional imagistic association (going back at least to the Egyptians) of the triangle with the tip of a flame (pyramid and obelisk being stone flames above a grave) and thus with eternal life.

Since Scharlach knows from the newspaper accounts that Lönnrot began his investigation of the murders by reading Yarmolinsky's works on cabalism, and since one of these is a study of Robert Fludd's mystical philosophy, it seems likely that the type of schema shown here was the model for Scharlach's labyrinth and that it is this cabalistic design which Lönnrot believes he is tracing on the landscape when in his initial surprise at finding Scharlach waiting at the fourth point of the compass he asks, "Scharlach, are you after the Secret Name?" (75).

Realizing that he has been outwitted and that he is about to be killed, Lönnrot tries to have the last word by finding a flaw in Scharlach's maze. Using a favorite ploy of mathematicians and logicians—that Scharlach's plan, though successful, violates the principle of economy of means—Lönnrot says,

> In your maze there are three lines too many. . . . I know of a Greek maze that is a single straight line. Along this line so many thinkers have lost their way that a mere detective may very well lose his way. Scharlach, when in another incarnation you hunt me down, stage (or commit) a murder at A, then a second murder at B, eight miles from A, then a third murder at C, four miles from A and B, halfway between the two. Lay in wait for me then at D, two miles from A and C, again halfway between them. Kill me at D, the way you are going to kill me here at Triste-le-Roy. (78)

In his note to the tale, Borges identifies "the straight-line labyrinth at the story's end" as a figure taken from "Zeno the Eleatic" (269). This closing image of infinite regression as the endless subdivision of a line inverts, of course, the figure of infinite progression evoked in the tale by the movement from a triangular to a quadrangular maze, which is to say, the figure of infinite progression as the endless addition of sides to a polygon—the figure that symbolizes the attempt to integrate the process of thinking into the content of thought as the attempt to incorporate an "objective" point of view outside a structure (e.g., the fourth point from which one views a triangle) into a more inclusive, more self-conscious formulation by making that viewpoint another angle of the structure (e.g., the progression from triangle to quadrangle).

As we noted earlier, in the mind's quest to comprehend itself totally, to be absolutely even or at one with itself, infinite progression and infinite regression represent reciprocal paths to the idealized ground of the self, to its original, essential unity—infinite progression pursuing an absolute unity figured as totality, infinite regression pursuing an absolute simplicity figured as indivisibility. Part of the numerical mystery of individual self-consciousness is that though it is only one thing in a world of many things, for its individual possessor it is one thing that is everything. And this absoluteness of individual self-consciousness for its possessor not only underlies the absolute means employed in quest of the self's origin (i.e., infinite progression/regression) but also projects itself naturally into the quest for a universal origin figured as a personified Absolute Consciousness, that Infinite Being whose consciousness is the one thing that is everything for every thing.

Translated into a religious context, infinite regression and infinite progression, as reciprocal modes of seeking an ultimate origin conceived as either a lower or an upper limit of consciousness, suggest the *via negativa* and the *via positiva* of mystical theology. In the *via negativa* one seeks an unmediated encounter with the divine origin by subtracting attributes from, by denying affirmative predicates to, the idea of God until one finally achieves a personal experience of the transcategorial nature of Being. Of this method Borges remarks, "To be one thing is inexorably not to be all the other things. The confused intuition of that truth has induced men to imagine that not being is more than being something and that, somehow, not to be is to be everything."[11] In the *via positiva* one takes the opposite path, constantly adding affirmative predicates to the concept of God until that concept becomes an absolute totality; though what one experiences in this path is once again the transcategorial nature of Being. In his essay "From Someone to No-body" in which he sketches the historical oscillations of the concept of the Judeo-Christian God, Borges describes the reciprocal character of these two methods as "magnification to nothingness" (*OI*, 147).

Given Borges's interest in the way that the classical pursuit of a microcosmic and a macrocosmic limit becomes the religious quest for the origin and end of all things, it is not surprising that as Lönnrot gets caught up in the quest for the sacred and unutterable Name of God, the meeting at the fourth point of the compass (a proleptic figure of infinite progression) comes to seem like a face-to-face encounter with the one, infinite, divine origin of all things. And inasmuch as Lönnrot will die at that fourth point, it does turn out to be the place where he will meet his maker (his mental double).

Agreeing to Lönnrot's request that he trap him in a straight-line labyrinth in their next incarnation, Scharlach takes a step back and shoots the detective with his own gun—shoots him in the head, one would guess, the right spot to drop a pure logician. In his note to the tale, Borges says, "The killer and the slain, whose minds work in the same way, may be the same man. Lönnrot is not an unbelievable fool walking into his own death trap but, in a symbolic way, a man committing suicide" (269). What with the presence of the color red in the names of slayer and slain and their talk of repeating their duel in another incarnation, one is reminded of Emerson's poem "Brahma" (which Borges cites in his 1947 essay on Whitman):[12]

> If the red slayer think he slays,
> Or if the slain think he is slain,
> They know not well the subtle ways
> I keep, and pass, and turn again.
>
> Far or forgot to me is near;
> Shadow and sunlight are the same;
> The vanished gods to me appear
> And one to me are shame and fame.

One question, however, still remains to be settled. Does Borges, in rewriting the numerical/geometrical structure of "The Purloined Letter" in "Death and the Compass," see that structure as threefold and triangular (as does Lacan) or fourfold and quadrangular (as does Derrida)? Certainly Scharlach's labyrinth seems to be fourfold and diamond-shaped. But inasmuch as the murder of Gryphius-Ginzberg was a ruse in which the criminal doubled as the victim, there were really only three crimes, and these three—the murders of Yarmolinsky in the north, Azevedo in the west, and Lönnrot in the south—form a triangle on the map. And if the labyrinth is really threefold and triangular, then all the obvious and simple clues indicating that there would only be three crimes are the correct ones. But if the correct number is three, then what becomes of the name that is being uttered letter by letter? If it is not the four-letter name of God that Borges means to evoke, then is it the three-letter name of Poe, the creator, the origin, of the detective genre?

Before deciding, however, that the structure is threefold and triangular, we should recall that there finally turns out to be three crimes only because one of the doubles correctly interprets all the arcane clues and presents himself at the fourth point at the expected moment. Is the numerical structure that Borges rewrites from "The Purloined Letter," then, that of the two interlocking pairs of words (simple/odd, even/odd), a structure in which three things are made to fill four spaces by doubling one of them—and all as part of the mind's quest for an original undivided one, for a mythic absolute simplicity? Inasmuch as Lönnrot's search for God's "Secret Name" (75) at the fourth point of the quadrangle symbolizes this quest for an original undivided one, it is significant that the Tetragrammaton, "God's unspeakable name" (68), has the same structure in all its various spellings (JHVH, IHVH, IHWH, YHVH, YHWH) as that of the two interlocking pairs of words in "The Purloined Letter," which is to say that three different letters are made to fill the four spaces of the name by doubling one of them (H). It is also worth noting that in the case of both the sacred name and the interlocking pairs of words the repeated letter or word occupies the second and fourth spaces—the numbers characteristically associated with doubling. (One might also note, given the quadrangular aspect of Scharlach's maze, that two is the only number for which doubling and squaring are the same operation.)

Borges's rewriting of the numerical/geometrical structure of "The Purloined Letter" in "Death and the Compass" assumes an even greater significance when we realize that it was part of a larger project in which he set out to double Poe's three Dupin stories a century later with three detective stories of his own. But with this difference: where Poe's detective solves the mystery and outwits the culprit, Borges's detectives or pursuers are outwitted by the people they pursue, are trapped in a labyrinth fashioned from the pursuer's ability to follow a trail until he arrives in the chosen spot at the expected moment. We should note, however, that in these stories Borges consistently undercuts the notion that the culprit's triumph, his being one up on his opponent, ultimately makes any real difference. "And one to me are shame and fame" might almost be the motto of these encounters.

The first Dupin story, "The Murders in the Rue Morgue," was published in 1841; Borges's first detective story, "The Garden of the Forking Paths," was published exactly one hundred years later in 1941. As Howard Haycraft, the historian of the detective genre, notes, there were "several events which marked the Centennial of the Detective Story in 1941": one was the first issue of *Ellery Queen's Mystery Magazine,* another was the publication of Haycraft's own magisterial *Murder for Pleasure: The Life and Times of the Detective Story.*[13] And yet another, it seems certain, was the publication of Borges's first detective story, which, he recalls, "won a second prize in *Ellery Queen's Mystery Magazine*" (*Aleph,* 273). The second Dupin story, "The Mystery of Marie Rogêt," first appeared in 1842–1843 in serial form; while Borges's second detective story, "Death and the Compass," was first published in 1942. This story was also submitted to *Ellery Queen's Mystery Magazine* but, as Borges ruefully notes, "was flatly rejected" (273).

The third Dupin story, "The Purloined Letter," was published in 1844, but Borges's third story, "Ibn Hakkan al-Bokhari, Dead in His Labyrinth," was not published until 1951. In his note to the story Borges accounts for this break in the pattern, commenting that after his "first two exercises of 1941 and 1942" his third effort "became a cross between a permissible detective story and a caricature of one. The more I worked on it, the more hopeless the plot seemed and the stronger my need to parody" (274). It is as if in reaching the third term of this series Borges realized that his effort to double Poe's three analytic detective stories— perhaps with the idea of going one up on the inventor of the genre— had gone awry and that he was himself trapped in the triangular/quadrangular labyrinth that Poe had constructed in "The Purloined Letter."

Certainly, in Borges's final detective story the allusions to "The Purloined Letter" are numerous, culminating in an explicit reference. In the tale, two friends, Dunraven and Unwin, try to decipher the mystery of Ibn Hakkan al-Bokhari's death in his own labyrinth. At one point Unwin says, "Don't go on multiplying the mysteries. . . . They should be kept simple. Bear in mind Poe's purloined letter, bear in mind Zangwill's locked room." To which Dunraven replies, "Or made complex. . . . Bear in mind the universe" (116). I assume that the name "Dunraven" is an allusion to the author of "The Raven," as the name "Unwin" is to the unwinnable game of trying to be one up on a double, assumptions supported by the fact that Dunraven is a poet and Unwin a mathematician. These occupations recall as well the discussion of the dual character of the Minister D____ in "The Purloined Letter." Thinking that they have confused the Minister with his brother who has also "attained reputation in letters," the narrator identifies D____ as "a mathematician, and no poet." To which Dupin replies, "You are mistaken; I know him well; he is both. As poet *and* mathematician, he would reason well; as mere mathematician, he could not have reasoned at all, and thus would have been at the mercy of the Prefect" (3:986).

As we noted earlier, the Minister's dual character as poet and mathematician mirrors that "double Dupin" whose reciprocal powers ("the creative and the resolvent") reminded the narrator in "The Murders in the Rue Morgue" of "the old philosophy of the Bi-Part Soul" (2:533). Borges echoes this reciprocal relationship between the creative and the resolvent when he has the poet Dunraven suggest a mathematical solution to the mystery of the labyrinth and the mathematician Unwin counter with a poetic one. Dunraven asks whether, in trying to solve the mystery, Unwin has considered "the theory of series" or "a fourth dimension of space," and Unwin replies, "No . . . I thought about the labyrinth of Crete. The labyrinth whose center was a man with the head of a bull" (123). Borges adds that Dunraven, "steeped in detective stories, thought that the solution is always less impressive than the mystery itself. Mystery has something of the supernatural about it, and even of the divine; its solution, however, is always tainted by sleight of hand" (123).

Since the minimum number needed to constitute a series is three (even if there are only two items in a series, the idea of their serial relationship is already a third thing), Dunraven's question about whether the solution might involve "the theory of series" or "a fourth dimension of space" suggests in effect that the key to the mystery turns upon choosing between the numbers three and four. And this implied oscillation between three and four, combined with the image of the labyrinth, returns us to the triangular/quadrangular maze of "Death and the Compass" and to its origin in the numerical/geometrical structure of "The Purloined Letter"—in much the same way that Borges's remark about the solution always being less impressive than the mystery itself returns us to the simpleminded question that began this inquiry.

For by now it should be clear that that question was, in the spirit of the genre, framed so as to contain a clue, in reverse, to its answer. Which is to say, the question about how one writes the analytic detective story

as a rereadable form was, like Scharlach's maze, a device to focus attention in one direction while leading us in the opposite, leading us to the
point where that simpleminded question about the unlimited repeata-
bility of a form becomes an endlessly repeatable because constantly re-
formulated question about the simplicity of mind, a question always
about to be answered because it requires only one more step to complete
the analysis. Poe's genius in the invention of the genre was precisely to
understand that the analytic solution of a mystery always leaves us at the
end with the mystery of an analytic solution, the mystery of that solving
power that catches a partial glimpse of itself in the achievement of a
deductive conclusion but that, maddeningly enough, cannot gain a complete view of itself no matter how often it repeats the analytic moment,
cannot totally comprehend itself simply because in doubling back to
effect an absolute coincidence of the self with itself it finds that it is based
on an original noncoincidence. This paradox of a (non)self-including
self—that if the process of thinking and the content of thought ever
absolutely coincided, they would vanish in a condition of no-difference,
taking with them the differential entity that is the self—lies at the heart
of the detective genre which Poe invented. And within the dynamics of
the text, this ultimate condition of no-difference (the imaginatively projected goal of the self's attempt to be absolutely even with itself) makes
its presence felt in that ceaseless oscillation of differential poles associated
with specular doubling, that continual reversal of a signifying term into
its opposite which, in its fluctuating equation of opposing terms, produces a differentiation that seems to make no difference.

V

What tends to be overlooked in readings of "The Purloined Letter" that
treat it as a pretext for examining the analytic act in a specific discipline
such as psychoanalysis, or that make it the more or less naive starting
point for an agon of ever-increasing methodological self-awareness, is
just how self-conscious Poe was about the interpretive effect produced
by a literary text ("The Purloined Letter") that includes within itself a
symbolic text (the purloined letter) whose attributes are clearly those of
the literary text itself—"The Purloined Letter" presenting the purloined
letter which represents in turn "The Purloined Letter" in an endless
oscillation of container and contained, of outer and inner (like that projected by the turning of the letter *inside out within* the story). Indeed,
what tends to be ignored in such readings is how self-consciously Poe

thematized in the story itself the reader's interpretive interaction with the story and then proceeded to make the discovery of that thematization a further form of interaction with the reader, a subtler game of hide-and-seek, of clues and solutions.

Thus, for example, the solution to the mystery of the purloined letter (the mystery of its concealment in the Minister's house so that the Prefect cannot find it) is that the Minister has turned the letter inside out and hidden it in the open; but that trick of reversing the missing object and leaving it in plain view is also the solution to Poe's concealment, within the text of "The Purloined Letter," of the solution to the purloined letter's concealment in the Minister's residence. On his first visit to Dupin the Prefect presents us with the mystery of the purloined letter, which is to say, the manner of its theft and the fact of its continued nonappearance despite his repeated searches. But that standard scene in the analytic detective story (the presentation of the mystery) is in effect turned inside out by Poe, for in describing how the Minister took the letter, Poe simultaneously shows us the secret of the letter's subsequent concealment, indeed, hides it in plain view, by giving us the detail of the Queen's turning the letter over and leaving it in the open on a table to conceal it from the King.

Similarly, in Dupin's open presentation of the game of even and odd as a figure of the attempt to be one up on a specular double, Poe again hides in plain sight that other, subtler game of simple/odd, even/odd—the game figuring the reader's battle of wits with the author as a specular encounter in which the reader plays or tries to avoid playing the game of even and odd with Poe through the author's opposing masks of detective and criminal. Poe hides *this* game in plain sight by having Dupin pointedly note that the game of even and odd "is simple," a verbal gesture that directs us back to his earlier emphatic repetition of the Prefect's claim that the mystery of the letter was "simple and odd." If one were to represent in a geometric figure the opposing players in this game of simple/odd, even/odd, the basic form of the figure would look like this:

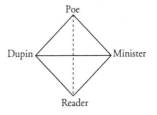

It is only through the battle of wits between Dupin and the Minister D_____ that the reader can engage in a battle of wits with Poe, can try to outwit the author for the interpretive possession of "The Purloined Letter" (much as Dupin outwits the Minister for the physical possession of the purloined letter). Because the reader cannot directly confront Poe (the man who concealed the purloined letter within "The Purloined Letter," as he concealed "The Purloined Letter" within the purloined letter), the reader has to confront him indirectly through his opposing masks in a triangular structure of reader, Dupin, Minister. And in a similar manner Poe can only confront the reader indirectly through these same masks in a triangular structure of author, Dupin, and Minister. Poe and the reader square off, then, as specular doubles, each meaning to outwit a self-projected image of the other, within a quadrangular figure composed of two triangles whose vertices point in opposite directions (Poe and the reader) but whose bases are a single line linking the opposing positions of Dupin and the Minister.

In this structure the reader is obviously at a disadvantage, for in having to match wits with Poe through the game of even and odd played by Poe's adversarial masks, the reader is in effect playing Poe's game. Yet the wish to avoid this game played through surrogates, in favor of a direct confrontation with the author, also seems to leave the reader playing Poe's game. For if, within that quadrangular figure representing the indirect confrontation of author and reader through the direct one of criminal and detective, we were to try to bring together the positions of Poe and the reader for a direct confrontation (like that between the specular doubles Lönnrot and Scharlach at the fourth point of the compass), if we were to try to make the upper and lower vertices representing the opposing positions of author and reader coincide, then we would see that this figure is formed by a mirror-fold. To visualize this, imagine the quadrangular figure as a flat surface like a sheet of paper that can be folded and unfolded along the horizontal line forming the base of the two triangles: folded, the figure is a triangular shape composed of two identical triangles hinged at their base, with one doubled back on top of the other so that their vertices coincide; unfolded, the quadrangle which we have described.

Not surprisingly, it is a form of this same operation—the geometric projection of a triangle (whose vertex points downward) from the base of a triangle (whose vertex points upward)—that Lönnrot uses in "Death and the Compass" to discover the location of the fourth point in Scharlach's maze, the point at which the doubles will confront each other face-to-face. Using a pair of dividers, Lönnrot measures the length of one side of the equilateral triangle inscribed in red ink on the city map sent to Treviranus. Maintaining this same length, he swings an arc downward from each end of the triangle's base line, and where the arcs intersect he discovers the villa Triste-le-Roy. It is as if the red triangle on the map were flipped downward, were unfolded 180 degrees, to produce a double, an inverted mirror-image, of itself. Appropriately enough, this quadrangular maze (composed of two identical triangles joined at their bases by a mirror-fold and with their vertices facing Janus-like in opposite directions) was conceived by Scharlach during that period of delirious convalescence at Triste-le-Roy when he "swore by the god who looks with two faces and by all the gods of fever and of mirrors" that he would "weave a maze around the man" who sent his brother to prison (76). And it is also appropriate that when Lönnrot arrives at the villa one of the first things he sees is the statue of a "two-faced Hermes" which casts "a monstrous shadow" (74)—the single mirror-fold of doubling that produces the two-faced Hermes (the god of mirrors) being doubled again by its shadow image to produce the fourfold.

Like Scharlach's diamond-shaped maze (which is indebted to it), the quadrangular figure representing the indirect confrontation of author and reader through the direct one of criminal and detective in "The Purloined Letter" involves a mirror-fold that doubles identical triangular shapes back upon themselves, and as such it serves as a geometric representation, an emblem, of self-identity. The figure represents the differential unity, the sameness-in-difference, of specular self-consciousness as a simplicity, a single fold, that in doubling an entity back upon itself calls it into existence as a self-conscious unit by introducing into it a difference with itself. But this *difference with itself* is by no means a *division within itself,* for as distinguished from the material (divisible) body, the ground of self-consciousness (mind, spirit, soul) is understood within the tradition in which Poe operates to be indivisible, to be a simple substance. And we can see from this figure, which is three-sided when folded back upon itself but four-sided when unfolded, why the oscillation between the numbers three and four (between the first odd number and the even number associated with doubling) lies at the heart of the game of simple/odd, even/odd, that game in which three words derived from numbers (simple [one], even [two], odd [three]) are made to fill four spaces by doubling one of them (odd). For of course what this game of numerically rooted words evokes is the doubling of a four-sided figure back upon itself to produce the coincidence, the evenness, of two three-sided figures, two identical shapes created as it were by the simplicity of a mirror-fold—the oscillation between three and four symbolizing the folded and unfolded states of this geometric representation of self-consciousness.

Having thematized in the geometrical structure of the game of simple/odd, even/odd, the indirect confrontation of author and reader through the direct one of criminal and detective, Poe makes the discovery of this thematization a further form of interaction with the reader by planting in the text clues to that oscillation between three and four that evokes the mirror-fold of the quadrangular figure. I will cite but two of the several instances of this in the tale.

In the very first sentence of "The Purloined Letter" the narrator gives us the complete street address of Dupin's residence in Paris, a level of specificity that in the economy of a Poe story usually signals the encryption of significant information, particularly where numbers are concerned. The address is *"au troisième, No. 33, Rue Dunôt, Faubourg St. Germain"* (3:974). Now we already know from the first Dupin story that the house is located in the Faubourg St. Germain, an authentic section of Paris. The street name, however, is Poe's own invention and is perhaps an appellation that, in echoing the sound of an elided "don't know," is meant to suggest, like Samuel Butler's *Erewhon*, the nonexistent character of the place it names. More significantly (for reasons that will be apparent in our second example), the name of the street begins with the letter D.

The crucial information, however, which Poe provides in this address is that Dupin lives *"au troisième"* at *"No. 33."* No annotated edition of the tale ever fails to point out that the French *"au troisième"* (*le troisième étage*), the third floor, is what Americans call the fourth floor. The custom in France, of course, is to call the floor at street level *"le rez-de-chaussée"* (the ground floor) and begin the numbering of floors with the level above that, so that what we call the second floor the French call the first floor, and so on. Dupin resides, then, in a numerically ambiguous spot—on a floor that in France is called the third but in America the fourth. And it is only appropriate that this third/fourth floor should be located in a building whose street number is 33, for in the folding back upon itself of that quadrangular figure symbolizing specular self-consciousness, the doubled figure that results is three-sided, a doubling of a triangular shape that is paralleled in the game of simple/odd, even/odd by that distribution of three words in four spaces achieved through the doubling of the word "odd," the word whose root is the Old Norse *oddi,* a triangle.

That Borges understood the clue hidden in the detail of Dupin's re-
siding *au troisième* at No. 33 can be seen from a detail in "Death and
the Compass." The murder of Rabbi Yarmolinsky, the first in the series,
takes place at the Hôtel du Nord in the rabbi's "room on floor R, across
from the suite occupied . . . by the Tetrarch of Galilee" (66). Now since
the name of the hotel is French, one assumes that the designation of its
floors follows the French custom and that the R of "floor R" is the first
letter of *rez-de-chaussée* (much as in this country the letter M in a building
directory stands for mezzanine or B for basement). The first murder
occurs, then, on a floor which the French call the ground floor and
Americans call the first floor, a difference in the naming/numbering of
the first term in a series that gives rise (and in this case is certainly meant
to allude) to the numerical ambiguity of Dupin's residence *au troisième*.
It is only appropriate, of course, that Yarmolinsky's murder on floor R
(the first floor) should *initiate* a series of events that ultimately brings
Lönnrot, who thinks of himself as "a kind of Auguste Dupin" (65), to
that fourth point of the compass where the third murder will occur as
the two doubles, who "may be the same man," confront one another.
And appropriate as well that the first murder in this series was the chance
result of the jewel thief Azevedo's mistaking Yarmolinsky's room for
"the suite occupied . . . by the Tetrarch of Galilee," for as we noted
earlier the title Tetrarch of Galilee derives from the historical division of
a realm into four parts in order to distribute it among three persons,
two of whom each received a quarter while the third received a half.

The second instance that I would cite of Poe's planting a clue in
the text to this three/four oscillation figuring the mirror-fold of specular self-consciousness is the naming of Dupin's rival, the Minister
D_____. In a tale entitled "The Purloined Letter" any manipulation of
a letter, such as the substitution of an initial for a name, should attract
our attention. Since Dupin and the Minister are antithetical doubles, it
is only fitting that the Minister's name begins with the same letter as
Dupin's, and more fitting still that the Minister's initial is also the first
letter of the word "double." There is, however, even more at work in
Poe's choice of this letter. If we were to examine the letter's roots (as
we did those of the words "simple," "even," and "odd"), we would
find that the shape of our capital D derives from the shape of the capital
delta (Δ) in Greek, which is to say, from a triangle. In the Greek alphabet,
delta is the fourth letter, as D is in ours; but in Greek, *delta* (Δ) also
serves as a sign for both the cardinal and ordinal forms of the number
four.[14] The initial of the Minister's name derives, then, from a triangular-

shaped Greek letter that stands for the number four, the same initial as that of his double who lives on the third/fourth floor at No. 33 Rue Dunôt. We should also note in this connection that *delta* is the root of the Greek word *deltos*, *"a writing-tablet,* from the letter Δ (the old shape of tablets)" (*Lexicon*, 178), the letter D thus being a doubly appropriate designation for the purloiner and the recoverer of the letter (themselves characters composed of letters) in this drama of inscribed surfaces.

That Borges spotted the clue concealed in the Minister's initial can be judged from Lönnrot's parting flourish in "Death and the Compass." Trapped in Scharlach's quadrangular labyrinth, Lönnrot makes one last attempt to best his enemy intellectually by proposing a simpler, more economical labyrinth composed of "a single straight line" (78). But Lönnrot's ploy is a trick, his labyrinth's vaunted economy more apparent than real. For what is at issue here is not the number of lines in a geometric figure but the number of steps in a mental operation. And just as there are four steps in Scharlach's labyrinth designated by the four points of the compass, so there are four steps in Lönnrot's labyrinth designated by the first four letters of the alphabet. In Scharlach's maze the doubles confront each other at the fourth point of the compass in the south; in Lönnrot's proposed maze they are to meet at the fourth letter of the alphabet. Lönnrot says, "Lay in wait for me then at D, two miles from A and C, again halfway between them." Lönnrot's suggestion that their specular duel will be replayed again in a future existence is simply Borges's implicit acknowledgement that this meeting of doubles at the letter D (Δ, four) has already been played in a previous incarnation.

VI

That Borges deciphered the game of simple/odd, even/odd in "The Purloined Letter" and then reencrypted it in "Death and the Compass" seems beyond doubt. What still remains to be noted in closing the circle of this essay is the distinct possibility that it was Borges's tale which originally directed Lacan's attention to the numerical/geometrical dimension of the story and thus suggested "The Purloined Letter" as an ideal text for an analysis of psychoanalysis that would project the structure of the Oedipal triangle onto the reciprocity of blindness and insight in the psychoanalytic encounter. The evidence of this influence is circumstantial, but certainly no psychoanalyst should object to that.

One of the first promoters of Borges's work in France was Roger

Caillois, the noted critic and sociologist whose writings influenced Lacan. In his biography of Borges, Rodríguez Monegal notes that Borges's friend Victoria Ocampo had invited Caillois to lecture in Argentina on the eve of the Second World War and that Caillois remained there for the duration. With Ocampo's help, he started a magazine in Buenos Aires called *Lettres Françaises,* and in its October 1944 issue he published French translations of two Borges stories, "The Babylon Lottery" and "The Library of Babel." The relationship between Caillois and Borges, not an entirely friendly one, turned in part upon their mutual interest in the detective genre. Rodríguez Monegal notes that Borges wrote "a rather catty article in *Sur* (April 1942) reviewing one of Caillois' pamphlets, on the detective novel. Against Caillois's statement that the detective story was born when Joseph Fouché created a well-trained police force in Paris, Borges observes that a literary genre invariably begins with a literary text and points out that the text in question is one of Edgar Allan Poe's stories. An exchange of notes ensued, and the relationship between Borges and Caillois cooled considerably. That did not affect Caillois's admiration for Borges's writing. He continued to promote Borges unflinchingly."[15] In 1951 Caillois published in Paris a translation (by P. Verdevoye and Nestor Ibarra) of Borges's *Ficciones,* the collection that contains both "The Garden of the Forking Paths" and "Death and the Compass" (Rodríguez Monegal, 420).

There was, then, a translation of "Death and the Compass" widely available in France under the aegis of Caillois some five years before the publication of Lacan's "Seminar on 'The Purloined Letter.'" Given Caillois's interest in the detective story, his ongoing promotion of one of the genre's most distinguished modern practitioners, the influence of his writings on Lacan, and the psychoanalyst's natural interest in analytic detection, it seems hard to believe that Lacan had not read "Death and the Compass" sometime in the early 1950s. Such a knowledge of the story on Lacan's part would at least go a long way toward explaining the extremely odd reference which he makes to Borges in a footnote to the "Seminar on 'The Purloined Letter.'"

In presenting the purloined letter as a model of the Lacanian floating signifier, Lacan points out the letter's property (as the signifier of an absence) of simultaneously being and not being present in a particular place, adding that "between *letter* and *place* exist relations for which no French word has quite the extension of the English adjective: *odd*" (53). He asks, "Must a letter then, of all objects, be endowed with the property of *nullibeity*: to use a term which the thesaurus known as *Roget* picks up from the semiotic utopia of Bishop Wilkins?" To which question he appends this curious note: "The very one to which Jorge Luis Borges, in works which harmonize so well with the phylum of our subject [dans son oeuvre si harmonique au phylum de notre propos], has accorded an importance which others have reduced to its proper proportions. Cf. *Les Temps modernes,* June-July 1955, pp. 2135–36 and Oct. 1955, pp. 574–75" (53). The citation of the June-July issue of *Les Temps modernes* refers us to the opening pages of a French translation of Borges's "The Analytical Language of John Wilkins" (one of a group of six short essays by Borges in that issue), while the citation of the October issue refers us to a letter to the editor from an M. Pobers commenting on Borges's essay. In "The Analytical Language of John Wilkins" (1941), Borges describes the universal language proposed by the seventeenth-century Englishman Wilkins, bishop of Chester and first secretary of the Royal Society, in his book *An Essay towards a Real Character and a Philosophical Language* (1668). Borges notes that in this language "each word defines itself": "Wilkins divided the universe into forty categories or classes, which were then subdivisible into differences, subdivisible in turn into species. To each class he assigned a monosyllable of two letters; to each difference, a consonant; to each species, a vowel. For example, *de* means an element; *deb,* the first of the elements, fire; *deba,* a portion of the element of fire, a flame" (*OI,* 102). In his letter to the editor commenting on Borges's essay, M. Pobers points out that this philosophical language, which replaces arbitrary words and expressions with a system of letters and syllables each having a particular sense, was not original with Wilkins. It had been invented by another Oxford scholar, George Dalgarno, and Wilkins's work simply completed and perfected the project presented in Dalgarno's 1661 treatise *Ars Signorum vulgo character universalis et Lingua Philosophica.*

Now it is always nice to learn new things simply for their own sake, and yet one cannot help but wonder what it is exactly that Lacan's footnote to Borges is meant to note. There is, according to Lacan, this special property possessed by a signifier (the present sign of an absence) of simultaneously being and not being present in a particular place, an odd relationship between letter and place; and to evoke this property he has found the perfect word, "nullibeity" (the condition of being nowhere existent), a word which Roget's *Thesaurus* tells him was first used in a work by John Wilkins. And by the way, says Lacan, this is the same John Wilkins whose universal analytic language Borges has discussed in an essay that "harmonizes so well with the phylum of our subject." Is the point of this footnote, then, simply to note a coincidence, this footnote which Lacan has appended to an essay he considered important enough to place at the start of the *Écrits?* Or is it meant to acknowledge (though it does not say so) some debt of influence to, or sense of priority of, Borges as regards a knowledge of Wilkins's work?

Perhaps, for example, Lacan, in discovering from Roget's *Thesaurus* that the word "nullibeity" had originated with Wilkins, recognized who Wilkins was because he had read Borges's essay. Such a debt would have been minor, easy enough to acknowledge, and yet in the last analysis no less trivial a matter than the noting of a coincidence. So why did Lacan go to the trouble of including this footnote? Though the property which the word "nullibeity" designates is important for Lacan's notion of the signifier, the word itself is not that important; he has described this property of the signifier often and with other words as good. Still less important and less obvious is the word's connection with Wilkins, and least important and least obvious of all is Wilkins's connection with Borges—both of which Lacan goes to the trouble of pointing out to the reader.

Clearly, there is something odd about this footnote, an uncanny feeling that the author has gone out of his way to emphasize a point at once gratuitous and trivial, the kind of uncanny feeling that is usually the aura of an unconscious mechanism, of a repression and a return. For while it is not at all clear that Borges's essay on Wilkins "harmonizes so well" with the subject of Lacan's "Seminar" that it was worth calling attention to that essay in a footnote, it is quite clear that another work of Borges's harmonizes only too well with the subject of Lacan's "Seminar," and it is that work, "Death and the Compass," of which, I would suggest, the essay on Wilkins reminds Lacan at crucial moments.

We can see just such a moment in the passage quoted above in which Borges illustrates Wilkins's analytic language by constructing the word for flame, *deba.* He starts with the two-letter *de,* an element; then in the second step adds the consonant *b* to specify the element fire; and in the third step adds the vowel *a* to specify a portion of that element, a flame— a three-step process to produce a four-letter word that cannot help but remind us of the way that the successive murders in "Death and the Compass" each add, as part of a supposed cabalistic rite, another letter to the spelling of a four-letter name composed of three different letters, the Tetragrammaton. The resemblance between essay and story in this regard seems even more striking when Borges remarks that in "the words of John Wilkins's analytical language . . . every letter is meaningful, as the letters of the Holy Scriptures were meaningful for the cabalists," the analytical language being "a universal key and a secret encyclopedia" (*OI*, 103).

One recalls the cabalistic texts which Lönnrot read in trying to solve the mystery of the murders: a work on "the magic and the terror of the Tetragrammaton, which is God's unspeakable name," another on "the doctrine that God has a secret name in which (as in the crystal sphere that the Persians attribute to Alexander of Macedonia) His ninth attribute, Eternity, may be found—that is to say, the immediate knowledge of everything under the sun that will be, that is, and that was. Tradition lists ninety-nine names of God; Hebrew scholars explain that imperfect cipher by *a mystic fear of even numbers*; the Hasidim argue that the missing term stands for a hundredth name—the Absolute Name" (68, italics mine). This Absolute Name, which is "the immediate knowledge" of everything that is, was, or will be, is in effect "a universal key and a secret encyclopedia"; it is the apotheosis of that linguistic totality of representation which Wilkins sought in his analytical language, and as such it confronts us with the paradox of self-inclusion on the cosmic level. For the Absolute Name, like "the crystal sphere that the Persians attribute to Alexander" or that other crystal sphere that Borges named the Aleph, is a faithful representation of everything in the universe, but it is also one of the things contained in that universe.

Consequently, any Aleph-like object, as a representation of all the things in that universe of which it is itself one minute part, must contain within its compass a faithful representation of itself, and that representation must contain within itself another, and so on, Aleph within Aleph, in an infinite progression of representations that is also an infinite regression as each successive representation is reduced in size to maintain the proportional relationship between the original representation and the universe. This ultimate vanishing of signification in the infinite as one pursues an absolute coincidence between the cosmos and its self-contained image probably accounts for the cabalists' "mystic fear of even numbers," the fear that the secret Absolute Name of God, that hundredth name representing a symbolic apotheosis of evenness, invokes the condition of zero difference, the condition where ubiquity and nullibeity are the same.

Given the several resemblances between "Death and the Compass" and "The Analytical Language of John Wilkins," one can see that Lacan's reference to the Wilkins essay may indeed represent the return of a repressed content, which is to say, the surfacing of Lacan's sense of how much his own reading of "The Purloined Letter" either owed directly to, or was anticipated by, Borges's reading/rewriting of the Poe story in "Death and the Compass." And certainly if Lacan had any misgivings, any anxiety about the originality of his reading, such misgivings could not help but have been increased and given focus by M. Pobers's "letter" to the editor pointing out that the analytical language which Borges attributed to Wilkins did not originate with him but was the invention of another man. Might another Pobers write a letter pointing out that Lacan's reading of "The Purloined Letter" did not originate with him, a letter arguing that Lacan's reading had either been influenced, or at the very least anticipated, by Borges's reading/rewriting, so that Lacan's reading, like the purloined letter itself, was out of place, not the first but the second instance of this particular interpretation of the tale?

If this originality anxiety existed for Lacan, then his footnote to Borges would be the trace of an inner division, the visible mark of his inability, on the one hand, *to acknowledge consciously* a debt of influence to, or the simple priority of, Borges in a matter so central to his interpretation of Poe's tale, and of his equal inability, on the other hand, *not to acknowledge unconsciously* his sense of this debt or priority. Or perhaps it is less a matter of Lacan's unwillingness to acknowledge Borges as a precursor than of his reluctance as a psychoanalyst—that is, as a scientist, a writer of nonfiction prose—to acknowledge an interpretive influence or priority originating in a work of fiction, since such an acknowledgment would seem to undermine the privileged, "scientific" status of Lacan's reading of Poe by suggesting the imaginative (not to say, fictive) component of psychoanalytic interpretation. If this were the case, then the footnote could be an unconscious compromise that lets Lacan acknowledge Borges not by citing one of his stories but by referencing one of his analytic essays, a nonfiction work whose veiled resemblance to "Death and the Compass" allows it to serve as a screen figure for the tale. In either case—originality anxiety or the privileging of psychoanalytic discourse—the result would be the same: the oddly gratuitous footnote pointing out a trivial coincidence.

That the structures of specular self-consciousness elaborated in Borges's "Death and the Compass" and in Lacan's "Seminar on 'The Purloined Letter'" involve essentially the same geometric configuration—a figure formed by the mirror-doubling of a triangle—can be seen quite clearly in a diagram which Lacan included as part of a commentary on the "Seminar" in his *Écrits*. Discussing "the dialectic of intersubjectivity" presented in the "Seminar," Lacan identifies its central mechanism as that reciprocal imaginary objectification of self and Other found in the Lacanian mirror stage.[16] According to Lacan, the mirror stage in human development occurs between the sixth and the eighteenth months when the child, lacking motor control of his body, "anticipates on the imaginary level the future acquisition and mastery of his bodily integrity." This "imaginary integration . . . brought about through identification with the image of a similar being . . . as a total form . . . is illustrated and realized in the concrete experience in which the child perceives his own image in a mirror."[17] To illustrate the specular nature of "the dialectic of intersubjectivity" in the "Seminar," Lacan uses the following diagram:

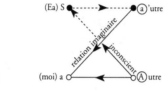

SCHEMA L:

(Écrits, 1:66)

This figure representing the mirror-doubling of two triangles is the reciprocal of the geometric shape that Borges uses in "Death and the Compass" to figure the face-to-face meeting of the two men "whose minds work in the same way" and who "may be the same man." The difference is that Borges represents the mirror-doubling of a triangular structure as the projection downward of a second triangle from the base of the first, while Lacan represents this same mirror-doubling inherent in "the dialectic of intersubjectivity" as the projection upward of a second triangle from the vertex of the first:

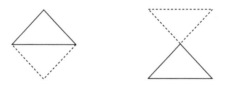

VII

Since the self-including structure of "The Purloined Letter" has the effect of drawing into its progressive/regressive vortex any interpretation of it,

I am resigned to my part in the casual comedy, ready to feign astonishment should some future interpreter point out that just as Lacan and Derrida in reading the tale replayed the game of even and odd in the critical register, so I have in reading the tale replayed Lönnrot's geometrical response to Scharlach's quadrangular maze. Which is to say that in writing an essay about Poe's "Purloined Letter" and the readings of it by Lacan, Derrida, and Johnson (i.e., in observing the quadrangular hermeneutic figure formed by the literary text and a cumulative series of three interpretations), I have in effect added one more side to that hermeneutic figure, a fifth side adumbrating an infinite progression of interpretations, while at the same time I have, like Lönnrot with his regressive straight-line labyrinth, introduced between points A and B in the hermeneutic figure (between Poe's tale and Lacan's reading) another story/interpretation, Borges's "Death and the Compass," that adumbrates an infinite regression of influence/priority in the interpretive tradition of the analytic detective genre. In pursuing this regression, one could, for example, introduce between "Death and the Compass" and "The Purloined Letter" Israel Zangwill's *The Big Bow Mystery* (1892); and between Borges and Zangwill, H. G. Wells's "The Plattner Story" (1897); and between Zangwill and Poe, Lewis Carroll's *Through the Looking Glass* (1872), and so on endlessly. But that is another task for a different work. For the present, I stand ready, should someone unmask my replaying of Lönnrot's maneuver, to slap my forehead with the palm of my hand (like Clarence Day on reading in his morning paper that there had been another wreck on the New Haven) and exclaim, "Oh gad!"

Wendy B. Faris

Marking Space, Charting Time: Text and Territory in Faulkner's "The Bear" and Carpentier's *Los pasos perdidos*

> . . . woods for game and streams for fish, . . . a
> refuge and sanctuary of liberty and freedom from
> what you called the old world's worthless
> evening . . .
> —William Faulkner, *Go Down, Moses*

> . . . un mundo remoto . . . un apacible concierto de
> tareas que eran las de una vida sometida a los
> ritmos primordiales . . .
> (. . . a remote world . . . a harmonious concert of
> duties that were those of a life moving to a
> primordial rhythm . . .)
> —Alejo Carpentier, *Los pasos perdidos* (*The Lost Steps*)

The moral and aesthetic force of the new American land continues as a powerful element in the shaping of fictions in both the United
States and Latin America, even as the actual land is developed unrec-
ognizably beyond its original state. According to Charles Sanford, for
example, "the Edenic myth . . . has been the most powerful and comprehensive organizing force in American culture."[1] Sanford is speaking
here for North America, and while it may be true that the Edenic myth
operates with more consistency in the North, perhaps because in the
South the land has been a greater physical obstacle to settlement, his
statement applies in large part to Latin America as well, the myth of
the promised land spanning the two continents. Juan Durán, for example, claims that throughout its literary history, Iberoamerica, in its

natural primitivism, "cannot exist except by comparison with the Edenic world."[2] Two central texts that illustrate this phenomenon with particular intensity are William Faulkner's "The Bear"[3] and Alejo Carpentier's *Los pasos perdidos (The Lost Steps)*.[4] Neither Faulkner nor Carpentier proposes the myth of paradise as the basis for a clear plan of action; it is rather an encounter with it—even a critique of it—that they offer; but in each case it remains an essential touchstone of experience. I intend to compare these two fictions closely in order to weave with them a web of connections between North and South, thereby proposing that the Americas possess a common literary tradition grounded, as it were, in the ground.[5]

Alfonso Reyes provides an interesting example of this close connection between text and territory early in the twentieth century. Reyes defines utopia (from the Greek via Quevedo) as "no hay tal lugar" ("there is no such place"). This formula emphasizes, as do the two works I analyze here, the imaginary nature of the place. Furthermore, Reyes's essay embodies two kinds of correspondence between text and terrain. First, Reyes initially read his essay at a law school in Mexico City and later (as he himself reports) "al aire libre sobre una mesa y bajo un arbol, en la Escuela de Agricultura de Chapingo" ("in the open air on a table under a tree, at the Agricultural School in Chapingo"), the description of the reading affirming a connection between the text and the natural world.[6] Second, the trajectory of presentation that Reyes describes duplicates that of the essay itself, which considers first man's attempts to imagine utopian societies and their laws, and then investigates man's memories of past arcadias, thus implying a connection between the laws and the lands. Nevertheless, while Reyes is an important figure in this context, given my emphasis on the land, his neoclassical spirit, his interest in utopias rather than in the pastoral, in culture rather than in nature, makes him less central to this discussion than writers in the romantic tradition.

The particular aspect of the land which will focus my discussion here is the idea of its appropriation, because issues of appropriation and ownership join terrestrial and textual concerns in many ways. Most importantly, writing itself, particularly the portrayal of place, involves a symbolic appropriation of sorts.[7] Thinking in more concrete historical terms, another aspect of the connection between text and terrain is the fact that appropriating and keeping track of lands motivated some of the first texts created in the new world. And the issue has remained alive; two earlier texts that document the point are Cooper's *The Pioneers* and

Gallegos's *Doña Bárbara,* both of which revolve in similar ways around the question of landownership. This primitive American bookkeeping is what Ike in "The Bear" still encounters in the ledgers of his "uncles" Buck and Buddy McCaslin, where he finds "a chronological and much more comprehensive though doubtless tedious record than he would ever get from any other source, not alone of his own flesh and blood but of all his people, not only the whites but the black ones too, who were as much a part of his ancestry as his white progenitors, and of the land which they had all held and used in common and fed from and on and would continue to use in common without regard to color or titular ownership" (268).

In both these texts, however, the question of legality receives a similar paradoxical twist. Ike is the character who possesses the land most meaningfully, but he is the very one who relinquishes legal possession. He possesses the woods in his identity as they possess him; they exist in a mutual embrace, just as Boon and Lion embrace in their sleep. The same is true of Carpentier's narrator and the people living in the heart of the jungle with whom he joins temporarily; in that environment they all possess and are possessed by the jungle irrespective of any document attesting ownership. In both cases the principle of natural right prevails, and in both cases that natural ownership would seem to be nontransferable; neither man has any children to whom he will pass on any land because he possesses it significantly only in spirit, literal possession bringing too many problems.

Both Faulkner and Carpentier confront this issue in concrete terms by parodying the principle of individual ownership in the new world. In "The Bear," Major de Spain tells several swampers that they are welcome to join in the bear hunt, since "he's more your bear than ours." But of course in the cosmic scheme of things he is nobody's bear, just as (Ike maintains) the American land is nobody's to buy or to sell: "Nobody shot Old Ben that day. No man saw him" (223). Similarly, in *Los pasos perdidos,* Carpentier includes what we perceive as an ironic detail: the Adelantado legislates in Santa Monica de los Venados, a town espousing communal ownership of land and game, with notebooks that have printed on their covers "Perteneciente a" ("Property of . . .")—a designation which has little meaning in that environment (215, 185–86).

Before entering on a detailed comparison of these two texts, we need to note two basic differences, one general, the other specific. First, if one were to survey the literatures of North and South America, the importance of the land as such would loom larger in the North; the reasons for this are hard to define, though they may have to do with different patterns of colonization, the widespread distribution of territories providing more of a national priority in the U.S. than in Latin America, where land was often granted by the crown to large *latifundistas* and remained in their hands until relatively recent times.[8] Second, the land appropriation in question is not identical in "The Bear" and *Los pasos perdidos*. In Ike's case it involves his inheritance of actual land from his ancestors, an inheritance he believes is corrupt since the Indians had no right to sell it in the first place, and since the official inheritance takes no account of his half siblings. In the case of Carpentier's narrator, his appropriation of the land is primarily symbolic; he attempts to include its rhythms in his music, and also to live there himself, but without owning any actual land. His possession does have some practical dimensions, however, in his collection of primitive instruments to take back to the city, a more concrete kind of appropriation, not of the land itself but of its indigenous artistic creations. His situation thus bears comparison with Ike's.

In both "The Bear" and *Los pasos perdidos,* the central question of land appropriation motivates an elaborate set of dualities that particularizes the division between civilization and wilderness. In tracing out some of these dichotomies, in noting their variety and insistence, we can observe how spatial perceptions of territory structure American fiction ideologically. Two systems—the mythic, Edenic, indigenous absolute, and the historical, compromised, colonized contingencies (singular and plural visions, really)—do battle within the texts. In both cases, the war zones are clearly delineated: the line of trees in "The Bear" separates woods from civilization; the notches in the tree trunk in *Los pasos perdidos* mark off the accessible from the inaccessible realms of the jungle. As usual, in Carpentier's case one needs to qualify such a division. The notches are really a polyvalent sign: they can lead into the jungle, joining man and nature, in addition to denying him access to it by their absence, foregrounding the difference between them. Both bear tracks and notches are primitive forms of writing on the land—messages—but only to be read by certain people or in certain seasons. In any case, in both novels, the characters who learn to sense the power of the wilderness in the core of their beings are shown as progressively shedding the accoutrements of civilization as they proceed into that wilderness. Ike sheds his gun, then watch, and finally compass; Carpentier's narrator sheds not so much his own possessions but history, proceeding backwards through what he perceives as equivalents of the Middle Ages to the classical period and the ages of the horse, the dog, the bird, to the earth before man inhabited it, adopting increasingly more primitive forms of locomotion: plane, bus, donkey, foot.[9] As they progress in this direction, primordial rhythms are the ones they both aspire to, revealing, of course, an implicit romantic connection between man's inner self and nature.

First of all, these spaces are distinguished specifically over and over again as such. "The tall and endless wall of dense November woods" in "The Bear" contrasts in every way with the minimal rooms and bars, with "the new jerrybuilt bungalow" that Ike inhabits in town (281). "The wilderness soared, musing, inattentive, myriad, eternal, green; older than any mill shed, longer than any spur line" (322). Carpentier's narrator dwells at length on the majestic trees and foliage in the jungle in contrast to the miniature fake magnolias on the stage set in the city and the one puny geranium plant in his apartment there. In the jungle, "la naturaleza que aquí nos circunda es implacable, terrible, a pesar de su belleza. Pero los que en medio de ella viven la consideran menos mala, mas tratable, que los espantos y sobresaltos, las crueldades frías, las amenazas siempre renovadas, del mundo de *allá*" ("no doubt . . . the nature surrounding us was implacable, terrible, in spite of its beauty. But those whose life was spent with it found it less evil, more friendly, than the terrors and alarms, the cold cruelties, the never-ending threats of the world back *there*" [203, 175]).

In the wilderness, time is eternal, mythic: the woods "did not change, and timeless, would not, any more than would the green of summer and the fire and rain of fall"; time is tied meaningfully to place by the passage of the seasons (323). Clouds in the jungle are "semejantes a sí mismas, desde los tiempos inmemoriales," "tiempos inmutables" ("resembling themselves since time immemorial," [in a place of] immutable rhythms" [174, 151]), where the narrator has left off thinking about what time it is, and where "el descubrimiento de que mi reloj está sin cuerda me hace reir a solas, estruendosamente, en esta llanura sin tiempo" ("the discovery that I had not wound my watch made me laugh out loud, alone there on that timeless savanna" [117, 101]). That land contrasts with the city where he belongs to "la única raza humana que está impedida de desligarse de las fechas [, . . .] la raza de quienes hacen arte" ("the only human race to which it is forbidden to sever the bonds of time [, . . .] that race of those who create art" [286, 249]). Time in Faulkner's woods is opposed to "town time," ordered by arbitrary hours and routine, like those by which Carpentier's narrator and his wife make love only on Sundays (309). Carpentier typically blurs the distinctions in this area as elsewhere; his wilderness world is more relentlessly temporal than Faulkner's, and it is connected with the world of the city through a progression of ages. The narrator does reach what he thinks of as "el mundo anterior al hombre" ("the world that existed before man"); but even there, time doesn't really stop (though it has slowed down in comparison to time in the city), for he thinks that once arrived there, "si retrocediéramos un poco más, llegaríamos adonde comenzara la terrible soledad del Creador, . . . cuando la tierra era desordenada y vacía, y las tinieblas estaban sobre la haz del abismo" ("if we go back a little farther, we will come to the terrible loneliness of the Creator, . . . when the earth was without order and empty, and darkness was upon the face of the deep" [193, 168]). As if to further blur this distinction, there is even a kind of eternity in his city; but it is an eternity of stagnation, where events, like the action in his wife's long-running play, repeat themselves over and over meaninglessly, "dentro de una prisa que solo servía para devolverme, cada mañana, al punto de partida de la víspera" ("in breathless haste that served only to bring [me] back each morning to the point of departure of the previous evening" [64, 54]).

Actions—both collective and individual—in these different settings are contrasted repeatedly. Rituals in the wilderness are solemnly performed and implicitly understood, whereas in city or town they may be nonexistent or devoid of meaning. Sam coaches and drills Ike in the solemn ritual of hunting, in which he is "humble and proud" to take part, and after which Sam is buried according to the rituals of his ancestors. We see no such rituals in town in "The Bear," and organized religion is even evoked there as the source of "fiery Christian symbols" used by Klan lynch mobs (290). If town rituals exist, somewhat softening this dichotomy, they lack the pristine quality of those in the wilderness. The funerary rite Miss Worsham enacts for Benjamin in "Go Down, Moses," for example, is only minimally dignified, perhaps even degraded, the hearse "going fast in a whining lower gear . . . with an unctuous, an almost bishoplike purr" (382). In the natural gothic of the jungle, Rosario lives her religion, traveling hundreds of miles to bring a devotional image to her father, and participating in a funeral which incarnates "las más nobles formas del rito milenario" ("the noblest forms of a millenary rite" [137, 119]). In contrast, the narrator goes to a church in the city where the worshippers no longer understand the Latin words, and gazes in the window of an antique store at African idols whose appeal to clients is only aesthetic.

The activity of dignified hunting in the woods which we see at the beginning of "The Bear," practiced by "the men, not white nor black nor red but men, hunters, with the will and hardihood to endure and the humility and skill to survive," contrasts with the less reverently portrayed farming, commerce, and banking in the town, where Mc-Caslin has "one foot straddled into a farm and the other foot straddled into a bank" (250). And Ike's boyhood trips to the woods contrast with the rest of his life in town: then "he was in the woods, not alone but solitary"; now, we infer, he is in town, alone but not solitary. Those contrasts are comparable to the contrast in *Los pasos perdidos* between the narrator's employment in the city and his activities in the jungle. Before he leaves on his trip we hear that although he is a composer he has become discouraged and gone from studying ethnomusicology to a job in an ad agency, definitely a downward movement, indicating a climate of ennui. In the jungle, on the contrary, a sense of discovery and newness pervades the atmosphere; rather than doing a meaningless job, he embarks on a meaningful search for his identity, a rediscovery of his own musical inspiration—decidedly an upward trajectory. The same is true on a more general level; routine and unfulfilling activities in the city, particularly the repeated theatrical performances which exhaust the narrator's wife, contrast with "la soberana precisión" ("the superb precision") of a jungle fisherman, "un ser humano llegado a maestro en la totalidad de oficios propiciados por el teatro de su existencia" ("[one of the] human beings who were masters of the skills required on the stage of their existence" [180, 156]). That the narrator—unlike Ike—eventually realizes he needs to return to civilization does not cancel the power of the jungle as a center of rejuvenation for him.

The same kind of contrast structures descriptions of the food people eat, the clothes they wear, and the tools they use. In "The Bear," liquor even seems to change from a debilitating brew, when Boon drinks it in town, to "some condensation of the wild immortal spirit" that the hunters drink "moderately, humbly even" in the camp in the woods (192). In *Los pasos perdidos*, liquor the narrator repeatedly consumes to stave off depression and boredom in the city bars contrasts not only with the water Rosario brings him from the jungle streams, but also with the liquor in the jungle which achieves a reawakening of his urban self—an unwelcome but ultimately necessary and meaningful reawakening. The clothes Faulkner's men wear in the woods are old, soft, and worn; in town they are new, starched, and stiff. When Ike visits Major de Spain in his office, he sees him "in sober fine broadcloth and an immaculate glazed shirt whom he was used to seeing in boots and muddy corduroy, unshaven, sitting the shaggy powerful long-hocked mare" (317). In similar fashion, Rosario laughs at the narrator's overly refined and stylish shirt, claiming that "tales prendas eran mas propias de hembras" ("such garments were for women, not men" [119, 103]). She herself wears clothes that are "fuera del tiempo, . . . todo muy limpio y almidonado, . . . con algo de costurero romántico" ("of no period, no time . . . all clean and starched, . . . something out of an old-fashioned sewing box" [89, 76]). Her black braids gleaming from her morning bath contrast with Mouche's tinted hair falling into disrepair in the jungle.

The dichotomy of realms includes not only men but animals and objects to match. Faulkner shows us real bears in the woods, and bears that eat quiche—or rather "ice cream and ladyfingers," according to Boon—in the town zoo (234–35). In Carpentier's jungle a pact unites men and the dogs who help them to hunt, a pact cemented by "un mutuo complemento de poderes, que les hacía trabajar en hermandad" ("a mutual complementing of powers which made their relation a brotherhood" [126–27, 109]). In the town, dogs are simply superfluous, mentioned only when the narrator reads a good omen in a dog who allows himself to be stroked in the park. Tools in the wilderness are guns and dogs of one kind or another; in "The Bear" the magnificent "tool" of Lion and the venerable guns of the hunters contrast with the tools carpenters use in town to build houses—either too elaborate or too flimsy. In Los pasos perdidos, Marcos can use the rifle to kill a leper who has molested a girl, while the narrator cannot, his only functional utensil being his pencil.

Contrasts in the kind and use of verbal tools provide other important points of similarity. Records in the wilderness are kept in minds and hearts, not in ledgers or on paper. Stories are oral and ancient, not printed and recent. "For six years now he had heard the best of all talking. It was of the wilderness, the big woods, bigger and older than any recorded document . . . the voices quiet and weighty and deliberate for retrospection and recollection and exactitude" (191–92). This talking and the lore Ike learns from Sam Fathers—which, as we learn in "Delta Autumn," he has passed on—contrast in both dignity and form with the history he reads in the ledgers. Those words unspoiled by historical documentation correspond to the primitive threnody unspoiled by later developments and notation which so inspires the narrator in Los pasos perdidos: he earlier goes searching for "una expresión musical que surgiera de la palabra desnuda, de la palabra anterior a la música" ("a musical expression that should come from the unadorned word, from the word prior to music"), which he imagines after hearing "un ritmo . . . que se crea en las frondas, . . . una música prodigiosa de lo verde" ("a rhythm . . . that is created in the branches, . . . a prodigious music of green" [219–22, my trans.]). Furthermore, the Adelantado carries the originally oral *Odyssey* with him wherever he goes, reading it over and over again, and Rosario's slow and literal reading of the ancient tale of Geneviève de Brabant contrasts with Mouche's quick absorption of her sophisticated contemporary novel as they travel side by side on the bus.

This contrast of superficiality in civilization with depth in the wilderness continues in the more general terms of both intellects and passions. In Faulkner, education in schools from "what some hired pedagogue put between the covers of a book" is specifically denied or bypassed in favor of the wisdom a person "was born knowing" or has acquired in the natural world (250). In Carpentier the corresponding contrast is between art forms in the city and those in the jungle: the rhythm of a barefoot harpist in Los Altos, for example, contrasts with the twelve tone compositions imported from the urban world. And it even has a moral effect, inspiring the narrator to collect the instruments for which he has been paid rather than simply using the money for a vacation. In part because of this kind of education and its aesthetic products, men live in woods and jungle in harmony with cosmic forces; in city and town we hear of discord—civil war in "The Bear" and revolution in *Los pasos perdidos.* On a more individual level, love is passionate and eternally new in the wilderness. In Faulkner it tends to exist between men and animals or men and men more easily than between men and women, though Ike and his wife "were married and it was the new country," their new love associated with the new world. In any case, the essential ingredient is the freedom of the gift of love. The subsequent barter of land for nude love that Ike's wife attempts is specifically located in a room in the town. In the narrator's encounters with Rosario he is clearly coupling idyllically with the freshness of the land; the first instance takes place in a pile of leaves on the ground, and in it he relives the first embraces of his youth. They contrast with civilized love—either his now old and tired weekly marital embraces or his tempestuous quarrels with his mistress.

The list of comparisons is virtually endless, so I will end it here, with two further qualifications. In "The Bear" the dichotomy between wilderness and civilization, between old and new orders, is more clearly established from the start and more rigorously exploited. It lacks the transition from capital through progressively smaller and less civilized towns to the originary jungle village that we experience through the narrator's journey from the Lands of the Horse, through the Lands of the Dog, to the Lands of the Bird in *Los pasos perdidos*. One cannot go too far with this difference, however; we do see Ike in "Delta Autumn" measure the passage of time in himself as he recalls earlier hunting trips. But even here the significant division between Jefferson and the wilderness hunting grounds, while considerably damaged and heavily ironized, is still preserved. The train which travels through space from town to woods in "The Bear" marks the division between those spatiotemporal realms rather than the progressive changes of the narrator's voyage in *Los pasos perdidos*. This difference indicates the somewhat larger presence of the idea of history in Carpentier, the relatively greater force of "old universal truths" and the ways in which they are eroded by actual historical change in Faulkner.[10] In addition, to compare the narrative situations of the two novels is difficult also, because in "The Bear" we have the ledgers and then the rest of the text, whereas in *Los pasos perdidos* we have only the diary (though it is introduced by a short frame). If we compare Faulkner's ledgers and the diary of Carpentier's narrator, we can see that both are attempts at the appropriation of land by text that are ultimately unsatisfactory, not only because of flawed motivations but because of the impossibility of the task. Most importantly, however, Faulkner's text, with its grandly dignified style and stately cadence, analogous to the "weighty and deliberate" voices in the woods, stands in opposition to the barely literate, decidedly ungrand ledgers, and in implicit substitution for them; the enormity of the task of appropriation is thus somewhat diminished by its existence. In Carpentier's case, the one text must absorb both misguided attempts at appropriation of the land and positive effects of identification with it.

Beyond these differences, however, both protagonists take stands with regard to the dichotomy of forest and town, siding with the wilder space, desperately attempting to mediate the dichotomy in their own persons. In "The Bear," Ike attempts to bring the ethos of the wilderness into town, taking up the biblical trade of carpenter and relinquishing his inheritance. Carpentier's narrator tries to bridge the same gap by proceeding in the opposite direction: adapting himself to life in the jungle, reflecting its rhythms in his music, and planning to marry Rosario. Both men fail in their attempts, however, and the dichotomy is finally mediated only by the texts we are reading. Words bridge the gap between the two realms, giving access to the truths of the heart and the rhythms of nature learned in the primordial realm so that they are remembered in the city or town. But those words are necessarily imbued with the lies they have told and the texts they have created; this makes them less pure than we would like, but it makes it possible for us as historical beings to comprehend them. The dichotomy is thus simultaneously delineated and bridged by the narration, which holds in suspension—as its fictional speakers find it so hard to do—both the compelling force and the ultimate impossibility of the American dream of paradise.[11]

In the attempts of these characters to achieve a satisfactory integration of realms, we see that even though the self may not be able to center itself completely in the wilderness, individual identity is tied to the land.[12] In both cases, initiatory trials—competence in tracking and hunting in "The Bear," survival of insects and storms in *Los pasos perdidos,* for example—confirm the importance of the land in the search for identity. Both "The Bear" and *Los pasos perdidos* exemplify Ainsa's concept of the centripetal hero, the man who desires to find his nascent identity in the temple in the forest. But this identification is paradoxical: as Sanford has put it, "the image of Paradise, taken by itself, would seem to be at once an image of desire and an image for the release of desire, an image for the realization and fulfillment of self and an image for the surrender of self."[13] The self in the wilderness encounters just this dilemma. Ike's initial experience with this dilemma is implicit and fleeting: the conflict between his desire to kill the bear to affirm himself and the feeling of a close kinship with the animal. The dilemma of Carpentier's narrator is less clearly delineated and less fleeting: his conflict centers on whether to merge his creative self with the atemporal life of the jungle or to affirm his life as a composer in time. Thus the problem is similar, although Ike ultimately decides in favor of relinquishment, Carpentier's narrator for artistic self-assertion.[14] Furthermore, the project of merging the two separate realms of nature and culture is problematic, and can reveal elements of self-deception. Close identification with the land and its values in the end provokes an awareness of its own impossibility, of historical difference displayed in spatial terms. Because of his age, Ike is permitted only a glimmer of ironic self-scrutiny in this regard; the narrator of *Los pasos perdidos* comes to a more explicit recognition of his delusions.[15]

In any case, the power of the identification with the land, indeed, the power of the land itself as a rejuvenating force, acts as a magnetic pole that causes the needle of individual and cultural development to swerve in its direction; neither man can live in the wilderness, but we all wish he—and we—could. The "Romantic monism," "the emergence of master forms from the desired communion of Mind and Nature," which

Roberto González Echevarría detects in *Los pasos perdidos,* appears in "The Bear" as Ike's absorption of values from the woods.[16] The naive and sentimental view of the Edenic wilderness and its value as a model for living is simultaneously upheld and denied.[17] Though subverted, it nevertheless remains, an ever-present ideal to civilization in its discontents.[18] Significantly, in both cases the symbol of the primordial realm provides the title for the book that records its triumph and its eclipse.

In addition to these questions of ideology and narrative structuring, the conjunction of terrestrial and territorial appropriation in these texts has metafictional ramifications as well. In this sense, "crossing" the mountains or "charting" the terrain takes on additional resonance. First of all, close connection with the land is artistically enabling. Ike's honorable relation to the land implicitly motivates the stately style of the text that chronicles it, just as the narrator's reverential connection to the jungle and its inhabitants in *Las pasos perdidos* enables him to write music again: "ante la visión de un auténtico treno, renació en mí la idea del *Treno*" ("at the memory of an authentic threnody, the idea of the *Threnody* revived in me" [224, 194]). The fact that neither man can remain successfully in permanent idyllic contact with the land does not negate its enabling power.[19] Looking more closely, however, we realize that an honorable relationship to the land in this context as in others has its problems and paradoxes. Since landscape only exists as a function of vision, of pictorial or verbal appropriation, the very act of writing about the unspoiled land is problematic. This is the textual analogue for the problem of identity we encountered above: whether to merge with and surrender to nature or to mark it with self-assertion. Thus two movements—to edit the landscape or to leave it unedited, to appropriate the land with words or to relinquish it—coexist here.[20] Conquering the wilderness, and the profound self-doubt that results from that conquest, stand at the heart of the literatures of both Americas. As Roderick Nash asks, "if God speaks to us in the sublimity of Nature, then was not the flood of pioneers a devilish stratagem for drowning the voice of God?"[21]

This issue—how to write of the pristine world without tarnishing it or distorting it too much—surfaces briefly in both texts. It is implicit when Ike touches on the problems of transcribing God's truth in familiar human terms, of expressing eternal truths of the heart with historical words of the world (260), and elsewhere in "The Bear" as well (see, for example, the passage I will quote later on where God's writing on the Southern land with the passage of the seasons is compared to man's writing on it with the Civil War). In *Los pasos perdidos,* it appears in the contrast between the natural "green music" of the jungle and the narrator's need for paper on which to write his own music inspired by it (of which more in a moment).

In this respect we can see that much writing in the two Americas that is linked closely to the land exists in the literary space between the search for uninhabited paradise and the impulse to colonize the wilderness—in literary terms, between the wish to leave the blank page of the land blank and the urge to write on it. The image of leisure in paradise, of "material ease without labor," of the desire "to transcend all that is merely human and temporal," is only half the story; this ancient ideal has been modified by the experience of colonization, of inscribing man's will on the land, which required integration of the paradisal impulse with the hard work necessary for survival in the American wilderness, not always a paradise.[22] This image is further modified by the desire for self-assertion, as Carpentier's narrator finds out when he wishes to continue composing in the jungle. Even as he is irresistibly attracted to it, Nash points out, man "by definition is alien to wilderness, and even the most careful camper leaves the marks of his passage on the land."[23] I am not sure I agree that man is entirely alien to the wilderness, but the conservationist sentiments Nash expresses help to explain why, even as we sympathize with the disappointment of the narrator, we are somewhat gratified when the waters have temporarily erased man's marks on the jungle, preventing his reentry into it, and why we relish the feebleness of Faulkner's train as it chugs through the woods as well as the repeated inability of the hunters to entrap the bear.

The problem of how to write about the land without spoiling or falsifying it is further complicated by the fact that these particular texts follow several centuries of literary appropriation of the land through description. Paradoxically enough, earlier, more purely descriptive texts that treat landscape as other have made possible the greater aesthetic integration of character and environment that characterize later ones like "The Bear" and *Los pasos perdidos*. In both those stories, we may note in passing, a valued merging of character and scene is celebrated by a certain idealization of the indigenous inhabitants for whom that seems "naturally" the case. But the realization of that very integration in later texts seems in some cases to induce a nostalgia for the virgin, unappropriated land whose disappearance is a condition of their very existence as texts that integrate man and scene. Thus the writer of texts in and on the wilderness is conflicted over and over.

Within this dialectic, *Los pasos perdidos* continues the tradition of exploration, of describing the heretofore undiscovered, of spatial enumeration. The Latin American novel, especially, developed significantly while serving as a vehicle for the literary appropriation of the land in the form of the infamous *novela de la tierra,* which Fuentes claims was itself devoured as text by the land it portrayed. Thus the Latin American novel has suffered to some extent from the lack of human orientation that would organize space meaningfully rather than being overwhelmed by it.[24] In Carpentier there remains a larger residue of that horror of the void which motivates extensive geographical description and which recalls the same tendency in earlier American writers like Cooper and Twain, whose treatment of the land precedes Faulkner's.[25] But Carpentier comes late enough for this literary appropriation to have already taken place—in large part through the rhetoric of Romanticism evoked in *Los pasos perdidos*—and so nature appears primarily as a friendly counterweight to the alienating civilization the narrator has just fled—a generally auspicious and recognizable even if at times a dangerous and insecure space. Such an appropriation of nature is clearly more advanced in North American literature, as we see in Faulkner, just as the destruction of the natural world is also more complete.

Let us dwell on this difference for a moment. The fear of the machine as the enemy of the pastoral dream is a stronger literary tradition in North America than in Latin America—indeed, Faulkner's small snake of a train puffing punily and yet insistently in the wilderness is a prime example of it. In Carpentier the machine is less important, perhaps because it is still less potent in the jungle; the narrator destroys his own pastoral ideal from the inside, and the flying machine lifts him back out into the historical reality he subsequently realizes he must inhabit. There is no equivalent in *Los pasos perdidas* for the sale in "The Bear" of timber rights to a lumber company, which heralds in no uncertain terms the end of the old order, perhaps because the equivalent of an analogous expropriation (as well as its impact) has not yet entered the Latin American literary imagination.[26]

In "The Bear," the old order is nearly extinguished by the new; in *Los pasos perdidos,* the orders are located in clearly different spaces, one not replacing the other, except as the home of the narrator, the primordial jungle remaining protected by the lost marks (though not forever). The primordial realm is an alternative living space for the narrator, but not one he can choose in good faith; the same is not true for Ike, which may explain why he relinquishes it less willingly than does Carpentier's narrator. Furthermore, and this is perhaps the most important difference between these two texts, the reason for passage from the old to the new order in Carpentier is not primarily greed associated with original sin, as it is in part in Faulkner (although we do get glimpses of greedy miners in the jungle, who bode ill for its future), but rather the relentless march of history and our necessary existence in time—also an important factor in "The Bear," of course. The moral issue of land appropriation as such is thus less central to Carpentier's novel; it is primarily a drama of personal choice, whereas "The Bear" also enacts a sense of national guilt.[27]

Carpentier's narrator encounters the land as it was before the conquest and leaves it as it is, and Faulkner's Ike wishes to restore the land to its original unconquered state; in both cases, the profound respect for the virgin land is striking.[28] Both novels end with a symbolic preservation of the wilderness—the land asserting its power over the invaders and would-be possessors of it. In *Los pasos perdidos* the waters obscure the passage into the jungle, and Rosario marries a man from her own milieu, obscuring her temporary colonization by the narrator (though we do wonder about the paternity of her unborn child). "The Bear" ends with Boon sitting under a tree filled with scampering and chattering squirrels, warning everyone else away by shouting " 'Get out of here! Don't touch them! Don't touch a one of them! They're mine!' " But his voice is "hoarse and strangled," and his gun is in pieces around him; they are clearly no match in their petty desire of appropriation for the squirrels who fill the tree. He cannot possibly have them all, as he seems to wish, for once he shoots (if he ever gets the gun together to do it!), even if he hits one, the others will retreat to safety. Furthermore, the implicit equation of the "frantic squirrels" who make the tree a "maelstrom of mad leaves" and Boon's "frantic abandon of a madman" as he hammers, further incapacitates man in the face of the natural wilderness by absorbing him into its rhythm even as he attempts to appropriate its creatures.[29]

The respect for the wilderness that these images reveal also includes a religious sense of awe, which is attested to in both novels by shrines. In "The Bear," Sam's and Lion's graves with their relics are "secret and sunless places with delicate fairy tracks," where the two beings are "not held fast in earth but free in earth and not in earth but of earth," and on which Ike deposits an offering (328). A similar talisman representing the value of the wilderness inheritance is the horn Ike gives to the woman who has borne Cass Edmonds's grandson's child in "Delta Autumn"— "covered with the unbroken skin from a buck's shank and bound with silver" (363). The horn contrasts with the money which she thrusts into her slicker pocket "as if it were a rag, a soiled handkerchief," before lifting down the horn (362). Once she has it in her hand, she says to Ike, who has been cynically advising her how to get on in the world and get revenge for her situation, "Old man, . . . have you lived so long and forgotten so much that you don't remember anything you ever knew or felt or even heard about love?" (363). It is as if through the horn she reaches back to the moral strength the wilderness used to embody, a strength that comes across in her words even though the wilderness has vanished. She is certainly not a virgin, but the unpierced skin over the horn still is. In *Los pasos perdidos* the narrator sees in blocks of granite what "parecían ruinas de templos muy arcáicos" ("seemed the ruins of archaic temples" [143, 125]), and recognizes in a primitive clay idol what he thinks is "más que Dios: es la Madre de Dios" ("more than God, it is the Mother of God" [189, 165]).

These shrines bear out Ainsa's contention that the sense of center is strong in American literature, and that American narrative often searches for temples that constitute sacred spaces. But his notion that these sacred centers are islands in vast unnamed and threatening spaces, while true for *Los pasos perdidos,* is really reversed in "The Bear" because of its more colonized scene. There it is the whole space of the woods which is itself the island in the sea of surrounding civilization and which is represented by the shrine. In any case, the dichotomies spanned by Ike and Carpentier's narrator mean that their existences embody the transition from a centered teleological view of culture to a decentered modernist perspective. The narrative voices of these texts exist not at the center the protagonist wishes to inhabit, but in the verbal spaces between that desired and denied telluric center and the more civilized and avowedly profane peripheries of cities and towns. In the end, then, as in the beginning (though perhaps for different reasons), there is still a "lack of 'hearths,' temples and fixed points from which everything can organize itself in a coherent space" in the American literary landscape.[30]

In both texts, then, while the land is extremely important, it is no longer the virtually autonomous force it was in earlier literature, molding character in unique ways—as the pampa, for example, is shown to mold the lonely and wandering souls of the gauchos in Ricardo Güiraldes's *Don Segundo Sombra.* Neither is it a mirror of the protagonist's soul. The closeness of character and land in "The Bear" and *Los pasos perdidos* represents the appropriation already effected in numerous ways—political, economic, literary; the distance that remains between them takes account of the irony with which that very appropriation is viewed in these texts.

The sense of betraying the land through words that perturbs both Ike and Carpentier's narrator obviously reinforces their sense of terrestrial betrayal through discovery and colonization. We might also note in this context that verbal appropriation of American landscape has often taken place from a foreign perspective; as we hear again and again, the new world was first described with and for the eyes of the old. Both Faulkner's and Carpentier's texts are implicated in this European betrayal of American reality: the use of European forms to tell of the land is analogous to the usurpation of that land, and both authors work solidly and avowedly in the European tradition, cementing the connection with intertextual allusions. But one could also argue that these particular texts use foreign forms to restore the autonomy of the land. Thus they make retribution in the only way they can—by offering themselves as the verbal spaces in which terrestrial appropriation is recorded, confronted, criticized, lamented, and thereby in some sense mitigated. In this enterprise it is important that the forms of that critique, like the ideologies and weapons of the appropriation, are clearly of European origin yet now serve a different end: the desire to undo in some sense the previous appropriation as well as to celebrate the land. In Faulkner the ritualistic tone is more clearly marked by the ceremonial language of repetition in the discourse itself; in Carpentier the frequent allusion to specific pieces of music serves a celebratory function, as do the baroque descriptions of the land.

In *Los pasos perdidos* the aesthetic appropriation of space is a central issue, an issue that is largely absent from "The Bear," but one which is analogous in many respects to the problem of actual landownership that absorbs Ike. We might say that Faulkner and Carpentier are looking ultimately for different things—Faulkner for moral laws, Carpentier for aesthetic inspiration—but that they find them in the same wild place, and, not inconsequentially, in that place the two aims often tend to merge.[31] In *Los pasos perdidos,* the narrator's companion Mouche is the primary culprit in this respect, for she is unable to appreciate most of what she sees of the new land without aesthetic glosses from the familiar—is unable, finally, to experience nature without culture. The problem becomes more complicated the more closely one investigates it, for even the narrator's enthusiasm for nature and primitive civilization is mediated substantially by cultural tradition—his studies in ethnomusicology, for example, and his reading of literature. Faulkner allows Ike a relatively untroubled reading of the holy words of nature in his communion with the woods and the bear, one that Carpentier denies his narrator, who recognizes that his jungle is not only for him an inevitably mediated but often a deceitful text: "la selva era el mundo de la mentira, de la trampa y del falso semblante; allí todo era disfraz, estratagema, juego de apariencias, metamorfosis" ("the jungle is the world of deceit, subterfuge, duplicity; everything there is disguise, stratagem, artifice, metamorphosis" [173, 149]). But not always, particularly in the aesthetic realm; at one point he wonders whether "las formas superiores de la emoción estética no consistirán, simplemente, en un supremo entendimiento de lo creado" ("the highest forms of the aesthetic emotion do not consist merely in a supreme understanding of creation" [219, 190]). The narrator's extreme overvaluation of the primordial realm is finally seen to be his delusion—and yet . . . the charm of it remains strong and brings back his ability to compose. So back and forth we go.

The effort to create texts appropriate to the land they describe coexists with the search for "'that inscription of the earth's initials' [of which we hear in Neruda's poem "Love, America (1400)"]—for the writing that precedes writing," a coexistence that is explicitly presented in the narrator's efforts to compose a symphony that would reflect the rhythms of the jungle, and in Carpentier's own descriptions of that jungle.[32] In "The Bear" this correspondence between land and text is rarely thematized, but we sense it implicitly in the stately and pristine language used to describe the hunt and the unspoiled woods. In this context the ending of Doña Bárbara provides a contrasting image of the desired relationship between territory and text in the barbed wire that represents "the straight line of man within the curved line of nature."[33] That barbed wire marks among all "los innumerables caminos, por donde hace tiempo se pierden, rumbiendo, las esperanzas, uno solo y derecho hacia el porvenir" ("the innumerable ways, where for ages hopes wandered and lost themselves, a single straight one toward the future"). Here the land needs to be tamed not matched by the word—the perspective of the Enlightenment rather than of romanticism.

That the correspondence between text and terrain can have negative as well as positive connotations, is another similarity between these two novels. A problematic relationship to the land can trouble the process of inscription, causing disruptions in textual production in both thematic and structural ways. Just as the narrator in Los pasos perdidos cannot find the right piece of earth to inhabit, trying to live the life of the jungle as his own, an attempt which even he will finally judge to be an inauthentic project, so he cannot find the paper—the artistic ground—on which to write the music inspired by that very jungle. He searches for the continental blank page on which to write his symphonies and finds that it is not really so blank either for him or for its inhabitants, and that even if it were, he needs pages with lines for writing music ruled on them— lines that have been traced symbolically by history. A similar disruption of text by a problematic relation to terrain appears in the fourth chapter of "The Bear," where the ledgers in which Ike reads the history of his misappropriated ancestral lands are stunningly illiterate and fragmen- tary—barely legible, minimal and distinctly underdeveloped as texts. This basic and problematic correspondence between text and terrain ap- pears at the heart of that section:

> The cotton was long since picked and ginned, and all day now the wagons loaded with gathered corn moved between field and crib, processional across the enduring land. "Well, maybe that's what He wanted. At least, that's what He got." This time there was no yellowed procession of fading and harmless ledger pages. This was chronicled in a harsher book and McCaslin, fourteen and fifteen and sixteen, had seen it and the boy himself had inherited it as Noah's grandchildren had inherited the Flood although they had not been there to see the deluge: that dark corrupt and bloody time while three separate peoples had tried to adjust not only to one another but to the new land which they had created and inherited too. . . . (289)

The seasonal procession, enduring like the land itself on which it writes, contrasts with the undignified procession of ledger pages, a degraded, perhaps, but not really a harmless text. Both the stately writing of the seasons (God's text) and the feeble scratchings in the ledger (the Mc- Caslin family's attempt at recording their own procession across time and space) are contrasted with the brutal text inscribed by the Civil War on the land. Shortly after this, Ike briefly and implicitly detaches the historical text from the land on which it is written. First we hear that "'this land is, indubitably, of and by itself cursed': and he / 'Cursed:' and again McCaslin merely lifted one hand, not even speaking and not even toward the ledgers: . . . so did that slight and rapid gesture establish in the small cramped and cluttered twilit room not only the ledgers but the whole plantation in its mazed and intricate entirety—the land, the fields. . . ." But soon this is rectified, and we hear that it is "not the land, but us"; presumably we bear the curse which the land merely records (298). "[B]y itself" it is potential not accomplished action, just as the blank page before the text is written exists as potential; once the writing, like the history Ike is recalling, takes place, page and text are inseparable (though not indistinguishable). McCaslin lifts his hand to symbolically write action on the land, and thereby evokes the plantation—the primary historical text inscribed irrevocably in the South. Here again Carpentier is more relentlessly historical in his philosophy, inscribing the passage of time and history on the land with his portraits of different ages the narrator passes through, time and history that start in the natural world before human habitation.

As I have implied throughout this discussion, the idealization of the land in these works, especially in "The Bear," is obviously the American version of the universal myth of paradise, of the search for the sacred center, for the temple with its grail—alternatives to the wasteland.[34] Such a search also belongs to the pattern of romance or, in Joseph Campbell's formulation, to the pattern of "a separation from the world, a penetration to some source of power, and a life-enhancing return."[35] The problem in both these cases is largely in the return. Within these broad categories, Carpentier's narrator remains closer to the contemplative European pastoral ideal, which, as Poggioli points out, never includes hunting; Ike, as American woodsman, represents the more active North American version of the pastoral. Part of the difference between these visions may stem from the cultural pretexts behind these texts: Carpentier inspired by accounts of discovery, Faulkner growing up amidst concerns for recovery.[36] In any case, both belong to what Leo Marx calls "complex pastoralism," which, while invoking the image of the green land as "a symbolic repository of meaning and value," acknowledges the power of opposing forces, not the least of which is history itself.[37]

A central point in this comparison, one which is important enough to be reflected in my title but which is too large to be pursued here, is the way in which the persistent concern with space in these new world fictions manifests itself as spatialization of time.[38] As has been implicit in much of my discussion, the spatial realms in both "The Bear" and *Los pasos perdidos* are clearly visions of temporal difference, and vice versa. Although in Latin America the expenditure of time is less tied to the ruination of space than in the U.S., the gaps in chronology in *Los pasos perdidos* and the difficulty of reconstructing genealogy and past events in "The Bear," for example, are temporal analogues for the problematic spatial history the texts dramatize, therefore not necessarily in the "ordered immortal sequence" of the seasons, but in man's disrupted temporal script (*Moses*, 312).

Another important point of comparison that I will mention only briefly is the role of women in this textuality of appropriation.[39] In both texts we see Adam and Eve in the garden momentarily, happily possessed and possessing. In Faulkner, for one brief instant Ike's wife functions similarly to Rosario in enabling Ike to experience an Edenic relation to woman as she personifies the land; when

> they were married and it was the new country, his heritage too as it was the heritage of all, out of the earth, beyond the earth yet of the earth because his too was of the earth's long chronicle, his too because each must share with another in order to come into it and in the sharing they become one: for that while, one: for that little while at least, one: indivisible, that while at least irrevocable and unrecoverable, living in a rented room still but for just a little while and that room wall-less and topless and floorless in glory for him to leave each morning and return to at night (311–12),

there is not too much of a discrepancy between their coupling and Ike's statement that "still the woods would be his mistress and his wife" (326). Note here how even though they are in a room, at the idyllic moment that room does not belong exclusively to them and opens out into space. But that moment of common union and mutual possession of bodies and lands is so brief that if we don't look carefully we might miss it; that idyll has already disintegrated even as Ike speaks, for his wife makes the acquisition of the ancestral lands to which he feels unentitled the condition for possession of her body, interjecting a kind of economic imperative between their love and their land, appropriating with corrupt flesh the very earth Ike wishes to cleanse. Thus this Eve quickly becomes temptress, incarnating the greed for property that transformed the Edenic South into its current degraded state.

Rosario, since she represents the land itself, plays a more passive role in the action (though not symbolically): "entre su carne y la tierra que se pisaba se establecían relaciones escritas en las pieles ensombrecidas por la luz" ("relationships became established between her flesh and the ground we were treading, relationships proclaimed by sun-darkened skins" [113, 97]). For a moment the narrator lets us glimpse himself and Rosario as Adam and Eve in their paradise "donde nos bañamos desnudos, los de la Pareja" ("[where] we bathed, naked, we, the Couple" [205, 177]), but ultimately it is he who cannot replay the simple solution of Rómulo Gallegos's *Canaima,* which ends with the union of foreigner and forest/woman producing a *mestizo* son who will carry forth the best of both traditions. Rosario, on the other hand, is one of those women in Latin American literature who, as Ainsa claims, seem to be born from the union of the river with the jungle; for the narrator, union with her gives the illusion that "a native woman encloses in her heart the secret of 'rootedness' and that it is possible to build, around their love, a *center* in the forest."[40]

These sexual differences are important culturally, even though the land represents a similarly rejuvenating force in both Americas. Another significant difference typical of the two literatures is that Carpentier's narrator finds both a community and union with a woman in his wilderness. Ike finds neither; his experience is more solitary in nature, his primary communion being with the bear as a symbol of the wilderness untouched by human hands. In addition, while sexual identities seem to be conflated in the North (as Leslie Fiedler has pointed out at length), the same is not generally true in the South.[41] The vision of Boon and Lion embracing in sleep contrasts with Rosario's fierce rejection of what she perceives to be Mouche's lesbian advances as they are bathing in the river. These characters, unlike Huck Finn, are not about to come back to the raft with someone of their own sex. Perhaps this is why the symbol of the wilderness in Faulkner is essentially masculine (the bear), and Carpentier feminine (Rosario). Even so, both writers—albeit Faulkner rather more than Carpentier—continue an American tradition of metaphorical association of the female body and the land, and of postromantic figurations of desire which associate the beloved to the land and then exclude her from its exploration. Even Carpentier belongs here in his way, for he divides the female presence in two here, personifying the land in Rosario and denying Mouche the power to explore it.

In both cases two visions of woman compete to represent man's relationship to the land. We have already seen Ike's wife as Edenic companion or grasping temptress. Similarly, on one level the rather primitive battle between Rosario and Mouche is a fight for reigning deity of the land—is she to be an autochthonous earth goddess or an imported cultural object?—and on another it is the symbolic struggle between two theories of writing in and on the new world—will it be of native or imported origin? Characteristically, Faulkner's concern with the land here is largely moral, Carpentier's largely aesthetic.

There has now developed a modern tradition of Latin American essays which contrast the two Americas—from Sarmiento and Rodó through Paz, O'Gorman, Fuentes, and Fernández Retámar, among others. This comparative tradition is less marked in North American writing because less powerful nations have a vested interest in understanding their more powerful neighbors, whereas the reverse is not generally the case. My comparison of these two texts, like others which investigate similarities between Faulkner and any number of Latin American writers with whom he has many affinities, softens some of the traditional distinctions between North and South. Faulkner, for example, retains in the generally sympathetic person of Ike some of the moral rigidity that Edmundo O'Gorman claims presided over the English program of taming the natural environment and providing a program of action and individual freedom, but puts it at the service of an opposing plan of restitution rather than the original project of appropriation. At the same time, however, Ike's sense that "there is only one truth and it covers all things that touch the heart," while imperfectly implemented, remains an ideal which approximates the project of the Spanish colonists who, O'Gorman maintains, wished to establish "ecumenical unity with the moral kingdom of Catholic truth, believed and lived as absolute and eternal" (*Moses,* 260).[42] Carpentier, on the other hand, depicts a more pragmatic approach, not going so far as to propose improvements in nature, but implying the validity of different systems of knowledge and values for different times and places. In the end, then, while it does not conflate the Anglo-Saxon and the Hispanic traditions, this comparison nevertheless joins North to South in significant ways, suggesting that the Americas do indeed have a common literature.

René Prieto

In-Fringe: The Role of French Criticism
in the Fiction of Nicole Brossard
and Severo Sarduy

> Tout écrivain qui, par le fait même d'écrire n'est pas conduit à penser: je suis la révolution . . . en réalité n'écrit pas.
> —Maurice Blanchot, *Le livre à venir*

The essays in this collection have, at the very least, one feature in common: they focus on the literary traffic that flows between the Americas. My design is both similar and different, at once broad and reductive. I, too, speculate on the commerce across the isthmus, but the line I draw is an arc of the horizon, an azimuth that brings together three parts of the world rather than two. *Do the Americas Have a Common Literature?,* like most human endeavors, is all about spills and spurts—styles and schools and tendencies that flow over borders and make contact, directly or indirectly. Indirectly, because two authors need not exert an unmediated influence upon each other but take inspiration, more often than not, from a common source. After all, as Wellek and Warren so pertinently point out, "Western literature . . . forms a unit, a whole," which is to say that we are bound to talk about global relationships rather than direct influences in any comparative study.[1]

A case in point is that of Nicole Brossard and Severo Sarduy, whose work I propose to study in this essay. They do not arrive at comparable ends from an acquaintance with each other's writing (even though they know each other) but rather through the French connection that drew them both to the theoretical reflections of critics, linguists, and philosophers who rallied around and published in the French quarterly *Tel Quel* during the 1960s and 1970s.

It is not surprising that Nicole Brossard (b. 1943), at the vanguard of Quebecois literature since the publication of her first volume of poetry, *Aube à la saison* (1965), and whose early novels—*Un livre* (1970), *Sold Out* (1973), *French Kiss* (1974)—had been influenced by the *nouveau roman* writers, should look toward France and the critical coterie clustering around *Tel Quel* for inspiration as well as for kinship. Sarduy, bird of a different feather, flocked to the quarterly through the vagaries of history. In 1959 he traveled to France to study art history with a grant from the Cuban government. Barely twenty-two, he was bursting with eagerness after the first six months of the Cuban Revolution, heady from two years of skylarking among Havana's literary firebrands (as a publishing member of *Ciclón* and, starting in March 1959, of the arts and literature weekly, *Lunes de Revolución*).

Planning to take Paris by storm, Sarduy was instead absorbed by the city that has mesmerized so many generations of Latin American writers. Once his grant from the Cuban government ran out, he stayed in France, a decision which, as Roberto González Echevarría points out in his groundbreaking *La Ruta de Severo Sarduy*, should not be seen as a "desertion."[2] I argue, in fact, that he stayed in Paris because, at that stage of his career, his commitment to art, to writing, and to his own growth concerned him far more than making a statement of political allegiance.

The truth of the matter is that for Sarduy, as for Brossard, writing *is* the revolution. Their disturbing originality stems from an ability to sever themselves from the literary language of the past, impressing their work with a uniqueness which is, after all, the essence of art. Brossard's writing, like Sarduy's, is a perpetual search for limits to transcend; it is an *oeuvre* in both senses of the French word: not only a substantial body of work but a task, a construction which in both cases forestalls psychological and chronological development to concentrate on language instead. In a nutshell, Sarduy and Brossard set out to transgress the canonical formulas of the art they practice. She, militant feminist, cofounder and coeditor of Quebec's avant-garde monthly, *La Nouvelle Barre du Jour*,[3] declares, with a twinge of glee that cannot escape the reader, "Lois, interdits sont sans efficacité devant le possible à transgresser,"[4] a statement which echoes Sarduy's own earlier declaration of independence: "La escritura es el arte de descomponer un orden y componer un desorden."[5] Their unswerving iconoclasm invites a number of reflections that can be summed up in three questions: where does such commitment to transgress originate? where does it lead our two authors? and, last but not least, does it evolve in a direction that is distinctively American?

As all roads led to Rome in the world of the ancients, all inquiries concerning the literature of the twentieth century lead us, of necessity, to the writing of Joyce. This may seem like a sally from our subject when it is, in fact, an entry through its widest door. What can come after *Finnegans Wake*? and how should it be written? are questions that must sooner or later face all writers worthy of the name. Inheritor and propounder of a transgressive legacy that has its greatest forerunners in Rabelais, Hölderlin, and Lautréamont, Joyce, more than any modern author, has disrupted the law—which is to say that he has first questioned and then symbolically done away with the father, emblem of power and order.[6] Such transgression, innovation, sacrifice—call it what we will— opens the way in turn to a subversive discourse which, to paraphrase Kristeva,[7] shatters ideologies and even "natural" language in order to reformulate the relationship between subjective and objective, between reality and the symbolic. Kristeva and the entire team of *Tel Quel* are drawn to the Irishman's "languo of flows"[8] because his literary practice is a compendium of all the notions and features that have fascinated the editorial board of this journal since its foundation. Notions, such as *sujet en procès,* which derail Cartesian logocentrism by casting doubts on the idea of the text as Truth and which substitute for the subject's foregone certainty, unity, and unquestionability, Lacan's notorious maxim: "Je ne pense pas là où je suis, et je ne suis pas là où je pense." Notions such as paragrammatic writing, *écriture,* and the relationship between body and text; in short, notions that refer to and sum up the transformation of linguistic codes which the process of *twentieth-century* writing entails.

More precisely, we could say that Joyce is to practice what *Tel Quel* is to theory or, to take up Lacan's words once again, that Joyce is what happens "quand on refuse l'analyse." He is the symptom which *Tel Quel* has been laying on the couch for the last two decades. Which brings me to say that if we examine this group's *Théorie d'ensemble,* we will end up in a privileged position on both sides of the looking glass: with the origin (Joyce) on one side, and the marriage of theory and practice (in the writing of Sarduy and Brossard) on the other. But let me not light the wick before loading the barrel. Let us travel rather from the specific to the general in a circular journey that will bring us back to the beginning. Let us compare Sarduy's writing to Brossard's, pointing out features shared with or borrowed from *Tel Quel* in the hope that, once gleaned within the symptom that is their writing, these features will shed some light on the creative process and the originality of our two radically modern American authors.

But why *these* authors? Why, in particular, Sarduy and Brossard? Why not Quebecois literature and Cuban literature or, taking our distinctions one step further, Cuban literature outside of Cuba? Simply because if both or all three are, arguably, offshoots from the mainstream, then the two authors we have chosen are each in their own way at the helm of the flagship, at the forefront of a literary "movement" which dodges even this label. Neither Anne Hébert nor Marie-Claire Blais in French Canada, neither Reinaldo Arenas nor, even, the genial Guillermo Cabrera Infante (among the Cubans writing outside of Cuba) has made such a thorough commitment to transgression and disruption in their innovation. Which is not to say that their writing is not exciting, engaging, unique; but simply that what I propose to do is to compare the most "liminal," the most extreme, the ones who, in every sense, revolutionize and reinvent literary language. It is this notion of literature as revolution that gives us direct entry into the more empirical section of our essay, but not before making one last stop: in order to discuss what is revolutionary, we must consider the literary traditions that are being questioned.

According to Philippe Sollers, the notion of artistic "creation" is one of the greatest myths of bourgeois ideology.[9] Sollers is referring to the neoromantic notion that enthrones or canonizes writers by attributing to them the power to read events from the storehouse of their mind in a linear, coherent, mimetic fashion; in other words, to trace a frieze of life from the blueprint they carry fully outlined in their brain. Sollers questions not only the idea of individual and exclusive authorship, but that of *oeuvre* as well. In his eyes—as in the eyes of all "Telquelians"— the text is a production which brings together reader and writer in a symbiotic process referred to as *"lecture-production."* The author of *Logiques* further argues that it is impossible to study writing (*l'écriture*) by means other than through writing itself (72). Writing is a process that unveils its secrets in the doing, in the production. Putting into perspective Althusser's definition of the notion of theory ("a specific form of practice"),[10] Sollers suggests that what we refer to as literature is a notion that belongs to the past, while that of *écriture* (i.e., the theoretical or theorizing exercise) is the vocation of our times (72). Kristeva, for her own part, equates *écriture* with *connaissance* indicating that writing is a process of (self) knowledge which writer and reader mother together as they unravel the text.[11] Building on these notions, Brossard elaborates her own artistic credo: "Je dis qu'il est difficile d'écrire la vérité—qu'elle est impossible—," she admits, "et que si je transgresse c'est par plaisir, pour en connaître davantage sur moi, ça, les personnes, les systèmes."[12]

Writing is—search, (re)search, of oneself, of the word, of the other. Writing is—has always been—a quest but, unlike the *littérature* of the past, hers and Sarduy's is an *écriture* in perpetual process of evolution, never firm-set or complete because it involves the reader in an ongoing and creative communication. Furthermore, the text is caught up in a process of *dépense* (or "expenditure" in the sense Bataille gives to this term), "it burns at all levels," and is therefore the opposite of an entity that is full, closed-off, complete.[13] It is for these very reasons that Kristeva suggests, "l'écriture est la crête où s'affirme le devenir historique du sujet, c'est à dire un sujet a-psychologique, a-subjectif, un sujet historique. L'écriture pose donc un autre sujet pour la première fois" (25). The subject described by Kristeva is both new and "historical" because it evolves through each reading. As Sollers goes on to indicate, the text belongs to everyone and to no one in particular; it is not a finite product and should be seen as the sign of a productivity that contains its own annulment (71).

Kristeva's and Sollers's reflections concerning the text-in-process might seem like minor concerns to some, like hairsplitting Bulgarian style to others, and like a digression on my part to most. The truth of the matter is that the statements of fact made by these critics are, first and foremost, momentous; second, directly related to our subject; and, third, the pearly gates through which *any* reflection on contemporary writing must endeavor to sail. What may sound like *Tel Quel* magniloquence boils down to one simple gesture: with a sweep of the hand, Kristeva and Sollers put to bed conventional expectations concerning unity and coherence of plot and character. "Putting them to bed" is actually a gross exaggeration. What *Tel Quel* does do is publicize how, in the process of *écriture,* the writer breaks away from the subjection to the *histoire,* with its "actors" (Greimas) and its narrative logic. The focus of interest shifts instead to what Benveniste labels the *discours;*[14] in other words, the world in which a tale is being told becomes more important than the world vision portrayed. It is at this point that Sarduy and Brossard reenter our discussion. It is they, along with the equally versatile Sollers, who are forging this new *écriture,* who are revolutionizing the state of the art by breaking with all the conventions of story-telling and casting the linguistic sign as protagonist of their fiction.

Suffice it to look, for example, at Sarduy's most *Tel Quel*–inspired novel, *Cobra.* This cock-and-bull farce of a transvestite bent on parting from his privates is literally shattering. Shattering because it introduces the notion of impermanence as a narrative a priori to the reading public in Latin America (or at least to the small reading public who does not reject a fiction in which each narrative phase turns out to call the lie to the ones that precede and follow it); shattering because the characters are in perpetual process of transformation (to wit: the slippery Dr. Ktazob, hard on Cobra's tracks, evolves from a morphine addict [96] to a "midwife" and a "chondrologist" [97], all in spite of the fact that a dancer at the Festival had earlier suggested that the protean surgeon "no existía" [96]).

Brossard's characters are similarly involved in a process of transformation, but unlike Sarduy's, the change they undergo is a response to passing time, changing readers, and sign association: "Le temps qui change. L'horizon blesse, brise dans sa suite logique. L'horizon est à l'oeuvre disait une petite fille à sa mère pour qu'elle inscrive la phrase dans son cahier d'adulte."[15] The little girl's "grown up ledger" suggests the process of *devenir,* to borrow Barthes's[16] and Kristeva's word, and it is but one of the many indications that all characters in the works of this author are adrift like the aptly named Claire *Dérive* in *Picture Theory* (my emphasis). Drifting away from the linear fictions of the past, Sarduy and Brossard allow parameters other than the logical development of the *histoire* to guide and generate their tales. For the Quebecoise author, the space of fiction is "le terrain sans frontière prévisible de l'imaginaire, de la dérive. . . ."[17] A certain referential level remains, nonetheless, in the work of both Sarduy and Brossard. One could, without much effort, summarize the gist of *Picture Theory* and of *Cobra*; in spite of the ongoing process of negation inherent in this last, a story (or rather, *many* stories) is (are) being told. But both authors de-emphasize this narrative level and bank on the actual discourse, on the mechanisms of textual production and generation.

As we know, traditional texts are those in which the rules of syntax, semantics, and pragmatics are respected. The literal aspect—the armature—of such texts is hidden and the fiction creates an illusion based on reality. No such concerns exist, however, in the semiotic writing of Brossard and Sarduy. In their work, the relationship between signs, the relationship of signs to objects and to their users ("sender" and "receiver") is dissected in full view. In fact, it is this transparent process of dissection that comes to be the essence of their art. Which is why an early and seldom quoted short review by Sarduy entitled "Cubos" (about the paintings of Larry Bell but primarily concerned with the Cuban's own method) is so important.[18] The author of *Cobra* begins by decrying the persistent prejudice in our culture that wills the armature out of every finished composition: "Un prejuicio persistente de nuestra cultura quiere que, de toda producción del arte, sea obliterado el *soporte*" (97). By "support" he means the canvas, the pigments, the plaster, and, in literature, "la página y el grafismo" (97)—the very "body" upon which the artistic message is composed. The obliteration of this support comes as no surprise to the Cuban author because, as he convincingly argues, "our civilization—and especially Christian thought—vows the body to oblivion, to sacrifice" (97). This is why everything that refers to the body, everything that emblematizes it, becomes, by definition, transgressive.

This statement speaks directly to the understanding of Sarduy's own narrative aims. After all, couldn't we argue that his fiction after *Gestos* always contains a sublimation of the body at the core of its message? Doesn't the character of Cobra function as a metaphor for the phallus?[19] Doesn't the whole of *Colibrí* function as a dramatization of the narrator's longing to be identified with the maternal body?[20] Can't we say then that Sarduy, by his own definition, transgresses one of the most sacred principles of our culture in baring *both* the body of the narrative subject *and* the armature of the text? Not only can we say it, we will go one step further by documenting how the terms of this transgression warrant further comparison between the Cuban author and his Quebecoise counterpart.

On the discursive level, Sarduy and Brossard apply themselves directly to exposing the signified; they rely on homonyms, antonyms, paronyms, and parasynthesis to further their fictions along the syntagmatic axis, often independently from the paradigmatic development of the *histoire*. In other words, language (the expanding sign) motivates the text as much as the events in more traditional fiction. In Sarduy's *Cobra,* for example, the sign "trompa" (25) refers to the Eustachian tube ("laberinto de la oreja") described earlier (13). And since one of the protagonists (the masseur of the "Doll's Lyrical Theater") is named "Eustaquio," it refers equally to him but more exactly to his prodigious sex organ, which reminds the Señora of Ganesha, the elephant god in Indian mythology (21). The elephant's entry into the fiction allows Sarduy to come closer to his objective. The sex organ is likened to a trunk and because its outlandish proportions prick the doll's curiosity and rouse them to their ruin, the Señora is prompted to lament the fact that her establishment has been wrecked by "la trompa de Eustaquio" (i.e., the Eustachian tubes, the elephant's trunk, the masseur's towering penis). A comparable handling of homonyms takes place in *Picture Theory* with

Brossard's usage of the term *"langue"* to refer indistinctly to "language" and "tongue," the bodily organ. Such commingling allows in turn the marriage of body (the narrator's, the characters') and text—a notion which is the essence of her narrative conception.

In all instances, the textual body of these authors is dressed with signs motivated by their context and not by the intrigue. For instance, a word in Spanish or French may lead to a cognate foreign term that furthers the fiction through association, as in Brossard's poetic chain in *Picture Theory,* "Cosmos osmose cosmos annule, avive, a-vide, gravite, l'affame la mère la femme la femme: (human mind) ——— ——— lap/ ensée. . . . C'est toujours ainsi que ça produit l'imagination tentée par l'impossible, débordée par l'utopie, utter, dutter, K.O., métaphysique" (115). Sarduy's transformations in *Cobra* are of a somewhat different order; his writing is peppered with foreign terms (not necessarily paronyms) wedged into Spanish to expand the semantic field: "adolece de la hipérbole tapageuse, el rococó abracadabrante y la exageración sin coto" (47), "Calzaba otra vez los coturnos" (33), "entiché" (59), "una pause-café" (78). In a similar manner, intertextual references penetrate his fiction although, in contrast to Brossard's serious allusions to other works, they are mostly parodic: "las muy Derridianas" (53), "borgesco espejeo" (53), "aparecen calderonianos" (57), or the blatant parodies of Lezama Lima in *Maitreya.*[21] The overall effect is that of a verbal collage in which language is in a perpetual process of expansion while the "rational" development of the *histoire* is being eroded.

Antonyms are an even more corrosive tool in the transgressive arsenal of both writers because the mimetic contract is perpetually subverted by statements that deny what has been previously stated. For instance, in *Cobra* the hero "reía sin reír" (80) while Pup, his alter ego "huye sin huir, aúlla sin sonar" (70). In *Picture Theory,* Brossard one-ups Sarduy by developing antonyms as a network of signifieds after translating the original or nuclear signifier from French to English. A case in point is the isotope *"Paravent"* translated into the ambivalent English term, "Screen" (a word that designates both a means to project [or reveal] and one to withhold from view [or conceal]). This kind of ambiguity holds true as well in the next terms of Brossard's associative chain: SKIN: SCREEN (the isotope generated by *paravent* telescopes far into the text, 130). SKIN, like the first term in the network of associations, connotes antonymous signifieds since it designates both the body's wrapping and its exposed state—its nakedness.

But this is merely the tip of Brossard's linguistic iceberg. Since a screen is also a partition, the author of *Picture Theory* associates it with the word *fente* (crack, crevice, split, slit), setting off a complete network of sexual associations in the process. *Fente* is thereafter linked to the female narrator, "M. V.," a woman who is capable of holding a "screen" between herself and her "true feelings" (127). "Paravent/translucide: la matière luisante et polie aux couleurs vives présentait *comme* M. V. une ouverture en forme de fente dans sa vie" (my emphasis, 147). Elsewhere we are told how M. V. manages to overcome pain by thinking about words, words which do not glide away because they have been screened off by an "Écran de sélection" (127). The narrator expresses the wish to pierce through this screen in a state of sexual arousal since "it is humid, saliva and salt" (127). The female sex is also, then, an *écran* or screen, and a *fente*. And so, metonymically, is woman: "FEMME SKIN" (127).

The original *paravent* functions, therefore, as "double densité" (127), weaving, as it unwinds, a rich tapestry of associations—"SCREEN: SKIN: SPIN: SCREAM: SKEIN" (127–29)—too elaborate to follow through in any greater detail within the limited space of this essay. But even without hearing the full delivery of Brossard's very pregnant isotope (there is no end to it, of course, as she argues. "Dans le concret de l'écriture, l'abstraction continue" [127]), what must be seen and said is that the development of *Picture Theory* relies not on the casual encounters of five women on a beach and in Montreal but, more importantly, in the coming together—and apart—of words which are, as Paz would say, "signos en rotación."[22] The intrigue, after all, is a mere fiction: "On invente un climat, une plage ou un hiver" (127). What is real is the *langue* which bares to view the narrative body and artistic tool encapsulated and released in the sign.

Sarduy's and Brossard's handling of parasynthesis is a case in point of this *langue* in search of an author. (It should be obvious that I do not use this term in the Saussurean sense but with Brossard's unique acceptation of a double meaning: language/body.) Both form words by adding a derivative ending and prefixing a particle in a manner which has everything to do with ludic transgression and nothing to do with the telling of a conventional adventure story. Words become their own adventure. For instance, when Sarduy, alluding to the snake of the title and to Paz's poem writes, "Se recobra. Se enrosca. (la boca obra.)" (118), or when Brossard drifts in *Picture Theory* from "Machines à tout faire" to "machine gun" to "machisme pensant" (96), the equation of terms is only part of the design. Of course, Brossard is making a political statement by identifying "machine" with "gun" with "machisme" (as is Sarduy by homologating language with snake with phallus with power), but such messages are the trace left on the page when signs are cultivated for their own sake in what amounts to an unprecedented verbal revolution.

Unprecedented, but not without lineage. Both authors play with the myriad possibilities of the linguistic sign as Mallarmé, Joyce, Artaud, and Bataille have done before them: they strip the word from its classical sense of plenitude, their narrative discourse no longer a reflection of the world. What was heretofore a specular relationship between signifier and signified becomes frayed, pluralized. Their aim, in the words of Brossard, is "Faire que le texte invente uniquement pour le plaisir et que son imagination l'éloigne des circuits de valeurs qui favorisent l'économie, l'accumulation, la thésaurisation" (47). This is why a tone of epistemological self-mockery aimed at the naive pretensions of bourgeois rationality is such an important ingredient in their fiction.

Sarduy and Brossard let their imaginations run free with the very matter they handle: words, sentences, syntax, chronology, character development. Rather than abide by establishment rules they invent their own and in the process forge a new literary language different from everything that has been written since *Finnegans Wake*. Their fiction relies upon one of the two modes of expression which Kristeva defines as *le sémiotique* and picks out in the exclamations and vocalizations of infants as well as in the rhythm, prosody, punning, "nonsensical sense," and laughter of adult discourse.[23] We could summarize Kristeva's idea by saying that the *sémiotique* is a nonexpressive articulation while the *symbolique* refers to the domain of signs, to language, to the relationship between signifier and signified. Of particular interest is the fact that in order to transcend from one modality or type of articulation to the other, the infant must internalize the paternal law (what Lacan terms the "Nom du Père") forbidding the body of the mother. When this occurs, the subject begins to articulate a type of discourse which is understood by those who surround him, a language that abides by the conventions of grammar, syntax, and the recognized correlation of given signifiers to given signifieds.

When we peruse the history of Western narrative, we immediately discover that the greatest schism in its development takes place when authors (Mallarmé, Joyce, Artaud) scale down or even abrade the *symbolique* by transgressing all of the conventions it imposes, and allow the characteristically maternal *sémiotique* to flood back into their discourse.[24]

We think immediately of Joyce's punning, word association, and use of homonyms and vocalizations (in the "Sirens" episode of *Ulysses,* for example) as we witness the deployment of similar effects in the work of Sarduy (Eustaquio episode) and Brossard (the *Paravent* sequence). But one feature distinguishes the radical revolution of our two authors from the voice of the masters. Joyce and Mallarmé generate and abrade language in order to charge it with meaning to the utmost degree without being necessarily conscious of the theoretical and/or psychoanalytic implications underlying their experimentation. Sarduy and Brossard, writing after *Tel Quel,* play a different semantic game. Let us not forget for one moment that the journal has dedicated a good number of special issues to transgressive language (numbers 34, 54, 78, 81, and 89, to name but a handful), not to mention Kristeva's own doctoral dissertation on Mallarmé, *La révolution du langage poétique.*[25] Brossard and Sarduy have both incorporated and shared in the theoretical findings disclosed by the avant-garde journal. Their writing, like Mallarmé's, charges language with meaning to the utmost; their writing, like Joyce's, tells a story, but in their case confabulation gives way to discourse in more ways than one.

It is not merely that signs motivate the development of the plot but so, too, that our American authors reveal and revel in the steps of narrative conception, steps that enter into the warp and woof of their writing when they tell us (as part of the "fiction") what it is that they do with words and why. Let us recall Sarduy's canonical pronouncements followed by practical demonstrations in *Cobra*: "la escritura es el arte de la elipsis" (15), "La escritura es el arte de la digresión" (16), "La escritura es el arte de recrear la realidad" (17); as well as Brossard's own "Les mots fonctionnent indéfiniment (l'évanouissement de la personne) à perte de vue en tout sens" (115). In short, Sarduy and Brossard bare the body of the text to the naked eye of the reader. Its machinery becomes their machination, the most blatant illustration of *écriture* as Sollers and Althusser define it—a theory that is a specific form of practice. And if theory is a form of practice, then the mimetic novel's greatest cynosure—verisimilitude—falls by the wayside. What used to be hidden becomes apparent: characters detach themselves from the fiction (Claire Dérive in *Picture Theory,* for instance, asks questions from "outside the text" [51]), the action casts doubts on itself and changes course in midstream, even the narrator of *Cobra* stands aside to address his characters: "Yo (que estoy en el público): Cállese o la saco del capítulo" (26).

Like Duchamp's notorious broken window, the fiction is "mise à nu":

Sarduy and Brossard merely print and bare it. Teasers at heart, they strip not only the narrative machinery but luxuriate in writing "the emotion of body in text,"[26] as they transgress every rule in the book. And since transgression is a defiance of the law and the law springs from the father—the figure which makes symbolic discourse possible—we can emphatically conclude that these two authors challenge, above all else, the phallocy of Western literature. As a result of this challenge the tower house of fiction does not topple but it is drastically transformed because the characteristically maternal *sémiotique* is allowed to take the helm.

It is to this type of rhythm, prosody, "nonsensical sense," and laughter that the Quebecoise feminist refers when she writes, "Les écrivains jouent à la femme pour pouvoir transgresser,"[27] a statement which floodlights in turn the nature of Sarduy's typical and topical transformations. Still, you wonder: in what way is transgressing the law an innovation? After all, doesn't modernity exist, as Paul de Man maintains, "in the form of a desire to wipe out whatever came earlier"?[28] We need to know, then, what makes the performing self-consciousness and self-reflexiveness of our two authors distinguishable from that of other postmodernists from both sides of the Atlantic. Can we even pretend that our two *enfants terribles* are unique or, to recapitulate the question out of which grew this essay, distinctly American in some respect? The answer to both questions is "yes" even though, in order to prove it, I must start by stating the obvious.

Insofar as all literature raises the question "what is language?" and the issue of language is in turn inextricable from the burden of culture and history, it is evident that each and every writer—issuing from a different set of experiences—will be a priori unique. Beyond this original distinction, however, writers drift toward sets, brotherhoods, and coteries, a fact that compels us to perceive them as members of a school or perpetrators of a style (realists, romantics, modernists). They are drawn to these coteries on the basis of shared experiences or common interests (a reaction against the nineteenth-century bourgeois social order, a spirit of anarchy, a cult of art for art's sake). While being unique, each and every one, they are also grouped together under generic labels that attempt to categorize the link that binds them. For instance, Sarduy and Brossard share many of the features that have come to signify the stock in trade of postmodernism—placing the emphasis on language and technique instead of on straightforward traditional content, or using parody in order to call into question the canonical function of literary action. What is it, then, that distinguishes them from fellow iconoclasts?

To begin with, and before going any further, let me say that there are times when even a compelling label stops us from staring into the face of truth. Here we are, attempting to circumscribe the purported originality of a given area while adhering to a label that is full of holes. The term "Literature of the Americas" has more of a connection with geography (specifically, with a sense of boundaries) than with history (the reason for and consequence of these boundaries). The particular type of idiolect that typifies Sarduy and Brossard could have been produced in India, Senegal, or in any colonial country fathered and smothered by a culture that functions as model of identification and object of rejection simultaneously. The postcolonial experience as a whole rather than the limiting label of "Literature of the Americas" is what distinguishes the extraordinary innovation of our two authors.

Being both part of a culture and linguistic tradition (respectively French and Spanish) and an offshoot from this tradition translates in their work as a return of the repressed that figures rejection as its cornerstone. It is this same rejection that Octavio Paz underscores in his authoritative arguments concerning the spurious origins of modern Mexicans, to whom he refers in terms that are equally applicable to other postcolonial offspring: "hijos de la nada" ("children of nothingness").[29] France and Spain may have given us language and the law, but they engendered us with a difference, a feature not unlike the legendary tail of the Buendías. This difference translates itself as a rejection of the origins that we simultaneously identify with and results in a torn, dialogical subject that is consistently and obsessively portrayed in our literature in one of two ways: on the one hand, by means of the doppelgänger (from Fabio Cáceres and Don Segundo Sombra to Marito and Pedro Camacho); on the other, by means of protagonists shown to be split between two ontological options ("Borges y Yo," or the heroes of Los pasos perdidos and El recurso del método).

Since our aim in this book is to grasp the uniqueness of the literature of the Americas, we cannot fail to specify one of its most distinctive features: I refer to this standing tradition of paired antagonists that illustrate in their schizoid split the dilemma of the negation of origins which Paz describes with such poignancy in El laberinto de la soledad. As the Mexican poet-philosopher so convincingly argues, "El mexicano no quiere ser ni indio, ni español. Tampoco quiere descender de ellos. Los niega" (78–79). And further, "Es pasmoso que un país con un pasado tan vivo, profundamente tradicional, atado a sus raíces, rico en antigüedad legendaria si pobre en historia moderna, solo se conciba como negación de su origen" (79). It is on this last point that I take issue with Paz: it is not *at all* astonishing that a country such as Mexico (or all of Latin America, for that matter) should conceive itself as a negation of its origins because the language and traditions we live with have been imposed upon us and become transformed, generating in the process new cultural and linguistic milieux that resemble the original medium but with the added twist of a different message. Such denial and transformation do not mean, at the same time, that our roots do not extend clear across the Atlantic. Spain and France are objects of rejection while continuing to be magnets and models of identification. Our postcolonial cultures—like the heroes in our literature—are split apart in this game of give and take. It only stands to reason that, as the literature of the Americas continues to evolve, this split will affect its language as it has its thematic development.

This is exactly what has happened in the fiction of Sarduy and Brossard. The paradox joining together identification and its contrary in unholy matrimony has been translated in their work in three related features: first and foremost, as a rejection of the symbolic, which is to say, of all that embodies the law of the father, the norm; second, as an apotheosis of the maternal impulse, the *sémiotique*; and third—because this struggle is written on the blood and marrow that we read—as a portrayal of the text as a dismembered *body* undergoing an autopsy that dramatizes the demise of phallic discourse. Sarduy's and Brossard's semiotic revolution is a logical outcome of the denial of origins which typifies our literature, but these authors have taken the disruption of the norm so far in form and content that we can speak of their innovation as the greatest upheaval in literary history since the publication of *Ulysses*.

If Sarduy and Brossard are so violently rejected by so many readers it is because their brand of action is too hot to handle, unbearable in every sense because it overturns the entire edifice of literature as we know it. It is not until we grasp their revolutionary and drastically innovative commitment to the semiotic modality that we begin to understand why they take such care to de-phallicize their narrative discourse in ways which include the aforementioned disruptions of the linear flow as well as more explicit scenes of castration and sapphic love from which the autocratic male figure is tellingly absent.

What is portrayed as a revealing absence in *Picture Theory* is even more plainly stated through Cobra's denial of self. Sarduy's protagonist embodies the paradox of being and not wanting, and conversely, of wanting and not being—in the sense that, as a transvestite, he spends the better part of the novel trying to dispossess himself from what he has and does not need even though it paradoxically defines him. Sarduy carries this identification to the point of likening Cobra to the phallus (describing the body of the transvestite with a "cabeza triangular que corona un arco," an "ojiva de bulbos babosos" capable of contraction and dilation and of spouting "chorros de jugos corrosivos, salivazos fénicos," makes this amply clear [120–21]), and designating the mutilated body after the castration ceremony with the third person singular pronoun, the voice that Benveniste refers to as the "non-personne."[30] In other words, without the phallus which signifies him (since Cobra is a metonymy for the male organ), the protagonist loses its identity.

What's more, all of Sarduy's characters after *Gestos* are in pursuit of this loss, a desire which translates itself as an identification with the female body. It is also a desire that defies the most fundamental law—that of nature—and one that is mirrored in this author's defiance of literary conventions. Defiance because even though Sarduy and Brossard use a language inherited from the father, it is a language they contaminate with neologisms, anglicisms, and gallicisms until they tear it apart. Of course, there is nothing new or unique about tearing language apart. Joyce did it and so did Artaud, and in both instances their destruction revealed—as it does for Sarduy and Brossard—a determination to transgress the symbolic discourse stationed by the "Name of the Father." What is new and therefore unique in the case of our postmodernists is that their own version of the tale of rejection is dramatized as an erotic metaphor which brings together body and language.

In fact, their novels can be said to be a bare for all because to them body is text, text is body. And this is no mere rhetorical formulation. When Brossard writes about "the passages" of Claire Dérive in *Picture Theory* she alludes explicitly to the labyrinths of her lover's physical being as well as to her station within the body of the text. "Claire Dérive du dedans de cette fiction se retournait vers moi, ayant compris qu'aucun passage ne m'était interdit" (159). Such double allusions abound in *Picture Theory* because, in the eyes of the Quebecoise, works of fiction are a duplication of image, a *dédoublement* of their author, the place where ink and voice flow together. Sarduy could not be more in agreement. In fact, the body is an even more persistent feature of his fiction because the hero of his allegory on the theme of castration is a characterization of the phallus. Cobra's lust for loss translates the author's own determination to transgress symbolic discourse. It would be a gross simplification, therefore, to view the hero's pursuit of castration as a restricted figuration of homosexuality and to ignore the fact that the refusal of the phallus is, in Sarduy's language, a metaphoric postulate of the kind of normative stance he aspires to obliterate. It is such abrogation that pinpoints the uniqueness of his work. It is by tearing apart the erotic body portrayed as fiction that our two authors show their determination to forge a semiotic language which, while appearing to deny its origins (Spanish, French, Telquelian theory), is in fact recasting the old blocks of the edifice of fiction in a unique and purely personal manner that deserves to be recognized as the furthest limb of the literary tree growing in America today.

Jonathan Monroe

Mischling and Métis: Common and Uncommon Languages in Adrienne Rich and Aimé Césaire

. . . progress in poetry has never consisted of anything but the annexation into the poem of a vast range of 'unwelcome' material [*de vastes étendues 'ingrates'*] torn away by a fortunate violence [*heureuse violence*] from the 'non-poetic.'
—Aimé Césaire, Preface to René Depestre's *Végétations de Clarté*

In their long-standing engagements with the politics of negritude and radical feminism, and in the more recent inflections of their work toward a politics of the *métis* and *Mischling,* Aimé Césaire and Adrienne Rich have both contributed significantly to expanding the range of what is common to poetry. To the extent that poetry itself continues to function, however, as a realm of the uncommon, the exceptional, a realm of privilege, its relationship to the commonplace, commonality, community, and what Rich has called "the dream of a common language" must remain deeply problematic. Such a dream points on the one hand to a shared wealth of linguistic resources and broad access to a wide range of discursive possibilities, the potentialities of an acquired idiom, and on the other to the homogenizing tendency and debased functionality of the cliché.

The line between idiom and cliché, between an enabling and a disabling discourse, is often not easily drawn, and assessments of the always relative commonness or uncommonness of a poet's work necessarily depend to a large extent on a variety of "inter-" and "extra-" (con)textual factors. In the United States, Rich's unquestioned technical facility with received poetic forms and her skillful recourse to these early in her career made her seem to many an agreeable newcomer to a common poetic tradition. Having begun her career as an uncommon insider, an exceptional woman allowed into a mostly male preserve, Rich has of course long since transgressed the bounds of what many have regarded and still regard as common poetic decorum by moving toward a woman-centered aesthetics and politics which call into question the putative universality of a poetic tradition dominated by white Anglo-American men. Given the assumptions behind her initial reception, it is hardly surprising that over the quarter century since she began to take what were at the time rather uncommon formal liberties, engaging herself at the same time more explicitly with political subject matter, her detractors have sometimes accused her work of being common in a more pejorative sense.

As a consequence in part of the profound differences between the two poetic traditions that welcomed them, Césaire's work has been spared a reevaluation of the kind Rich's has undergone. Thanks largely to Breton's enthusiastic reception of the now classic *Cahier d'un retour au pays natal* (*Notebook of a Return to the Native Land*), Césaire found himself legitimated as a poet, like Rich, while he was still in his twenties.[1] Unlike Rich, however, Césaire was able to position himself from the very beginning in relation to a tradition running from Baudelaire and Rimbaud to the surrealists that allowed for and even demanded a revolt *against* poetry from "within" poetry. Thus, speaking of the strategic mix of prose and verse in *Notebook* in an interview with the exiled communist Haitian poet René Depestre, Césaire describes himself as "liberated literally beginning at that moment when I decided to turn my back on poetry. In reality . . . I became a poet in renouncing poetry. . . . Poetry was for me the only means available to break with the standard French [*la forme régulière française*] that was suffocating me."[2]

Where the most common reservations voiced about Rich's work have had to do with the sense that the political commitment manifest in her work over the last three decades has somehow driven the poetry out of her poetry, Césaire has often been criticized for writing a hermetic poetry that makes his political commitment largely inaccessible to the public on whose behalf he has wanted to speak. Thus, although both Rich and Césaire have demonstrated a common commitment to articulating connections between poetry and what Rich has called the "history of the dispossessed,"[3] their personal and political situations have yielded quite different poetic strategies and relationships to audience. In order to explore more concretely what is common and uncommon in the poetry and poetics of Césaire and Rich and the implications of their work for the question of a common literature of the Americas, this essay will focus on two poems, "Le verbe marronner" ("The Verb 'Marronner' ") and "North American Time," which open onto a number of critical issues informing each writer's project.

Where Rich has waged her struggles by and large on the margins of the political establishment, Césaire has been not only the dominant cultural figure in Martinique but also the island's preeminent public official. As mayor of Fort-de-France and as Martinique's deputy in the French legislature over the last forty years, for the first ten as a member of the French Communist party and for the last thirty as the head of the Parti Progressiste Martiniquais which he founded two years after his break with the French Communist party in 1956, Césaire has served as a representative voice in more than a symbolic sense. From the vantage point of the United States, where the dominant view held by poets and nonpoets, by professional critics and nonreaders of poetry alike, is that poetry and politics have or should have little or nothing to do with each other, the coincidence of tangible cultural and political influence exemplified in Césaire's career is particularly striking. Although Césaire may seem to occupy an enviable position from the perspective of the comparatively rare poet from the U.S. such as Rich who shares with Césaire a sustained interest in combining poetry and politics, his situation is not altogether as privileged as it may first appear to an outsider. As is suggested by the recent publication of two ample collections of essays devoted to his work, Le Soleil éclaté (1984) and Aimé Césaire: ou l'athanor d'un alchimiste (1987), and bilingual editions of his poetry published in the U.S. by Clayton Eshleman and Annette Smith (1983), and by Gregson Davis (1984),[4] the audience for Césaire's literary productions among French and English speakers continues to broaden. His cultural prestige notwithstanding, however, in his political role as the representative of a small island department far from the French mainland Césaire has exercised comparatively little influence. As Césaire himself has put it: "I am not a head of state; I am only a poor mayor, and a poor deputy. I have very few means at my disposal."[5]

In "Le verbe marronner," reprinted in the 1976 collection Noria, Césaire has produced an exceptionally focused and forceful text concerning the discursive means available to a black Caribbean French-language poet writing in the mid- to late-twentieth century. First published as "Réponse à Depestre, poète haïtien (Eléments d'un art poétique)" ("Response to Depestre, Haitian Poet [Elements of an Ars Poetica]") in 1955—a year before Césaire's "Lettre à Maurice Thorez" ("Letter to Maurice Thorez") announced his formal withdrawal from the French Communist party—and subsequently renamed "Lettre brésilienne" ("Brazilian Letter") following a voyage he made to Brazil in 1963, the poem Césaire has come to call "Le verbe marronner" remains dedicated and directly addressed to Depestre, whom Césaire first met during a seven-month visit to Haiti as a lecturer in 1944.[6] As the current title's focus on a single word and its dedication suggest, an accurate plotting of the poem's coordinates must be at once philological, biographical, and historical. Functioning as a kind of vortex and *Vortext* of all that follows, the verb "marronner" ultimately reminds us that these areas of concern remain for Césaire, as they do for Rich, inseparable.

With its associational leaps, idiosyncratic punctuation, and complex spatial organization, "Le verbe marronner" both invites and defies critical representation. In these respects, the poem displays tendencies that have persisted to varying degrees in Césaire's work from *Notebook* to the present, including a certain resistance to representation which is heavily indebted to the poetic projects, so diverse and heterogeneous in themselves, of Baudelaire, Rimbaud, Mallarmé, and Breton. Re-presenting to some extent aesthetic struggles already waged by these poetic precursors, Césaire's work also reminds us, however, that an adequate account of the specificity of his or any poetic project cannot avoid considering that project's particular historical and aesthetic overdeterminations. "Le verbe marronner" provides, among other things, a powerful injunction to think these two terms together.

With this aim in mind, and in light of Émile Benveniste's emphasis on pronouns as an organizational principle of discourse,[7] we may identify three distinct moments in what is without any doubt a deliberately unruly text. The first of these moments, encompassing the twenty-three lines from the opening "C'est une nuit de Seine" ("It is a Seine night") to "Le sang est un vaudoun puissant" ("Blood / is truly a powerful vodun") involves a persistent alternation among three pronouns: the first person singular (*moi, je*), the familiar second person singular (*tu, ton*), and the first person plural (*nous, nos, notre, le nôtre*). The central section, extending over the following nineteen lines from "C'est vrai ils arrondissent cette saison des sonnets" ("Is it true this season that they're polishing up sonnets") to "au fait est-ce que Dessalines mignonnait à Vertières" ("as a matter of fact *did* Dessalines prance about at Vertières") is marked by the initial intrusion of the third person plural (*ils*), a subsequent return to the alternation of the first person singular (*me, moi, je*) and the second person singular familiar (*te*), and the appearance of the first person plural now in both the declarative and imperative modes (*nous*, "rions buvons marronnons"). The twenty-eight lines of the poem's final section, from the direct address "Comrade Depestre" to the closing phrase, "d'un rut sommaire d'astres moudangs" ("with a succinct rutting of moudang stars") stage the most complex pronominal interaction, including the familiar second person singular in both the declarative and imperative modes (*te, toi, bats-nous*), the impersonal collective third person singular (*l'on*), first person singular and plural (*je, mon, me, nous*), and three forms of the third person plural (*tous, ceux, leur*).

Together with the poetic devices mentioned earlier, the complex interactions figured by these pronominal shifts make interpreting the text a demanding project for even the most skilled readers of Césaire's own linguistic and cultural background. From the perspective of a background as far removed from Césaire's own as that of a still predominantly white, middle-class, English-speaking United States, however, "Le verbe marronner" poses additional difficulties of a different order.[8] To approach the poem from this perspective is to run up against the limits of our cultural vision and the challenge of uncovering layers of aesthetic and historical material that have not generally been held to belong to the common heritage of the U.S. any more than they have been considered a part of the common heritage of "poetry" or "literature."

C'est une nuit de Seine
et moi je me souviens comme ivre
du chant dément de Boukmann accouchant ton pays
aux forceps de l'orage

DEPESTRE

Vaillant cavalier du tam-tam
est-il vrai que tu doutes de la forêt natale
de nos voix rauques de nos coeurs qui nous
    remontent amers
de nos yeux de rhum rouges de nos nuits incendiées
se peut-il
que les pluies de l'exil
aient détendu la peau de tambour de ta voix

marronnerons-nous Depestre marronnerons-nous?
Depestre j'accuse les mauvaises manières de notre sang
est-ce notre faute
si la bourrasque se lève

et nous désapprend tout soudain de compter sur nos doigts
de faire trois tours de saluer

Ou bien encore cela revient au même
le sang est une chose qui va vient et revient
et le nôtre je suppose nous revient après s'être attardé
à quelque macumba. Qu'y faire? En vérité
le sang est un vaudoun puissant

(It is a Seine night
and as if in drunkenness I recall
the insane song of Boukmann delivering your country
with the forceps of the storm

DEPESTRE

    Courageous tom-tom rider
    is it true that you mistrust the native forest
    and our hoarse voices our hearts that come back up on
      us bitter
    our rum red eyes our burned out nights
    is it possible
    that the rains of exile
    have slackened the drum skin of your voice?

shall we escape like slaves Depestre like slaves?
Depestre I indict the bad manners of our blood
is it our fault
if the squall hits
suddenly unteaching us to count on our fingers
to circle three times and bow

Or else it boils down to the same thing
blood is a thing that comes and goes
and ours I suppose comes back on us after having spent time
in some macumba. What can be done about it? Blood
is truly a powerful vodun)

Invoking "as if drunk" the "insane song" of Boukmann, the black Haitian slave who led revolts in 1791, Césaire recalls both a common heritage of poetic revolt that looks back to such writers as Baudelaire and Rimbaud and a common history of political struggle exemplified in the revolution of black slaves that led to Haitian independence in 1804.

In 1947, three years after Césaire and Depestre had met in Haiti, Depestre would travel, as Césaire had done over a decade earlier, to study in Paris. While Césaire's experiences in France and Haiti proved pivotal, however, to his triumphant return as a public figure in Martinique, Depestre's travel abroad would absent him permanently from his native land. Writing Depestre from Paris in 1955, Césaire had already served nine years as a deputy to the French legislature; living at the time in Brazil, by contrast, Depestre was already in the eighth year of his exile from Haiti and the third year of his exile from Cuba, to which he would return four years later. Thus, when Césaire writes "It is a Seine night," and again near the end of the poem, "from the Seine I send you my greetings in Brazil," the differences between their personal fortunes are at least as striking as their similarities.

Although Césaire's invocation of Boukmann has the intended function of establishing a common aesthetic, historical, and political frame of reference, the direct address to Depestre in the following section opens on to as yet unstated personal and ideological tensions between the two poets which constitute the major focus of what I have identified as the first of the poem's three major moments. As the place where, in the words of *Notebook*, "negritude rose for the first time and stated that it believed in its humanity" (CP, 46–47), Haiti occupies a special status in the history of black struggle.[9] Though Haiti's importance to Césaire in this regard is amply attested to throughout his oeuvre, most notably in the extensive historical and biographical study *Toussaint L'Ouverture* (1960) and in the play *La Tragédie du Roi Christophe* (*The Tragedy of King Christopher*, 1963), his relationship to the independent island country remains fundamentally that of an outsider. As is clear from the five-question series that organizes the remainder of this section, what is primarily at stake for Césaire is solidarity, the sense of a common strategy for overcoming colonial domination: "est-il vrai que tu doutes . . ." ("is it true that you mistrust . . ."); "se peut-il . . ." ("is it possible . . ."); "marronnerons-nous Depestre marronnerons-nous?" ("shall we escape like slaves Depestre like slaves?"); "est-ce notre faute" ("is it our fault"); "Qu'y faire?" ("What can be done?"). The mildly oxymoronic epithet with which Césaire first addresses Depestre, "Vaillant cavalier du tam-tam" ("Courageous tom-tom rider") already contains within itself the fundamental opposition between European and primitive civilizations that structures the section's subsequent elaboration. Against the white European culture that wanted slaves with good manners who would be obedient enough "de compter sur nos doigts / de faire trois tours de

saluer" ("to count on our fingers / to circle three times and bow"),
Césaire aligns himself implicitly with those who look for inspiration to
"the native forest" and the common blood of black African descent
which he regards as a "powerful vodun." Like the "as if" of "comme
ivre," Césaire's invocation of rum and vodun blood and his wry in-
dictment of the bad manners of black slaves and their descendants are
ambiguous and highly charged. Heuristically figuring, on the one hand,
a non-European position from which to oppose the imposition of conventional European schemes of order, the poem's invocation of the primitive suggests the possibility of a true escape or *marronnage* from colonial
oppression. Less positively, however, the "burned out nights" spent
drinking "in some macumba" suggest a form of empty escapism and
self-delusion.

Whatever is to be done will likely entail something resembling the
intoxicated state of lucidity or lucid state of intoxication figured by Boukmann delivering Haiti "with the forceps of the storm." As the second
major section of the poem suggests, the common cause of resistance to
French colonial culture demands for Césaire a refusal of conventional
French verse forms. In opposition to Depestre's recently announced solidarity with the former surrealist Louis Aragon's call on behalf of the
French Communist party for a revival of such forms, Césaire compares
the well-turned sonnet to the "jus sucré que bavent là-bas les distilleries
des mornes" ("sugary / juice drooled over there by the distilleries on the
mornes"). Refusing to participate in what he takes to be a form of
complicity between this kind of poetry and one of the principal indus-
tries of the French colonial economy, Césaire rejects the image of the
poem as a "mill for / grinding sugar cane." Simultaneously playing with
and against the return to conventional poetic devices advocated by Aragon and agreed upon in principle by Depestre, Césaire figures a complex
relationship to the ostensibly revolutionary means and ends of Aragon's
program:

> et si les rimes sont mouches sur les mares
> > sans rimes
> > toute une saison
> loin des mares
> > moi te faisant raison
> rions buvons et marronnons
>
> (and if the rhymes are flies on ponds
> > without rhymes

                    for a whole season
        away from ponds
                                    under my persuasion
        let's laugh and escape like slaves)

While the spatial distribution of these lines on the page figures the comic reversal of a lock-step dialectic ending in the stagnant, fly-infested waters of the "mares," their propositional content also affirms the value of reaching back behind these devices to the primitive sources of poetry in laughter, drinking, and freedom. As the euphonic repetition and liquidation of "mares" in "marronnons" suggests, the goal is to get things moving by refusing to accept the constraints of received forms, especially those received by colonial imposition. In the lines that follow Césaire offers conspicuously mythopoetic images that may be read as ironic emblems of the utterly unpoetic condition of slavery and the physical constraints it entails:

        avec au cou le collier de commandement de la lune
        avec autour du bras le rouleau bien lové du lasso du soleil
        la poitrine tatouée comme par une des blessures de la
            nuit
        aussi je me souviens

    au fait est-ce que Dessalines mignonnait à Vertières

        (the necklace of the Order of the Moon around my neck
        the tightly wrapped coil of the sun's lasso around my arm
        my chest tattooed as if by one of night's wounds
        I too remember

    as a matter of fact *did* Dessalines prance about at Vertières)

As the placement of these lines immediately after the poem's renunciation of the sonnet indicates, the idea of returning to conventional forms of poetry would be comparable for Césaire to a willingness to submit once again to the shackles formerly placed around the necks and arms of slaves caught trying to escape. In this context the allusion to the great Haitian revolutionary Jean-Jacques Dessalines prancing about during the assault he commanded on Fort Breda in November 1803 figures a Dionysian resistance to any and all constraints on poetic freedom, including those imposed in the name of Communist solidarity and what Césaire perceived to be a mechanistic dialecticism.

Following the preceding section's renunciation of the sonnet as synecdochic of the unwanted constraints of all conventional poetic forms, the third and final moment of the poem raises its implied critique of Aragon's aesthetic program to the more general theoretical level of the "rapports de la poésie et de la Révolution" ("relation between poetry and Revolution"). With its opening direct address, "Comrade Depestre," this section may appear to begin on a conciliatory note. Although Césaire would withdraw from the Communist party within a year, he was in 1955 still Depestre's "comrade" in a strict formal sense. In light of the critique of formal constraints just articulated, however, the double-edged tone of Césaire's address to Depestre is unmistakable. Thus, when Césaire writes that the relationship between poetry and Revolution is "undoubtedly a very serious problem," the emphatic "undoubtedly" [*assurément*] may be read at one and the same time as a straightforward affirmation of the problem's seriousness and as an ironic, tongue-in-cheek dismissal of it as an overblown or distorted issue. As the difference between the lowercase "poetry" and the uppercase "Revolution" suggests, Aragon's formulation of the problem on behalf of the party risks subsuming aesthetic under political considerations in a way that betrays both. Flatly and ambiguously affirming the familiar claim that "le fond conditionne la forme" ("the content determines the form"), Césaire keeps his distance from a Stalinized aesthetic program that would have the effect of suffocating poetic and political freedom.

> et si l'on s'avisait aussi du détour dialectique
> par quoi la forme prenant sa revanche
> comme un figuier maudit étouffe le poème
>
> (and what about keeping in mind as well the dialectical
> backlash by which the form taking its revenge
> chokes the poems like an accursed fig tree)

Indicating a profoundly ambivalent attitude on Césaire's part toward the French Communist party and the Marxist dialectic, these lines may be interpreted, in one sense, as expressing a resistance to any "detour" that would inhibit "true" dialectical progression. Césaire's reservations about the aesthetic proposed by Depestre, Aragon, and the French Communist party would thus be in keeping with a desire to preserve both the party and the dialectic from corruption, distortion, or deviation. In another sense, however, the idea of enforcing strict adherence to a putatively revolutionary program that prohibits any and all detours, poetic or otherwise, may be seen as a serious problem in itself.[10]

In opposition to the notion of a straightforward progression and radical break commonly associated with political uses of the word "Revolution," Césaire deploys the term once again, this time with a lowercase "r," in the alternative sense of a cyclical return.

> mais non
>> je ne me charge pas du rapport
> j'aime mieux regarder le printemps. Justement
> c'est la révolution
>> et les formes qui s'attardent
> à nos oreilles bourdonnant
> çe sont mangeant les pousses
>> de gras hannetons hannetonnant le printemps.

> (but no
>> a report on this is none of my business
> I'd rather look at the spring. Precisely,
> it is the revolution
>> and the forms which linger
> humming in our ears
> are, eating the new which sprouts
> eating the shoots,
>> fat cockchafers cockchafing the spring.)

In reading this passage it would be a mistake to interpret Césaire's provocational nonchalance as either aesthetically or politically naive. In certain contexts, the impulse to turn away from the problem of the relationship between aesthetics and politics to praise the advent of spring might well be regarded as an index of complacency. In the United States especially, where the dominant tendency has been to ignore the problem altogether, such a gesture would be all too predictable. In the context of Césaire's concerns regarding Depestre, Aragon, and the Communist party, however, the affirmation of "revolution" against "Revolution" is calculated to call attention to differing aesthetic and political modalities that may not be so easily harmonized with one another. Recalling the poem's earlier ambivalent evocation of the vodun blood which "comes and goes / and . . . comes back on us after having spent time / in some macumba," the "revolution" that marks the return of spring and the "forms which linger / humming in our ears / . . . eating the new which sprouts / eating the shoots" serves as a reminder of, on the one hand, the continuing political importance of a certain aesthetic lingering and, on the other, the potentially repressive character of any aesthetic or political program that imposes strict guidelines for the sake of a rigidly dialectical progression toward the "new."

Given the evident pleasure and importance Césaire attaches to the idea of a cyclical return, his implicit refusal of all conventional European forms leaves him open to the accusation of a rather dogmatic antiformalism. This accusation notwithstanding, in such phrases as "si les rimes sont mouches sur les mares / sans rimes" and "de gras hannetons hannetonnant le printemps,"[11] and in the homonymous play on "mares" and "marronnons," "Le verbe 'marronner'" consistently displays that uncommon ability Césaire has manifested throughout his career to activate the common poetic pleasure of reveling in the sheer sounds of words. In the poem's closing lines, Césaire surpasses himself in this regard with a powerfully incantatory passage, itself a kind of chant dément worthy of Boukmann, which exemplifies the possibilities of a heightened aesthetic and political lucidity alluded to earlier.

Depestre

de la Seine je t'envoie au Brésil mon salut
à toi à Bahia à tous les saints à tous les diables
Cabritos cantagallo Botafogo
bate
batuque
à ceux des favellas

Depestre
bombaïa bombaïa

crois-m'en comme jadis bats-nous le bon tam-tam
eclaboussant leur nuit rance
d'un rut sommaire d'astres moudangs.

(Depestre

from the Seine I send you my greetings in Brazil
to you to Bahia to all saints to all devils
Cabritos cantagallo Botafogo
bate
batuque
to all those in the favellas

Depestre
bombaïa bombaïa

believe me as in the old days beat the good tom-tom for us

splashing their rancid night
with a succinct rutting of moudang stars.)

Returning to the poem's earlier references to the Seine, the "tam-tam,"
and the question concerning Depestre's "doutes de la forêt natale" ("mistrust (of) the native forest"), these closing lines return to the issue of
Césaire's relationship to Depestre in an effort to underscore the solidarity
that exists or might exist between them despite their quite different
personal situations and their opposing views on Aragon's aesthetic program. In effect, Césaire is attempting to persuade Depestre to join him
in giving higher priority to their shared racial identity than to their
allegiance to a white European-based political movement which he had
come to regard by 1955 as not necessarily serving their best interests,
whether as blacks, poets, or revolutionaries.[12]

Césaire has often been criticized, particularly within the last decade
by the younger generation of Martinican writers who began to gain
prominence in the 1980s, for not making greater use of Creole in order
to make his work more accessible to those whose political interests he
has represented. Although such criticisms carry an undeniable force, they
need to be historically situated in terms of the profound differences between Césaire's cultural and political situation in 1955 and the situation
of Martinican writers today. Acknowledging in a 1984 interview with
Jacqueline Leiner the importance of the current interest in Creole among
Martinican intellectuals, Césaire argues that the unavoidable first task of
his generation was to master the language of the dominant culture in
order to challenge that culture's dominance on its own terms.[13] In light
of this claim, the closing lines of "Le verbe marronner" are particularly
interesting. Reversing the dialectical *re*gression figured earlier in the
poem's renunciation of the sonnet, the spatial distribution of these lines
enacts a progressive movement in keeping with the poem's call for racial
solidarity and its insurrectionary appeal on behalf of those living in the
slums of Brazil whose "rancid night" contrasts so sharply with the more
pleasantly auratic "Seine night" that was the scene of Césaire's writing.
In articulating this appeal, and in disengaging itself in the process from
the aesthetic program of the French Communist party, which Césaire
had once affirmed as the most promising collectivity the dominant culture had to offer, the poem bursts out of the standard French and conventional poetic constraints Césaire once described as suffocating him
to embrace a poly- and heteroglot speech drawn from the Spanish Caribbean ("Cabritos"), Brazil ("cantagallo Botafogo / bate / batuque /

. . . favellas"), Haiti ("bombaïa"), and Africa ("moudangs"). With their intense concentration of occlusive consonants, their dynamic verbal *métissage,* and the appeal to a violent uprising signaled by the Haitian rallying cry "bombaïa," these explosive closing lines provide a formidable model of what a truly revolutionary poetry might be.[14]

The problem with the French Communist party in 1955 from Césaire's point of view lay especially in its obliviousness to the particularity of black struggle. In the same year in which he wrote "Le verbe marronner," Césaire addressed this issue in two complementary texts, the justly famous *Discours sur le colonialisme (Discourse on Colonialism)* and the somewhat less well-known but no less impressive *Culture et colonisation (Culturation and Colonization).* Where the first of these offers a powerful polemic against a false universalism based exclusively on white European values, the second warns more guardedly against a simple choice between the universal and the particular. By contrast, at the close of the 1959 essay "L'homme de culture et ses responsabilités" ("The Man of Culture and His Responsibilities"), Césaire's desire to contribute toward the founding of a "universal humanism" once again reasserts itself. In the context of Césaire's lifelong attempt to negotiate strategically between these extremes, the value of negritude lay first and foremost in what he has since called its "resistance to the politics of assimilation" and its corollary insistence on a coming to consciousness of the "numerous historical singularities" of blacks that would be "concrete and not abstract."[15]

In the 1700s, at the height of the black slave trade, *marronnage* had come to be recognized, as Louis Sala-Molins points out, as a serious threat to the foundations of colonial society and the most efficient way possible for blacks to come to an awareness of their revolutionary potential *en masse.*[16] Already in widespread usage in the 1720s throughout the French-speaking Caribbean as an alternative to *fugitif* (the official term for runaways used in the French monarchy's *Code Noir*), the word *marron* has its origins in what is perhaps the most familiar of white racist analogies. As the French missionary Margat explains in a letter dated February 2, 1729, the same year in which a royal edict issued guidelines raising the stakes of punishment for attempted escapes from whipping and shackling to bodily mutilation and death: "the term *marron* . . . comes from the Spanish *simarron*; (more precisely: *cimarrón*), which means monkey. . . . It is the name the Spanish have given to escaped slaves" (CN, 166). Like monkeys, so the analogy goes, slaves who are "unhappy with their masters" or who have been punished for one reason or another "flee into the woods and the mountains, where they hide during the day, and disperse at night . . . to gather provisions and make off with whatever they can get their hands on." Attesting to the revolutionary potential of these marauding bands, which led the 1729 edict to establish a fine of 300 pounds of sugar for whites caught housing runaways, Margat's letter continues: "Sometimes, when they've managed to get hold of fire-arms, they even gather into mobs during the day, set ambushes, and attack passers-by so that it is often necessary to send out large detachments to stop their collective plundering and bring them to justice." Designating what was at the time a common practice in all the colonies populated by black slaves—whether in Louisiana, where so-called *chasses aux marrons* (slave hunts) were organized at will by the French king's subjects (CN, 168), in Martinique, or elsewhere— the word *marronnage* carries within it an entire history of revolutionary activity among black slaves throughout the Caribbean and the Americas. Reversing the charge of the originally pejorative noun *marron* by turning it into the verb *marronner,* Césaire subjects the word to much the same kind of positive transvaluation he contributed to in coining the word *négritude.* In so doing, he focuses attention above all on a common language of struggle shared by all descendants of black slaves which cuts across issues of national, regional, gender, or class identity.

As Césaire put it in the Leiner interview quoted earlier: "I am first of all the man of a historically situated community. . . . I feel in solidarity with all men [*tout les hommes*] who struggle for freedom . . . who suffer and above all with those who have suffered the most and who have too often been forgotten, I mean the Blacks" (NA, 11). Yet as the transnational, multiracial colonial context of the *marron* suggests, *négritude* itself may be considered a less than adequate term for describing the concrete struggles of black slaves and their descendants in the Americas. Thus, where Césaire has defined his situation most consistently in relation to the two poles of France and Africa, increasing numbers of young Caribbean writers have followed such writers as Depestre and Edouard Glissant in emphasizing *créolité* and *métissage* as more accurate terms for describing the multiracial context of the Americas in general and of the Caribbean in particular.[17] Creole, the indigenous, heterogeneous language of the *métis,* has its origins, in Depestre's words, in the event of a "marronnage culturel" where "at a certain moment one flees into the woods from the culture of the masters and, out of contempt, expresses oneself in a language they cannot understand."[18] After years of manipulating the master's language with an erudition and resourcefulness that have had the ironic effect of placing him at a large cultural remove from the vast majority of those he has represented politically, Césaire has displayed in recent years an increased willingness to acknowledge the importance of Creole and the multidimensional heritage of Martinique which he has characterized as a source of its "wealth . . . and its difficulties" (NA, 13). At a time when *créolité* and *métissage* have come to challenge and even supplant *négritude* as the rallying cries of writers of color belonging to the generation of Césaire's grandchildren, the hybrid speech of "Le verbe marronner" provides an impressive example of a text situated acutely in the present that draws its poetry not only from the past, but from the future.

"North American Time"

Although Rich has not played an official political role comparable to Césaire's, she too has come to be regarded as the representative voice of a large community. After roughly two decades of consistently identifying herself and her writing with radical feminism, she remains for this particular audience as well as for many others, as Paula Bennett has noted recently, the most important woman poet writing in America.[19] Troubled by what she has called the "level of ritual assent" accorded to her poetic language by her most uncritical admirers (MFC, 90), Rich has in recent years sharpened her critical position toward the relationship between language and political action generally and toward her own role in particular as a poet and spokeswoman. In the process, expanding her identification with those who are engaged in a common effort to "transform an oppressive order," Rich has not turned away from what she has called a "woman-identified" aesthetics and politics any more than Césaire has turned away from negritude (MFC, 90; CH, 51). Yet in visualizing an audience for her work that would include, among others, "parents, brothers, lovers . . . academic colleagues . . . Black feminists," she has opened onto a broader field of aesthetic and political activity (MFC, 91). As the conclusion of "Le verbe marronner" anticipates the shift of emphasis from *négritude* to *métissage* that has asserted itself increasingly in recent years among younger generations of Martinican writers, the attention Rich has devoted in her most recent poetry and prose to what she has called "identity politics" and a "politics of location" points from a more exclusive preoccupation with radical feminism toward an aesthetics and politics of what she has called the "Misch-ling."[20]

To be a *métis* or *Mischling* is above all to have a common sense of being, in Rich's words, "split at the root" (SR, 100–123). Having learned as a child that "'common' was a term of deep opprobrium," a word "'common' white people might speak of 'niggers'" (SR, 100), Rich has now begun to explore especially the common and uncommon compli-cations of having "seen too long from too many disconnected angles: white, Jewish, anti-Semite, racist, antiracist, once-married, lesbian, middle-class, feminist, exmatriate southerner . . ." (SR, 122). Thus the tripartite arrangement of her most recent collection of poems, *Your Native Land, Your Life,* does not have as its trajectory the hopeful synthesis implied by the "dream of a common language."[21] Passing instead from the first section's primary focus on the ways in which her personal past has shaped her present identity ("Sources") to the second section's concern with situating the present self in a broader geographical, social, political, and historical context ("North American Time"), Rich concludes in the section entitled "Contradictions: Tracking Poems" by calling attention to ongoing irresolution, division, and the continuing need for a ques-tioning of self and others.

In the second section's title poem, Rich's self-revisions focus most insistently on the relationship between what she calls "verbal privilege" and national identity. Writing in a country where, as she has noted in a recent essay, "'politics' is mostly a dirty word" and "political poetry is suspected of immense subversive power, yet accused of being, by defi-nition, bad writing, impotent, lacking in breadth," Rich offers a strong challenge to what she has called our "particular history of hostility both to art and to socialism" (BBP, 178–79, 183). Yet although her sense of herself as participating in a movement that encourages artists to think aesthetics and politics together has allowed her to continue resisting the still dominant tendency in the United States to think them apart, this tendency has itself resulted in a polarized reception of her work. While it is easy enough to find critical essays and reviews praising or con-demning Rich's poetic practice, it is considerably more difficult to find assessments of her work, whether "for" or "against," which take it seriously enough to elaborate extensive close readings of individual poems. What one critic describes as powerfully "straightforward" may be easily dismissed by another as distressingly common. Yet what has been most surprising given Rich's own careful, sustained attention to the possibility poetry provides for a "critique of language" is, as she herself has recently suggested, how cursorily her own verbal constructions have been treated by admirers and detractors alike (BBP, 90–91).[22]

It is significant in this regard that one of the most sustained and illuminating readings of Rich's poetry to date has been produced by Myriam Diaz-Diocaretz in connection with her translations of Rich's poetry in Spanish. Diaz-Diocaretz's emphasis on person deixis in particular offers a useful basis for comparing what is common and uncommon to the ways in which Césaire and Rich articulate the relationship between language and politics.[23] Like "Le verbe marronner," "North American Time" is structured primarily around first and second person pronouns.[24] As for Césaire, the positioning of these pronouns in relation to each other is above all a way of exploring problems of language as they pertain to questions of individual agency, personal responsibility, and community. Thus, the poem's focus shifts from the first persons singular and plural in the first two sections, respectively, to the predominant emphasis of sections III–V on the second person, to the sixth section's inclusion of both first and second person references, and finally to a renewed focus in sections VII–IX on the first person.

Like "Le verbe marronner," "North American Time" is concerned with the possibility of escaping from unwanted constraints. Unlike the constraints Césaire recalls through the figure of Boukmann, however, those evoked by Rich stem from a sense of having fallen into a form of self-censorship.

> When my dreams showed signs
> of becoming
> politically correct
> no unruly images
> escaping beyond borders
> when walking in the street I found my
> themes cut out for me
> knew what I would not report
> for fear of enemies' usage
> then I began to wonder

As this first section suggests, Rich envisions poetry, like Césaire, as a mode of resistance to reified political positions, including those with which she feels most closely allied. Through the mobility and open-endedness brought about by the suppression of conventional punctuation and the strategic use of enjambments to call the speaking subject's status into question from one line to the next, these lines figure a struggle against any use of language that would demand strict adherence to a preestablished grammar or ideology and thus cut off, in effect, the very possibility of a radical personal and social transformation. In contrast to "Le verbe marronner," however, which asserts much the same, as we have seen, in renouncing Aragon's call for a return to received poetic forms, "North American Time" posits a speaker struggling primarily with herself and, by implication, with the acquired audience that has come to expect her to perform reliably in her role as spokeswoman for a common cause. Refusing to rule out such "unruly images" as the aesthetically and politically suggestive "escaping beyond borders," Rich encourages a use of language that does not turn away expediently from divisions *within* in order to focus exclusively on divisions *between,* but instead allows for a certain wonder or wandering, as in the drift of dreams in signs and signs in dreams, which the ready-made themes of the politically correct "report" cannot contain.

It is implicitly only on the basis of this recognition of an internally divided self whose very dreams are traversed by the signs and discourses of others like and unlike itself that the second section is able to posit the collective "we." As the section's opening lines make clear, however, this movement from the "I" to the "we" brings its own complications. If the critical problem of the "I" in the first section is that of the subject's inscription in the reified language of a political program that represses or disallows new possibilities in the name of ideological purity, the problem of the "we" of the second section resides in its recognition that even the most "politically correct," well-intentioned, precise, and imaginative uses of language cannot control their reception.

> Everything we write
> will be used against us
> or against those we love.
> These are the terms,
> take them or leave them.
> Poetry never stood a chance
> of standing outside history.

For the politically minded poet, the final two lines of this passage might be read as indicating both resignation and affirmation. If poetry has always been inscribed within history, then perhaps the possibility remains open that poetry might contribute in some way to history's positive transformation. Yet, as the ambiguous use of the common phrase, "take them or leave them," suggests, we are at once free and not free to do with language what we will. The possibilities for "escaping beyond the borders" are endless, yet nowhere to be seen. The common and the uncommon, the enabling idiom and the disabling cliché, the line of graffiti and the line of poetry may appear the same or different, depending on how we use or abuse them.

> One line typed twenty years ago
> can be blazed on a wall in spraypaint
> to glorify art as detachment
> or torture of those we
> did not love but also
> did not want to kill
> We move   but our words stand
> become responsible
> for more than we intended
>
> and this is verbal privilege

However rigorous or responsible we attempt to be in using language, our "own" words and intentions both precede and exceed us. In this sense, although poetry's intended function may be tightly controlled, its dissemination makes it no less susceptible to being used either "for" or "against" us than any other mode of discourse. Even where poetry can focus our attention, as here, on the unstable ironies of its own "verbal privilege," the implied self-critique may be used either to deny or to reassert that privilege. If it is poetry's privilege to offer a self-critique, then this capacity may itself seem grounds for a willingness to continue granting it a certain privilege. If poetry is perceived, on the other hand, as having abused its privileges, as having led us with "poetic licence" to forget that words may be used not merely to "glorify" but to "torture," then even the most rigorous self-critique might appear too late. To "become responsible" with words appears both impossible and necessary, beyond us yet within no one's grasp but our own.

But whose privilege is "this"? And who is "we"? What is perhaps most conspicuous about the rhetoric of the second section is its comparatively high level of abstraction, the floating pronominal context that takes in everyone in general and no one in particular. In Section III, by contrast, turning away from the first person pronouns singular and plural in the first two sections, Rich lays down an invitation/imperative to join in the act of imagining herself and ourselves in a more concrete setting.

> Try sitting at a typewriter
> one calm summer evening
> at a table by a window
> in the country, try pretending
> your time does not exist
> that you are simply you
> that the imagination simply strays
> like a great moth, unintentional
> try telling yourself
> you are not accountable
> to the life of your tribe
> the breath of your planet

In its opening lines, this beautifully structured passage appears to offer an innocent instantiation of one of the most privileged of poetic genres, a pleasant rural scene perceived by a writer from within cozily domestic surroundings. As the imagining of this scene moves from "sitting" to "pretending," however, each apparently innocent suggestion turns ironically against itself. To try to pretend "that your time does not exist / that you are simply you / that the imagination simply strays / like a great moth, unintentional," is to be reminded unmistakably that you are in time, that in some sense you are not "simply" you, and that the imagination does not "simply" stray, "unintentional." Similarly, to "try telling yourself / you are not accountable" is to be reminded of just the opposite. On the one hand, then, the experience of "verbal privilege" may lead to an increased sense of personal accountability. As the following section suggests, however, an increased awareness of this kind may lead in precisely the opposite direction.

> It doesn't matter what you think.
> Words are found responsible
> all you can do is choose them
> or choose
> to remain silent.   Or, you never had a choice,
> which is why the words that do stand
> are responsible
>
> and this is verbal privilege

Implicit in the "or . . . / Or . . . which is why. . . ." structure of this section is the temptation to rationalize away a condition of relative powerlessness by denying that very accountability which it was the function of the previous section to make more tangible. To come to an awareness of a position of relative privilege may be trying enough, but to have a sense that what you say from that privileged position also "does matter" for the "tribe" or the "planet" may be still more uncomfortable. The rationalizations are themselves, of course, not altogether implausible. Like the specific suggestions in section III, however, each one tends to call forth its opposite. Thus, the second line's abrupt recourse to the passive voice in "Words are found responsible" reminds us that the author has in fact made a deliberate stylistic decision. Similarly, the generalized "all you can do" of line three and the "never" of line five taken together with the insistent references to choice and responsibility in lines two through seven are likely to make the reader consider just how limited and abstract a realm of verbal privilege the section has in fact presented. Were the section merely to indicate how strongly overdetermined are the verbal choices of even the most privileged, it might avoid collapsing into self-irony. As the words "stand," however, they tend toward a linguistic determinism Rich implicitly rejects as apoetic for those who would continue to take the responsibilities of verbal privilege seriously.

Distancing itself decisively at the outset from the abstract, mutedly ironic formulations of section IV, the pivotal fifth section establishes a concreteness of detail which sets the tone, albeit still in the hypothetical imperative mode of section III, for the remainder of the poem.

> Suppose you want to write
> of a woman braiding
> another woman's hair—
> straight down, or with beads and shells
> in three-strand plaits or corn-rows—
> you had better know the thickness
> the length   the pattern
> why she decides to braid her hair
> how it is done to her
> what country it happens in
> what else happens in that country
>
> You have to know these things

Recalling the evocation at the close of Wallace Stevens's "Of Modern Poetry" of "a man skating, a woman dancing, a woman / Combing,"

Rich raises questions about the claims of privileged white male authors to speak authoritatively about what will suffice for imagining the everyday words and activities of those whose lives differ profoundly from their own in crucial respects. As is clear from the second and third lines, "a woman braiding / another woman's hair," a certain "woman-centeredness" remains at the core of Rich's reflections on identity. In the section's subsequent distinction, however, between "three-strand plaits" and "corn-rows," Rich suggests the importance of considering questions of gender together with questions of race. In addition to these questions, moreover, which must be taken into account if we are to understand "why she decides to braid her hair" and "how it is done to her," the speaking subject must have some sense, as the passage further implies, of the significance of her activities taken not in isolation but in relation to other activities within the same country. "You have to know these things" in order precisely to be able to write concretely and thus responsibly about them and not give in to the abstract linguistic resignation ironized in the preceding section.

Having opened at this point in the poem onto a multidimensional concept of identity that includes gender, race, and nationality, Rich addresses herself and her situation still more concretely:

> Poet, sister: words—
> whether we like it or not—
> stand in a time of their own.
> No use protesting. *I wrote that*
> *before Kollontai was exiled*
> *Rose Luxemburg, Malcolm,*
> *Anna Mae Aquash, murdered,*
> *before Treblinka, Birkenau,*
> *Hiroshima, before Sharpeville,*
> *Biafra, Bangladesh, Boston,*
> *Atlanta, Soweto, Beirut, Assam*
> —those faces, names of places
> sheared from the almanac
> of North American time

Beginning with the direct address "Poet, sister" and concluding with the poem's first explicit reference beyond the title to North America, this section locates the activity of writing within a chronotope that is at once local and international. Echoing the emphasis in the second and fourth sections on the potentiality of words to take on a certain autonomy and initiative of their own, the self-divided speaker nevertheless no longer describes them at this point as being or becoming "responsible," but only as standing "in a time of their own." The difference is subtle but crucial; "whether we like it or not" that words inevitably exceed our intended uses of them, the responsibility for using or abusing them in particular contexts remains. And though there may be "No use protesting" that words have failed us where we have most needed to use them effectively, as the litany of lines five through eleven suggests, a decision *not* to protest this failure and seek to use words as responsibly as possible would be still more troubling. Thus, in opposition to the impersonal, official "almanac" time of a privileged continent that often tends to view past and present victims of history within and without its borders with a mix of indifference and myopic self-interest, the speaker posits for poetry the task of shearing away specific "faces" and "names of places" in order to activate an individual and collective counter-memory that would envision the entire planet as a community in which violence and oppression anywhere ought to be of concern to people everywhere.

Having passed through the self-questioning, second-person mode of the previous four sections, the poem returns in section VII to a first person perspective informed by a more particularized understanding of the issues involved in holding ourselves accountable for words:

> I am thinking this in a country
> where words are stolen out of mouths
> as bread is stolen out of mouths
> where poets don't go to jail
> for being poets, but for being
> dark-skinned, female, poor.
> I am writing this in a time
> when anything we write
> can be used against those we love
> where the context is never given
> though we try to explain, over and over
> For the sake of poetry at least
> I need to know these things

Sharpening her focus still further from the concrete yet large-scale continental and global emphasis of the preceding section, in section VII Rich explores "thinking . . . in a country" and "writing . . . in a time" that bring her still closer to home. In the U.S. of the 1980s, where political violence and oppression tend to assume the comparatively subtle, bureaucratized forms suggested by the passive voice verbs of lines two, three, nine, and ten, it does in fact become that much more difficult to say where the primary responsibility for injustice lies. In this situation, the poet may well feel, as Rich clearly does here, a special sense of urgency about contributing to the struggle to reappropriate or steal back what she elsewhere calls "the oppressor's language"[25] as a participant in the interrelated discursive and material struggles for "words" and "bread." Yet however much poets may want to assume responsibility for their own discourse, it is the "verbal privilege" of poets in the U.S. to be accorded a status that is at once risk-free and of comparatively little consequence. Poets are free to say whatever they please, to speak as commonly or uncommonly, as responsibly or irresponsibly as they wish, but only with the understanding that what they say is not likely to be taken seriously into account by those with the power to make far-reaching decisions. Thus, although the poet may call attention to discrimination within her own country based on race, gender, and class— "being / dark-skinned, female, poor"—it is a part of her ambiguous privilege as a poet that she will not have to suffer for doing so. On the other hand, as the section's concluding lines indicate, the fact of poetry's relative inconsequence in the U.S. at the present time does not finally diminish the importance of gaining as precise an understanding, through poetry and whatever other discursive means are available, of the verbal and material mechanisms of oppression and marginalization. Although the context is never given and, as Jacques Derrida has pointed out, the fact that no context is ever "absolutely determinable" means there are, in effect, "*only* contexts without any center or absolute anchoring (*ancrage*)" (my emphasis),[26] the inextricably interrelated tasks of explaining, dismantling, constructing, and reconstructing particular contexts for the concrete production and reception of particular utterances are not thereby rendered less important. On the contrary, "For the sake of poetry at least," and arguably for the sake of any discursive practice that measures the comparative risks of holding itself accountable for words, these tasks must be engaged that much more intensively.

To be actively engaged in this process, to "try to explain, over and over" in order to acquire a precise understanding of context that is as necessary as it is impossible, is to become aware of an identity politics that is not carried out in the realm of timeless abstractions but within specific times and places which themselves undergo constant change and redefinition. Thus, even the most abstract and detached of contexts, the context of a white, middle-class North American time that allows us to make sense of the phrase "Words are found responsible," is itself a particular context with a particular history that bears representing. Such a representation needs to account not only for such specific world-wide mechanisms of marginalization as gender, race, and class, but also for an asynchronic development between, say, Martinique and the U.S., or between North America and the Third World generally, which complicates what Rich has called elsewhere a "simultaneity of oppressions."[27]

Continuing in the eighth section the poem's interrogation of the privilege which has been accorded her and which she has accorded herself as poet and spokeswoman, Rich locates her own situation still more concretely:

> Sometimes, gliding at night
> in a plane over New York City
> I have felt like some messenger
> called to enter, called to engage
> this field of light and darkness.
> A grandiose idea, born of flying.
> But underneath the grandiose idea
> is the thought that what I must engage
> after the plane has raged onto the tarmac
> after climbing my old stairs, sitting down
> at my old window
> is meant to break my heart and reduce me to silence.

In this, the only one of the poem's nine sections that is not left open-ended, the conjunction of the final word, "silence," and the ensuing period marks a provisional culmination to the project of an identity politics and a politics of locations, the journey of individual and collective self-definition and self-contextualization, which was initiated with the generalized, abstract "I" and "we" of the poem's first two sections. Having moved from this beginning through the alternately concrete and abstract articulations of the "you" and "she" in sections III–V, the increasingly concrete shift of focus from "you" back to "I" in section VI and from "I" to "we" and back to "I" in section VII, the poem narrows its focus in section VIII still further. After identifying herself in section VI as a North American, and in section VII as a citizen of the United

States, the speaker in section VIII locates herself even more explicitly by returning to New York City and her own house, "my old stairs . . . / . . . my old window." In returning to this specific place, the speaker returns to a sense of the importance of a politically engaged poetry that has stripped itself of any lofty or "grandiose" notions it might have had concerning its status as a putatively transcendent discourse, as well as of inflated ideas concerning its capacity to bring about change. Simultaneously affirming, undercutting, qualifying, and reaffirming the poet's role as "messenger," the section calls attention to the anger that drives this particular poet to write—"what I must engage / after the plane has raged onto the tarmac"—within an enlarged yet specific aesthetic and political context that threatens to reduce her to a resigned silence.

In the poem's final section, the sources of this tension between engaged anger and silent resignation become increasingly clear.

> In North America time stumbles on
> without moving, only releasing
> a certain North American pain.
> Julia de Burgos wrote:
> *That my grandfather was a slave*
> *is my grief; had he been a master*
> *that would have been my shame.*
> A poet's words, hung over a door
> in North America, in the year
> nineteen-eighty-three.
> The almost-full moon rises
> timelessly speaking of change
> out of the Bronx, the Harlem River
> the drowned towns of the Quabbin
> the pilfered burial mounds
> the toxic swamps, the testing-grounds
>
> and I start to speak again

What prevents Rich from falling into a powerless silence and allows her instead to turn her anger into an engaged poetry at this point in the poem is above all her sense of herself as participating in an expanded field of aesthetic, discursive, historical, and political struggle that is at once personal, local, social, and international. It is, implicitly, only through a timely effort to bring the intersection of these contexts concretely into focus that the specifically "North American Time" of a stumbling immobility of pain without progress can open onto the poetic promise of the "almost-full moon. . . ." Thus, in its specific allusion to "A poet's words, hung over a door / in North America, in the year / nineteen-eighty-three," the same year as the date of composition indicated at the poem's conclusion, Rich underscores both her sympathy for the Puerto Rican poet who died in 1953, as Rich's notes tell us, "on the streets of New York City," and the acute sense she shares with Césaire of the concrete materiality and historicity of all aesthetic production and reception, including those texts that are conceived by their always historically situated authors and readers as most "timeless." As the juxtaposition of de Burgos's words with Rich's own in lines thirteen through sixteen of the closing section suggests, to speak "timelessly . . . of change" is to speak ambiguously, to ask in effect what has really changed and what has not.

In focusing "North American Time" and the question of change on the grief and shame of slave and master, Rich's appropriation of de Burgos's words calls attention to a common heritage described by Edouard Glissant as perhaps the central preoccupation of all the literatures of the Americas. In describing the attempt of writers on the American continents to come to terms with the "shame [*hantise*] of what happened, with the way in which this mixing [*mélange*] occurred, the way in which its cultures cross-bred [*se sont métissées*]," Glissant notes that the American search is not "for a distant source but for a source right there, close by, which one feels one is just now able to touch but which one doesn't really manage to see clearly because of the obfuscations of the colonial situation."[28] One of the more immediate sources of "North American Time"—as also of the two companion essays from the same year, " 'Going There' and Being Here" and "North American Tunnel Vision," and the 1984 essay "Blood, Bread, and Poetry: The Location of the Poet"—was Rich's summer 1983 visit to Nicaragua. The consequences of this visit, Rich's first to Latin America and the occasion of what she has called an expanded "hemispheric education" (NA, 161), are particularly visible in lines thirteen through fifteen of the closing section of "North American Time." In her recourse to the words of a woman poet, Rich attests once again to the importance of questions of gender. In alluding to a black woman, however, a slave's descendant from Puerto Rico, and to "the Bronx, the Harlem River / the drowned towns of the Quabbin / the pilfered burial mounds," Rich calls attention to a common history of suffering among women, Latin Americans, Jews, Blacks, American Indians, and other ethnic groups both living and dead, within and outside of North America, which expands and complicates the earlier frame of reference of her identity politics from radical feminist to *Mischling* in much the same way the conclusion of "Le verbe marronner" enlarges its focus from *nègre* to *métis*. What is most common to the Americas, that "cultural arena formerly organized around the plantation system," is the liquidation, as Glissant points out, of its indigenous peoples and their replacement by a mixed population from all corners of the world (15). Resembling the conclusion of "Le verbe marronner" in its emphasis on a Pan-American context, the closing section of "North American Time" brings in view the shameful past of this mixed culture, as well as the precarious promise of a present in which power relations have changed less decisively from those of master and slave than we might have wished.

Mischling, Métis, and Community

In an America of "toxic swamps" and "testing-grounds," what escapes "beyond borders" may not be to everyone's liking. Mixing is not necessarily in itself either poison or cure, however, but may turn out to be predominantly one or the other depending on how it is handled, contained, or liberated in specific contexts. Accordingly, as "North American Time" indicates, although speaking or attempting to speak "responsibly" guarantees nothing, it remains a common task of critical importance both "inside" and "outside" literature. In their very different idioms, and with very different audiences, both Rich and Césaire demonstrate a common desire to write a poetry that would engage history and the "oppressor's language" in order to move beyond existing power relations in the Americas and elsewhere. For all that remains untranslatable in their experiences of language and discourse, they share a sense of the importance of poetry in particular and of language in general as a field of struggle in which there is no escaping accountability, whether for oneself and one's "own" discourse, or for the Americas, or for the planet as a whole.

But what does it mean to be "accountable"? And as Rich says at the close of the essay, "Notes toward a Politics of Location": "Once again: Who is *we*?" (231). As we have seen, the very different contexts of "Le verbe marronner" and "North American Time" suggest equally different answers to both of these questions. For the Césaire of the mid-1950s, Aragon's statements on behalf of an increasingly Stalinized French Communist party advocating a return to conventional metrical forms demanded a counteraccountability that refused the party line in the name of a certain poetic autonomy and the particularity of the black Caribbean experience. Faced with what he regarded as a demand for aesthetic conformity grounded in a mechanistic dialecticism, Césaire reasserts the political and aesthetic importance of allowing for the productive and nonproductive detours of poetry. Similarly, in the case of "North American Time," the poet's questions concerning the consequences of attempting to be "politically correct" lead to an emphasis on the need to ground poetry's "critique of language" more concretely so as to avoid as much as possible overly abstract (mis)representations of both the individual and the social. Thinking and writing in the North American time of the middle to end of Ronald Reagan's first term, however, Rich necessarily encounters different problems of accountability than does Césaire. Thus, where "Le verbe marronner" establishes from the outset through its dedication to Depestre and its allusions to Paris, Boukmann, and Haiti a concrete context of discursive struggle that serves as a common frame of reference for assessing the French Communist party's abstract formulations concerning the "relation between poetry and Revolution," Rich begins with an abstractly situated "I" and "we" and works her way toward a more concrete understanding of what it might actually mean to be aesthetically and politically accountable from a point of view that resists the "'deadly sameness' of abstraction" that tends to be a part of what she elsewhere calls "North American Tunnel Vision."

Reflecting in a different context on what he has called "le partage de la communauté" ("the sharing-dividing of community"), Jean-Luc Nancy has written that the authentic "communication" of this sharing-dividing would not be that of either a communion or a fusion, but rather that of a common dis-location and resistance to fusion that constitutes the community's very "being-in-common."[29] Since this sharing-dividing which is the being-in-common of community is always and already everywhere and nowhere to be found, it is, says Nancy, "not a work to be completed" ("pas une oeuvre à faire"), but rather "an infinite task at the heart of finitude. (A task and a struggle, that struggle Marx had in mind [*dont Marx eut le sens*] . . . (which) is not at all to be confused with a 'communist' teleology" (59, 88–89). Yet if it is the task of writing in general and of a "literary communism" in particular, as Nancy argues, to inscribe and articulate the sharing-dividing of community (164–65) and in the process to "open the community to itself, rather than to a destiny or a future" (198), this task itself needs to be defined more concretely and historically than the abstract register of Nancy's particular articulation of the "communauté désoeuvrée" will allow.

If it is no longer communism but "the disappearance, the condemnation, or the impossibility of communism" which now constitutes for us, as Nancy claims, "le nouvel horizon indépassable" ("the new unsurpassable horizon," 28), this situation may have arisen in large part as the result of a collective failure to see the community Marx envisioned as one formed "by an articulation of 'particularities'" (186). In just this sense, however, the abstract, universalizing tendency of Nancy's attempt to redefine communism not as a project or teleology but as the ongoing task of a sharing-dividing of community (64) remains open to objections similar to those leveled by Césaire thirty years ago against a communist party so caught up in its theoretical articulations that it overlooked or underestimated the particularity of black struggle. Given that, as Nancy concedes, there is no such thing as a "pure non-project" (55), the particular oppressions of blacks, women, and the inhabitants of Third World countries may lend to the idea of community-as-project—with its implicit demand for radical changes, if not absolute "ends"—a sense of urgency and timeliness that the notion of community as an "*infinite* task" (my emphasis) tends, perhaps despite itself, to undermine. Thus, looking forward in "L'homme de culture et ses responsabilités" to the project of bringing about cultural and political decolonization, Césaire speaks of the need for writers to hold up to the universal the "particular situation of our peoples" and ask: "What kind of world are you preparing for us?"[30]

Like Césaire, Rich attempts to think the complex particularity of the "I" together with the "difficulty of saying 'we'" (PL, 224), and like Césaire as well, she has devoted a considerable portion of her energies to a "struggle against free-floating abstraction" (PL, 218). While she continues to see herself as working toward the "creation of a society without domination"—a project that remains in her view a common element of both Marxism and radical feminism—she has herself emphasized the "deadendness" of the "faceless, sexless, raceless" categories of both the "proletariat" and "'all women'" (PL, 218–19). Although as Rich points out, "Black and other dark-skinned people, Jews and women have haunted white Western thought as Other, as fantasy, as projected obsession" (IN, 203), the comparatively abstract, homogenizing notion of Otherness may itself lead to an obfuscation of the particular histories and struggles of each group. As Toril Moi has noted recently:

> What is repressed is not *Otherness,* but specific, historically constructed agents. Women under patriarchy are oppressed because

they are women, not because they are irredeemably Other. Anti-Semitism is directed against Jews, and South African racism against blacks, not simply against abstract otherness. The promotion and valorization of Otherness will never liberate the oppressed. It is, of course, hopelessly idealist to assume that Otherness somehow causes oppression. The fact that the oppressors tend to equate the oppressed group with ontological Otherness, perceived as a threatening, disruptive, alien force is precisely an ideological manoeuvre designed to mask the concrete material grounds for oppression and exploitation. Only a materialist analysis can provide a credible explanation of *why* the burden of Otherness has been placed on this or that particular group in a given society at a given time.[31]

Poetry, for both Césaire and Rich, is a chronotope for articulating, not abstract Otherness, but the concrete locations and dis-locations of the "I" and "we" in particular, historically overdetermined contexts. Descendants of two different diasporas and heirs to very different linguistic and cultural heritages, both poets recognize the risks of choosing between what Césaire has called a "walled segregation in the particular" and the "dilution of the universal."[32] Thus, in the poem "Natural Resources,"[33] Rich writes:

> There are words I cannot choose again:
> *humanism   androgyny*
>
> Such words have no shame in them, no diffidence
> before the raging stoic grandmothers:
>
> their glint is too shallow, like a dye
> that does not permeate
>
> the fibers of actual life
> as we live it, now

In attempting to come to terms both with their own uncommon privileges as poets and representative figures and with the simultaneity of oppressions in life in the Americas and elsewhere, Rich and Césaire each attempt to articulate differences and commonality so as not to betray either. In this sense, their very different idioms contribute toward and participate in that "literary communism" Nancy has described as "inaugural, not final" (169), which remains in specific ways and in distinct contexts at once a project and a task. In a passage from *Notebook* that anticipates the complex identifications of *métis* and *Mischling* politics, yet is conspicuous in the context of Rich's work for its male inflection, Césaire writes:

> Comme il y a des hommes-hyènes et des hommes-panthères,
> je serais un homme-juif
> un homme-cafre
> un homme-hindou-de-Calcutta
> un homme-de-Harlem-qui-ne-vote-pas
>
> l'homme-famine, l'homme-insulte, l'homme-torture, on
> pouvait à n'importe quel moment le saisir,
> le rouer de coups, le tuer—parfaitement le tuer—sans avoir
> de compte à rendre à personne, sans avoir
> d'excuses à présenter à personne
> un homme-juif
> un homme-pogrom
> un chiot
> un mendigot
>
> (As there are hyena-men and panther-men, I would be a jew-man
> a Kaffir-man
> a Hindu-man-from Calcutta
> a Harlem-man-who-doesn't vote
>
> the famine man, the insult-man, the torture man you can grab
> anytime, beat up, kill—no joke,
> kill—without having to account to anyone, without having to
> make excuses to anyone.
> a jew-man
> a pogrom-man
> a puppy
> a beggar . . .) [CP, 42–43]

As the conditional tense that begins this catalogue suggests, the context for a sharing-dividing of literature and the Americas is itself not a given, but depends on the active choices we make as readers and writers in construing it. Although every language may be regarded as in some sense "a map of our failures" (BP, 119), there remains a choice of emphasis within, between, and among the heterogeneous discourses of the common and the uncommon, community and difference. The Americas and their literatures are there to see, together or apart, *Mischling* and *métis,* together and apart in constructing ourselves.

Gustavo Pérez Firmat

The Strut of the Centipede: José Lezama Lima and New World Exceptionalism

In the spring of 1957, José Lezama Lima delivered a series of four lectures at the Centro de Altos Estudios in Havana under the collective title *La expresión americana*. Although the lectures were sparsely attended and little commented, their printed version has become in recent years a central text in contemporary reflections about Latin American culture. In spite of the opulent obscurity and enigmatic allusiveness of Lezama's prose, *La expresión americana* is now widely regarded as perhaps the most important meditation on the theme of Latin American identity since Octavio Paz's *El laberinto de la soledad* (1950).[1]

Less often remarked, however, is the extent to which *La expresión americana* fits only uneasily in the tradition of Latin American self-reflection. For one thing, unlike most other works in that tradition, Lezama's focus is not on *identidad* (identity) but rather, as he makes clear from the title, on *expresión* (expression); his emphasis is rhetorical rather than ontological, and this sets Lezama apart from such philosophers as Leopoldo Zea, for example, whose project is an ontological definition of Latin American culture.[2] Lezama's stress on expression is highlighted further by the several uses he makes of the term. In the most narrow sense, *expresión* designates an idiom or a set phrase, as when Lezama discusses the linguistic idiosyncrasies of gaucho poetry; in a second, more general sense, the term refers to literature and other varieties of artistic production; in the third, most general sense, it alludes to something like inclination or temperament, what in Spanish may be called *talante,* a word that signifies both ability and propensity, talent as well as temperament. In this context, *expresión* designates not the product of the artistic process but the temper or quality of the American creative imagination, not only expression but also expressiveness.[3] Thus imparting a kind of onomastic coherence to Lezama's essay, *expresión* functions as a connector that binds the most narrowly linguistic features with the temper of mind that produced them.[4]

Lezama also deviates from the tradition of self-reflection in that he views American culture from a hemispheric perspective. The *americana* in his title is no less revisionary than the *expresión,* for Lezama intends the adjective in the broad, inter-American sense. So that, unlike such thinkers as José Enrique Rodó or José Vasconcelos, Lezama is trying to elaborate a theory not only of Spanish or Latin American culture but of hemispheric American culture. And indeed, one of the attractive things about the book is that, although most references and citations allude to Latin American texts, one finds also substantial comments on such North American authors as Melville and Whitman. The most striking instance of this, perhaps, occurs in the last, recapitulatory essay, "Sumas críticas del americano" ["Critical Summas of the American"], where in one brave bravura paragraph Lezama goes from nativist Argentine poetry to North American popular music, literally from the gauchos to the Gershwins, both of which are said to emerge from the same cultural matrix.

Taking my cue from Lezama's title, what I should like to do here is rationalize and nuance Lezama's departures from the tradition of Latin American self-reflection in order to document more fully the book's relevance to a discussion of New World culture. This will mean drawing out of the text what I take to be a kind of "invisible argument,"[5] that is, a line of thought that, if not incompatible with the work's overt theses, is at least separate from them. My presentation will have two parts, the first devoted to the book's visible claims, the second to the covert or invisible ones.

American Hermeneutics

Most studies of *La expresión americana* have centered on Lezama's conviction that the baroque lies at the heart of Latin American culture. The titles of the first two chapters, "Mitos y cansancio clásico" [Myths and classical weariness] and "La curiosidad barroca" [Baroque curiosity] set up symmetrical binomials: on one side, weariness and classicism; on the other, curiosity and the baroque. Just as curiosity offsets weariness, the baroque counters the classical. In Lezama's scheme, weary classicism has produced a "crepuscular criticism" [*crítica crepuscular*], whose representative exponent is T. S. Eliot. To this he would oppose the "matinal hermeneutics" of baroque curiosity embodied in the works of the American expression. The excluded term in these oppositions is *mitos* (myths), the first word in the title of the first chapter. But myth escapes these oppositions because it is actually their fulcrum, since the contrast between the baroque and the classical turns on their treatment of myth. The crepuscular criticism of a neoclassical aesthetics recycles old myths, a tack that Lezama traces back to Eliot's mythical method. Matinal hermeneutics, on the contrary, invents new myths by the happy and even haphazard mutation of old ones.

The problem with these neat oppositions is that, upon closer inspection, Lezama's baroque actually contains two different claims about the uniqueness of the American expression. His "matinal hermeneutics" embraces two different moments or operations, and only one of them fits this scheme. In keeping with Lezama's terminology, I will call the first moment "hermeneutic." As I just suggested, hermeneutics in the Lezamian sense involves the rearrangement of cultural blocks—natural phenomena, historical events, works of art, or myths—into novel configurations. Even though this procedure is certainly not privative of American culture, Lezama argues that the American artist—as a part of and apart from European tradition—is ideally placed to undertake these manipulations. Unlike his European counterpart, the American artist—Lezama calls him abstractly "the metaphorical subject" [*el sujeto metafórico*], that is, the subject that generates metaphors—commands Western culture without being dominated by it. This combination of foreignness and familiarity allows him to play freely, even irresponsibly, with literary and cultural tradition—somewhat as Lezama himself does in many of his texts. His term for this operation is "creative assimilation," with the noun construed in the most literal sense possible, since Lezama clearly conceives of the operation in alimentary terms. Indeed, one of the book's central passages illustrates the American capacity for assimilation by putting together a "literary banquet" whose many courses consist of prandial scenes from a brilliantly heterogeneous group of texts. Thus, the metaphorical subject feasts on culture, his curiosity a species of voracity. As Lezama puts it, the American artist is defined by "el afán, tan dionisiaco como dialéctico, de incorporar el mundo, de hacer suyo el mundo exterior, a través del horno transmutativo de la asimilación ("the dialectical and Dionysian need to incorporate the world, to make it one's own through the transmutative oven of assimilation" [388]).

In a recent book, *José Lezama Lima's Joyful Vision*, Gustavo Pellón summarizes this line of thought by asserting that Lezama's voracity obliterates the age-old distinction between nature and culture.[6] In Lezama's thought culture is or becomes nature, by which Pellón means, I think, that the metaphorical subject does not distinguish between the categories of the natural and the artificial, the mediated and the unmediated, or the evidentiary and the hearsay. For the metaphorical subject, presentation and representation exist at the same level; a represented tree enjoys the same status as the tree, and Lezama himself routinely fails to distinguish between what he has witnessed and what he has only read about, with the result that *La expresión americana* contains any number of misleading assertions of firsthand knowledge. The point is not so much that Lezama bears "false" witness but rather that his idea of testimony does not countenance distinctions between the primary and the secondary. There is in Lezama a kind of gullibility that allows him to assimilate information without too much regard for its status. The metaphorical subject is liable to swallow anything: the raw, the cooked, and even the half-baked.

In the light of this, it is tempting to adopt Pellón's equation of culture and nature. The problem, however, is that in *La expresión americana* "nature" is precisely what resists acculturation. Lezama's nature does not encompass the whole gamut of natural phenomena; rather, he restricts the term to that set of natural phenomena that cannot be turned into facts of culture. In other words, nature is what resists the hermeneutic manipulations of the metaphorical subject. Nature is the residue of hermeneutics, a category of objects and events that cannot be cooked inside the transmutative oven or that the metaphorical subject finds indigestible.

This opposition between nature and culture is mediated by a third term, *paisaje* (landscape). Landscape is the product of the subject's intervention in nature, an intervention that is not necessarily physical or material. Indeed it seems primarily perceptual, for it consists of an act of apprehension, of framing, of fitting objects and events into a cognitive field that renders them suitable for human consumption. As he puts it: "El paisaje es una de las formas del dominio del hombre, como un acueducto romano, una sentencia de Licurgo, o el triunfo apolíneo de la flauta. Paisaje es siempre diálogo, reducción de la naturaleza puesta a la altura del hombre" ("Landscape is one of man's forms of domination, like a Roman aqueduct, a dictum by Lycurgus, or the Apollinean triumph of the flute. Landscape is dialogue, a reduction of nature to bring it to the stature of man" [433]). And again: "Ante todo, el paisaje nos lleva a la adquisición del punto de mira, del campo óptico y del contorno" ("Above all landscape leads us to the acquisition of a point of view, of an optical field and a context" [433]). Rephrasing Pellón, it is perhaps more accurate to say that, in *La expresión americana,* it is landscape, and not nature, that is equated with culture. Landscape is a second nature constituted by the activity of the metaphorical subject and which includes both natural phenomena and cultural facts.[7] In an essay entitled "Pascal y la poesía," Lezama states, "Hay inclusive como la obligación de devolver la naturaleza perdida. De fabricar naturaleza, no de recibirla como algo dado" ("We even have the obligation to return our lost nature, to fabricate nature rather than receiving it as something given" [145]).[8] The paradox of a "fabricated nature," which exploits and explodes the distinction between the natural and the artificial, defines Lezama's notion of *paisaje.* The purpose of hermeneutic operations is to fabricate nature, and fabricated nature is second nature or, more simply, landscape. Landscape in turn creates culture: "Lo único que crea cultura es el paisaje" ("The only thing that creates culture is landscape" [376]).

An aphorism that occurs in another of Lezama's works, *Tratados en La Habana,* will help us summarize the principal components of hermeneutics. It reads, "El gozo del ciempiés es la encrucijada" ("The joy of the centipede is the crossroads").[9] The phrase derives its meaning from a kind of motor fantasy: since the centipede has a hundred legs, it is able to traverse several roads at once; consequently, crossroads are its utopia. For our purposes the relevance of the aphorism emerges, first of all, from the fact that crossroads are sites of culture, points of cultural convergence, and as such, a suitable emblem for the place of hermeneutics. Indeed, the crossroads may be seen as Lezama's mutation of Borges's library; just as the Argentine's imaginative universe takes the shape of a Babel-like *biblioteca,* Lezama's is best seen as a well-travelled crossroads, a notion whose aptness is enhanced by Cuba's location and history. Moreover, if the crossroads are the locus of culture, the centipede is Lezama's version of the culture vulture, his idea of the bookworm; and *gozo* (joy) is what the centipede feels as he traverses cultures. Lastly, in rhetorical terms, the image of the crossroads suggests that the trope associated with hermeneutics is chiasmus, the figure of the cross. Because the metaphorical subject operates by grafting and combining items from diverse texts and cultures, his activity is chiasmic. In its rhetorical aspect, the American expression relies on chiasmic crossings.

We should note further that, for Lezama, hermeneutics furnishes a way out of the dilemma of belatedness. Odd as it may seem, the centipede is an adamic figure. Its chiasmic joy is inaugural. Speaking of Whitman and Melville, Lezama remarks that they established in the middle of the nineteenth century "the epoch of the first men" ("la era de los hombres de los comienzos" [438]). The reason for this is that their distance from European culture allowed them to begin anew, to place themselves at the head of the line. Lezama would make a similar claim about his own theory and practice of writing. Hence the "matinal" hermeneutics. In Lezama's case, however, the sense of initial achievement does not arise from the severance of ties with the past or tradition; rather, it emerges from the metaphorical subject's ability to consume the past, in both senses of the verb. Lezama's Adamism is a function of his belief in what he termed "the serene and infinite possibility of assimilation" (*Tratados,* 216). In this respect it differs significantly from the attitude often predicated of North American culture, and specifically, of such founding figures as Emerson, with whom Lezama allies himself.[10] In fact Lezama's reference to the protagonists of the American Renaissance dissimulates the large distance between the American Adam and the "Cuban" American Adam. Unlike Emerson, Lezama would hardly ejaculate, "Here's for the plain old Adam, the simple genuine self against the world."[11] And not only because Emerson's opposition of self and world elides Lezama's mediating notion of landscape; but also because Lezama's metaphorical subject is far from being "plain" or "simple." The metaphorical subject is cultured through and through, he is compacted from culture, the cruxes and crossroads of culture are his grounds. If Emerson's adamism may be called precultural, since it seeks not assimilation but dissimilation, the preemption of culture, Lezama's can be called postcultural, since it is the posture of someone who *comes after* culture, in the two senses of the verb. In a programmatic passage from his first book, *Nature* (1836), Emerson speaks of "casting off the years."[12] As we have seen, in Lezama the operative term is not casting off but assimilation, and the past is not unloaded but consumed. What in Emerson is a kind of repugnance or anorexia, in Lezama is appetite.

The difference between Emerson and Lezama is clear also in their treatment of mediation: Emerson seeks an unmediated hold on nature, a hold based not on tradition but on insight (Emerson's terms). This project may well grow out of an anxiety about mediation; it is because mediation degrades experience that one needs what Emerson calls "an original relation to the Universe"—original here meaning unmediated by culture or tradition (7). Knowing that relations are always distant, Lezama, on the other hand, feels no nostalgia for unmediated facts or original relations; and this lack of nostalgia manifests itself as a dismissal of the entire problematic. Thus, if Emerson longs after innocence, Lezama relishes something more akin to irresponsibility. In his postcultural posture, Adam is not innocent but irresponsible—the sort of attitude reflected in Lezama's disregard for temporal and causal links, for example. Rather than Adam, a more appropriate personification for postcultural adamism may be Caliban, since Lezama's voraciousness toward Western culture would seem to fit better with what we now take to be the significance of Shakespeare's character.[13] Like Caliban, the metaphorical subject steals the books; his hermeneutic practice is conflictual, predatory, invasive. The crossroads are also a battleground.

American Ecstasies

The line of argument I have followed so far essentially restates the "book" on *La expresión americana*. When scholars speak of Lezama's "baroque" or "neobaroque" aesthetics, they are thinking of the kinds of operations that I have grouped under hermeneutics. In my view, however, hermeneutics is only one part of the book. The other part produces a rather different Lezama, a less postcultural Lezama if you will, one more plain and simple. If the hermeneutic Lezama reminds us of the distance that separates Concord from Trocadero, the ecstatic Lezama sometimes seems very much a part of the house of Emerson.

The lineaments of this other Lezama become visible in the opening chapter. This chapter parses into three sections that adhere closely to a traditional pattern of exposition: an initial presentation of Lezama's thesis, a statement of the principal objection to this thesis, and the refutation of this objection. In a dazzling display of erudition and imagination, Lezama begins by making connections between a medieval book of hours, paintings by Van der Weiden, Jan Van Eyck, and Martini, and a line of Chinese poetry. The result is "an erudite polyphony" and "a dizzying and dialectical cavalcade" ("una cabalgata tan alucinante como dialéctica" [371]). After these initial fireworks, Lezama asserts that the distinctiveness of American culture resides in being able to put on such performances. Having instanced and asserted his thesis, he then rebuts the objection that his display may well amount to nothing more than one of the hackneyed "combinatory games" typical of weary classicism. If this is so, his demonstration is nothing more than another symptom of belatedness, and Lezama's metaphorical subject is indistinguishable from a "crepuscular critic" like Eliot. Lezama's answer is that his procedure, unlike Eliot's, is not "critical" but "fictional," and that instead of repeating old myths it creates new ones.[14] In fact, for Lezama the objection itself betrays the "terrible complex of the American," the fear that American artists cannot add anything new to Western culture. To this Lezama answers in language reminiscent of the opening of Emerson's *Nature*: since America offers the same possibilities for original expression as Europe, Americans have nothing to envy Europeans. The American artist who labors under an inferiority complex, says Lezama, "ha olvidado lo esencial, que el plasma de su autoctonía, es tierra igual que la de Europa" ("has forgotten the essential thing, that the plasma of his autochthony is soil like Europe's"). And he adds: "Lo único que crea cultura es el paisaje y eso lo tenemos de maestra monstruosidad, sin que nos recorra el cansancio de los crepúsculos críticos" ("The only thing that creates culture is landscape and ours is masterfully monstrous, so that we need not feel traversed by the fatigue of critical twilights" [376]). Consequently, the metaphorical subject in no way resembles the crepuscular critic; indeed, he "destroys the pessimism hidden in the theory of artistic constants" (376).

Lezama devotes the rest of the first chapter to illustrations of the myth-making potential of America, all taken either from Amerindian mythology or from the accounts of the first Spanish settlers. The "elemental imagination" present in works like the Popol Vuh or the chronicles of discovery and conquest bears witness to the ability for "joyful creation" available to the American artist (381). In this way the general assertions at the center of the chapter are framed by complementary illustrations. The opening examples show how a modern artist, Lezama, can revitalize old myths and traditions; the closing illustrations indicate the mythopoetic power of the earliest American artists.

The problem is that these two sets of examples are not consistent with each other, for the references to the *cronistas* suggest a creative stance far different from that of the metaphorical subject. We can begin to see these differences if we look closely at the following passage:

> Es muy significativo que tanto los que hacen crónicas sin letras, un Bernal Díaz del Castillo, como los misioneros latinizados y apegados a las sutilezas teologales, escriben en prosa de primitivo que recibe el dictado del paisaje, las sorpresas del animal si descubierto, acorralado. Se percibe en las primeras teogonías americanas, aun en los cantos guerreros, un no resuelto, un quedarse extasiado

ante las nuevas apariciones de las nubes. Es muy curioso que en las tribus precortesinas hay el convencimiento de que alguien va a venir, se está en la espera de la nueva aparición. Sin embargo, en los cronistas el asombro está dictado por la misma naturaleza, por un paisaje que ansioso de su expresión se vuelca sobre el perplejo misionero, sobre el asombrado estudiante en quien la aventura rompió el buen final del diploma de letras (381).

(It is very significant that those chroniclers like Bernal Díaz del Castillo who lack a formal education as well as those latinized missionaries who are attached to theological subtleties write in the prose of a primitive who receives the dictates of nature, the surprise of the animal who has been discovered and cornered. One perceives in the first American theogonies, even in war chants, a lack of resolution, an ecstasy before the new apparitions of the clouds. It is very curious that among pre-Cortesian tribes there is the conviction that someone is going to come, they await the new apparition. Nonetheless, in the chroniclers astonishment is dictated by nature itself, by a landscape that, eager for its expression, descends on the perplexed missionary, on the astonished student in whom adventure interrupted the completion of the diploma of letters.)

The first thing to remark here is the affect produced by these earliest encounters with American nature. Rather than *gozo* (joy), it is ecstasy, wonder, perplexity, astonishment—a very different complex of emotions. Speaking of Rimbaud, Lezama formulates the distinction rather precisely: "Su imaginación parece mostrar incesantemente el nacimiento del que llega y el asombro no nace de dos naturalezas dispares unidas en un tumulto *foudroyant,* sino en la adecuación a un mundo que se acaba de arribar" ("His imagination seems to show incessantly the birth of he who arrives and the astonishment is not born of two unlike natures joined in a thundering tumult, but of the adjustment to a world where one has just arrived" [*Tratados,* 83]). The lightning generated from the conjunction of unlike things names hermeutic illuminations—a different phenomenon from the wonder produced by the arrival to a new world.

Behind this difference in affect lie cognitive differences. The hermeneutic scenario posits an active, indeed a devouring, subject. By contrast, the "ecstasy" of this scene offers a passive subject, one that is seized by nature's power and monumentality. Unlike hermeneutics, ecstasy is triggered by the perceiver's *in*ability to assimilate. Nature "descends" or "converges" on the perceiver, leaving him stunned, perplexed, in a state of cognitive blankness. Unlike joy, perplexity and wonder are passive emotions, readerly emotions, as it were; instead of taking nature's measure, instead of reducing it, the perplexed student and the stunned missionary are caught and cornered, like the animal in the quotation. Even though Lezama in this passage uses the terms "nature" and "landscape" interchangeably, I think it is clear that what acts on these figures is a force that escapes hermeneutic monitoring. One telling detail is the silence with which these figures meet nature. As Lezama's own writing testifies, the metaphorical subject is nothing if not garrulous. His joy is voluble, conversational, dialogic. But the scene of ecstasy is monologic: nature "dictates" (a word that occurs twice in the quoted passage) and man does no more than "receive nature's *dictado*"—its dictation but also its dictates. Unlike the metaphorical subject when he is in the throes of joy, the subject of wonder does not speak. For this reason, we can say that the rhetorical figure of ecstasy is aposiopesis, a falling silent. If hermeneutics is chiasmic, ecstasy is aposiopetic. When nature talks, the metaphorical subject listens—silently.

Lezama's portrayal of the chroniclers suggests further differences between ecstasy and hermeneutics. The first sentence of the quoted passage states that the chroniclers "escriben en prosa de primitivo que recibe el dictado del paisaje" ("write in the prose of a primitive that receives the dictation of the landscape"). The issue is the status of primitive prose in Lezama's poetics. Is primitive prose also characteristic of the American expression? Is Lezama's own prose "primitive"? Is that dialectical cavalcade at the beginning of the book an example of American primitivism? To the extent that Lezama uses "primitive" in the sense of first or original, we can answer these questions affirmatively. New World literature is indeed supposed to be inaugural, primitive in the etymological sense. (And here one is reminded of Lezama's assertion that Melville and Emerson established "the epoch of the first men"). But Lezama seems to be using the concept also in its more conventional meaning. As he says a bit later, the primitive is someone who is able to "feel wonder" because he lacks "humanistic insistences";[15] that is to say, someone who writes without the aid of cultural or literary grids, someone whose transactions with nature are unmediated. This kind of writer, Lezama concludes in the last sentence of the chapter, "advances into nature accompanied only by the sound of his own natural steps" (383).

The contrast between this view of the American artist as an untutored primitive, as a natural man, and that set forth at the beginning of the essay in the description of the metaphorical subject, could not be sharper. The metaphorical subject is nothing if not bookish; of the centipede's many steps, none is "natural." As the title of the last chapter of Lezama's own book attests, the metaphorical subject manufactures critical summas, he works by accretion and revision, not by renunciation. Referring to the eighteenth-century writer Fray Servando Teresa de Mier, Lezama states that Fray Servando's American achievement is to reform rather than break with tradition: "Reformar dentro del ordenamiento previo, no romper, sino retomar el hilo" ("To reform within the previous order, not to break, but to pick the thread up again" [402]). This is typical: when Lezama speaks of hermeneutics, he thinks of it not as rupture but as reform; and yet his discussion of the chroniclers presupposes rupture, as shown by the last sentence of the passage under discussion, which states that for some of the *cronistas* "la aventura rompió el buen final del diploma de letras" ("adventure interrupted the completion of the diploma of letters"). The adventure of discovering a new world occasions a "break" with Old World culture, here symbolized by the classical education. Both educated and uneducated chroniclers, those with "letters" as well as those without, shed their European learning, their "humanistic insistences," when encountering American nature. Primitive prose is what results from such encounters.

This means that primitives do not so much write as transcribe. Rather than the source of original utterances, they are the medium for nature's speech. For this reason, the primitive is neither an author nor an authority figure. Unlike the centipede, whose hundred legs figure its ability to take possession, to cover and command, the primitive derives his authority from an agency other than himself. As Lezama puts it, primitives "write because landscape dictates" (421).[16] In primitive prose nature is the subject, both in the sense that it provides the authoring impulse and that it constitutes the topic of discussion. Primitive prose is heterological, for it takes authority from the "other" it represents.[17] By contrast, hermeneutic discourse takes authority from itself; this is precisely the impression created by Lezama's opening "cavalcade," which is deployed without preparation or justification. The metaphorical subject does not seek validation from any external agency; his discourse asks to be taken at its word. But the primitive, whose modest footsteps cannot match the centipede's strut, acts as repository and relay for the words of nature.

His one inflection of nature's words is to accent them with wonder or perplexity. As often happens in the literature of the sublime (to which

Lezama's ecstasy bears a significant relation), in the ecstatic situation the subject's role is limited to, on the one hand, receiving the stimulus and, on the other, registering the affective response. There is no sense here of "reducing" or "dominating" nature by entering into dialogue with it, as happens in the hermeneutic situation. No longer is Lezama offering the bookworm as the ideal American artist; now his figure is a "natural man" whose lack of a humanistic education enables him to feel and convey nature's power.

Lezama is here making a very different case for American exceptionalism from that which he made earlier. His stance is no longer that of the revisionist but that of the visionary. Ecstasy differs from hermeneutics point by point: its subject is not a bookworm but a primitive; its affect is not joy but wonder; its rhetorical protocol is not chiasmus but aposiopesis; and, lastly, its place is not the crossroads but the pampas. In the course of working out the distinction between nature and landscape, Lezama provides a panorama of what he considers to be landscapes: the bay of Havana, the Andes, the valley of Mexico. In the middle of this list he inserts the pampas and then asks abruptly, "¿la pampa es paisaje o naturaleza?" ("Are the pampas landscape or nature?" [434]). His answer is ambiguous, for even as he discusses the ways in which the language of the gauchesque poem *Martín Fierro* "runs through them," as he puts it, he recognizes their intractability. In *La expresión americana,* and perhaps in other of Lezama's works as well,[18] the pampas figure as a space beyond man's reductive control, and we can usefully contrast the vast and void expanses of the pampas with the well-travelled crossroads. If the centipede rejoices at the crossroads because he can master the possibilities, in the pampas he does not know whether he is coming or going. Instead of strutting with joy, he squirms with apprehension. The crossroads are a point of convergence, a reduction in the etymological sense; but the pampa is a space of dispersal—what Lezama labels a "leviathan of extensiveness" capable of "swallowing" [*engullir*] man (434). This choice of words is significant: Lezama employs the same alimentary relationship he had used earlier but with the poles reversed; in front of nature, the metaphorical subject is not the consumer but the consommé. If hermeneutics gives us an active, voracious subject, ecstasy gives us a subject in danger of consumption. And the agent of consumption is nature, what Lezama labels a "gengiskanesca barbarie" ("Genghis Khan-like barbarism" [433]).[19]

Ecstasy may then be described as the barbaric instance in the text, the place in Lezama's thinking where culture cracks. If hermeneutics is postcultural, ecstasy may well be paracultural, for it strives after an unmediated encounter with nature. I should make clear that although Lezama's text discloses this possibility, Lezama seems to have mixed feelings about it. Ecstasy appears in his work not necessarily as a desirable end but rather as the by-product of a certain type of cognitive failure. When he experiences *asombro,* the centipede loses his legs. Instead of strutting, he squirms. This is the reason why Lezama repeatedly phrases the encounters between man and recalcitrant nature in military terms.[20] For a writer as inveterately cultured as Lezama, culture crack cannot appear as anything other than vanquishment. But my point is that even as Lezama distinguishes between land and landscape in order to come down on the side of landscape, his discussion sketches out the outlines of a different poetics, a poetics of wonder rather than joy, one based on the supersession of culture rather than on its consumption.

Let me now round out my description of ecstasy and suggest the wider relevance of the concept by taking my final examples from a text not by Lezama, Alejo Carpentier's *Los pasos perdidos* (1953), which is one of the great fictional attempts to define Latin American identity. This novel is about an exiled Latin American artist who, after an absence of many years, returns to South America in search of primitive musical instruments. His voyage is a quest for origins—both personal and continental—and in his encounters with American culture there is a great deal of hermeneutic wrangling. The novel contains a couple of moments, however, when hermeneutics breaks down. One of these occurs when the narrator comes upon some monoliths in the jungle. As he approaches these *moles,* his first impulse is to proceed as he does elsewhere and naturalize them by calling up resemblances between the monoliths and images stored in his memory. Thus the monoliths remind him of some structures in paintings by Bosch.[21]

Lezama, who asserts that memory and analogy are the two principal mechanisms in hermeneutics, would call the narrator's operation "mnemonic analogy," and would see it as an instance of creative assimilation. In the scene with the monoliths, however, analogy fails, since the reference to Bosch is followed by a recognition that such comparisons are inadequate: "Y aun cuando encontraba una analogía, tenía que renunciar a ella, al punto, por una cuestión de proporciones" ("And even when I found an analogy, I had to renounce it immediately because of the question of proportions" [233]). Just like the pampas, the monoliths are too large to be dominated by reduction. This renunciation of analogy is succeeded by what the narrator regards as a noninterpretive encounter with nature: "el ánimo, pasmado, no buscaba la menor interpretación de aquella desconcertante arquitectura telúrica, aceptando sin razonar su belleza vertical e inexorable" ("my spirit, awestruck, did not seek the least interpretation of that disconcerting telluric architecture, accepting without reasoning its vertical and inexorable beauty" [233]). A patient reading of this sentence would squeeze four words in particular: *pasmado,* awestruck, a cognate of Lezama's *asombro; interpretación,* interpretation, a loaded term considering that the narrator moonlights as an interpreter; *desconcertante,* disconcerting, an equally loaded term since the narrator is a musicologist by training and his father was a concertmaster; and *aceptación,* acceptance, which one would relate to the "renunciation" of analogy mentioned a few sentences earlier: Carpentier's narrator renounces analogy and accepts *asombro,* astonishment. But the fact that the narrator, even in the middle of his trance, finds a name for what he observes—he calls it a "disconcerting telluric architecture"—suggests how frail and fleeting ecstatic trances really are. Because the attempt to move beyond culture always fails (this is in fact the message of Carpentier's novel), ecstasy exists as a limit concept, a concept that is not susceptible to full articulation and manifests itself by its logoclastic effects on discourse. As long as one remains in the arena of language, the cracks of culture are glimpsed and then just as quickly covered.

It is appropriate, for this reason, that the second passage I will mention shows Carpentier's narrator opting for silence. Again he is deep in the jungle; it is the middle of the night, and he is trying to assign names to the sounds he hears. This activity is by no means innocent, since by his own admission the adamic task of the Latin American writer is precisely to give names to new realities; Carpentier himself, in a well-known essay, has asserted as much.[22] On this particular occasion the narrator gets off to a good start: "Alguien, no sabía dónde, empezó a probar la embocadura de un oboe. Un cobre grotesco rompió a reír en el fondo de un caño. Mil flautas de dos notas, distintamente afinadas, se respondieron a través de las frondas. Y fueron peines de metal, sierras que mordían leños, lengüetas de harmónicas, tremulantes y rasca-rasca de grillos, que parecían cubrir la tierra entera" ("Somebody, somewhere tried out the mouthpiece of an oboe. A grotesque brass set up a laugh in a hidden glade. A thousand flutes of two differently tuned notes answered each other through the leaves: There were metal combs, saws whining through wood, harmonica reeds, the quavering stridulation of the crickets, which seemed to cover all the earth" [224]). Musicologist that he is, the narrator arranges the noises of the jungle into a symphonic piece. But then—uncharacteristically—words begin to fail him. First, his analogizing mechanism loses its precision. The next sentence no longer asserts exact equivalences: "Hubo como gritos de pavo real" ("There were cries somewhat like those of peacocks" [225]). Immediately thereafter, he gives up trying to identify the source of the sounds altogether and settles for calling them only "cosas" ("things"). "Hubo como gritos de pavo real, borborigmos errantes, silbidos que subían y bajaban, *cosas* que pasaban debajo de nosotros, pegadas al suelo; *cosas* que se zambullían, martillaban, crujían" ("There were cries somewhat like those of peacocks, errant growls, whistles that rose and died away, *things* that passed beneath us, flat to the ground, *things* that dived, hammered, creaked"). By relying on the catchall *cosas,* the onomateur nearly lapses into aphasia, and after this sentence he stops describing the concert of noises and switches instead to naming his own feelings. "Estaba aturdido, asustado, febril. . . . Cuando el sueño venció el temor a las amenazas que me rodeaban, estaba a punto de capitular—de clamar mi miedo, para oír voces de hombre" ("I was dazed, frightened, feverish. . . . When sleep finally overcame the fear of the threats I felt on every side, I was on the verge of capitulation—of speaking my fear— for the sake of hearing human voices" [225]).

Although it may seem like stretching it to connect this episode with Lezama's scene of ecstasy, the similarities are broad and significant. In both cases there is a transition from stimulus to affect that culminates in a loss of language. What the narrator feels here is the *asombro,* the bewilderment that takes place when one walks into nature accompanied only by the sound of one's natural steps. It is significant that when he thinks of asking for help, he describes this as "speaking my fear," "clamar mi miedo." In such a situation, escape or avoidance is tantamount to linguistic articulation. What the narrator terms "capitulation" (an echo of Lezama's military phrasing) is equated with giving voice, *clamar.* And we should not overlook the etymological relation between *clamar,* to call out, and *llamar,* to call or name, of which the former is the learned doublet. The threat here, more than the physical harm, is language loss, the possibility of unnameable *cosas* filtering through the cracks of culture. The narrator fears nature's address, what Lezama would term its *dictado.* Thus when he alludes at the end to "voces de hombres" ("human voices") the term *voces* activates its two meanings in Spanish—*voz* as voice but also *voz* as word. *Voces de hombres* are not only human voices but human words, language. It may seem paradoxical, perhaps, that a passage that moves relentlessly toward aposiopesis should have such a dense verbal texture. But the density of the narrator's language is a symptom of culture's alarm at its vulnerability. Just as the antidote to jungle noises is human voices, the antidote to ecstasy, the way to combat culture crack, is to landscape nature with language. This is no less true of Lezama than it is of Carpentier. Ecstasy culminates in an aposiopetic trance from which we are saved by hermeneutic gab. This is what happens repeatedly in Lezama's essay and in Carpentier's novel. Language comes to the rescue and seals the cracks of culture. Ecstasy dissolves into expression.

I will close with two brief general observations. The first is that the two notions I have outlined not only help to organize Lezama's thought in *La expresión americana*; they also represent the two fundamental ways in which the distinctiveness of New World culture has been conceived. Claims of American exceptionalism have always invoked one or another version of these two options: we are either centipedes at the crossroads, or we are centipedes in the wilderness; we strut, or we squirm. At the crossroads, in the hermeneutic camp, we can place such notions as Severo Sarduy's neobaroque (much of it built from Lezama's own ideas), the "signifying" of Afro-American literature, and various Creole versions of Bakhtin's dialogical imagination.[23] In the wilderness, one finds North American Adamism, the *criollismo* of such novels as *La vorágine* (1924) and *Doña Bárbara* (1929), and the magical realism of some contemporary Latin American novelists.

I also believe that what I have termed ecstasy sometimes gets short shrift in contemporary discussions of this topic. Indeed, my attempt to recover an ecstatic instance in both Lezama and Carpentier is intended to counter the dominant readings of these important figures. Contemporary criticism likes to "deconstruct" wonder, to argue that it is actually joy in disguise. Ecstasy is then seen as a naive or unself-conscious hermeneutics. This is, for example, the gist of Roberto González Echevarría's influential analysis of Carpentier's *lo real maravilloso* ("marvelous American reality").[24] From my perspective, however, such attempts to acculturate wonder should be placed alongside the fear experienced by Carpentier's narrator: perhaps they also betray culture's anxiety about its supersession. Spirited revisions of ecstasy may themselves be symptoms of culture crack.

Now it should be clear from what I have just said that, as for myself, I'd rather squirm than strut, although I certainly am sensitive to the charm and effect of the centipedal swagger. I want to end, however, by insisting on the exemplariness of *La expresión americana*: Lezama's text is a privileged site for the display of these two powerful ways of specifying the uniqueness of American culture; it is both crossroads and *pampa*. The achievement of *La expresión americana* is to juxtapose hermeneutics and ecstasy, joy and wonder, so that the lure and allure of *both* options become visible. The crux of the matter is style: strutting or squirming, the American centipede will never be confused with an Old World mole.

Notes

Note: Unless otherwise indicated, translations are those of the respective authors.

Introduction: Cheek to Cheek

1. The most interesting recent works in this area are: José Ballón, *Autonomía cultural de América: Emerson y Martí* (Madrid: Pliegos, 1986); Bell Gale Chevigny and Gari Laguardia, eds., *Reinventing the Americas: Comparative Readings of Literature of the United States and Spanish America* (Cambridge: Cambridge University Press, 1987); Vera Kutzinski, *Against the American Grain: Myth and History in William Carlos Williams, Jay Wright, and Nicolás Guillén* (Baltimore: Johns Hopkins University Press, 1987); Alfred MacAdam, *Textual Confrontations: Comparative Readings in Latin American Literature* (Chicago: University of Chicago Press, 1987); Lois Parkinson Zamora, *Writing the Apocalypse: Historical Vision in Contemporary U.S. and Latin American Fiction* (Cambridge: Cambridge University Press, 1989).

2. Herbert Eugene Bolton, "The Epic of Greater America," reprinted in *Do the Americas Have a Common History?*, ed. Lewis Hanke (New York: Alfred A. Knopf, 1964), 67–100.

3. Roberto Fernández Retamar, *Para una teoría de la literatura hispanoamericana,* 3rd ed. (Mexico City: Nuestro Tiempo, 1977), 135.

The Usable Past:
The Idea of History in Modern U.S.
and Latin American Fiction

To minimize the necessarily cumbersome process of dual citation in English and Spanish, I cite passages from Hispanic works of *nonfiction* in English only.

1. David Hume, *Letters to William Strahan* (Oxford: Clarendon Press, 1888), 155.

2. Hannah Arendt, "The Concept of History," in *Between Past and Future* (1961; rpt. New York: Viking Press, 1969), 68.

3. Georg Lukács, *The Historical Novel,* trans. Hannah and Stanley Mitchell (1962; rpt. New York: Penguin, 1981), 20. This book was orginally written in 1936–37 and published in Russia shortly thereafter. Subsequent references are cited in the text.

4. Georg Wilhelm Friedrich Hegel, *The Philosophy of History,* trans. J. Sibree (New York: Willey Book Co., 1944), 87. The lectures which comprise this book were first delivered in 1822–23, again in 1824–25 and in 1831, the year of his death. Subsequent references are cited in the text.

5. Roberto González Echevarría writes, "The main theme of Latin American thought has been the question of identity" (*The Voice of the Masters* [Austin: University of Texas Press, 1985], 12). Nina Baym also discusses the ways in which the "idea of essential Americanness" has been pursued in U.S. literature and criticism in "Melodramas of Beset Manhood: How Theories of American Fiction Exclude Women Authors," in *The New Feminist Criticism,* ed. Elaine Showalter (New York: Pantheon Books, 1985), 63–80. See also Russell Reising's discussion of literary critical theories of the uniqueness of U.S. identity in *The Unusable Past: Theory and the Study of American Literature* (New York: Methuen, 1986).

6. Carlos Fuentes, *Latin America: At War With the Past* (Montréal: CBC Enterprises, 1985), 9. This is a published series of lectures broadcast by the Canadian Broadcasting Company in 1984. Fuentes explicitly defines the term North American as meaning the U.S., and in discussing Fuentes's opposition, I too refer only to the U.S.

7. Octavio Paz embodies the contrasting attitudes toward the past in contrasting attitudes toward the present: "North Americans consider the world to be something that can be perfected, and . . . we consider it to be something that can be redeemed" *The Labyrinth of Solitude: Life and Thought in Mexico* (1950, rev. ed. 1959), trans. Lysander Kemp (New York: Grove Press, 1961), 24. Paz pursues this opposition in "Reflections: Mexico and the United States," *The New Yorker,* 17 Sept. 1979, 137–53.

8. Carlos Fuentes, "La violenta identidad de José Luis Cuevas," in *Casa con dos puertas* (Mexico City: Joaquín Mortiz, 1970), 239–79; I cite from the bilingual edition, *El mundo de José Luis Cuevas,* trans. Consuelo de Aerenlund (New York: Tudor Publishing Co., 1969), 8.

9. For a more complete discussion of Fuentes's work in these terms, see chapter 7 of my book, *Writing the Apocalypse: Historical Vision in Contemporary U.S. and Latin American Fiction* (Cambridge and New York: Cambridge University Press, 1989). The Cuban novelist, Alejo Carpentier, was also influenced by Vico's historiography. According to Roberto González Echevarría, Vico re-

placed Spengler as the historiographic basis of Carpentier's later work: "If Spengler posited a circular history whose cycles were repeated throughout the universe, Vico offers an idea of return that does not deny historicity, but affirms it" (*Alejo Carpentier: The Pilgrim at Home* [Ithaca, N.Y.: Cornell University Press, 1977], 259).

10. Carlos Fuentes to Jonathan Tittler, *Diacritics* 10, 3 (1980): 49. The phrase is in the context of Fuentes's definition of Mexican temporality:

> it is a time which conceives itself in a perpetual present, one that is not alienated by the pursuit of the future, a future that we can never reach. . . . This bastardization of the philosophy of the Enlightenment is common to both the capitalist and the socialist bureaucratic systems—the promise of a future, of the paradise on earth. The mythical time, which as I say is a present, does not admit the past as such. It considers what we call the past—in the Western linear system—as a present which is accreting, which is constantly enriching the moment, the instant. The past is never condemned to the past in a mythical system.

A recently published collection of essays on the historical consciousness of North American Indian groups suggests a radical difference of indigenous and Western time concepts in North America as well. See Calvin Martin, ed., *The American Indian and the Problem of History* (Oxford: Oxford University Press, 1987).

11. Carlos Fuentes to Christopher Sharp in *W*, a supplement to *Women's Wear Daily* 29 (October 1976): 9. See also Fuentes's essay, "La novela como tragedia: William Faulkner," in *Casa con dos puertas,* 52–78.

12. Carlos Fuentes, *Una familia lejana* (Mexico City: Joaquín Mortiz, 1980), 163–64; *Distant Relations,* trans. Margaret Sayers Peden (New York: Farrar, Straus, Giroux, 1982), 170. Subsequent references are cited in the text.

13. Baym, "Melodramas of Beset Manhood," 71.

14. J. Hillis Miller, "Presidential Address 1986: The Triumph of Theory, the Resistance to Reading, and the Question of the Material Base," *PMLA* 102, 3 (1987): 287. Miller's observation reiterates the critical attitude of Van Wyck Brooks's essay, "On Creating a Usable Past," except that Miller treats the thinness of American culture as an essential liability, whereas Brooks treats it as a literary opportunity. Brooks writes, "The present is a void and the American writer floats in that void because the past that survives in the common mind is a past without living value. But is this the only possible past? If we need another past so badly, is it inconceivable that we might discover one, that we might even invent one?" Quoted in Reising, *The Unusable Past,* 13. I am indebted to both sources, and implicitly refer to both, in the "usable past" of my own title.

15. In *The Voice of the Masters,* González Echevarría discusses this analogous aspect of Latin American literary theory, what he calls the "concept of culture" (36ff.).

16. My concern in this essay is with American historiography after Hegel. Before Hegel—that is, before the independence of the American states from

Spain and England—it is possible to speak in relatively unified terms of historical understanding in the colonial Americas. Despite enormous differences in the social and institutional patterns of the Catholic and Protestant settlement of the Americas, there nonetheless existed a common historiographic conception based on the linear, teleological, apocalyptic historiography of Judeo-Christianity. John Leddy Phelan discusses the similarity between sixteenth-century Spain's sense of its messianic historical mission in the New World and the Puritans' theological vision of a new heaven and new earth, though he notes that the immediate sources of the visions were different. Spain's sense of its historical mission was an extension of the Joachimite Messiah-Emperor myth of the later Middle Ages, whereas the English settlers were impelled primarily by Martin Luther's apocalyptic interpretations of the Reformation. See his *The Millennial Kingdom of the Franciscans in the New World* (1956; rev. ed. Berkeley and Los Angeles: University of California Press, 1970), 21.

17. George Bancroft, "The Progress of Mankind," in *Literary and Historical Miscellanies* (New York: Harper and Brothers, 1855), 517.

18. Geoffrey H. Hartman, "Towards Literary History," in *Beyond Formalism: Literary Essays 1958–1970* (New Haven: Yale University Press, 1971), 356.

19. Useful comparative studies are Charles Frederick Harrold, *Carlyle and German Thought: 1819–1834* (Hamden: Archon Books, 1963); Kenneth Marc Harris, *Carlyle and Emerson: Their Long Debate* (Cambridge: Harvard University Press, 1978). Further sources on Carlyle's historiography are John D. Rosenberg, *Carlyle and the Burden of History* (Cambridge: Harvard University Press, 1985); Hill Shine, *Carlyle's Fusion of Poetry, History, and Religion by 1834* (1938; rpt. Port Washington, N.Y.: Kennikat Press, 1967).

20. Cather implicitly acknowledges her affinity for the German tradition when she begins her essay on Carlyle: "Perhaps no man who has ever stood before the public as an English author was [so] thoroughly un-English as Thomas Carlyle. His life, his habits, and his literature were most decidedly German" ("Concerning Thomas Carlyle," in *The Kingdom of Art: Willa Cather's First Principles and Critical Statements, 1893–1896,* ed. Bernice Slote [Lincoln: University of Nebraska Press, 1966], 421). See Patricia Lee Yongue's useful discussions of Carlyle and Cather's historiography in *Death Comes for the Archbishop,* in "Willa Cather on Heroes and Hero-Worship," *Neuphilologische Mitteilungen* 79, i (1978): 59–66; and "Search and Research: Willa Cather in Quest of History," *Southwestern American Literature* 5 (1975): 27–39. William M. Curtin discusses William James and Cather in "Willa Cather and *The Varieties of Religious Experience,*" *Renascence* 27 (1974): 115–23. Cather's education in English and American romanticism is well known; it is generally documented in Susan J. Rosowski, *The Voyage Perilous: Willa Cather's Romanticism* (Lincoln: University of Nebraska Press, 1986). I want here to thank Loretta Wasserman for her helpful suggestions about Cather's historiographic assumptions.

21. Although not comparative studies, relevant thematic discussions of U.S.

literature which include Cather's fiction are by Cecil Robinson, *Mexico and the Hispanic Southwest in American Literature* (Tucson: University of Arizona Press, 1977), and Raymund Arthur Paredes, "The Image of the Mexican in American Literature," Diss., University of Texas, 1973.

22. Cather was writing during the years of Turner's greatest acceptance. Turner's thesis, published in 1893, that the U.S. democracy was formed in the crucible of the frontier, provided an easily acceptable explanation for the difference between Americans and Europeans. Like Turner and Whitman (and Crèvecoeur before them), Cather asks the question, "What is an American?" But her novelistic response is more complex than Turner's historical thesis because her concerns are metaphysical as well as territorial. And more complex too than Walt Whitman's, because she posits the attraction backward to the Old World as well as forward to the New, the repulsion of the West as well as its lure. Though Cather is often associated with Whitman (her title *O Pioneers!* is of course from Whitman's 1865 poem, "Pioneers, O Pioneers"), her depictions of the historical problematics of the frontier are considerably more subtle than Whitman's.

23. Thomas Carlyle, *On Heroes, Hero-Worship, and the Heroic in History*, ed. Archibald MacMechan (Boston: Ginn and Company, 1901), 1: "the history of what man has accomplished in this world, is at bottom the History of Great Men who have worked here."

24. Angel Rama compares the two areas of heaviest European immigration in nineteenth-century America, the U.S. and the area of the Río de la Plata, stating that the immigrants and their descendants did not stamp the national ideology of Argentina as they did in the U.S., a fact

> which becomes clear if one evokes the extraordinary diffusion of the myth of the pioneer in the United States . . . and then seeks some equivalent entity in South America. Its absence forces us to realize the constricting force which the oligarchic landowners exercised. The "conquering of the desert" in Argentina follows closely upon the "conquering of the West" in the United States, but the former was achieved by the army and the oligarchy, while the latter is owed in large part to immigrants, who were compensated for their efforts with land.

See *La ciudad letrada* (Hanover, N.H.: Ediciones del Norte, 1984), 76, my translation. Subsequent passages from this study are cited in the text in my translation.

25. Thomas Carlyle, "Characteristics," in *Critical and Miscellaneous Essays,* 3:39.

26. The name of Thea's German piano teacher is Wünsch, which means "wish" in German; the name may be connected to the religious significance which Carlyle gives to desire in *Heroes and Hero-Worship*. In his description of "The Hero as Divinity," Carlyle refers to Norse mythology: "But perhaps the notablest god we tell of is one of whom Grimm the German Etymologist finds trace: the God Wünsch, or Wish" (28).

27. Willa Cather, *The Song of the Lark* (1915; rev. ed. 1937; New York: Houghton Mifflin, 1983), 251. Subsequent references are cited in the text.

28. William James, *The Principles of Psychology*, 2 vols. (London: Macmillan and Co., 1890), 1:234. Cather was, according to a close contemporary, "a devoted disciple" of James. See George Seibel, "Miss Willa Cather from Nebraska," *New Colophon* 2, 7 (1949): 202. Curtin, in "Willa Cather and *The Varieties of Religious Experience*," notes: "The period of Willa Cather's apprenticeship coincided with the dominant influence of William James upon her whole generation, from the publication of *The Principles of Psychology* in 1890 to his death in 1910, when his essay 'The Moral Equivalent of War' appeared in *McClure's Magazine,* of which Cather was then the editor" (115).

29. Leopoldo Zea, *The Latin American Mind* (*Dos etapas de pensamiento en Hispanoamérica,* 1949), trans. James H. Abbott and Lowell Dunham (Norman: University of Oklahoma Press, 1963), section 2, "The New Order," 135–289. Other relevant studies by Leopoldo Zea are *El positivismo en México* (1943; Mexico City: Fondo de Cultura Económica, 1968) and *Apogeo y decadencia del positivismo en México* (Mexico City: El Colegio de México, 1944).

30. See Karl Löwith, *Meaning in History* (Chicago: Phoenix Books, 1949), 67ff.

31. Herbert Spencer in *Social Statistics* (1851): "always toward perfection is the mighty movement—toward a complete development and a more unmixed good, subordinating in its universality all petty irregularities and falling back, as the curvature of the earth subordinates mountains and valleys" (New York: Robert Schalkenback Foundation, 1954), 263.

32. See Zea, *The Latin American Mind,* 269–89.

33. See H. Stuart Hughes, "The Decade of the 1890's: The Revolt against Positivism," in his *Consciousness and Society: The Reorientation of European Social Thought, 1890–1930* (New York: Knopf, 1958), 33–66. Hughes notes the antipathy toward and yet the reliance on European positivism by early twentieth-century theorists who attempted to free themselves from their nineteenth-century philosophical heritage. Barbara Foley surveys the philosophical rejections of positivism which shaped representational strategies of the modernist novel in Europe and the U.S. in *Telling the Truth: The Theory and Practice of Documentary Fiction* (Ithaca, N.Y.: Cornell University Press, 1986), 212–21. See also James Longenbach, *Modernist Poetics of History: Pound, Eliot, and the Sense of the Past* (Princeton: Princeton University Press, 1987), for a discussion of the antipositivist or "existential historicism" of Pound and Eliot, which manifested itself not in an interest in communal or cosmic historical patterns so much as in the relationship between the individual interpreter and the representation of the past.

34. Michael A. Weinstein, *The Polarity of Mexican Thought: Instrumentalism and Finalism* (University Park, Pa.: Pennsylvania State University Press, 1976). Subsequent page references are cited in the text. Among Mexican intellectuals, besides José Vasconcelos and Antonio Caso, Weinstein discusses Samuel Ramos,

Lucio Mendieta y Núñez, Emilio Uranga, Agustín Basave Fernández del Valle, Leopoldo Zea, and Octavio Paz. I am indebted to Carla Cooper for bringing Weinstein's book to my attention.

35. Nevertheless, Ortega made extended visits to Argentina, one from 1939 to 1942, and declared that he considered himself "half Argentinian." See Franz Niedermayer, *José Ortega y Gasset,* trans. Peter Tirner (New York: Ungar, 1973), 94.

36. At the time of Ortega's death in 1955, Carpentier stated: "The influence of Ortega y Gasset on the thinking and the artistic and literary orientation of the men of my generation was immense." Borges, on the other hand, stated that he hardly knew Ortega's writings (an assertion contradicted by his references to Ortega elsewhere in his own work): "The stoics declared that the universe forms a single organism; it is quite possible that I, by force of the secret sympathy that unites all of its parts, owe much or something or everything to Ortega y Gasset, whose works I have barely skimmed." Here, Borges's involuted homage to and dismissal of Ortega may be attributed in part to Ortega's problematic attitude toward America, mentioned above. See Roberto González Echevarría, "Borges, Carpentier y Ortega: Dos textos olvidados," *Revista Iberoamericana* 43 (1977): 697–704.

Paz has reiterated Carpentier's sense of Ortega's influence:

> His influence marked profoundly the cultural life of Spain and Hispanic America. For the first time, after an eclipse of two centuries, Spanish thought was listened to and discussed in Hispanic American countries. They not only renewed and changed our ways of thinking and our information: Ortega y Gasset and his circle also left their mark on literature, the arts, and the sensibility of the period. Between 1920 and 1935, in the enlightened classes, as they said in the nineteenth century, there predominated a *style* which came from the *Revista de Occidente.* I am sure that the thought of Ortega will be rediscovered, and soon, by new generations of Spaniards.

From "José Ortega y Gasset: El cómo y el para qué," in *Hombres en su siglo y otros ensayos* (Barcelona: Seix Barral, 1984), 104, Paz's italics. For a general consideration of Paz's relation to twentieth-century Spanish literature and philosophy, see Peter G. Earle, "Octavio Paz y España," *Revista Iberoamericana* 141 (1987): 945–53.

37. Niedermayer comments, "Around the *Revista* Ortega assembled a group of translators not unlike the famous twelfth-century College of Translators of Toledo" (45).

38. José Ortega y Gasset, *History as a System and Other Essays toward a Philosophy of History,* trans. Helene Weyl (1941; New York: W. W. Norton, 1962), 216, 217, Ortega's italics. Subsequent references are cited in the text.

39. Ortega wrote this phrase many times, beginning with his first full-length book, *Meditaciones del Quijote* (1914): *Obras completas* I (Madrid: Revista del Occidente, 1966), 51–52. For a discussion of Ortega's relation to Husserl and Hei-

degger, see Philip W. Silver, *Ortega as Phenomenologist: The Genesis of* Meditations on Quixote (New York: Columbia University Press, 1978).

40. Paz, "El cómo y el para qué," 102. Subsequent references are cited in the text.

41. I am indebted to Ewell E. Murphy, Jr., for making available to me his unpublished study, "Waiting for the Barbarians: The Future of the West in the Historical Philosophy of José Ortega y Gasset," presented to the Houston Philosophical Society, February 16, 1978. See also Harold Raley, *José Ortega y Gasset: Philosopher of European Unity* (University, Ala.: University of Alabama Press, 1971), especially chapters 1 and 4.

42. Karl Marx, Afterword to the second German edition of *Das Kapital* (1873), in *The Marx-Engels Reader,* ed. Robert C. Tucker (New York: W. W. Norton, 1978), 302.

43. Weinstein, *The Polarity of Mexican Thought,* 17. Weinstein cites Alejandro Korn, "Bergson en la filosofía contemporánea," in *Filósofos y sistemas* (Buenos Aires: Colección Claridad, n.d.), and Alejandro O. Deústua, "El orden y la libertad," in *La filosofía latinoamericana contemporánea,* ed. Aníbal Sánchez Reulet (Washington, D.C.: Unión Panamericana, n.d.), as important statements of the influence of Bergson on Latin American antipositivism.

44. Bergson's ideas have been far more influential on literature and philosophy than on politics or psychology: they are rarely, and then only briefly, mentioned in standard histories of modern psychology, whereas their presence in European and American literature has been voluminously documented. See, for example, Shiv Kumar, *Bergson and the Stream of Consciousness Novel* (London: Blackie, 1962), and Leon Edel, *The Modern Psychological Novel* (New York: Grosset and Dunlap, 1964). Wendy B. Faris discusses the influence of Bergson, via Proust, on Carpentier's work: "Alejo Carpentier à la recherche du temps perdu," *Comparative Literature Studies* 17, 2 (1980): 133–54.

45. Octavio Paz, *Postdata* (Mexico City: Siglo Veintiuno, 1970), 116–17, my translation. Alejo Carpentier has also written of American identity in terms of indigenous architectural forms in his famous essay of regional self-definition, "Lo barroco y lo real maravilloso," in *La novela latinoamericana en vísperas de un nuevo siglo* (Mexico City: Siglo Veintiuno, 1981), 123–24.

46. Fuentes, "La violenta identidad de José Luis Cuevas," 14.

47. Henri Bergson, *Creative Evolution,* trans. Arthur Mitchell (1907; rpt. New York: Modern Library, 1944), 45. Subsequent references are cited in the text.

48. The prevalence of this idea in postmodernist criticism is suggested by the strongly antigeneric positions taken by Roland Barthes and Jacques Derrida. See Roland Barthes, "Historical Discourse," in *Introduction to Structuralism,* ed. Michael Lane (New York: Basic Books, 1970), 145–55; and Jacques Derrida, "Limited Inc abc," in *Glyph: Johns Hopkins Textual Studies 2* (Baltimore: Johns Hopkins University Press, 1977), 162–254.

49. For an explicit statement of this view, see E. L. Doctorow, "False Doc-

uments," *American Review* 26 (Nov. 1977): 215–32. I discuss contemporary U.S. and Latin American documentary fiction in "Novels and Newspapers in the Americas," *Novel* 23, 1 (1989): 44–62.

50. The relativity of factual and fictional narrative was, by the middle of the eighteenth century, a well-established idea. See Ian Haywood, *The Making of History: A Study of the Literary Forgeries of James Macpherson and Thomas Chatterton in Relation to Eighteenth-Century Ideas of History and Fiction* (Rutherford, N.J.: Fairleigh Dickinson University Press, 1986), 31–35.

51. "El escritor argentino y la tradición" was collected in *Discusión* (1932; Buenos Aires: Emecé Editores, 1964). That Borges conceived Latin American literature in profoundly comparative and intertextual terms is once again confirmed by the recent anthology of his magazine reviews, primarily of English and German literature. See *Textos Cautivos: Ensayos y reseñas en "El Hogar" (1936–1939)* [*Captive Texts: Essays and Reviews in "El Hogar" (1936–1939)*], ed. Enrique Sacerio-Garí y Emir Rodríguez Monegal (Barcelona: Tusquets Editores, 1986). In his reviews, Borges's activity of cultural mediation parallels in a number of ways Ortega's work in the *Revista de Occidente*: sometimes the very texts and writers which the two introduce to Hispanic audiences coincide. This parallel makes Borges's avowal of ignorance of Ortega's work all the more intriguing.

52. An exception is Borges's treatment of Emerson, whose historical vision he implicitly indicts as rigidly linear, and which he opposes to his own complex historiography of repetition and recurrence. In his story, "La otra muerte" ("The Other Death"), Borges describes a character's imaginative revising and reliving of multiple lifetimes. The story begins with a reference to Emerson's poem, "The Past," a poem which describes the absolute impossibility of revising the monolithic past—just the opposite of the multiple pasts which the story dramatizes. See *El aleph* (Buenos Aires: Emecé Editores, 1957), 71–80. Borges's poem entitled "Emerson" ends with Borges's own imaginative revision of Emerson's lifetime: he makes his "tall New Englander" dissatisfied with his progressive, unrepeatable history: "No he vivido. Quisiera ser otro hombre" ("I have not lived. I want to be someone else"). In *Selected Poems, 1932–67*, ed. Norman Thomas di Giovanni (New York: Delta, 1979), 170–71.

53. "Prólogo," in *Discusión*, 9. The phrase quoted in the preceding sentence is found in the final paragraph of "Pierre Menard, autor del Quijote," which was first published in 1939 in *Sur*.

54. Jorge Luis Borges, *Otras inquisiciones* (Buenos Aires: Emecé Editores, 1960), 213; *Other Inquisitions*, trans. Ruth L. C. Simms (Austin: University of Texas Press, 1964), 167. Subsequent references are cited in the text.

Form and Function in the New World Legend

1. Northrop Frye, "Literature and Myth," in *Relations of Literary Study*, ed. James Thorpe (New York: Modern Language Association, 1967), 30.

2. Kenneth W. and Mary W. Clarke, *Introducing Folklore* (New York: Holt, Rinehart and Winston, 1963), 11.

3. See, for example, the *Dictionnaire de l'Académie Françoise,* 5th ed. (Paris, 1811), vol. 2: "Se dit aussi par dénigrement, d'une liste, d'une longue suite de choses, et signifie ordinairement une liste ennuyeuse"; or Sheridan's *General Dictionary of the English Language* (London, 1780), vol. 2: "A chronical or register of the lives of saints; any memorial or relation; an incredible unauthentick narrative; any inscription, particularly on medals or coins."

4. Published in Berlin in two volumes, 1812–1815.

5. The first edition, in five volumes, appeared in Gotha between 1782 and 1787; the Wieland version, also in five volumes, was published in Vienna, 1815–1816.

6. Otmar is Nachtigal's pseudonymous narrator. The first German edition is Bremen, 1800.

7. Published in Leipzig in 1812.

8. Published in two volumes in Berlin, 1816–1818.

9. Stith Thompson, *The Folktale* (Berkeley and Los Angeles: University of California Press, 1977), 8.

10. Ibid., 8–9.

11. For the relationship between popular literary forms and early German romanticism, see Klaus Weissenberger, "Mythopoesis in German Literary Criticism," in *Literary Criticism and Myth,* ed. Joseph P. Strelka (University Park: Pennsylvania State University Press, 1980), 242–44; and A. Leslie Willson, "Romantic Neomythology," in *Myth and Reason,* ed. Walter D. Wetzels (Austin: University of Texas Press, 1973), 43–69.

12. Cited in Thompson, *The Folktale,* 370.

13. Nathaniel Hawthorne, *The Marble Faun.* The *Leyendas* appeared in periodicals from 1858 to 1864. See Gustavo Adolfo Bécquer, *Leyendas,* ed. Pascual Izquierdo (Madrid: Ediciones Cátedra, 1986), 90–91. Also see Rubén Benítez, *Bécquer tradicionalista* (Madrid: Editorial Gredos, 1971).

14. Nathaniel Hawthorne, *The Marble Faun,* vol. 4 of *The Centenary Edition of The Works of Nathaniel Hawthorne,* ed. William Charvat et al. (Columbus: Ohio State University Press, 1968), 3.

15. Washington Irving, *The Sketch Book of Geoffrey Crayon, Gent.,* ed. Haskell Springer (Boston: Twayne, 1978), 308. The page references in the text are to this edition.

16. Walter A. Reichart, *Washington Irving and Germany* (Ann Arbor: University of Michigan Press, 1957), 26–29.

17. Cited in Reichart, *Washington Irving and Germany,* 25–26.

18. Ibid., 28.

19. See, among many others: Martin Roth, *Comedy and America: The Lost World of Washington Irving* (Port Washington, N.Y.: Kennikat Press, 1976), 156–58; Philip Young, "Fallen From Time: The Mythic Rip Van Winkle," *Kenyon*

Review 22 (1960): 547–73; Allen Gutman, "Washington Irving and the Conservative Imagination," *American Literature* 36 (1964): 165–73; and Alessandro Portelli, *Il re nascosto* (Rome: Bulzoni, 1979), 25–48.

20. The spelling is "Kaatskill" in the text of the story, "Kaatsberg" or "Catskill" or "Kaaters-kill" in the postscript.

21. Notes to the *Sketch Book,* 308.

22. Much of what I have said about "Rip Van Winkle" is equally applicable to Irving's other masterpiece, "The Legend of Sleepy Hollow" (272–97): the frame attributing the text to Knickerbocker, the cultural community from old Teutonic to Indian to Dutch (273); and the defeat of Ichabod Crane—symbol of Yankee invasion, book learning, and the ideal of national progress and expansion (280)—by the ludic, ignorant, but irresistible forces of the Hudson Valley Golden Age.

23. References to *Iracema* in the text are to the *Romances Ilustrados* edition of Alencar's novels (Rio de Janeiro: José Olympio, 1967), 1:257–309.

24. One indication of the fidelity of New World authors to the traditional definition of the legend as a description of events which took place within historical time (that is, after Christ) is that almost all American legends dealing with the Indian world are set after 1492 (that is, after the arrival of Christianity).

25. Cited by M. Cavalcanti Proença, *José de Alencar na Literatura Brasileira,* 2nd ed. (Rio de Janeiro: Civilização Brasileira, 1972), 42.

26. Cited by Eugénio Gomes, *Aspectos do Romance Brasileiro* (Bahia: Pregoresso, 1958), 14.

27. From the preface to *Ubirajara,* in the *Romances Ilustrados,* 1:376.

28. Alencar's notes to *Iracema* appear in the *Romances Ilustrados,* 1:310–19.

29. "La fiebre amarilla" was first published in *El Monitor Republicano* on June 28, 1868, but was extensively revised for republication in Sierra's 1898 *Cuentos románticos.* Both the *Monitor* and the *Cuentos* versions appear in Sierra's *Prosa literaria,* ed. Francisco Monterde (Mexico: UNAM, 1948), 128–33 and 436–42 respectively. I have used the revised version here; page references in the text are to Monterde's edition.

30. Alejo Carpentier, "De lo real maravilloso americano," in his *Tientos y diferencias* (Montevideo: Editorial Arca, 1967), 115.

The Dialectics of Our America

Note: This essay was completed during my tenure as a Visiting Ford Foundation Postdoctoral Fellow at the Stanford Center for Chicano Research, Stanford University, in 1986–1987. Of inestimable value as I pursued the ideas and materials discussed here have been the helpful comments and suggestions on earlier versions of this piece by Fernando Alegría, Houston Baker, Jr., Sacvan Bercovitch, Héctor Calderón, Gustavo Pérez Firmat, Paul Lauter, José Limón, Steven Mailloux, and the reviewers for Duke University Press.

1. See the critical anthology, *Ideology and Classic American Literature,* ed. Sacvan Bercovitch and Myra Jehlen (Cambridge: Cambridge University Press, 1986). See also Sacvan Bercovitch, *Reconstructing American Literary History* (Cambridge, Mass.: Harvard University Press, 1986); and Mary V. Dearborn, *Pocahontas's Daughters: Gender and Ethnicity in American Culture* (New York: Oxford University Press, 1986). For a general discussion of ideology in American literary history, see Sacvan Bercovitch, "The Problem of Ideology in American Literary History," *Critical Inquiry* 12 (Summer 1986): 631–53.

2. See, e.g., Sacvan Bercovitch's comments on "dissensus" in "America as Canon and Context: Literary History in a Time of Dissensus," *American Literature* 58, 1 (March 1986): 99–107. See also Bercovitch, "The Problem of Ideology," 632–33. Finally, see Mikhail M. Bakhtin's radical reconceptualization of the novel in *The Dialogic Imagination: Four Essays,* ed. Michael Holquist, trans. Caryl Emerson and Michael Holquist (Austin: University of Texas Press, 1981). According to Bakhtin, the novel is a genre, in contradistinction to such fixed genres as epic and lyric, which has the ability to speak out in the most diverse and often conflicting voices. Put plainly, the novel, says Bakhtin, is "dialogic," that is, an interaction of utterances, a "polyphonic" multiplicity of voices and meanings.

3. Some of the more interesting studies in American literary history and canon formation have been done by the Reconstructing American Literature Project directed by Paul Lauter. For a summary of this project, see Paul Lauter, "Reconstructing American Literature: A Synopsis of an Educational Project of the Feminist Press," *MELUS* 11 (Spring 1984): 33–45. See also Paul Lauter, "Society and the Profession, 1958–1983," *PMLA,* Centennial Issue (May 1984): 414–26; and his "History and the Canon," *Social Text* 12 (Fall 1985); 94–101. See also the following: Herbert Lindenberger, "Toward a New History in Literary Study," *Profession 84* (Modern Language Association): 16–24; Annette Kolodny, "The Integrity of Memory: Creating a New Literary History in the United States," *American Literature* 57, 2 (May 1985): 291–307; Bruce Novoa, *Chicano Poetry: A Response to Chaos* (Austin: University of Texas Press, 1982); Houston A. Baker, Jr., *Blues, Ideology, and Afro-American Literature* (Chicago: University of Chicago Press, 1984); and Jane P. Tompkin, *Sensational Designs: The Cultural Work of American Fiction, 1790–1860* (New York: Oxford University Press, 1985).

4. See Fredric Jameson, *The Political Unconscious: Narrative as a Socially Symbolic Act* (Ithaca, N.Y.: Cornell University Press, 1981); Frank Lentricchia, *Criticism and Social Change* (Chicago: University of Chicago Press, 1983); Hayden V. White, *Tropics of Discourse* (Baltimore: Johns Hopkins University Press, 1978); and Edward W. Said, *Orientalism* (New York: Pantheon Books, 1978), and *The World, the Text, and the Critic* (Cambridge, Mass.: Harvard University Press, 1983).

5. The following new American histories are most relevant to my study:

Ronald T. Takaki, *Iron Cages: Race and Culture in Nineteenth-Century America* (New York: Knopf, 1979); Arnoldo De Leon, *They Called Them Greasers: Anglo Attitudes Towards Mexicans in Texas, 1821–1900* (Austin: University of Texas Press, 1983); Mario T. García, *Desert Immigrants: The Mexicans of El Paso, 1880–1920* (New Haven: Yale University Press, 1981); Albert Camarillo, *Chicanos in a Changing Society: From Mexican Pueblos to American Barrios in Santa Barbara and Southern California* (Cambridge, Mass.: Harvard University Press, 1979); Francis Jennings, *The Invasion of America: Indians, Colonialism, and the Cant of Conquest* (Chapel Hill: University of North Carolina Press, 1975); Winthrop D. Jordan, *White Over Black: American Attitudes Toward the Negro, 1550–1812* (Chapel Hill: University of North Carolina Press, 1968); and Annette Kolodny, *The Land Before Her: Fantasy and Experience of the American Frontiers, 1630–1860* (Chapel Hill: University of North Carolina Press, 1984).

6. See Friedrich Nietzsche's figure of the genealogist in *On the Genealogy of Morals*, ed. Walter Kaufman (New York: Vintage Books, 1967). Like Nietzsche's figure of the intellectual-genealogist, Martí and Fernández Retamar, I contend, are heroic, struggling, and oppositional intellectuals. Of relevance here is Michel Foucault's classic essay, "Nietzsche, Genealogy, History," in *The Foucault Reader*, ed. Paul Rabinow (New York: Pantheon Books, 1984): 76–100. For Foucault, "Genealogy is history in the form of concerted carnival" (94).

7. Jean Franco, *An Introduction to Spanish American Literature* (Cambridge: Cambridge University Press, 1969), 118.

8. Enrico Mario Santí, "José Martí and the Cuban Revolution," *Cuban Studies* 16 (1986): 139–45.

9. The work of the American historian William Appleman Williams stands behind my reading of American imperialism. According to Williams,

> . . . our Revolutionary and Founding Fathers knew the ideas, languages, and reality of empire from their study of the classic literature about Greece and Rome (and about politics in general); they used the word regularly in their talk about England. . . . [Later generations] talked even more about "extending the area of freedom," supporting such noble principles as "territorial and administrative integrity," and "saving the world for democracy"—even as they destroyed the cultures of the First Americans, conquered half of Mexico, and relentlessly expanded their government's power around the globe. Empire became so intrinsically our American way of life that we rationalized and suppressed the nature of our means in the euphoria of our enjoyment of the ends. Abundance was freedom, and freedom was abundance. The democratic City on the Hill. Hence we projected our imperium outward upon others—avowed friends as well as damned antagonists.

From his *Empire as a Way of Life: An Essay on the Causes and Character of America's Present Predicament, Along With a Few Thoughts About an Alternative* (New York: Oxford University Press, 1980), viii–ix. For a good overview of how Martí has been appropriated by the 'right' and 'left,' see John Kirk, *José Martí: Mentor of the Cuban Nation* (Tampa: University Presses of Florida, 1983), especially ch. 1, "From Místico to Revolutionary," 3–18.

10. Roberto Fernández Retamar, "The Modernity of Martí," in *José Martí, Revolutionary Democrat,* ed. Christopher Abel and Nissa Torrents (Durham, N.C.: Duke University Press, 1986), 6.

11. Andrés Iduarte as quoted in Ramón Eduardo Ruiz, *Cuba: The Making of a Revolution* (New York: W. W. Norton, 1970), 62.

12. José Martí, *Obras Completas,* 2nd ed. (Havana: Editora Nacional de Cuba, 1963–1966), 4:168. The translation is mine.

13. Ralph Waldo Emerson, "The American Scholar," in *The Collected Works of Ralph Waldo Emerson.* Vol. 1, *Nature, Addresses, and Lectures,* intro. and notes by Robert E. Spiller (Cambridge, Mass.: Belknap Press, 1971), 56.

14. José Martí, "The Washington Pan-American Congress," *La Nación,* 19–20 Dec. 1889, in *Inside the Monster: Writings on the United States and American Imperialism,* ed. Philip S. Foner, trans. Elinor Randall, Juan de Onis, and Roslyn Held Foner (New York: Monthly Review Press, 1975), 355–56. Also relevant here is Abdul R. JanMohamed's analysis of "the manichean organization of colonial society" in his *Manichean Aesthetics: The Politics of Literature in Colonial Africa* (Amherst: University of Massachusetts Press, 1983). According to JanMohamed, the "colonial mentality is dominated by a manichean allegory of white and black, good and evil, salvation and damnation, civilization and savagery, superiority and inferiority . . . self and other, subject and object" (4).

15. See *Granma Weekly Review* (Havana), May 19, 1968.

16. See José Martí's "Our America" in *Our America by José Martí: Writings on Latin America and the Struggle for Cuban Independence,* trans. Elinor Randall, ed. Philip S. Foner (New York: Monthly Review Press, 1977), 3. All future references to this essay will be paginated in the text.

17. Martí, *Obras Completas,* 32:108.

18. See George M. Fredrickson, *White Supremacy: A Comparative Study in American and South African History* (New York: Oxford University Press, 1981). As Fredrickson tells us,

> The phrase "white supremacy" applies with particular force to the historical experience of two nations—South Africa and the United States. As generally understood, white supremacy refers to the attitudes, ideologies, and policies associated with the rise of blatant forms of white or European dominance over "nonwhite" populations. In other words, it involves making invidious distinctions of a socially crucial kind that are based primarily, if not exclusively, on physical characterizations and ancestry. In its fully developed form, white supremacy means "color bars," "racial segregation," and the restriction of meaningful citizenship rights to a privileged group characterized by its light pigmentation (ix).

19. José Martí, "A Glance at the North American's Soul Today," *La Nación,*

January 16, 1886. For an English translation see *Martí on the U.S.A.*, trans. Luis A. Baralt (Carbondale: Southern Illinois University Press, 1966), 197–98.

20. Carl N. Degler notes in *Out of Our Past: The Forces That Shaped Modern America,* 3rd ed. (New York: Harper and Row, 1984) that

> Historians usually credit John L. O'Sullivan, spread-eagle nationalist editor of the Jacksonian-Democratic organ *United States and Democratic Review,* for originating the phrase. In an article in 1845, justifying America's claims to the Oregon territory, O'Sullivan asserted that the American claim "is by right of our manifest destiny to overspread and to possess the whole of the Continent which Providence has given for the development of the great experiment of liberty and federated self-government entrusted to us" (118, n.4).

21. Martí, *Obras Completas,* 9:205–6. The translation is mine.

22. Andre Gunder Frank, *Capitalism and Underdevelopment in Latin America* (New York: Monthly Review Press, 1969).

23. Foner, *Inside the Monster,* 25.

24. In "Mexico and the United States," first published in *The New Yorker* (September 17, 1979), 136–53, Octavio Paz localizes and supplements Martí's thesis:

> [T]he opposition between Mexico and the United States belongs to the North-South duality as much from the geographical as the symbolic point of view. It is an ancient opposition which was already unfolding in pre-Columbian America, so that it antedates the very existence of the United States and Mexico. The northern part of the continent was settled by nomadic, warrior nations; MesoAmerica, on the other hand, was the home of an agricultural civilization, with complex social and political institutions, dominated by warlike theocracies that invented refined and cruel rituals, great art, and vast cosmogonies inspired by a very original vision of time. The great opposition of pre-Columbian America . . . was between different ways of life: nomads and settled peoples, hunters and farmers. This division greatly influenced the later developments of the United States and Mexico. The policies of the English and the Spanish toward the Indians were in large part determined by this division; it was not insignificant that the former established themselves in the territory of the nomads and the latter in that of the settled peoples (138).

More recently, Carlos Fuentes, at a conference at Michigan State University entitled "The Politics of Experience" (October 1985), said this about the essential North-South opposition: "There is a character in *One Hundred Years of Solitude* who decides that from now on it will always be Monday, and one has the impression in the relations between Latin America and the United States that it is always Monday, that nothing happens because the actual difference is never understood. But if there is a difference, it is the difference as regards the consideration of the past and memory. There is a tendency in this country to look too much towards the future and to forget the past" (*The Centennial Review* 30 [Spring 1986]: 133).

25. Juan Marinello pointed out that Martí did not think in "materialist"

terms. See his *Once ensayos martianos* (Havana, Cuba: Comisión Nacional Cubana de la UNESCO, n.d.), 193. But as Fidel Castro justly claimed, Martí was his mentor. A typical statement of Castro's debt to Martí is the following: "I carry in my heart the teachings of the Maestro. Martí is the instigator of the 26th of July Movement," quoted in Ramón Eduardo Ruíz, *Cuba: The Making of a Revolution* (New York: W. W. Norton, 1970), 58.

26. Ernesto Guevara, "The Most Dangerous Enemies and Other Stupidities," in *Che: Selected Works of Ernesto Guevara,* ed. Rolando E. Bonachea and Nelson P. Valdés (Cambridge, Mass.: MIT Press, 1970), 46.

27. Roberto González Echevarría, "Criticism and Literature in Revolutionary Cuba," *Cuban Studies/Estudios Cubanos* 11 (1981): 2. Of relevance here is Judith A. Weiss's summary of the *Mundo Nuevo* and the *Casa de las Américas* conflict. According to Weiss, *Mundo Nuevo,* edited by the eminent Uruguayan writer and critic Rodríguez Monegal, was a right-wing response to the leftist *Casa de las Américas.* See Weiss, *Casa de las Américas: An Intellectual Review in the Cuban Revolution* (Chapel Hill: University of North Carolina Press, 1977), especially 18–61.

28. See the following by José David Saldívar: "The Real and the Marvelous in Nogales, Arizona," *Denver Quarterly* 17, 2 (Summer 1982): 141–44; "The Ideological and the Utopian in Tomás Rivera's *y no se lo tragó la tierra* and Ron Arias's *The Road to Tamazunchale,*" *Crítica* 1, 2 (Spring 1985): 100–114; "Ideology and Deconstruction in Macondo," *Latin American Literary Review* (Special Issue on Gabriel García Márquez) 13, 25 (Jan.–June 1985): 29–43; and "Rolando Hinojosa's *Klail City Death Trip Series*: A Critical Introduction," in *The Rolando Hinojosa Reader: Essays Historical and Critical,* ed. José David Saldívar (Houston: Arte Pública Press, 1985), 44–63.

29. Ernest Mandel, *Late Capitalism* (London: NLB, 1975). According to Mandel,

> This new period [1940 to 1965] was characterized, among other things, by the fact that alongside machine-made industrial consumer goods (as from the early 19th century) and machine-made machines (as from the mid-19th century), we now find machine-produced raw materials and foodstuffs. Late capitalism, far from representing a postindustrial society, thus appears as the period in which all branches of the economy are further industrialized for the first time; to which one could further add the increasing mechanization of the sphere of circulation (with the exception of pure repair services) and the increasing mechanization of the superstructure (190–91).

Relevant here to my study are: Jean François Lyotard, *The Postmodern Condition: A Report on Knowledge,* trans. Geoff Bennington and Brian Massumi (Minneapolis: University of Minnesota Press, 1984); and Fredric Jameson, "Postmodernism, or the Cultural Logic of Late Capitalism," *New Left Review* 146 (July–Aug. 1984): 53–93.

30. Roberto González Echevarría, "Roberto Fernández Retamar: An Introduction," *Diacritics* (Dec. 1978): 70.

31. See Karl Marx and Friedrich Engels, *The Communist Manifesto,* in *The Marx-Engels Reader,* 2nd ed., ed. Robert C. Tucker (New York: Norton, 1978), 477.

32. See Domingo Faustino Sarmiento, *Facundo: Civilización y barbarie* (Buenos Aires: 1958). Sarmiento's hegemonic vision was very powerful among the ruling classes in Latin America, and echoes of Facundo can be found in José Enrique Rodó's *Ariel* (1900), another target of Fernández Retamar in *Caliban*. Rodó's *Ariel* was one of the first Latin American appropriations of Shakespeare's *The Tempest*. Rodó glorifies Prospero, whose advice to Latin American intellectuals is to preserve the aristocratic qualities of the mind, admire the greatness of the United States, and preserve the spiritualism of Ariel.

33. González Echevarría, "Fernández Retamar," 74.

34. Roberto Fernández Retamar, "Nuestra América y Occidente," *Casa de las Américas* 98 (1976): 36–57. I cite Fernández Retamar's essay in the collection entitled *Para El Perfil Definitivo Del Hombre* (Havana: Ediciones Vitral, 1981), 359. The translation is mine. All further references will be paginated in the text.

35. E. L. Doctorow, "False Documents," in *E. L. Doctorow: Essays and Conversations,* ed. Richard Trenner (Princeton, N.J.: Ontario Review Press, 1983), 16–27. Doctorow, like Roland Barthes and Hayden White, Gabriel García Márquez and Mario Vargas Llosa, Rolando Hinojosa and Ntozake Shange, challenges the distinction, basic to all historicism in all its forms, between "historical" and "fictional" discourse, between what he sees as the "power of the regime" (history) and "the power of freedom" (fiction/narrative). Doctorow's principal aim here is to attack the vaunted objectivity of Western historiography. And this is precisely what he does: he exposes the ideological function of the narrative mode of representation with which it has been associated. Although Doctorow has not been "canonized" by Fernández Retamar and the Cuban-Marxist school of the *nueva narrativa,* I believe that his work (from *Welcome to Hard Times* [1960] to *World's Fair* [1985], which are essentially Nietzschean in their semiological method), can be seen as part of the generalized negation by the American *nueva narrativa* which seeks to break down the distinction between the novel and history as institutions. See, for example, Jason Weiss, "An Interview With Carlos Fuentes," *Kenyon Review* 5, 4 (1983): 105–18; Fuentes remarks that "After all, history is only what we remember about history. What is fact in history? The novel asks this question" (106). More recently, the investigative narrator in Mario Vargas Llosa's *The Real Life of Alejandro Mayta,* trans. Alfred MacAdam (New York: Farrar, Straus and Giroux, 1986), tells one of the characters, "in my novels I always try to lie knowing when I do it. . . . And I think the only way to write stories is to start with History—with a capital H" (87). An interesting twist to this theme is seen in Arturo Islas's postmodernist Chicano novel, *The Rain God: A Desert Tale* (Palo Alto, Calif.: Alexandrian Press, 1984), where his Faulknerian

narrator, Miguel Chico, tells us that he "was the family analyst, interested in the past for psychological reasons, not historical reasons. Like Mama Chona, he preferred to ignore facts in favor of motives, which were always and endlessly open to question and interpretation" (28). If I were to make a totalizing proposition about the *nueva narrativa* in the Americas (from García Márquez to Hinojosa and Shange), it would echo Perry Anderson's thesis in *In the Tracks of Historical Materialism* (Chicago: University of Chicago Press, 1984): "Theory [in these narratives] now is History, with a seriousness and severity it never was in the past; as history is equally theory, in all its exigency, in a way that it typically evaded before" (26).

36. See Roberto González Echevarría, "The Case of the Speaking Statue: Ariel and the Magisterial Rhetoric of the Latin American Essay," in his *The Voice of the Masters: Writing and Authority in Modern Latin American Literature* (Austin: University of Texas Press, 1985), especially 12–14.

37. See Roberto Fernández Retamar, "Caliban: apuntos sobre la cultura en nuestra América," in *Para El Perfil Definitivo Del Hombre,* 219–90. For an English translation by Roberto Márquez, see "Caliban: Notes Toward a Discussion of Culture in Our America," *The Massachusetts Review* 15, 1–2 (1974): 7–72.

38. Ibid., 24. As Fernández Retamar tells us, "Our Symbol then is not Ariel, as Rodó thought, but rather Caliban. . . . I know no other metaphor more expressive of our cultural situations, of our reality" (Fernández Retamar, *Caliban,* 24).

39. Steve Hellman, "The Cuban Pulitzer," *The San Francisco Chronicle Review,* July 20, 1986: 2, 10. A local journalist from San Pablo, Steve Hellman is the first U.S. judge to participate in the Casa Prize since Rolando Hinojosa in 1980, and Allen Ginsberg in 1962.

40. Only two years after Rolando Hinojosa's new narrative, *Klail City y sus alrededores* (Havana: Casa de las Américas, 1976), was published in Cuba, Hinojosa's text from south Texas found its way into the Eastern bloc via the German Democratic Republic in a German version entitled *Klail City und Umgebund,* trans. Yolanda Julia Broyles (East Berlin: Volk und Welt, 1980). In recognition of the Chicano novel's merits, the Federal Republic of Germany's premier "canonical" publisher, Suhrkamp Verlag, adopted the East German edition for publication in the West, as *Klail City und Umgebund* (Frankfurt: 1981). In her essay on Hinojosa's novel, "Oral Culture and Print Culture," in *The Rolando Hinojosa Reader,* Broyles writes: "The [Frankfurt] publisher's only problem was whether to market the work as part of the Latin American program or as part of the United States literature program. . . . Indeed, the novel's firm footing in South American literature and United States literature defies the arbitrary political borders and the corresponding categories of national literatures. *Klail City* is a prime example of Chicano literature which is *sin fronteras*" (109). Ironically, Hinojosa's work is virtually unknown in the United States.

41. Werner Sollors, *Beyond Ethnicity: Consent and Descent in American Culture*

(New York: Oxford University Press, 1986), 14. Subsequent references are cited in the text.

42. See my comments on Doctorow's "False Documents" in n. 35.

43. Ntozake Shange, "Diario Nicaragüense," in *See No Evil: Prefaces, Essays & Accounts, 1976–1983* (San Francisco: Momo's Press, 1984), 62.

44. Ntozake Shange, interview with author, University of Houston, 5 May 1985.

45. Ntozake Shange, *A Daughter's Geography* (New York: St. Martin's Press, 1983), 19–21.

46. Russell A. Berman, *The Rise of the Modern German Novel: Crisis and Charisma* (Cambridge, Mass.: Harvard University Press, 1986), 3.

47. Some recent exceptions to this rule are: Marta Ester Sánchez, "Three Latin American Novelists in Search of 'Lo Americano': A Productive Failure," Diss., University of California, San Diego, 1977; and Ileana Rodríguez and Marc Zimmerman, eds., *Process of Unity in Caribbean Society: Ideologies and Literature* (Minneapolis, Minn.: Institute for the Study of Ideologies and Literature, 1983). See also Sandra E. Drake, "The Uses of History in the Caribbean Novel," Diss., Stanford University, 1977; and William Luis, ed., *Voices from Under: Black Narrative in Latin America and the Caribbean* (Westport, Conn.: Greenwood Press, 1984).

48. See Emir Rodríguez Monegal, ed., *The Borzoi Anthology of Latin American Literature,* Vol. 2: *The Twentieth Century from Borges and Paz to Guimarães Rosa and Donoso* (New York: Knopf, 1977), especially 687–89. Subsequent references are cited in the text. Also relevant here are: Emir Rodríguez Monegal, *El boom de la novela latinoamericana* (Caracas: Editorial Tiempo Nuevo, 1972), and José Donoso, *The Boom in Spanish American Literature,* trans. Gregory Kolovakos (New York: Columbia University Press, 1977).

49. For an analysis of Borges's influence on North American metafictionalists, see Tony Tanner, *City of Words: American Fiction, 1950–1970* (New York: Harper and Row, 1971). According to Tanner, "A part of the appeal that Borges has for American writers is his sense that 'reality' is an infinitely plural affair, that there are many different worlds and that the intersection points might not be so fixed as some people think, that the established ways in which we classify and order reality are as much 'fictions' as his stories" (42). See also John Barth, "The Literature of Exhaustion," *The Atlantic Monthly* 222 (Aug. 1967): 29–34. For an alternative analysis of Borges's impact on postmodernism in general, see Jean Franco, "The Utopia of a Tired Man: Jorge Luis Borges," *Social Text* 4 (Fall 1981): 52–78. According to Franco, "the graph of Borges' reputation" began to rise rapidly after 1961, "precisely the time when Gerard Genette, Foucault, Barthes, Derrida, the *Tel Quel* group, and others had begun to challenge the procedures of discourse and the assumption on which traditional narrative, history, metaphysics, and science based their authority. . . . Everyone surely wanted to join [Borges's] revolution which involved no bloodshed" (52).

50. Steven Mailloux, "Rhetorical Hermeneutics," *Critical Inquiry* 11 (June 1985): 630. Subsequent references are cited in the text. As a student of Stanley Fish and Edward Said, Mailloux contends, in his post–"Reader Response" American criticism, that the discipline of proper hermeneutic critique is argument. Like Fish and Said, Mailloux believes in the necessity of making your case. Mailloux's newer work thus stands behind my own inquiry into criticism's "institutional practice"; as colleagues at the Stanford Humanities Center during 1985–1986, I profited immensely from our many discussions on history and hermeneutics. See also Stanley Fish, "Demonstration vs. Persuasion: Two Models of Critical Acts," in *Is There a Text in This Class?: The Authority of Interpretive Communities* (Cambridge, Mass.: Harvard University Press, 1980), 356–73.

51. Robert Coover, "The Writer as God and Saboteur," review of *The Real Life of Alejandro Mayta,* by Mario Vargas Llosa, *The New York Times Book Review,* 2 February 1986, 1.

52. Marlise Simmons, "A Talk with Gabriel García Márquez," *New York Times Book Review,* 5 December 1982, 7, 60.

53. Gabriel García Márquez, "La soledad de Latin América," *Proceso* 319 (13 deciembre de 1982). In my essay, I cite Marina Castañeda's translation entitled "The Solitude of Latin America," in *The New York Times,* 6 February 1982, sec. 4, p. 17. Subsequent references are cited in the text.

54. Gabriel García Márquez, *One Hundred Years of Solitude,* trans. Gregory Rabassa (New York: Harper and Row, 1970), 383.

Through Blues

1. Langston Hughes, "IS IT TRUE?" in *ASK YOUR MAMA. 12 MOODS FOR JAZZ* (New York: Alfred A. Knopf, 1961), 57.

2. See Ishmael Reed, *Mumbo Jumbo* (New York: Doubleday, 1972), and the introduction of Houston A. Baker, Jr., *Blues, Ideology and Afro-American Literature. A Vernacular Theory* (Chicago: University of Chicago Press, 1984).

3. For the "unknown voice" see "La voz desconocida" ("The Unknown Voice") in *Obra poética de Nicolás Guillén,* vol. 1 (Havana: Editorial Arte y Cultura, 1974), 8. For the most complete "dictionary" of Afro-Cuban ritual writing see Lydia Cabrera, *Anaforuana: Ritual y símbolos de la iniciación en la sociedad secreta Abakuá* (Madrid: Ediciones R., 1975).

4. Martin Heidegger, "What Is Called Thinking?" trans. D. Wieck and J. Glenn Gray, in *Basic Writings* (New York: Harper and Row, 1977), 351.

5. For instance the cross-written cosmology of the Congo (Kongo).

6. This drum is also called *eribó, sesé-eribó,* or *seseribó.* See Lydia Cabrera, *La sociedad secreta abakuá narrada por viejos adeptos* (Miami: Editorial C. R., 1970), 148.

7. For the issue of scratchy sounds see Hughes, p. 3, and for the ritual act of *fragayar,* see Cabrera, *La sociedad secreta,* 119.

8. Charles Keil, "Peoples' Music Comparatively: Style and Stereotype, Class and Hegemony," in *Dialectical Anthropology* 10 (1985): 119.

9. Alejo Carpentier, *Obras completas* (Mexico City: Siglo XXI, 1983), 1:215–16.

10. Gustavo Pérez Firmat, "Carolina Blues," in *Triple Crown: Chicano, Puerto Rican and Cuban-American Poetry* (Tempe, Arizona: Bilingual Press, 1987), 113.

11. Octavio Paz, *Sombra de obras* (Barcelona: Seix Barral, 1983), 81.

12. Ibid.

13. Argeliers Léon, *Del canto y del tiempo* (Havana: Editorial Letras Cubanas, 1984), 123–24, 135.

14. Geneviève Calame-Griaule, *Etnología y lenguage: La palabra del pueblo dogón,* trans. Sol Assor Castiel (Madrid: Editora Nacional, 1982), 25–27.

15. Ibid., 34.

16. Ibid., 31.

17. For a discussion of the historical background and records of the "Son of Ma Teodora," see Alejo Carpentier, *La música en Cuba* (Mexico City: Fondo de Cultura Económica, Colección Tierra Firme, 1946), 18–21; and Natalio Galán, *Cuba y sus sones* (Valencia: Artes Gráficas Soler, 1946), 18–21. For a novelized version of the *son* as point of "origin" and philosophy of "being" [Cuban] see Severo Sarduy, *De donde son los cantantes* (Mexico: Joaquín Mortiz, 1967), which is discussed later on in this text.

18. For *muntu,* consult Janheinz Jahn, *Muntu: The New African Cultures,* trans Marjorie Grene (New York: Grove Press, 1979), particularly the section "The Four Categories," 99–104. For *mono,* consult entry "Macaco," in Fernando Ortiz, *Glosario de afronegrismos* (Havana: Imprenta "El Siglo XX," 1924), 293–96.

19. Morton Marks, "Uncovering Ritual Structures in Afro-American Music," in *Religious Movements in Contemporary America* (Princeton: Princeton University Press, 1974), 103.

20. José Piedra, "From Monkey Tales to Cuban Songs: On Signification," *Modern Language Notes* 100 (1985): 362–63, 379–90.

21. Sarduy, *De donde son los cantantes,* 9–21.

22. Enrico Mario Santí, "Textual Politics: Severo Sarduy," *Latin American Literary Review* 8, 16 (1980): 157. For the scene at the Self-Service (which occurs in the section "Curriculum Cubense") and the section called "Note" (which act as an "addendum" after the end of the "plot" of the book), see Sarduy, *De donde son los cantantes,* 14–18 and 151–53, respectively.

23. See Sarduy, 13, 20, and 19, respectively.

24. Langston Hughes, "Blues at Dawn," in *The Book of Negro Folklore,* ed. Langston Hughes and Arna Bontemps (New York: Dodd, Mead and Co., 1983), 556.

25. Juan Marinello, "Americanismos y cubanismos literarios," in *Ensayos* (Havana: Editora Arte y Libertad, 1977), 49.

26. David Levering Lewis, "Harlem My Home," in *Harlem Renaissance: Art in Black America* (New York: Harry N. Abrams, 1987), 85.

27. José Ortega y Gasset, "The Historical Significance of the Theory of Einstein," in *The Modern Theme* (New York: Harper and Row, 1961), 43.

28. Ibid., 45.

29. Reed, *Mumbo Jumbo*, 221.

30. For Mayombe, see Lydia Cabrera, *Vocabulario congo (El bantu que se habla en Cuba)* (Miami: Colección del Chicherekú en el exilio, 1984), 99. For the Mumban-Jumban society, see Raymond Nina Rodrigues, *O animismo fetichista dos negros bahianos* (Rio de Janeiro: Bibliotheca de Divulgaçao Scientifica, 1935), 156–57.

31. Baker, *Blues, Ideology, and Afro-American Literature*, 1–4.

32. Hughes, *ASK YOUR MAMA*, Introduction, n.p. Subsequent references will be cited in the text.

33. Guillén, "La voz desconocida" ("The Unknown Voice"), *Obra poética,* 1:85.

Plagiarized Authenticity: Sarmiento's Cooper and Others

1. Jorge Luis Borges, "Pierre Menard, Author of the Quixote," in *Labyrinths,* ed. Donald A. Yates and James E. Irby (New York: New Directions, 1964), 42.

2. Ibid., 44.

3. The opportunity for misreadings, even in so didactic and heavy-handed a novel as Cooper's, is the only point at which I depart from Jane Tompkins's excellent *Sensational Designs: The Cultural Work of American Fiction, 1790–1860* (New York and Oxford: Oxford University Press, 1985). Her welcome and rather convincing defense of best-sellers as indicators and arbiters of our political culture tends, nonetheless, to underestimate the likelihood that messages may be processed differently even when they are passionately put forth. "The text succeeds or fails on the basis of its 'fit' with the features of its immediate context, on the degree to which it provokes the desired response, and not in relation to unchanging formal, psychological, or philosophical standards of complexity, or truth, or correctness" (xviii). I would add that the standards are so changeable that the responses a text provokes may vary quite a bit. Literary ambiguity, and especially the particular usefulness that a reader may have in mind, do not belong exclusively to modernist or poststructural readings.

4. Martin Green, *The Great American Adventure* (Boston: Beacon Press, 1984), 23.

5. Walt Whitman, "Song of Myself," in *The Portable Walt Whitman,* selected and with notes by Mark Van Doren, revised by Malcolm Cowley (New York: Penguin Books, 1981), 92.

6. All page references to James Fenimore Cooper are from *The Last of the Mohicans* (New York: Signet Classic, New American Library, 1980).

7. Domingo Faustino Sarmiento, *Facundo: Civilización y Barbarie*, 8th ed.

(Buenos Aires: Espasa-Calpe Argentina, 1970), hereinafter cited as Sarmiento, *Facundo*; Domingo Faustino Sarmiento, *Life in the Argentine Republic in the Days of the Tyrants; or, Civilization and Barbarism*, trans. Mrs. Horace Mann (New York: Hurd and Houghton, 1868), hereinafter cited as Sarmiento, *Life in the Argentine Republic*.

8. Sarmiento, *Facundo*, 24 (Sarmiento, *Life in the Argentine Republic*, 25).

9. Nina Baym, "The Women of Cooper's Leatherstocking Tales," *American Quarterly* 23 (1971): 696–709. Baym observes (698) that women are the "chief signs, the language of social communication between males"; and thus the basis for male civilization. To develop this we might say that the ideal basis for Cooper's civilization was the transparent, unmarked language that Alice represented rather than the polyvalent traces that Cora bore.

10. Annette Kolodny explores the Land-as-Woman metaphor and Americans' self-defeating relationships to it. See her *The Lay of the Land* (Chapel Hill: University of North Carolina Press, 1975), 90–97. She points out an inevitable slippage from our pastoral desire to regress to a pre-Oedipal and "passive" love for the Land-as-Mother, through the fear of castration and enclosure, to an aggressive post-Oedipal desire to dominate her, a desire I identify with romance. Despite this repeated move (farther and farther West), Kolodny continues to plead for a pastoral America. The scene at Glenn's Falls (*Mohicans*, 66–63) shows the extended company of heroes and helpers hiding in Nature's caverns, which open conveniently from the front and the back (96–97). See also Cecilia Tichi, *New World, New Earth: Environmental Reform in American Literature from the Puritans to Whitman* (New Haven: Yale University Press, 1979), 173.

11. The assumption of female stability that "grounds" male activity is provocatively developed by Luce Irigaray in *Speculum of the Other Woman*, trans. Gillian C. Gill (Ithaca: Cornell University Press, 1985). See especially the essay "Any Theory of the 'Subject' Has Always Been Appropriated by the 'Masculine'" (133–46):

> Subjectivity denied to woman: indisputably this provides the financial backing for every irreducible constitution as an object: of representation, of discourse, of desire. Once imagine that woman imagines and the object loses its fixed, obsessional character. As a benchmark that is ultimately more crucial than the subject, for he can sustain himself only by bouncing back off some objectiveness, some objective. If there is no more "earth" to press down/repress, to work, to represent, but also and always to desire (for one's own), no opaque matter which in theory does not know herself, then what pedestal remains for the existence of the "subject"? If the earth turned and more especially turned upon herself, the erection of the subject might thereby be disconcerted and risk losing its elevation and penetration" (133).

12. Michel Foucault, *The Order of Things: An Archaeology of the Human Sciences* (New York: Vintage Books, 1973), especially 55–63, where the Classical episteme is shown to treat language as transparent. It orders knowledge through

mutually exclusive comparisons, as opposed to the sixteenth-century supposition of correspondences, and thus produces an exhaustive categorical arrangement of knowledge through the "justified arbitrariness" (63) of the sign system. See also the section on "taxonomia" (71–76): "The project of a general science of order; a theory of signs analyzing representation; the arrangement of identities and differences into ordered tables: these constituted an area of empiricity in the Classical Age that had not existed until the end of the Renaissance and that was destined to disappear early in the nineteenth century" (71). Foucault also points out that "from the nineteenth century, History was to deploy, in a temporal series, the analogies that connect distinct organic structures to one another" (219).

13. Tompkins, *Sensational Designs,* is at least one recent North American reader who might agree with Sarmiento's brutally lucid reading of Cooper. She notes that Charles Brockden Brown's *Arthur Mervyn* is about cross-cultural marriage as resolution to social tension; the hero marries a Portuguese-Jewish widow (94). This is the kind of mix that doesn't happen in *The Last of the Mohicans.* She claims that most critics try to apologize for Cooper's plots and characters, but Tompkins wisely attends to the obvious and conventional racism in Cooper. The subject of *The Last of the Mohicans* is cultural miscegenation (114). And the lesson, especially at Fort William Henry, is that when social controls start to break down the ultimate consequence is a bloodbath (117).

14. See Leslie A. Fiedler, *Love and Death in the American Novel,* rev. ed. (New York: Stein and Day, 1966). Fiedler reads *The Wept of Wish-Ton-Wish* as "the first antimiscegenation novel in our literature." He continues that "*The Last of the Mohicans* must be reread in its light" (204).

15. Her father confesses to Heyward that in the West Indies, "[I]t was my lot to form a connection with one who in time became my wife, and the mother of Cora. She was the daughter of a gentleman of those isles, by a lady whose misfortune it was, if you will, . . . to be descended remotely from that unfortunate class who are so basely enslaved to administer to the wants of a luxurious people. Aye, sir, that is a curse entailed on Scotland by her unnatural union with a foreign and trading people" (187–88). Tompkins's excellent chapter in *Sensational Designs,* "No Apologies for the Iroquois," makes too simple a case for Cora's whiteness. The danger of her confrontation with Magua is compounded, I think, by the fact that she is already a corrupt category, porous to his darkening effect. Wayne Franklin even surmises that she feels an erotic attraction to Magua. See his *The New World of James Fenimore Cooper* (Chicago: University of Chicago Press, 1982), 224.

16. In *The Lay of the Land* (90–97), Kolodny shows that Cooper's relationship to the organizing metaphor of the American pastoral offers a good case for reading both the self-defeating dimension of Land-as-Woman and the reifying dimension of Woman-as-Land. Like many of the authors Kolodny studies, Cooper has his share of ecological guilt that predicts either barrenness or Nature's revenge by entrapping the despoilers in her womb.

17. Sarmiento, *Life in the Argentine Republic*, 1.

18. Typically, this is an image that Mann judiciously substitutes for dead metaphors in English: "penetrates its very heart." See Sarmiento, *Facundo*, 9: "El mal que aqueja a la República Argentina es la extensión: el desierto la rodea por todas partes, se le insinúa en las entrañas; la soledad, el despoblado sin una habitación humana. . . ."

19. Roberto González Echevarría reminds us of Sarmiento's secondhand nativism and develops an argument about the travelogue nature of *Facundo,* which like other books of its genre, takes care to produce an identification with civilized readers at home by distancing the narrator from the strange or wonderful scenes beheld. See his "Redescubrimiento del mundo perdido: El *Facundo* de Sarmiento," *Revista Iberoamericana* 54, 143 (April–June 1988): 385–406. "Todas estas inversiones han preparado al lector para lo inusual, lo inesperado, la 'escena extraña' que se va a relatar, en la que el hombre es el objeto de la caza, y no al revés" (403). Nevertheless, this traveler at home identifies most intimately with marvelous and monstrous Facundo (406).

20. Sarmiento, *Facundo,* 12 (my emphasis). He continues: "No siendo esto posible, demos por bien hecho lo que de mano del Maestro está hecho."

21. Sarmiento, *Life in the Argentine Republic*, 6.

22. Ibid., 1–2: "Its own extent is the evil from which the Argentine Republic suffers; the desert encompasses it on every side and penetrates its very heart; wastes containing no human dwelling are, generally speaking, the unmistakable boundaries between its several provinces."

23. Ibid., 27.

24. Ibid., 2. Mann's chaste version reads "velvet-like" while the Spanish word *velludo* is unmistakably associated with pubic hair.

25. Sarmiento, *Facundo,* 10–11.

26. Sarmiento, *Life in the Argentine Republic,* 10. "[A] homogeneous whole has resulted from the fusion of the three above named families [Spaniard, Indian, Black]. It is characterized by love of idleness and incapacity for industry. . . . To a great extent, this unfortunate result is owing to the incorporation of the native tribes, effected by the process of colonization. . . . But the Spanish race has not shown itself more energetic than the aborigines."

27. See Leopoldo Zea's classic work, *The Latin American Mind* (Norman: University of Oklahoma Press, 1963), and his prologue to the anthology he edited, *Pensamiento positivista latinoamericano* (Caracas: Biblioteca Ayacucho, 1979).

28. See Sylvia Molloy's excellent "Sarmiento, lector de sí mismo en *Recuerdos de Provincia,*" *Revista Iberoamericana* 54, 143 (April–June 1988): 407–18, especially 415 and 417.

29. For the most passionate and playful guide to hearing that multiplicity and the conflict with the gaucho genre of poetry that also constitutes *Facundo,* see Josefina Ludmer, *El género gauchesco: Un tratado sobre la patria* (Buenos Aires: Editorial Sudamericana, 1988). She writes, "Sólo el texto da Sarmiento, el otro

padre de la patria (alongside historian Mitre), es a la vez un clásico de la literatura, de la política y de la historia." Elizabeth Garrels notes that Sarmiento chose to publish *Facundo* during 1845 in the new section for serialized novels in *El Progreso,* the newspaper he edited in Santiago between 1842 and 1845. By contrast, he published his perhaps comparable biography of Aldao in the "Sección Correspondencia." See her "El *Facundo* como folletín," *Revista Iberoamericana* 54, 143 (April–June 1988): 419–47.

30. For this powerful observation, I am indebted to Carlos Alonso's excellent paper, "Reading Sarmiento: One More Time, with Passion," delivered at the 1988 MLA meeting. "[T]he successive projects that would subsume Latin America under the mantle of modernity are simultaneously and paradoxically engaged in the affirmation of a radical cultural difference, a cultural claim to exception from the demands of modernity that is the expression of a discursive will-to-power—and an attempt to stave off the rhetorical disenfranchisement with which modernity threatened the Latin American writer at every turn" (11). See also Julio Ramos, "Saber del otro: Escritura y oralidad en el *Facundo* de D. F. Sarmiento," *Revista Iberoamericana* 54, 143 (April–June 1988): 551–69, especially 561. There Ramos reviews the criticism of *Facundo* by Valentín Alsina, who objected to Sarmiento's poetic flights in a book that should have been objective and "true social history." But Sarmiento's defense of his spontaneous (poetic or barbarous) style in the modernizing project underlines his practice as an American writer.

31. Ludmer, *El género gauchesco,* makes a similar point: "La barbarie no sólo dramatiza el enfrentamiento con 'la civilización' sino un segundo enfrentamiento, interior, consigo misma. El lugar tenso y dual de la barbarie en *Facundo* es ése hostil a la sociedad civilizada y hostil a sí misma. . . . La doble tensión, hacia afuera y adentro de sí es la mejor definición de *Facundo,* el texto de Sarmiento."

32. Sarmiento mentions this early (6); but later he is more explicit (217): "La idea de los unitarios está realizada; sólo está de más el tirano; el día que un buen gobierno se establezca, hallará las resistencias locales vencidas y todo dispuesto para la *unión.*"

33. Sarmiento, *Facundo,* 24; Sarmiento, *Life in the Argentine Republic,* 24 (with my adjustments for a more literal translation).

34. More than from Cooper, Sarmiento probably learned about the "American" sublime from François-René de Chateaubriand's chapter "To America" in his *Memoirs,* trans. Robert Baldick (New York: Alfred Knopf, 1961), 114–61. About Niagara Falls, for example, he writes, "I was unable to express the thoughts which stirred me at the sight of such sublime disorder" (150).

35. Sarmiento, *Life in the Argentine Republic,* 25.

36. Ibid., 27: ". . . for the fables of the imagination, the ideal world, begin only where the actual and the commonplace end . . . simple act of fixing his eyes upon the horizon, and seeing nothing?—for the deeper his gaze sinks into that shifting, hazy, undefined horizon, the further it withdraws from him, the

more it fascinates and confuses him, and plunges him in contemplation and doubt . . ." Is it possible to imagine Alice, in her blankness, sublime, so colorless that, like Melville's "white," men get lost in her? Could Sarmiento have found Alice sublime? But this seems to stretch even our Borgesian fiction of possible misreadings.

37. While it is true that Cooper lamented the "corruption" of place-names in his 1826 preface, he also laments Cora's death, the Mohicans' demise, and the general disturbance of paradise. Yet the narrative shows him willing, for the time, to pay the price in order to establish his American family. Later, the more circumspect and less optimistic Cooper of *The Deerslayer* (1841) attempts to forswear the violence of naming, even as he writes about Glimmerglass, or Otsego Lake: "'I'm glad it has no name,' resumed Deerslayer, 'or, at least, no paleface name; for their christenings always foretell waste and destruction.'"

38. Octavio Paz, *El laberinto de la soledad* (Mexico City: Fondo de Cultura Económica, 1959), 40.

39. Sarmiento, *Life in the Argentine Republic,* 12. He reports that Walter Scott said: "'The vast plains of Buenos Aires . . . are inhabited only by Christian savages known as Guachos [gauchos, he should have said] whose furniture is chiefly composed of horses' skulls, whose food is raw beef and water, and whose favorite pastime is running horses to death. Unfortunately,' adds the good foreigner, 'they prefer their national independence to our cottons and muslins.'

"It would be well to ask England to say at a venture how many yards of linen and pieces of muslin she would give to own these plains of Buenos Ayres."

40. Ibid., 15.

41. Ibid.: "[T]he life of Abraham, which is that of the Bedouin of today prevails in the Argentine plains, . . ." But he also writes about a proprietor in Sierra de San Luis, "I seemed to be living in the times of Abraham, in his presence, in that of God, and of the nature which reveals Him" (19).

42. Peter Hulme, "Versions of Virginia: Crossing Cultures in Early Colonial America," in his *Colonial Encounters* (London: Methuen, 1987). See also Michael Rogin, who refers to the differences between the "northern tribes which were smaller and more numerous than the five southern Indian confederations. They were less settled than the southern tribes, and never developed so large-scale an agriculture or so complexly stratified a social structure." To locate Cooper in a general moment of Indian removal, see Michael Rogin, *Fathers and Children: Andrew Jackson and the Subjugation of the American Indian* (New York: Knopf, 1975), 166–67.

43. His most ferocious critic was Juan Bautista Alberdi, one of the original members of the Generation of 1837, later called "Young Argentina." These romantic, rebellious youths had pledged themselves to overcoming the fratricidal antagonism between Europeanizing Centralists called Unitarians, based in Buenos Aires, and the more autochthonous Federalists who were then in control under the dictator Rosas. As the dictatorship turned to terror, practically all of

the Generation of '37 retreated to Unitarian sectarianism, except for Alberdi. And his criticism of Sarmiento's *Facundo* revives the principle of flexibility and conciliation. See his *Cartas quillotanas* where Alberdi objects to Sarmiento's binary formulation of city and country desert:

> Ud. pone en los *campos* la edad media y el antiguo régimen español, y en las ciudades el siglo XIX y el moderno régimen.
>
> La vista nos enseña que no es así. La colonia, es decir, la edad media de la Europa, estaba en los campos y estaba en las ciudades, lo mismo que había existido en Europa. La revolución a su vez, es decir, el siglo XIX de la Europa, invadió todo nuestro suelo, abrazó los campos y las ciudades. De ambas partes salieron los ejércitos que conquistaron la independencia. Las ciudades dieron infantes, los campos cabellerías. Los *gauchos* nunca han sido realistas después de 1810.
>
> La localización de la civilización en las ciudades y la barbarie en las campañas, es un error de historia y de observación, y manantial de antipatías artificiales entre localidades que se necesitan y complentan mutuamente. (Quoted from *Historia de la literatura argentina* [Buenos Aires: Centro Editor de América Latina, 1967] 1:308.)

Moreover, Sarmiento knew he was being schematic. He admits, for example, that blacks have integrated well, but also rejoices over their near extermination in the wars. See the suggestive essay by William H. Katra, "Reading *Facundo* as Historical Novel," in *The Historical Novel in Latin America,* ed. Daniel Balderston (Gaithersburg, Md.: Ediciones Hispamérica, 1986), 31–46. "Mitre's and Sarmiento's writings, Alberdi stated, were examples of 'la historia forjada por la vanidad, una especie de mitología política con base histórica [history forged in vanity, a kind of political mythology with historical grounding]' " (36).

44. See Brook Thomas, *Cross-Examinations of Law and Literature: Cooper, Hawthorne, Stowe, and Melville* (Cambridge: Cambridge University Press, 1987), 23. "When Van Buren spoke against New York's 'aristocracy,' he was not making a claim for popular rule. The governing elite (to which Cooper belonged) was sustained by social position and family connection. Van Buren wanted to replace it with a new leadership of the rising powerful—the Albany Regency. The constitution that had ruled New York State from the Revolution until 1821 was an object of Van Buren's attack because it, along with residual elements of the old Dutch patroon system, protected the interests of what the Federalists called the 'guardian class.' "

45. Tompkins, *Sensational Designs,* 110.

46. Georg Lukács, *The Historical Novel,* trans. Hannah Mitchell and Stanley Mitchell (Boston: Beacon Press, 1963). "Gorky's fine analysis of Cooper's novels . . . shows the divided attitude of the classics of the historical novel clearly. They have to affirm the downfall of the humanly noble Indian, the straightforwardly decent, straightforwardly heroic 'leather-stocking,' treating it as a necessary step of progress, and yet cannot help seeing and depicting the human inferiority of the victors. This is the necessary fate of every primitive culture with which

capitalism comes into contact" (346). Katra, *The Historical Novel in Latin America,* 39, then reads Lukács through Sarmiento and concludes rather hastily that both celebrated this "pitiless march of progress," when, in fact, Lukács tries to draw a distinction between classical historical novels and those of the Popular Front that can accommodate the "primitive communism." Compare Lukács (347).

47. I am referring here to Michel Foucault's arguably schematic distinction in *The Order of Things: An Archaeology of the Human Sciences* (New York: Vintage Books, 1973). See note 12.

48. Sarmiento, *Facundo,* 26; Sarmiento, *Life in the Argentine Republic,* 26.

49. Ibid., 26.

50. See Sylvia Molloy's wonderfully probing discussion (416).

51. Domingo Faustino Sarmiento, *Recuerdos de provincia* (Barcelona: Ramón Sopena, 1931), 107–8. The passage continues: "Aquello, pues, que llamamos hoy plagio, era entonces erudición y riqueza; y yo prefiriera oír segunda vez a un autor digno de ser leído cien veces, a los ensayos incompletos de la razón y del estilo que aun están en embrión, porque nuestra inteligencia nacional no se ha desenvuelto lo bastante para rivalizar con los autores que el concepto del mundo reputa dignos de ser escuchados."

52. Sarmiento, *Recuerdos,* 161. "La vida de Franklin debiera formar parte de los libros de las escuelas primarias. Alienta tanto su ejemplo, está tan al alcance de todos lla carrera que él recorría, que no habría muchacho un poco bien inclinado que no se tentase a ser un Franklincito, por aquella bella tendencia del espíritu humano a imitar los modelos de la perfección que concibe."

53. William J. Nowak argues that the gesture to make himself representative of Argentina, the synecdoche for an entire country, meant that Sarmiento's self-portrait was purposefully impersonal. See "La personificación en *Recuerdos de provincia*: La despersonalización de D. F. Sarmiento," *Revista Iberoamericana* 54, 143 (April–June 1988): 585–601.

54. Carlos Altamirano and Beatriz Sarlo, "La estrategia de *Recuerdos de provincia,*" in *Literatura/Sociedad* (Buenos Aires: Hachette, 1983), 165.

55. Sarmiento, *Recuerdos,* 68 (my translation). Sarmiento wrote, "Oro ha dado el modelo y el tipo del futuro argentino, europeo hasta los últimos refinamientos de las bellas artes, americano hasta cabalgar el potro indómito; parisiense por el espíritu, pampa por la energía y los poderes físicos."

56. Ibid., 69.

57. Jean Baudrillard, *Simulations,* trans. Paul Foss, Paul Patton, and Philip Beitchman (New York: Semiotext(e), Inc., Columbia University, 1983), 11: "Whereas representation tries to absorb simulation by interpreting it as false representation, simulation envelops the whole edifice of representation as itself a simulacrum."

58. Ibid., 2.

59. Sarmiento, *Recuerdos,* 142 (my translation).

60. An extended discussion of these authors will appear in *Foundational Fic-*

tions: When History Was Romance in Latin America (forthcoming from University of California Press).

61. Historians of the period, most notably Bartolomé Mitre, were also writing biography as one of the most compelling kinds of history.

62. Michel Foucault, *The History of Sexuality*, Vol. 1, *An Introduction,* trans. Robert Hurley (New York: Vintage Books, 1980), 78.

63. For a succinct definition of this Gramscian concept, see Chantal Mouffe, ed., *Gramsci and Marxist Theory* (London: Routledge and Kegan Paul, 1979), 181. "[A] hegemonic class has been able to articulate the interests of other social groups to its own by means of ideological struggle. This, according to G, is only possible if this class renounces a strictly corporatist conception . . ."

64. Sarmiento, *Life in the Argentine Republic,* trans., 24–25: "[I]t cannot be denied . . . that this state of things has its poetic side, and possesses aspects worthy of the pen of the romancer. . . . The only North American novelist [*romancista* in Spanish] who has gained a European reputation is Fenimore Cooper."

65. The tradition probably originated with Dr. Johnson's definition of romance as "a military fable of the middle ages; a tale of wild adventures in love and chivalry." The novel, on the other hand, was "a smooth tale, generally of love." But Walter Scott adjusted Johnson's definitions in his own article on romance (1823) for the Encyclopaedia Britannica, stressing the novel's "ordinary train of human events (in) the modern state of society." See Walter Scott, "Essay on Romance," in *Essays on Chivalry, Romance and the Drama,* ed. Leslie Fiedler (London: Frederick Warne, 1887), 65–108. That is to say, or imply, that it is a lesser genre, fit more for lady writers and readers than for robust men.

In the U.S., writers like Hawthorne and his admirer Melville picked up this distinction, and insisted they were writing romance as opposed to the novels of "female scribblers." Cooper, at least, suggested the connection between the public good and private desire when he boasted that the distinguishing characteristic of romance was that it aimed to deal poetic justice all around, and thus achieve a higher truth than any available from chronicles where too many heroes marry the wrong girls. (See Perry Miller, *Nature's Nation* [Cambridge: Belknap Press, 1958], 250). North American critics have also noticed that the apparently male romance and female novels keep very close company. Leslie Fiedler points out that only several years before he wrote his great romances, Cooper was training himself as a writer by imitating, not the manly historical romancer Walter Scott, but that English gentlewoman and mistress of the domestic psychological novel, Ms. Jane Austen. See Fiedler, *Love and Death in the American Novel,* 186, 190. In general Fiedler shows how the genres bleed into one another even in their own nineteenth-century terms.

For Myra Jehlen, the distinction would be moot, since all U.S. fiction of the nineteenth century was some variety of romance. She argues that our contemporary theories of the novel tend to distinguish it from nineteenth-century American works in general. If Bakhtin, Bloch, and Lukács are right to call the novel a self-conscious construction that resists a predictable closure, neither the high-minded adventure stories nor the sentimental tales of this hemisphere qualify as examples. Their desire is ultimately contained in the lap of family life. See Myra Jehlen, "New World Epics: The Novel and the Middle Class in America," *Salmagundi* 36 (Winter 1977): 49–68.

66. Sarmiento, *Facundo*, 126.

67. Simón Bolívar, in *Pensamiento Político de la Emancipación*, ed. José Luis Romero (Caracas: Biblioteca Ayacucho, 1977), 114 (my translation).

68. I detail this perhaps provocative reading in "*María*'s Disease: A National Novel (Con)Founded" (forthcoming).

69. Henry Nash Smith, "The Dime Novel Heroine," in his *Virgin Land: The American West as Symbol and Myth* (Cambridge: Harvard University Press, 1950), 126–35.

70. Baym, "The Women of Cooper's Leatherstocking Tales," 706.

71. For the definitive formulation of this idea see Eve Kosofsky Sedgwick, *Between Men: English Literature and Male Homosocial Desire* (New York: Columbia University Press, 1985).

72. Altamirano and Sarlo, "La estrategia de *Recuerdos de provincia*," 163–208.

73. Tulio Halperin Donghi, "Intelectuales, sociedad y vida pública en His-panoamérica a través de la literatura autobiográfica," in *El espejo de la historia: Problemas argentinos y perspectivas latinoamericanas* (Buenos Aires: Editorial Sud-americana, 1987), 58. "Denunciado como hombre de origen modesto, Sarmiento extrema la acusación y la transforma en reivindicación: no ha nacido en un barrio modesto y de familia oscura, como alegan sus enemigos; su origen es una po-blación marginal, y desde los quince años, por deserción de su padre, ha sido jefe de su propia familia: es, en otras palabras, y de acuerdo con la expresión llena de sentido que ha comenzado ya a ganar circulación, un hijo de sus obras. . . . Unos años después el mismo Sarmiento iba a dar de nuevo cuenta de sí mismo en *Recuerdos de provincia*, y aquí el hijo de sus obras abre literalmente el volumen con su árbol genealógico: su esfuerzo se define ahora como el de adaptar la tradición de la elite letrada al clima social e ideológico de la era republicana."

74. It is like the lost objects in Tlön that are later found enlarged and im-proved. I owe this reference to my colleague Antonio Benítez-Rojo. Borges writes, "No es infrecuente, en las regiones más antiguas de Tlön, la duplicación de objetos perdidos. Dos personas buscan un lápiz; la primera lo encuentra y no dice nada; la segunda encuentra un segundo lápiz no menos real, pero más ajustado a su expectativa. Esos objetos secundarios se llaman *hrönir* y son, aunque de forma desairada, un poco más largos. Hasta hace poco los *hrönir* fueron hijos casuales de la distracción y el olvido. Parece mentira que su metódica producción cuente apenas cien años, pero así lo declara el Onceno Tomo." "Tlön, Uqbar, Orbis Tertius," *Ficciones* (Buenos Aires: Alianza, 1982), 28–29.

The Accidental Tourist: Walt Whitman in Latin America

1. I am grateful to Octavio Paz and Stephen Schlesinger, secretary of the John Simon Guggenheim Memorial Foundation, for allowing me to cite my translation of Paz's unpublished 1943 proposal.

2. Octavio Paz, *The Bow and the Lyre*, trans. Ruth L. C. Simms (Austin: University of Texas Press, 1973), 274. This translation is based on the second revised (1967) rather than the first (1956) Spanish edition. Paz was alluding to Borges's classic essay "El otro Whitman" collected in *Discusión* (Buenos Aires: M. Gleizer, 1932). Borges's other famous essay, "Nota sobre Walt Whitman," appeared in *Otras inquisiciones* (Buenos Aires: Emecé, 1960), 97–104 (English translation in *Other Inquisitions, 1937–1952,* trans. Ruth L. C. Simms [Austin: University of Texas Press, 1964]), but I prefer to cite from my own translation of the text as it also appears in *Discusión,* where it has been collected in the most recent editions.

3. Doris Sommer, "Supplying Demand: Walt Whitman as the Liberal Self," in *Reinventing the Americas: Comparative Studies of Literature of the United States and Spanish America,* ed. Bell Gale Chevigny and Gari Laguardia (Cambridge: Cambridge University Press, 1986), 68–91. Sommer's essay is more a reading of Whitman than of his Latin American cult. Also, Fernando Alegría, *Walt Whitman en Hispanoamérica* (Mexico City: Colección Studium, 1954). Subsequent references are from this edition and are cited in the text. In the thirty years since publication of Alegría's study, the following supplements to his bibliography have appeared: Hensley C. Woodbridge, "Walt Whitman: Additional Bibliography in Spanish," *Walt Whitman Review* 12 (Sept. 1986): 70–71; Didier T. Jaén, trans. and ed., *Homage to Walt Whitman: A Collection of Poems from the Spanish,* foreword by Jorge Luis Borges (University: University of Alabama Press, 1969); José Benito Alvarez Buylla, "Whitman: poeta ibérico," *Filología moderna* 40–41 (1970): 43–65; Alberto Uva, "Notas para un estudio del 'Whitman' de José Martí," trans. Jean R. Langland, *Anuario de Filología* 8–9 (1969–1970): 199–212; Luís Eugénio Ferreira, *Walt Whitman: Vida e Pensamento* (Alfragide, Portugal: Galeria Panorama, 1970), "Whitman's Presence in Alvaro de Campos [Fernando Pessoa]," *Calamus* 7 (Feb. 1973): 2–9; Mauricio González de la Garza, *Walt Whitman: Racista, Imperialista, Anti-mexicano* (Mexico: Colección Málaga, 1971); Hensley C. Woodbridge, "González de la Garza: Anti-Whitman," *Walt Whitman Review* 17 (Dec. 1971): 142–43; Emilio Bernal Labrador, "El idioma de Whitman: su traducción," *Revista Interamericana de Bibliografía* 21 (1971): 46–63; Roger Asselineau and William White, eds., *Walt Whitman in Europe Today: A Collection of Essays* (Detroit: Wayne State University Press, 1972), 9–12, 32–33, 41; Sister Agnes V. McLaughlin, "Una comparación entre la poesía de Luis Llorens Torres y la de Walt Whitman," *Horizontes: Revista de la Universidad Católica de Puerto Rico* 31–32 (1973): 73–93; Roger Asselineau, "Spanish Leaves from Argentina," *Walt Whitman Review* 23 (June 1977): 94–96; Claire Paxton, "Unamuno's Indebtedness to Whitman," *Walt Whitman Review* 9 (March 1963): 16–19; Debra

Harper, "Whitman and Unamuno: Language for Immortality," *Walt Whitman Review* 25 (June 1979): 60–73; Luis Benito, *Walt Whitman, Poeta lírico* (Granada, 1975); Vilma Areas, "Uma Epopea para Vozes," *Actas do 20 Congresso Internacional de Estudos Pessoanos* (Oporto: Centro de Estudos Pessoanos, 1985): 47–59; Manuel Gómez-Reinoso, "Martí and Whitman," *West Hills Review* 3 (1981–82): 47–48; Horacio Peña, "Aproximaciones a Rubén Darío y Walt Whitman," *Káñina* 8 (1984): 165–76; José L. Caramés Lago, "Evocación de León Felipe en su centenario," *Arbor* 118 (July–Aug. 1984): 125–32; Neil Larsen and Ronald W. Sousa, "From Whitman (to Marinetti) to Alvaro de Campos: A Case Study in Materialist Approaches to Literary Influence," *Ideologies & Literatures* 4 (Sept.–Oct. 1983): 94–115; Angel Rama, "José Martí en el eje de la modernización poética: Whitman, Lautréamont, Rimbaud," *Nueva Revista de Filología Hispánica* 32 (1983): 96–135. Of interest also are Juan Ramón Jiménez's radio scripts on the subject of "El modernismo: Estados Unidos," unpublished until recently; see his *Alerta,* ed. Francisco Javier Blasco (Salamanca: Universidad de Salamanca, 1983), 127–35. (My thanks to Professor Howard Young of Pomona College for alerting me to these texts.) At least four Whitman translations of *Leaves of Grass* (*Hojas de hierba*), done since Alegría's pioneer study, are worth mentioning: Francisco Alexander (Quito: Casa de la Cultura Ecuatoriana, 1953); Jorge Luis Borges (Buenos Aires: Editora Juárez, 1969); Leonardo Wolfson (Buenos Aires: Ediciones Libreria Fausto, 1976); and E. M. S. Danero (Buenos Aires: Ediciones Macondo, 1969).

4. For the texts of this polemic see Lewis Hanke, ed., *Do the Americas Have a Common History? A Critique of the Bolton Theory* (New York: Knopf, 1964). O'Gorman's text, partially reprinted on 103–11, first appeared as "Hegel y el moderno panamericanismo," *Universidad de la Habana* 22 (Jan.–Feb. 1939): 61–74; English version in *Points of View* 3 (1941): 1–10. For a different, more recent critique of Hegel see the brilliant lectures by José Lezama Lima, *La expresión americana* (Havana: Instituto Nacional de Cultura, 1957), and Irlemar Chiampi's excellent introduction to her own translation and critical edition: *A expressão americana* (São Paulo: Editora Brasiliense, 1987), a model for whatever future English translation of Lezama Lima's important text.

5. I quote from "¿América es un continente?" (1941), collected in my edition of Octavio Paz, *Primeras Letras (1931–1943)* (Mexico City: Vuelta, 1988), 189–92. Twelve years before, in 1929 in "El otro Whitman" (51), Borges had remarked something uncannily similar: "Los hombres de la diversas Américas permanecemos tan incomunicados que apenas nos conocemos por referencia, contados por Europa" ("The people of the different Americas remain so out of reach that we hardly know each other by reference, counted by Europe"). My essay can be viewed as an extension of Borges's and Paz's common insight.

6. For Paz's version of his quarrel with Neruda, see his *Sombras de obras: Arte y literatura* (Barcelona: Seix Barral, 1983), 48–56; for his comments on the significance of their rupture, see *Primeras Letras,* 44–47.

7. See José Martí, "Walt Whitman," in *Martí on the U.S.A.*, trans. Luis A. Baralt (Carbondale: Southern Illinois University Press, 1966), 3–16; and Rubén Darío, *Azul . . .* (Valparaíso: Excelsior, 1888).

8. Borges, "Nota sobre Walt Whitman," 122–23.

9. See Betsy Erkkila, *Walt Whitman Among the French: Poet and Myth* (Princeton: Princeton University Press, 1980).

10. See Mikhail Bakhtin, *Rabelais and His World,* trans. Hélène Iswolsky (Cambridge: MIT Press, 1968).

11. ". . . la obra de Vasseur se merece un minucioso estudio analítico porque de todas las traducciones españolas [*sic*] del libro de Whitman es la que mayor influencia ha ejercido en los poetas y el público de España e Hispano América . . . la de Vasseur es la traducción que acompaña al movimiento modernista y post-modernista. Es el breviario en que aprendieron su Whitman Lugones y Chocano [*sic*], Barba Jacob y Neruda, Parra del Riego y de Rokha y la Mistral" ("Vasseur's work deserves a detailed analytic study because of all the Spanish translations [*sic*] of Whitman's book it is the one that has had the greatest influence on the poets and public of Spain and Spanish America . . . Vasseur's is the translation that accompanies the *modernista* and post-*modernista* movement. It is the breviary where Lugones and Chocano, Barba Jacob and Neruda, Parra del Riego and de Rokha and Mistral learned their Whitman" (Alegría, 349).

12. See *Cantos augurales* (Montevideo: O. M. Bertani, 1904), and Alegría (284). Vasseur noted his Italian source in his preface to the sixth edition of *Poemas: Walt Whitman* (Buenos Aires: Schapire, 1950), a text he also published in *Alfar* 89 (1951): [no pagination], from which I quote the following: "En 1902, en la librería Comini, en Montevideo, hallé los dos breviarios de la versión italiana, de las *Briznas* editados por Sonsogno [*sic*] (Milano, 1896). Algunos versículos aparecen al frente de uno o dos capítulos de *Cantos augurales* (Montevideo, 1904)" ("In 1902, in Montevideo's Comini Bookstore, I found the two volumes of the Italian version of the *Leaves* edited by Sonsogno in Italy [Milan, 1896]. Some of the verses appear at the beginning of one or two chapters of my *Cantos augurales*"). Elsewhere in the same essay, Vasseur explains how he was never able to take in "Anglo-Saxon words and tones," and how all translations from the original English were done by his wife and son, who "más lo asimilaron" ("took it in better") than he.

Compare, however, Vasseur's testimony in his preface with Alberto Zum Felde's recollection that "Vasseur no sabía inglés a fondo. . . . tuvo un gran auxiliar en el Dr. Vitale, un médico muy ilustrado y autor de algunos libros de Sociología y Economía Política. El Dr. Vitale dominaba a fondo el inglés y hacía la traducción literal que Vasseur arreglaba poéticamente" ("Vasseur did not know English well. . . . he had a great assistant in Dr. Vitale, a well-educated doctor and author of books on Sociology and Political Economy. Dr. Vitale knew English well and did the literal translations that Vasseur then fashioned poetically"). See Arturo Sergio Visca, "Conversando con Zum Felde," *Reportajes Culturales*

(Biblioteca Nacional, Montevideo), 1 (1969): 36. My thanks to Dr. Visca, President of the Academia Nacional de Letras de Uruguay, for this timely reference.

The bibliography of *Walt Whitman en Hispanoamérica* does note the sixth edition (418) of Vasseur's versions, but appears to be an add-on. In note 3 of chapter 6 (406) Alegría mentions that "existe una tercera edición publicada por Schapire, Buenos Aires, 1944" ("a third edition by Schapire has been published"), as if he knew none of the later ones. In 1910, when Vasseur began to work on his versions, the best-known Italian translations were those by Luigi Gamberale. See his *Canti Scelti* (Milan: Edoardo Sonzogno, 1881–1932, several reprints and editions) and *Foglie di erba* (Milan: Sandron, 1907). The former, published by Edoardo Sonzogno Editrice, is the one Vasseur handled; as far as I have been able to ascertain, two-volume editions were published in 1885, 1891, and 1932, but Vasseur is obviously citing from (fuzzy) memory. For information on Whitman's reception in Italy see *Walt Whitman Abroad* (Syracuse, N.Y.: Syracuse University Press, 1955), 187–98 and 278–79; and Gay Wilson Allen, ed., *Walt Whitman in Europe Today* (Syracuse, N.Y.: Syracuse University Press, 1955), passim.

It is interesting that in the same text (36) Zum Felde, a sometime Whitmanian poet as well as a well-known literary historian, observes that his own *El Huanakauri* (Montevideo: M. García, 1917) shows the dual influence of Whitman and Nietzsche but describes the latter's influence as earlier: "la influencia de Nietzsche en mí es muy anterior. Creo que fui a los veinte años el único nietzscheano en nuestro ambiente intelectual" ("Nietzsche's influence on me comes much earlier. When I was twenty years old I was the only Nietzschean in our intellectual circles"). Zum Felde was born in 1888.

On Vasseur, I have also found the following useful: Hugo Achugar, "Modernización, europeización: el lirismo social en Uruguay entre 1885 y 1911," in his *Poesía y sociedad (Uruguay 1880–1911)* (Montevideo: Arca, 1985), 137–69; Rafael Cansinos-Asséns, "Alvaro Armando Vasseur," in his *La nueva literatura* (Madrid: V. H. de Sanz Calleja, 1927), 81–100; Emilio Frugoni, "Prólogo," in Alvaro Armando Vasseur, *Todos los cantos (1898–1912)* (Montevideo: Clásicos Uruguayos, 1955), vii–xxiii; and "Tres polémicas literarias," in *La literatura uruguaya del 1900,* ed. Arturo Ardao, et al. (Montevideo: Imprenta Nacional Colorada, 1950), 315–20; and Alberto Zum Felde, *Proceso intelectual del Uruguay y crítica de su literatura* (Montevideo, 1930), 2:307–13. I thank my friend Enrique Fierro, Director of the Uruguay National Library, for alerting me to many of these items.

13. Jorge Luis Borges, "La doctrina de los ciclos" (1934), in *Historia de la eternidad* (Buenos Aires: Emecé Editores, 1953), 84. In "Nota sobre Walt Whitman" Borges also mentions Nietzsche in connection with Whitman's blurring of personal and factual history. On Nietzsche's reception in Spain and Latin America the standard works are Gonzalo Sobejano, *Nietzsche en España* (Madrid: Editorial Gredos, 1967), and Udo Rukser, *Nietzsche in der Hispania: Ein Beitrag*

zur Hispanischen und Geistesgeschichte (Bern: Francke, 1962). See especially the latter's bibliography (358–69) for a useful list of Spanish translations of Nietzsche which began in full force in 1900–1901. Significantly, Sobejano's "Final" note (664) quotes Blas de Otero's sonnet "Posición" which invokes equally Whitman's "hermoso libro dilatado" ("beautiful extensive book") and Nietzsche's "sombra, tan espléndida, tan llena" ("splendid, full shadow"). Nietzsche's general influence on a poetics of post-*modernismo,* especially as it affected late *modernista* poets in Argentina (Lugones and Martínez Estrada, for example), deserves a fuller treatment.

14. C. N. Stavrou, *Whitman and Nietzsche: A Comparative Study of Their Thought* (Chapel Hill: University of North Carolina Press, 1964), 193.

15. See Harold Bloom, *Poetry and Repression: Revisionism from Blake to Stevens* (New Haven: Yale University Press, 1976), as well as his *Agon: Towards a Theory of Revisionism* (New York: Oxford University Press, 1982), especially 330–36.

16. I have in mind, specifically, the readings by both Fernando Alegría ("¿Cuál Whitman?: Borges, Lorca y Neruda?" *Texto Crítico* 22–23 [1981]: 3–12) and Jaime Alazraki ("Neruda y Borges: Dos rostros de Walt Whitman," *Confluencia* 1 [Fall 1985]: 37–42). The common effort of such essays is to demonstrate how two such dissimilar authors join forces under the same fascination for Whitman. For an early vigorous discussion of their contrasts, on the other hand, see the lively three-way debate by Carlos Real de Azúa, Angel Rama, and Emir Rodríguez Monegal, "Evasión y arraigo de Borges y Neruda," *Revista Nacional* (Montevideo), 2° Ciclo, Año IV, No. 202 (Oct.–Dec. 1959): 514–31. For the latest example of such a "communal reading," see Jaime Concha's sentimental piece, "Borges, Neruda: dos poetas, dos destinos," in *Jorge Luis Borges: El último laberinto,* ed. Rómulo Cosse (Montevideo: Librería Linardi y Risso, 1987), 17–30. For a useful contrast, see Alexander Coleman's sharp "The Ghost of Walt Whitman in Neruda and Borges," *Mickle Street Review* 9 (1988): 76–89.

17. See "Vengo a renegociar mi deuda con Walt Whitman," in his *Obras Completas,* 4th ed. (Buenos Aires: Editorial Losada, 1973), 3:747; partially translated as "We Live in a Whitmanesque Age," *New York Times* 14 April 1972, 37. Neruda reviewed Torres-Rioseco's translations [*Walt Whitman* (San José, Costa Rica, 1922)] in the student magazine *Claridad* 86 (5 May 1923). My thanks to Hertha Berenguer L., of Santiago de Chile, for helping me secure photocopies of this and other Neruda texts from *Claridad.* For Neruda's additional comments on Whitman see his *Memoirs,* trans. Hardie St. Martin (New York: Farrar, Straus and Giroux, 1976), 262, 294. For comparisons of Neruda and Whitman see, in addition to Alegría (314–34) and the items noted in note 16, Djelal Kadir's excellent "Neruda and Whitman: Short-circuiting the Body Electric," *Pacific Coast Philology* 8 (1973): 16–22; Peter G. Earle, "Whitman and Neruda and Their Implicit Cultural Revolution," in *Proceedings of the Xth Congress of the International Comparative Literature Association,* ed. Mario J. Valdés (New York: Garland, 1985), 3:189–93; Guillermo Rothschuh, "Whitman, Darío y Neruda," *Encuentro*

(Sept.–Oct. 1973): 59–67; and Alain Sicard, "Camerado Neruda . . . (Notes sur le 'whitmanisme' de Neruda)," *Letterature d'America* 14–15 (1982): 177–87.

18. See Pablo Neruda, "Los libros: *Poemas del hombre: Libros del corazón, de la voluntad, del tiempo y del mar,* por Carlos Sabat Ercasty," *Claridad* 87 (12 May 1923). For Sabat Ercasty's views of Vasseur see his "La lírica de Vasseur," included in *Poesías,* Alvaro Armando Vasseur (Montevideo: Revista "Letras," 1933), 39–54.

19. See Pablo Neruda, "Algunas reflexiones improvisadas sobre mis trabajos," *Obras Completas* 3:708–14. For similar comments, see his *Memoirs,* 261–62, where "the tendency to stretch out in space" is linked to "Walt Whitman, my comrade from Manhattan."

20. For such a reading of *Canto general* see my *Pablo Neruda: The Poetics of Prophecy* (Ithaca, N.Y.: Cornell University Press, 1982), 176–205, and my introduction to Pablo Neruda, *Canto general* (Madrid: Ediciones Cátedra, 1990). Also, Gordon Brotherston, *Latin American Poetry: Origins and Presence* (Cambridge: Cambridge University Press, 1975), 27–55. It would be revealing to study the parallels between the tradition Brotherston so labels and the one in North American poetry studied by Roy Harvey Pearce in his classic, *The Continuity of American Poetry* (Princeton, N.J.: Princeton University Press, 1954), 59–136.

21. I quote from *The Aleph and Other Stories (1933–1969),* ed. Norman Thomas di Giovanni (New York: E. P. Dutton, 1970), 217–18. At a further point in the essay (251) Borges mentions Whitman in a list of his literary heroes. Besides Borges's own texts on Whitman, see Alexander A. Coleman, "Notes on Borges and American Literature," *Tri-Quarterly Review* 25 (1972): 356–77; Emir Rodríguez Monegal, *Jorge Luis Borges: A Literary Biography* (New York: E. P. Dutton, 1978), 147–49; Jaime Alazraki, "Enumerations as Evocations in Borges's Latest Poetry," *Poesis* 5 (1984): 55–68 (reprinted as "Enumerations as Evocations: On the Use of a Device in Borges's Latest Poetry," in *Borges, the Poet,* ed. Carlos Cortínez [Fayetteville: University of Arkansas Press, 1986], 149–57); Joseph John Benevento, "Self, Reader, Persona: Whitman, Borges and Their Experimental Trinity," Ph.D. Diss., Michigan State University, 1983, and "What Borges Learned from Whitman: The Open Road and Its Forking Path," *Walt Whitman Review* 2 (Spring 1985): 21–30; and María Luisa Bastos, "Whitman as Inscribed by Borges," in Cortínez, *Borges, the Poet,* 219–31. Borges does not figure at all in Alegría's 1954 study.

22. Borges, *The Aleph and Other Stories,* 220. For Borges's early poetry, see *Poesía juvenil de Jorge Luis Borges,* ed. Carlos Meneses (Barcelona: Olañeta, 1978).

23. Jorge Luis Borges, *Prólogos, con un prólogo de prólogos* (Buenos Aires: Torres Agüero, 1975), 174. We should recall that in "El otro Whitman" (52–53), Borges makes his point about Whitman's reticence and laconic quality by offering some of his own translations of such representative poems.

24. Jorge Luis Borges, "La nadería de la personalidad," in *Inquisiciones* (Buenos Aires, 1925), 90–93. Subsequent references are cited in the text. In the same

book Borges mentions Whitman in another essay on Ramón Gómez de la Serna (125).

25. Borges, "El otro Whitman," 52–53.

26. Borges, "Nota sobre Walt Whitman," 125. Subsequent references are cited in the text.

27. Borges, "The Aleph," in *The Aleph and Other Stories,* 173. Subsequent references are cited in the text.

28. For Borges's parody of Dante see Emir Rodríguez Monegal, *Borges: A Literary Biography,* 414–17, where he disputes Borges's dismissal of such an interpretation in his notes to the story included in *The Aleph and Other Stories* (263–64). In my view, however, Borges did not so much dismiss the Dante *coda* as clarify that his real theme was the ultimate identity between impersonality and totalization, which would include Dante as well as Whitman, among others. Hence Borges's remark, in the same notes, to the effect that "My chief problem in writing the story lay in what Walt Whitman had very successfully achieved—the setting down of a limited catalog of endless things. The task, as is evident, is impossible, for such chaotic enumeration can only be simulated, and every apparently haphazard element has to be linked to its neighbor by secret association or by contrast" (264). Borges has restated his ideas on Whitman in many interviews; among these restatements the clearest by far appears in the one in Rita Guibert, *Seven Voices,* trans. Frances Partridge (New York: Knopf, 1973), 97. For a nearly exhaustive reading of Borges's complex relationship to Dante, see Jon Thiem's "Borges, Dante, and the Poetics of Total Vision," *Comparative Literature* 40 (Spring 1988): 97–121. Thiem shows convincingly that in "The Aleph" Borges arrives at "the paradoxical conclusion that a method of *significant omission* is essential to a modern poetics of total vision" (108), and further that " 'Borges' succeeds precisely where Daneri evidently failed, namely in giving the reader the illusion of having experienced a total vision" (112). Thiem misses totally, however, that Borges's approach has as much to do with Whitman as with Dante, despite Borges's explicit acknowledgment in his 1970 "Commentaries."

29. See Richard Burgin, *Conversations with Jorge Luis Borges* (New York: Holt, Rinehart and Winston, 1969), 95–96.

30. For an early discussion of Neruda's Americanist project see Maurice Halperin, "Pablo Neruda in Mexico," *Books Abroad* 15 (1941): 164–68. In his book-length study (211–24) Alegría did discuss the important work on Whitman by Gilberto Freyre; but Freyre was a sociologist, not a poet, and it would be essential to learn whether Freyre's work was merely responding to an incipient Whitman cult, such as it appears in Brazilian poets like Sousândrade, or Portuguese ones like Alvaro de Campos (a heteronym of Fernando Pessoa). For some thoughts on this question, see especially Augusto de Campos and Haroldo de Campos, *Revisão de Sousândrade,* 2nd ed. (Rio de Janeiro: Editora Nova Fronteira, 1982), the essay by Larsen and Sousa (n. 16), and the study by Luis Eugenio

Ferreira, *Walt Whitman: Vida e Pensamento.* For Lezama Lima's views on Whitman see the last chapter of his *La expresión americana.* Larzer Ziff provides a reading of Whitman that is uncannily close to that of these poets; see his chapter "Poet of Death: Whitman and Democracy," in his *Literary Democracy: The Declaration of Cultural Independence in America* (New York: Viking, 1981), 244–59.

American Theriomorphia: The Presence of *Mulatez* in Cirilo Villaverde and Beyond

1. Sigmund Freud, "The Uncanny," in *The Standard Edition of the Complete Psychological Works of Sigmund Freud,* ed. James Strachey and Anna Freud (London: Hogarth Press, Institute of Psychoanalysis, 1953–1974), 17:237.

2. Around the centenary of *Cecilia* in 1982, a whole cycle of critical work appeared, including both reprints and fresh views: see *Acerca de Cirilo Villaverde,* ed. Imeldo Alvarez García (Havana: Editorial Letras Cubanas 1982); as well as Reinaldo González's informed and imaginative *Contradanzas y latigazos* (Havana: Editorial Letras Cubanas, 1983). Since first writing this essay in the fall of 1987, I have read Reinaldo Arenas's *Graveyard of the Angels,* trans. Alfred J. MacAdam (New York: Avon Books, 1987), whose satirical recasting of *Cecilia* as a surreal farce can be seen as a classic example of pariah excess.

3. Rudolph Binion, *Frau Lou: Nietzsche's Wayward Disciple* (Princeton, N.J.: Princeton University Press, 1968), 543, 548.

4. George Eliot, *The Mill on the Floss* (Oxford: Oxford Classics, 1983), 13.

5. I first became aware of this black polyphony while reading Lawrence Levine, *Black Culture and Black Consciousness: Afro-American Folk Thought from Slavery to Freedom* (New York: Oxford University Press, 1977), one of the few nonfiction books I am fond of rereading (it was while reading Levine that I first bumped into Claude McKay).

6. Bernard Sergent, *Homosexuality in Greek Myth,* trans. Arthur Goldhammer (Boston: Beacon Press, 1968), 221ff., offers a recent view of this youthful brood of hunters and warriors.

7. Mark Twain, *Pudd'nhead Wilson* (New York: Penguin, 1969), 61, 75.

8. Géza Róheim, *The Eternal Ones of the Dream* (New York: International Universities Press, 1945).

9. Borges remains frustrated by not having been able to find in any library a book called *Omphalos,* on which Gosse based his own speculations on geology and *Genesis.* See his "La creación y P. H. Gosse," in *Otras inquisiciones* (Buenos Aires: Emecé, 1960), 37.

10. James Joyce, *Ulysses* (New York: Random House, 1946), 39. On Adam Kadmon and Joyce, see Don Gifford and Robert J. Seidman, *Notes for Joyce: An Annotation of James Joyce's Ulysses* (New York: Dutton, 1974), 34.

11. Klein's understanding and explorations of archaic fantasies should be applied to any thorough account of theriomorphia. See Phyllis Grosskurth, *Melanie*

Klein: Her World and Work (New York: Knopf, 1986), 59*n*, 169–70, 317–20, 322–23. Skeptics about the value of psychoanalytic perspectives on the racist mind should read the historical account of Tom Dixon, his work, and family history given by Joel Williamson in *The Crucible of Race; Black-White Relations in the American South Since Emancipation* (New York: Oxford University Press, 1984), 140–79.

12. Carolyn L. Karcher writes: "In Saddle Meadows, where 'man and horse are both hereditary,' the descendants of General Glendinning's horse are 'a sort of family cousins to Pierre . . .' like the illegitimate mulatto children fathered by slaveholders" (see *Shadow Over the Promised Land: Slavery, Race, and Violence in Melville's America* [Baton Rouge: Louisiana State University Press, 1980], 101). Some recent important interpretations of *Pierre* include: Michael Paul Rogin, *Subversive Genealogy: The Politics and Art of Herman Melville* (Berkeley: University of California Press, 1979), 155–86; Eric Sundquist, *Home as Found: Authority and Genealogy in Nineteenth-Century American Literature* (Baltimore: Johns Hopkins University Press, 1979), 143–85; and Myra Jehlen, *American Incarnation: The Individual, the Nation, and the Continent* (Cambridge: Harvard University Press, 1986), 185–226.

13. Martín Morúa Delgado, "Las novelas del señor Villaverde," in *Acerca de Cirilo Villaverde*, 64–97. Reinaldo González offers a tolerant if condescending Marxist reading of Villaverde's romantic burdens; see his *Contradanzas*.

14. Gayl Jones, *Corregidora* (New York: Random House, 1975), quoted in Mary V. Dearborn, *Pocahontas's Daughters: Gender and Ethnicity in American Culture* (New York: Oxford University Press, 1986), 131.

15. Cirilo Villaverde, *Cecilia Valdés: novela de costumbres cubanas,* ed. Raymundo Lazo (Mexico City: Porrúa, 1979), 96. Subsequent references are cited in the text (all translations are my own).

16. George Washington Cable, *The Grandissimes* (New York: C. Scribner's Sons, 1908), 80. The quotation that follows appears on p. 60. The novel first appeared in book form in 1880. For an excellent discussion of the author and his work see Louis D. Rubin, Jr., *George Washington Cable: The Life and Times of a Southern Heretic* (New York: Pegasus, 1969). A new edition has just appeared in the Penguin Classics: see *The Grandissimes,* ed. Michael Kreyling (New York: Penguin Classics, 1988).

17. *Ion by Euripides: A Translation with Commentary,* ed. and trans. Anne Pippin Burnett (Englewood Cliffs, N.J.: Prentice-Hall, 1970). For a view of *Ion* as comedy, see Bernard Knox, "Euripidean Comedy," in his *Word and Action* (Baltimore: Johns Hopkins University Press, 1979), 250–74. On questions of race, see Arlene W. Saxonhouse, "Myths and the Origins of Cities: Reflections on the Autochthony Theme in Euripides' *Ion,*" in *Greek Tragedy and Political Theory,* ed. J. Peter Euben (Berkeley and Los Angeles: University of California Press, 1986), 252–73; and George B. Walsh, "The Rhetoric of Birthright and Race in Euripides' *Ion,*" *Hermes* 106, 2 (1978): 301–15.

18. Certainly not in any pedestrian sense, but as a cardinal virtue, I admire the theological egoism of the great and the anonymous among the Puritans. Ann Douglas has written that "Calvinism was a great faith, with great limitations: it was repressive, authoritarian, dogmatic, patriarchal to an extreme. Its demise was inevitable, and in some real sense welcome"; but she adds that "it deserved, and elsewhere and at other times found, great opponents," and that one "could argue that the logical antagonist of Calvinism was a fully humanistic, historically minded romanticism," of which she regards Melville and Margaret Fuller as rare examples; see her *The Feminization of American Culture* (New York: Knopf, 1977), 12–13.

19. Richard H. Brodhead, *The School of Hawthorne* (New York: Oxford University Press, 1986), 73. Subsequent references are cited in the text.

20. Carol Shloss, "Nathaniel Hawthorne and Daguerreotypy: *Disinterested Vision*," in her *In Visible Light: Photography and the American Writer, 1840–1940* (New York: Oxford University Press, 1987), 25–50.

21. Nathaniel Hawthorne, *The Marble Faun; or, The Romance of Monte Beni.* The Centenary Edition (Columbus, Ohio: Merill, 1969), 23. Subsequent references are cited in the text.

22. Binion, *Frau Lou,* 343.

Mysteries We Reread, Mysteries of Rereading: Poe, Borges, and the Analytic Detective Story; Also Lacan, Derrida, and Johnson

1. Raymond Chandler, "The Simple Art of Murder," in *Detective Fiction: Crime and Compromise,* ed. Dick Allen and David Chacko (New York: Harcourt Brace Jovanovich, 1974), 398.

2. Edgar Allan Poe, *Collected Works of Edgar Allan Poe,* ed. Thomas Ollive Mabbott, 3 vols. (Cambridge: Harvard University Press, 1969–1978), 2:521n. All subsequent quotations from Poe are taken from this edition.

3. Jorge Luis Borges, "Ibn Hakkan al-Bokhari, Dead in His Labyrinth," in *The Aelph and Other Stories, 1933–1969,* trans. Norman Thomas di Giovanni (New York: E. P. Dutton, 1978), 123. All subsequent quotations from Borges's fiction are taken from this edition.

4. Jacques Lacan, "Seminar on 'The Purloined Letter,'" trans. Jeffrey Mehlman, *Yale French Studies* 48 (1972): 41. Unless otherwise noted, all subsequent quotations from the "Seminar on 'The Purloined Letter'" are taken from this edition.

5. Barbara Johnson, "The Frame of Reference: Poe, Lacan, Derrida," in *The Critical Difference* (Baltimore: Johns Hopkins University Press, 1980), 118. All subsequent quotations from Johnson are taken from this edition.

6. Jacques Derrida, "The Purveyor of Truth," trans. W. Domingo, J. Hulbert, M. Ron, and M.-R. Logan, *Yale French Studies* 52 (1975): 100. All subsequent quotations from Derrida are taken from this edition.

7. *Webster's New World Dictionary of the American Language,* College Edition (Cleveland and New York: World Publishing Co., 1964), 1359, "simple." The etymologies of "even" and "odd" are also taken from this edition.

8. D. P. Simpson, *Cassell's Latin Dictionary* (New York: Macmillan, 1978), 556, "simplex."

9. *The Encyclopaedia Britannica,* 11th edition, 29 vols. (New York: Encyclopaedia Britannica Co., 1911), 27:254.

10. S. K. Heninger, Jr., *The Cosmographical Glass: Renaissance Diagrams of the Universe* (San Marino, Calif.: Huntington Library, 1977), 83, fig. 52b. All subsequent quotations referring to Fludd's diagram are cited from Heninger. This diagram was brought to my attention by my student James Boylan.

11. Jorge Luis Borges, "From Someone to Nobody," in *Other Inquisitions, 1937–1952,* trans. Ruth L. C. Simms (New York: Simon and Schuster, 1965), 148. All subsequent quotations from Borges's essays are taken from this edition, designated *OI* in the text.

12. Ralph Waldo Emerson, *The Complete Works of Ralph Waldo Emerson,* ed. E. W. Emerson, 12 vols. (Boston: Houghton Mifflin, 1903–1904), 9:195. See also Borges, *Other Inquisitions,* 69.

13. Howard Haycraft, *Murder for Pleasure: The Life and Times of the Detective Story* (New York: Carroll and Graf, 1984), xxi.

14. *An Intermediate Greek-English Lexicon* (Oxford: Oxford University Press, 1980), 171.

15. Emir Rodríguez Monegal, *Jorge Luis Borges: A Literary Biography* (New York: E. P. Dutton, 1978), 382. All subsequent quotations from Rodríguez Monegal are taken from this edition.

16. Jacques Lacan, *Écrits,* 2 vols. (Paris: Édition du Seuil, 1966), 1:66.

17. Jean Laplanche and J.-B. Pontalis, "Mirror Stage (Stade du miroir)," trans. Peter Kussell and Jeffrey Mehlman, *Yale French Studies* 48 (1972): 192.

Marking Space, Charting Time: Text and Territory in Faulkner's "The Bear" and Carpentier's *Los pasos perdidos*

1. Charles L. Sanford, *The Quest for Paradise: Europe and the American Moral Imagination* (Urbana: University of Illinois Press, 1961), vi.

2. For an investigation of this utopian tendency in Latin American literature, see Juan G. Durán, *Literatura y utopía en hispanoamérica* (Ithaca, N.Y.: Cornell University Latin American Studies Program Dissertation Series, 1972), 259. Like Alfonso Reyes and others, Durán emphasizes the correspondence of the discovery of America to European dreams of the promised land, so that America is, in Octavio Paz's words, a "premeditated creation" (Octavio Paz, "Literatura de fundación," in his *Puertas al campo* [Mexico City: Universidad Nacional Autónoma de México, 1966], 13; cited in Durán, 18). Following Leopoldo Zea, he believes that the utopian urge created a kind of maladaptive literary vision in

which Latin Americans continued this European desire to see their land as the promised one, writers thus continuing to supply what history was increasingly denying.

3. William Faulkner, "The Bear," in *Go Down, Moses* (1940; New York: Random House, 1973). Further references are given in the text. I have chosen to deal primarily with "The Bear," referring only minimally to the rest of *Go Down, Moses,* because it is in "The Bear" that we encounter a significant kernel of Faulkner's paradisal land-centered vision, and because I wish to emphasize the strength of that vision, which survives despite ironic undercuttings. The fact that "The Bear" has been so often anthologized and read as a separate piece implicitly attests to its force as a representative of the Edenic impulse in American fiction and justifies this intensive treatment. While it forms an integral part of *Go Down, Moses,* "The Bear" remains as a kind of monolith in that larger narrative stream, its primitivist themes reinforced by the two sections preceding and following it—"The Old People" and "Delta Autumn."

4. Alejo Capentier, *Los pasos perdidos* (1957; Mexico City: Compañía General de Ediciones, 1968), 180. Further references are given in the text. The English translation used is Alejo Carpentier, *The Lost Steps,* trans. Harriet de Onis (Hammondsworth, Eng.: Penguin Books, 1968), 156. Further references are given in the text.

5. As Fernando Ainsa suggests with his analysis of centripetal and centrifugal movements in Latin American literature, the complement to this attachment of text to terrain is the linking of literature and exile; the literature of both Americas shares this polarity, having developed in the space between them. See his *Los buscadores de la utopía* (Caracas: Monte Avila, 1977). I have found Professor Ainsa's book very helpful in preparing this essay, and therefore will refer to his ideas frequently.

6. Alfonso Reyes, *Obras completas* (Mexico City: Fondo de Cultura Económica, 1960), 6:338.

7. Julio Rodríguez Luis investigates another aspect of the importance of landownership in the development of Latin American fiction in an essay on "Persistencia del terrateniente," in his *La literatura hispanoamericana: Entre compromiso y experimento* (Madrid: Fundamentos, 1984).

8. I am grateful to Lois Parkinson Zamora for suggesting this general idea and others which were helpful to me in writing this essay.

9. Thanks to Gustavo Pérez Firmat for reminding me of this modal progression, and for several other helpful suggestions.

10. The words are Faulkner's—from his Nobel Prize speech.

11. Durán agrees that this novel itself is the narrator's memory of the utopia he encountered in the jungle; see his *Literatura y utopía en hispanoamérica,* 294.

12. Ainsa maintains that a lack of roots is more endemic to the American consciousness and that the search for them is thus more pervasive; see *Los buscadores de la utopía,* 123.

13. Sanford, *The Quest for Paradise*, 266.

14. Richard Poirier notes that Ike's action of relinquishing completely to the wilderness is foreshadowed by the log he encounters there, "almost completely crumbled now," in a state of "passionate and almost visible relinquishment" (199). See his " 'The Bear,' " in Harold Bloom, ed., *William Faulkner* (New York: Chelsea House, 1986), 50.

15. Ike is a problematic figure, but critical controversy over his relative virtues and vices doesn't negate the value of his experience in the wilderness as it is portrayed in the text, of the land as moral touchstone in the novel. For a recent reinterpretation of Ike as irresponsible and lacking in love, see Lyall H. Powers, *Faulkner's Yoknapatawpha Comedy* (Ann Arbor: University of Michigan Press, 1980), 175–80.

16. Robert González Echevarría, *Alejo Carpentier: The Pilgrim at Home* (Ithaca, N.Y.: Cornell University Press, 1977), 180.

17. It resembles the concept of origin as analyzed by Eduardo González: even though the fiction recognizes the irrecuperable nature of an origin, its epiphanic power remains strong. See his *Alejo Carpentier: El tiempo del hombre* (Caracas: Monte Avila, 1978), 194.

18. According to González Echevarría, "*The Lost Steps* and 'Manhunt' take to its limits and subvert the metaphor of nature as logos, of the fusion of creative consciousness and nature as the source of narrativity" (*The Pilgrim at Home*, 211). The continuing attraction of the wilderness region—in critical discourse this time—is attested also by the interpretation (erroneous, I believe) of René Jara Cuadra, who classifies Carpentier's narrator as a failed hero, incapable of disengaging himself from his urban habits and remaining in the promised land. See his "Tierra y mundo en la novela contemporánea," in *La naturaleza y el hombre en la novela hispanoamericana*, ed. Mauricio Ostría González (Antofagasta, Chile: Universidad del Norte, 1969), 65. Jara Cuadra makes a number of strong statements regarding Latin American attachment to the land, such as "the land is the place where being and existence are merged," and "man is neither whole nor authentic unless he is in contact with the land" (72, 74). These statements are significant as general cultural definitions (and I sympathize with them personally), but the problem with applying them to Carpentier is that even though he is writing out of this tradition and many of these feelings, he recognizes their limits as a basis for social and aesthetic action in the present.

19. Durán agrees that for the narrator, "the environment is purifying because it is in itself purer" (*Literatura y utopía en hispanoamérica*, 279.

20. Both Ainsa and González Echevarría take up this point in their discussions of new world writing (*Los buscadores de la utopía*, 90–91; *The Pilgrim at Home*, 171.

21. Roderick Nash, *Wilderness and the American Mind* (New Haven, Conn.: Yale University Press, 1967), 212.

22. Sanford, *The Quest for Paradise*, 18.

23. Nash, *Wilderness and the American Mind,* 236.

24. According to Ainsa, "it is the disorientation of man with respect to his surroundings and the lack of a selective dialogue between the center of his conscience and the environment, which prohibits the unfolding of a determined ordering of the world" (*Los buscadores de la utopía,* 111).

25. According to R. W. B. Lewis, " 'The Bear' is a work in the tradition of Cooper and Twain; another tale of a boy growing up and growing wiser along the border between the civilized and the still unspoiled." See his " 'The Bear': America Transcended," in *Faulkner: A Collection of Critical Essays,* ed. Robert Penn Warren (Englewood Cliffs, N.J.: Prentice-Hall, 1966), 208.

26. Gustavo Pérez Firmat has formulated another important difference between these two texts—that of the narrative time frame: "Set in the late 1800s, Faulkner's novella anticipated the destruction of the wilderness; it is a 'historical' novel with a prospective slant. Carpentier's novel is a 'contemporary' work with a retrospective or atavistic slant. 'The Bear' plants the seeds of alienation; [*The Lost Steps*] shows us the fruits." Professor Pérez Firmat made this point in a letter to me.

27. Ursula Brumm thinks that in recognizing the "inevitable, tragic conflict" between civilization and wilderness, Faulkner "comes to a conclusion which to my knowledge no European has ever drawn with such severity: at the root and beginning of civilization and all its achievements is rapacity, and civilized man has to bear the burden of this guilt always and everywhere." See her "Wilderness and Civilization: A Note on William Faulkner," in *William Faulkner: Three Decades of Criticism,* ed. Frederick J. Hoffman and Olga Vickery (New York: Harcourt Brace Jovanovich, 1960), 130.

28. Arnold Chapman also believes in this mutual concern. In his comparison of initiations in *Don Segundo Sombra* and "The Bear," he notes the importance of nature as "a refuge from the blighting routines of human society," and also confirms the common "American problems" the young men in the stories face in dealing with "the land as possession," with its contamination by colonization, and in "spanning the gap between a primitive world in equilibrium, apparently perfect in the harmony of its parts, and a clearly imperfect, changing, unhappy, hybrid society." See his "Pampas and Big Woods: Heroic Initiation in Güiraldes and Faulkner," *Comparative Literature* 11 (1959): 70–75.

29. James Guetti glosses the passage in this way: "as the killer of Old Ben, it may be that [Boon] now possesses the mystery, that he has apprehended the reality of the wilderness, and his passion of ownership can now take the form only of an intense and futile confusion." See his " 'The Sound and the Fury' and 'The Bear,' " in Bloom, *William Faulkner,* 60. Confusion, yes; apprehension, doubtful. I would say rather that Boon is possessed by the wilderness, which necessarily confuses issues of ownership.

30. Ibid., 196.

31. Lewis has aptly defined the value that permeates Faulkner's wilderness as "the honorable" (in Warren, *Faulkner,* 217).

32. The Neruda poem is cited in González Echevarría, *The Pilgrim at Home,* 161.

33. Rodríguez Luis, "Persistencia del terrateniente," 159.

34. According to González Echevarría, Carpentier's prologue to *El reino de este mundo* (*The Kingdom of This World*), and presumably *Los pasos perdidos* as well, belong to the "whole movement in Latin American literature whose central metaphor is the recuperation of the lost origin, that Edenic beginning of beginnings destroyed by the violent birth of history with the European invasion" (*The Pilgrim at Home,* 160).

35. Leo Marx cites Campbell's formulation in *The Machine in the Garden: Technology and the Pastoral Ideal in America* (New York: Oxford University Press, 1964), 228.

36. Nash locates the height of American deception with civilization and the related cult of the wilderness in the late nineteenth and early twentieth centuries; he cites numerous examples, including of course the essays of Frederick Jackson Turner, the Boy Scout movement, and the founding of the national parks (*Wilderness and the American Mind*). "The Bear" (with Ike as the ultimate boy scout?) grows out of this tradition. I am not familiar with a similar tradition in Latin America, except for the controversy over the Amazonian rain forest, which is only now building momentum. The *mundonovista* movement, of which Carpentier certainly forms part, was broadly cultural rather than conservationist in nature.

37. Marx, *The Machine in the Garden,* 362–63.

38. I have dealt with this aspect of Carpentier's work briefly in my article on "Alejo Carpentier à la recherche du temps perdu," *Comparative Literature Studies* 17, 2 (1980): 137–39.

39. Ainsa includes in his discussion a quotation from Vargas Llosa's *La casa verde* which masterfully unites the metaphorical association of woman and land with the problem of portraying unknown territory without familiarizing it too much: "'¿Te acuerdas como quemamos tus mapas?' dijo Aquilino. Pura basura, los que hacen mapas no saben que la Amazonia es como mujer caliente, no se está quieta" ("'Do you remember how we burnt your maps?' said Aquilino. Pure garbage, those who make maps don't know that Amazonia is like a desirous woman, they're never still" [*Los buscadores de la utopía,* 239]).

40. Ibid., 248.

41. According to Eric J. Sundquist, "The celibate marriage of hunter and beast in 'The Bear,' and in Cooper's *The Deerslayer* or in [Melville's] *Moby Dick,* for example, collapses the sexual identities of each in order to express an androgynous, self-generating and self-consuming union." See his *Faulkner: The House Divided* (Baltimore: Johns Hopkins University Press, 1983), 68.

42. Edmundo O'Gorman, "La gran dicotomía americana: Angloamérica e Iberoamérica," *Vuelta* 10 (Sept. 1977): 5–6.

In-Fringe: The Role of French Criticism in the Fiction of
Nicole Brossard and Severo Sarduy

1. René Wellek and Warren Austin, *Theory of Literature*, 3rd ed. (New York: Harcourt, Brace and World, 1962), 49.

2. Roberto González Echevarría, *La ruta de Severo Sarduy* (Hanover, N.H.: Ediciones del Norte, 1987), 36.

3. The original title of the journal, founded in 1965, was *La Barre du Jour.* *Nouvelle* was added to the title in 1972.

4. Nicole Brossard, *Double Impression* (Montreal: Éditions de l'Hexagone et Nicole Brossard, 1984), 44.

5. Severo Sarduy, *Cobra* (Buenos Aires: Editorial Sudamericana, 1972), 20. Subsequent references will be cited in the text.

6. Jacques Derrida, "La pharmacie de Platon," *Tel Quel* 32 (1968): 17.

7. Julia Kristeva, "Comment parler à la littérature," *Tel Quel* 47 (1971): 27.

8. James Joyce, *Finnegans Wake*, 3rd ed. (London: Faber and Faber, 1964), 621.

9. Philippe Sollers and Jacques Henric, "Écriture et révolution," in *Theorie d'ensemble* (Paris: Éditions du Seuil, 1968), 70. Subsequent references will be cited in the text.

10. Louis Althusser, *Pour Marx* (Paris: Libraire François Maspero, 1965), 189.

11. Kristeva, "Comment parler à la littérature," 28. Subsequent references will be cited in the text.

12. Brossard, *Double Impression*, 40.

13. Sollers and Henric, "Écriture et révolution," 75.

14. Émile Benveniste, *Problèmes de linguistique générale* (Paris: Éditions Gallimard, 1966).

15. Nicole Brossard, *Picture Theory* (Montreal: Nouvelle Optique, 1982), 120. Subsequent references will be cited in the text.

16. Roland Barthes, *Le grain de la voix* (Paris: Éditions du Seuil, 1982).

17. Brossard, *Double Impression*, 65.

18. Severo Sarduy, "Cubos," in *Ensayos sobre un cuerpo, Ensayos de crítica* (Buenos Aires: Editorial Sudamericana, 1969). Subsequent references will be cited in the text.

19. See René Prieto, "The Ambiviolent Fiction of Severo Sarduy," *Symposium* 39 (1985): 49–60, for a detailed discussion of the identification of Cobra and the phallus.

20. See René Prieto, "La Persistencia del Deseo: *Colibrí* de Severo Sarduy," *Revista Iberoamericana* (forthcoming), for a discussion of the narrator's longing to be identified with the maternal body.

21. Severo Sarduy, *Maitreya* (Madrid: Seix Barral, 1978).

22. Octavio Paz, *El laberinto de la soledad* (Mexico City: Fondo de Cultura Económica, 1959).

23. Julia Kristeva, *Polylogue* (Paris: Éditions du Seuil, 1977), 14.

24. Ibid., 16.

25. Julia Kristeva, *La révolution du langage poétique* (Paris: Éditions du Seuil, 1974).

26. Nicole Brossard, *Les strategies du réel: The story so far 6* (Toronto: Coach House Press, 1979), 9.

27. Brossard, *Double Impression,* 54–55.

28. Paul de Man, *Blindness and Insight: Essays in the Rhetoric of Contemporary Civilization,* 2nd ed. (Minneapolis: University of Minnesota Press, 1983), 148.

29. Paz, *El laberinto de la soledad,* 79. Subsequent references will be cited in the text.

30. Benveniste, *Problèmes de linguistique générale,* 256.

Mischling and Métis: Common and Uncommon Languages in Adrienne Rich and Aimé Césaire

Note: I am grateful to Cornell University for a Humanities Fellowship which enabled me to travel to Martinique to pursue research on Césaire. My special thanks as well to Émile and Yvonne Eadie, Raphäel Confiant, Patrick Chamoiseau, and Vincent Placoly for their generous hospitality during my stay in Fort-de-France and for discussions of the current reception of Césaire's work in Martinique which greatly contributed toward the essay's completion.

1. Following Breton's enthusiastic response to *Notebook* in 1941, Césaire's work received its second great boost with the publication in 1948 of Sartre's "Orphée noir" ("Black Orpheus"). First published in English in 1956, Sartre's essay is newly available in *"What Is Literature?" and Other Essays* (Cambridge: Harvard University Press, 1988). References to Césair's poetry, in French and in English, will be drawn from *Aimé Césaire: The Collected Poetry,* trans. Clayton Eshleman and Annette Smith (Berkeley: University of California Press, 1983). Additional references to the *Collected Poetry* will be indicated in the text by CP followed by page number.

2. René Depestre, *Pour la Révolution, pour la poésie* (Ottawa: Leméac, 1974), 157. *Notebook's* emphasis on mixing as a lexical, formal, thematic, and discursive principle is in keeping with the dialogizing mode I have examined in *A Poverty of Objects: The Prose Poem and the Politics of Genre* (Ithaca, N.Y.: Cornell University Press, 1987) in relation to the prose poem as it was developed by Baudelaire and Rimbaud. As Jonathan Ngaté has pointed out in his essay " 'Mauvais sang' de Rimbaud et *Cahier d'un retour au pays natal* de Césaire: la poésie au service de la révolution," *Cahiers Césairiens* 3 (Spring 1977): 25–32, intertextual resonances between Césaire and Rimbaud in particular are especially striking. Writing of Rimbaud's "dialogue with time and history" in her illuminating study, *The Emergence of Space: Rimbaud and the Paris Commune* (Minneapolis: University of Minnesota Press, 1988), Kristin Ross rightly describes Césaire as "the French-

speaking contemporary poet most in [Rimbaud's] lineage" (103). Césaire also drew inspiration early in his career from the poets of the Harlem Renaissance; see especially A. James Arnold, *Modernism and Negritude: The Poetry and Poetics of Aimé Césaire* (Cambridge: Harvard University Press, 1981), 27–33, and Michel Fabre, "Du mouvement noir à la négritude césairienne," in *Soleil éclaté*, ed. Jacqueline Leiner (Tübingen, Ger.: Gunter Narr Verlag, 1984), 145–59.

3. Adrienne Rich, "Blood, Bread, and Poetry: The Location of the Poet" (1984), in *Blood, Bread, and Poetry: Selected Prose 1979–1985* (New York: Norton, 1986), 176. Subsequent references to the title essay will be indicated by BBP followed by page number. Other essays in *Blood, Bread, and Poetry* will be referred to in the text as follows: "Compulsory Heterosexuality and Lesbian Existence" (1980) = CH; "Toward a More Feminist Criticism" (1981) = MFC; "Split at the Root: An Essay on Jewish Identity" (1982) = SR; "'Going There' and Being Here" (1983) = GT; "North American Tunnel Vision" (1983) = NA; "If Not with Others, How?" (1985) = IN; "Notes Toward a Politics of Location" (1984) = PL.

4. In addition to providing detailed commentary for each of the twenty Césaire poems he has translated and included in his book *Non-Vicious Circle* (Palo Alto, Calif.: Stanford University Press, 1984), Davis offers a useful introduction situating Césaire's work in relation to both French surrealism and Latin American magical realism (3–28).

5. Cited by Keith Warner in "De l'écrivain devenu leader politique: à la recherche d'un héros antillais," in *Soleil éclaté*, 429.

6. Joan Dayan, *A Rainbow for the Christian West: René Depestre* (Amherst: University of Massachusetts Press, 1977), provides an excellent introduction to Depestre's work.

7. See Émile Benveniste, "The Nature of Pronouns" and "Subjectivity in Language," in *Problems in General Linguistics*, trans. Mary Elizabeth Meek (Coral Gables, Fla: University of Miami Press, 1971), 1:217–22 and 223–30. For a discussion of poetic subjectivity and the figure of woman as intimate other in Césaire's work in light of Benveniste's work on pronouns, see Ronnie Leah Scharfman, *Engagement and the Language of the Subject in the Poetry of Aimé Césaire* (Gainesville: University Presses of Florida, 1987), 65–73. Scharfman's discussion is reprinted in French and with some variation in *Aimé Césaire: ou l'athanor d'un alchimiste* (Paris: Editions Caribeénnes, 1987) under the title "Retour au/du sujet césairien: le sujet et l'autre intime" (86–97).

8. As a number of critics have pointed out in *Aimé Césaire: ou l'athanor d'un alchimiste*, what appears hermetic or exotic for white European or North American readers of Césaire may be part of a more familiar discursive landscape for readers from the Caribbean. See especially Michel Hausser, "Césaire et l'hermétisme" (33–52); Graziano Benelli, "L'écriture des libertés" (23–32); and Frederick Ivor Case, "Idéologie du discours esthétique césairien" (337–46).

9. Dayan, *Depestre*, 3–6.

10. See Arnold, *Modernism and Negritude*, 180–83, and Dayan, *Depestre*, 29–32.

11. On the political and personal resonances of the word *hanneton* in Rimbaud's "Chant de guerre parisien" and the same term's function as Césaire uses it here, see Ross, *Emergence of Space*, 145–47.

12. As Henock Trouillot, the Haitian author of *L'itinéraire d'Aimé Césaire* points out in "La présence d'Aimé Césaire en Haiti" (*Soleil éclaté*), Depestre was himself not persuaded. Offended, as Trouillot puts it, by Césaire's intervention and by his perception of the Martinican poet as conducting himself in a manner "more Haitian than thou" ("qui se veut plus haïtien que lui"), Depestre maintained his support for Aragon (412).

13. "Négritude et antillanité: Entretien avec Aimé Césaire," in *Notre Librairie* 74 (Apr.–June 1984): 11; hereafter referred to in the text as NA.

14. On the prevalence of occlusive consonants in Césaire's work generally and his use of their "harshly expressive tendency . . . to a strategic end," see Arnold, *Modernism and Negritude*, 236.

15. Depestre, *Pour la Révolution, pour la poésie*, 164 and 167.

16. Louis Sala-Molins, *Le Code Noir: ou le calvaire de Canaan* (Paris: Presses universitaires de France, 1987), 169. Additional references will be indicated by CN followed by page number.

17. See especially Edouard Glissant, *Le discours antillais* (Paris: Seuil, 1981).

18. Depestre, "Les Aspects créateurs du métissage culturel aux Caraibes," in *Notre Librairie* 74 (Apr.–June 1984): 63.

19. Paula Bennett, *My Life a Loaded Gun: Female Creativity and Feminist Poetics* (Boston: Beacon, 1986), 168.

20. See in particular the 1986 Foreword to *Blood, Bread, and Poetry*, xii, and, in the same collection, "North American Tunnel Vision" (1983), 165; "If Not with Others, How?" (1985), 203; "Notes Toward a Politics of Location" (1984), 216; and the title essay, 185.

21. *Your Native Land, Your Life* (New York: Norton, 1986); *The Dream of a Common Language* (New York: Norton, 1978).

22. As Cary Nelson points out in his chapter entitled "Meditative Aggressions: Adrienne Rich's Recent Transactions with History" (*Our Last First Poets: Vision and History in Contemporary American Poetry* [Urbana: University of Illinois Press, 1981]), Rich's reception has ranged "from uncritical enthusiasm for her courage in dealing openly with feminist issues to a patronizing nostalgia for the more genteel formalism of her first books" (148). While acknowledging the risks Rich's poetry began to undergo with *The Will to Change: Poems 1968–1970* (New York: Norton, 1971), Nelson nevertheless regards her characteristic juxtapositions of the public and the private "not as a weakness but a substantial accomplishment" (154). More recently, in an equally balanced and engaged response to Rich's work, Charles Altieri praises Rich for exploring a form of poetry in which "poems are intended to function as literal examples of living and writing

within what history makes possible and necessary" (*Self and Sensibility in Contemporary American Poetry* [New York: Cambridge University Press, 1984], 180). Less favorable assessments of Rich's attempts to develop a self-consciously political poetry from the late 1960s through the early 1980s register in Helen Vendler's "All Too Real," *New York Review of Books* (17 Dec. 1981), 32–35, and Marjorie Perloff's "Private Lives/Public Images," *Michigan Quarterly Review* 22 (Winter 1983): 130–42.

23. Myriam Diaz-Diocaretz, *Translating Poetic Discourse: Questions on Feminist Strategies in Adrienne Rich* (Amsterdam and Philadelphia: John Benjamins, 1985), 5; see also *The Transforming Power of Language: The Poetry of Adrienne Rich* (Utrecht: HES, 1984).

24. "North American Time," *Your Native Land, Your Life,* 33–36. The poem also appears as the closing text of *The Fact of a Doorframe: Poems Selected and New: 1959–1984* (New York: Norton, 1984), 324–28.

25. "The Burning of Paper Instead of Children," *The Will to Change* (1971), reprinted in *The Fact of a Doorframe,* 116–19; hereafter referred to as BP.

26. Jacques Derrida, "Signature Event Context," trans. Samuel Weber and Jeffrey Mehlman, in *Limited Inc* (Evanston: Northwestern University Press, 1988), 2 and 12. First published in the Weber and Mehlman translation in *Glyph* 1 (Baltimore: Johns Hopkins University Press, 1977), the essay also appears in *Margins of Philosophy,* trans. Allan Bass (Chicago: University of Chicago Press, 1982), 307–30.

27. See the Foreword, "North American Tunnel Vision," and "Notes Toward a Politics of Location," in *Blood, Bread, and Poetry,* xii, 165, and 227.

28. Edouard Glissant, "Préface d'une littérature future," in *Notre Librairie* 74 (Apr.–June 1984): 18; hereafter referred to in the text by page number only.

29. Jean-Luc Nancy, *La communauté désoeuvrée* (Paris: Christian Bourgois, 1986), 64 and 53–54; subsequent references will be included in the text.

30. "L'homme de culture et ses responsabilités," in *Deuxième Congrès des Ecrivains et Artistes Noirs* (Paris: Présence Africaine, 1959), 121–22.

31. Toril Moi, "Feminism, Postmodernism and Style: Recent Feminist Criticism in the U.S." (lecture delivered at Cornell University, 20 November 1987), 13–14.

32. "Lettre à Maurice Thorez," cited in Susan Willis, "Caliban as Poet: Reversing the Maps of Domination," in *Reinventing the Americas* (New York: Cambridge University Press, 1986), 103.

33. From *The Dream of a Common Language,* reprinted in *The Fact of a Doorframe,* 256–63.

The Strut of the Centipede: José Lezama Lima and New World Exceptionalism

1. Studies of *La expresión americana* include: José María Bernáldez, "*La expresión americana* de Lezama Lima," *Cuadernos Hispanoamericanos* 318 (Dec. 1976):

653–70; Oscar Collazos, "La expresión americana," in *Recopilación de textos sobre José Lezama Lima,* ed. Pedro Simón (Havana: Casa de las Américas, 1970), 130–70; Irlemar Chiampi, *"La expresión americana* de José Lezama Lima: La dificultad y el diabolismo del caníbal," *Escritura* 10 (Jan.–Dec. 1985): 103–15; Ester Gimbernat de González, "La curiosidad barroca," in *Coloquio internacional sobre la obra de José Lezama Lima* (Madrid: Fundamentos, 1984), 1:59–65; Julio Ortega, *"La expresión americana:* una teoría de la cultura," *Eco,* no. 187 (May 1977): 55–63. Also useful is Irlemar Chiampi's introduction to her Portuguese translation, *A Expressão Americana* (São Paulo: Editora Brasiliense, 1988). Page references to *La expresión americana* are taken from the version contained in José Lezama Lima, *El reino de la imagen,* ed. Julio Ortega (Caracas: Biblioteca Ayacucho, 1981).

2. For a succinct recent statement of Zea's position, see his "Identity: A Latin American Philosophical Problem," *The Philosophical Forum* 20, 1–2 (Fall-Winter 1988–89): 33–42.

3. Hence the book's gallery of the American artist types—the *señor barroco,* the *romántico desterrado,* the *señor estanciero.* Hence also Lezama's portraits of individual American artists—Sor Juana, Sigüenza y Góngora, Fray Servando Teresa de Mier, and the Indian sculptor Kondori, among others. In this respect *La expresión americana* may be seen as an ethopoeia of American genius.

4. I do not mean to imply that Lezama's emphasis on expression is entirely without precedent, only that it is not the norm. One important precedent for Lezama's use of this term is Pedro Henríquez Ureña's *Seis ensayos en busca de nuestra expresión* (Buenos Aires: Biblioteca argentina, 1927).

5. I take this phrase from Borges's "El arte narrativo y la magia," in *Discusión,* 7th ed. (Buenos Aires: Emecé, 1972), 81–91.

6. Gustavo Pellón, "Culture as Nature: An American Practice of Reading and Writing," in *José Lezama Lima's Joyful Vision* (Austin: University of Texas Press, 1989), 45–69.

7. Djelal Kadir has discussed some rhetorical antecedents of Lezama's notion of *paisaje* in *Questing Fictions: Latin America's Family Romance* (Minneapolis: University of Minnesota Press, 1986), 26–27.

8. *Tratados en La Habana* (Santiago de Chile: Orbe, 1970), 145. This is Lezama's gloss of one of Pascal's *Pensées:* "La vrai nature étant perdue, tout devient sa nature; comme, le véritable bien étant perdu, tout devient son veritable bien."

9. Lezama, *Tratados en La Habana,* 102.

10. I am thinking in particular of R. W. B. Lewis's classic study, *The American Adam* (Chicago: University of Chicago Press, 1955).

11. This is one of the epigraphs of Lewis's *The American Adam.*

12. *The Portable Emerson,* ed. Carl Bode (New York: Penguin Books, 1981), 10. Other page numbers refer to this edition.

13. On Lezama as Caliban, see Chiampi, *supra* n. 1, 106–7.

14. On Lezama's idea of a "técnica de la ficción," see Enrico Mario Santí, "Lezama, V.itier y la Crítica de la Razón Reminiscente," in *Escritura y tradición* (Barcelona: Laia, 1987), 182–88.

15. "Eran los hombres sin insistencias humanísticas los que podían captar el asombro, el nuevo unicornio, que no regresaba para morir" (383).

16. "Para un español, lector de la época áurea, el conocimiento de los cronistas de Indias, puede pasar como prosistas menores, que añaden un primor o una gracia de primitivo. Pero el americano encuentra en esos cronistas de Indias sus primeros prosistas, los hombres que hablan porque el paisaje les dicta" (421).

17. See Michel de Certau, *Heterologies* (Minneapolis: University of Minnesota Press, 1986), especially 68–69.

18. I am thinking of an essay included in *Tratados en La Habana*, "Penetraciones en la pampa," 148–50.

19. Lezama's choice of the pampas as an example of nature is suggestive also because it connects *La expresión americana* to other meditations on the pampa, especially Domingo Faustino Sarmiento's *Facundo* (1845). Sarmiento's thought is structured around the opposition between civilization and barbarism. The locus of barbarism was the Argentine wilderness. Although I will not do so here, one may well be able to nuance and refine Lezama's distinction between land and landscape by mapping it unto Sarmiento's antithesis.

20. "Ante todo, el paisaje nos lleva a la adquisición del punto de mira, del campo óptico y del contorno. Que la atención o una saetilla misteriosa se disparen sobre nosotros, que la mirada suelte sus guerreros en defensa de su territorio, y el contorno enarque sus empalizadas frente a zonas indiferentes o gengiskanesca barbarie" (433).

21. References are taken from Alejo Carpentier, *Los pasos perdidos,* ed. Roberto González Echevarría (Madrid: Cátedra, 1985). English translations are taken from *The Lost Steps,* trans. Harriet de Onís (New York: Avon Books, 1979). In some instances I have modified the English translation in order to give a more literal rendering.

22. Alejo Carpentier, "Problemática de la actual novela latinoamericana," in *Tientos y diferencias* (Montevideo: Arca, 1967), 5–41.

23. See Severo Sarduy, *Escrito sobre un cuerpo* (Buenos Aires: Sudamericana, 1969); Henry Louis Gates, Jr., *The Signifying Monkey* (New York: Oxford University Press, 1988); Emir Rodríguez Monegal, "Carnaval/Antropofagia/Parodia," *Revista Iberoamericana* 45 (1979): 401–12.

24. Roberto González Echevarría, *Alejo Carpentier: The Pilgrim at Home* (Ithaca, N.Y.: Cornell University Press, 1977).

Index

Contributors

Antonio Benítez-Rojo, Professor of Romance Languages at Amherst College, is a Cuban writer and literary critic. He is the author of several collections of short stories, two novels, and several critical anthologies. The essay included in this collection is part of a book entitled *La isla que se repite* (1989).

Wendy B. Faris teaches Comparative Literature in the English Department at the University of Texas at Arlington. Her publications include *Carlos Fuentes* (1983), *Labyrinths of Language: Symbolic Landscape and Narrative Design in Modern Fiction* (1988) as well as articles on modern and contemporary fiction in England, France, the United States, and Latin America.

Eduardo González is Associate Professor of Spanish at Johns Hopkins University. A specialist in modern Spanish-American literature, he is the author of *Alejo Carpentier: El tiempo del hombre* (1978) and *La persona y el relato: Proyecto de lectura psicoanalítica* (1985).

David T. Haberly is Professor of Portuguese at the University of Virginia. He is the author of *Three Sad Races: Racial Identity and National Consciousness in Brazilian Literature* (1982) as well as of numerous articles on North American, Spanish-American, and Brazilian literature.

John T. Irwin is the Decker Professor in the Humanities, Professor of English, and Chairman of the Writing Seminars at Johns Hopkins University. He is the author of *Doubling and Incest / Repetition and Revenge: A Speculative Reading of Faulkner* (1975), *American Hieroglyphics* (1980), and (as John Bricuth) *The Heisenberg Variations* (1976). His essay in this collection appeared in *MLN* 101 (1986).

Jonathan Monroe is Associate Professor of Comparative Literature at Cornell University. He is the author of *A Poverty of Objects: The Prose Poem and the Politics of Genre* (1987) and articles on Novalis,

Baudelaire, T. S. Eliot, and John Ashbery. His essay on Césaire and Rich is part of a book in preparation entitled *Contemporary Poetry and Social Transformation*.

Gustavo Pérez Firmat is Professor of Spanish and Literature at Duke University. He is the author of *Idle Fictions: The Hispanic Vanguard Novel, 1926–1934* (1982), *Literature and Liminality* (1986), *Carolina Cuban* (1986), *Equivocaciones* (1989), and *The Cuban Condition: Translation and Identity in Modern Cuban Literature* (1989).

José Piedra is Assistant Professor of Spanish at Cornell University. In addition to articles on Spanish-American and Afro-Hispanic literature, he is the author of a forthcoming book entitled, *Shadow Writing: The Afro-Hispanic Aesthetics of Alejo Carpentier*.

René Prieto is Associate Professor of Spanish at Southern Methodist University. A Stanford Ph.D. and student of Roland Barthes, Prieto has published widely on contemporary Spanish-American narratives and is now completing a book-length study of the fiction of Miguel Angel Asturias.

José David Saldívar is Associate Professor of American Literature and Cultural Studies at the University of California at Santa Cruz. A fellow of the Stanford Humanities Center during 1985–86, he is the author of the forthcoming book, *The Dialectics of Our America: Genealogy, Cultural Critique, and Literary History*.

Enrico Mario Santí is Professor of Spanish and Latin American Studies at Georgetown University, where he is also Associate Director of the Latin American Studies Program. In addition to many articles and reviews, he is the author of *Pablo Neruda: The Poetics of Prophecy* (1982), *Escritura y tradición: Texto, crítica y poética en la literatura hispanoamericana* (1988) and of *Rights of Poetry: An Intellectual Biography of Octavio Paz* (forthcoming in 1991).

Doris Sommer is Professor of Spanish and Women's Studies at Amherst College. She is the author of *One Master for Another: Populism as Patriarchal Rhetoric in Dominican Novels* (1984) and of many articles on comparative and Hispanic topics. Her *National Romance: Foundational Fiction in Latin America* is forthcoming.

Lois Parkinson Zamora, a Berkeley Ph.D. in Comparative Literature, is Professor of English at the University of Houston. She is the author of *Writing the Apocalypse: Historical Vision in Contemporary U.S. and Latin American Fiction* (1989) as well as of many articles on North and South American literature. Her current project is an interartistic study of Latin American narrative and the visual arts tentatively entitled, *The Inordinate Eye*.

Library of Congress Cataloging-in-Publication Data

Do the Americas have a common literature? / Gustavo Pérez Firmat,
editor.
Includes bibliographical references.
ISBN 0-8223-1054-6. —ISBN 0-8223-1072-4 (pbk.)
1. America—Literatures—History and criticism.   2. Literature,
Comparative—American and Latin American.   3. Literature,
Comparative—Latin American and American.   I. Pérez Firmat,
Gustavo, 1949–   .
PN843.D6   1990
809'.891812—dc20   90-33990
                                                                          CIP